D1265803

# SEARCH AND SEIZURE AND THE SUPREME COURT

## A Study in Constitutional Interpretation

# SEARCH AND SEIZURE AND THE SUPREME COURT

## A STUDY IN CONSTITUTIONAL INTERPRETATION

By

JACOB W. LANDYNSKI

BALTIMORE
THE JOHNS HOPKINS PRESS

Baltimore, Maryland 21218
Printed in the United States of America
Library of Congress Catalog Card No. 65-13523

TO MY PARENTS

# ACKNOWLEDGMENTS

In preparing this manuscript for publication, I have had the singular good fortune to receive a wealth of advice from a number of distinguished scholars. I wish first to express my gratitude to Professor Carl B. Swisher of The Johns Hopkins University for his unstinting help during my years of graduate work, and, in particular, for his comments on this study. Even when I imposed upon him beyond reason, he unfailingly responded with grace and good cheer.

Professors Gerald Gunther of Stanford Law School, C. Herman Pritchett of the University of Chicago, and David R. Manwaring of Hobart and William Smith Colleges all read an early version of the manuscript in its entirety, and Professor Francis A. Allen of the University of Chicago Law School read the first three chapters. I have derived much profit from their suggestions. My colleague at the New School for Social Research, Professor Felicia Deyrup, very kindly gave the entire manuscript the benefit of her meticulous scrutiny and saved me from many an error of omission and commission. Professors Samuel J. Konefsky and Martin Landau of Brooklyn College have given me valuable help with this study, and their friendship and unfailing assistance have meant much to me.

The completion of the manuscript was aided immeasurably by the forbearance of my colleagues in the Graduate Faculty of the New School, Dean Howard B. White and Professors Erich Hula, Saul K. Padover, and Adamantia Pollis.

Mr. James Backes, assistant librarian of the New York Law Institute, kindly helped me to locate needed research materials. Mrs. Jean Owen, of The Johns Hopkins Press, proved to be as wise and helpful an editor as any author could wish for. Mrs. Henny Greenberg and Mrs. Mae Gardner, secretaries in the office of the dean of the Graduate Faculty of the New School, have smoothed my path in many ways over the last three years. The typing of the manuscript was done, expertly and often on very short notice, by Mrs. Carol Grad and Miss Mabel Eddy.

Many judges, law enforcement officials, and teachers of law provided, either by interview or letter, information and perspective on the questions raised in this study. To all these persons, too numerous to name here, I wish to express my thanks.

My wife, Miriam, typed first drafts, read proof, and in a multitude of ways made herself indispensable to the preparation of this book, and my greatest debt is to her.

# CONTENTS

Acknowledgments ........ 9

Introduction ........ 13

Chapter

I. The Fourth Amendment: Its Origins and Significance ..... 19

II. The Boyd Case: The Fourth Amendment Broadly Construed . 49

III. The Federal Exclusionary Rule ........ 62

IV. Constitutional Searches without Warrant ........ 87

V. The Process That Is Due ........ 118

VI. The Exclusionary Rule and the States ........ 144

VII. The Exclusionary Rule and the Problem of Illegal Search ... 173

VIII. Eavesdropping and the Constitution ........ 198

IX. Administrative Invasion of Privacy ........ 245

X. The Supreme Court and the Fourth Amendment ........ 263

Selected Bibliography ........ 271

Index ........ 278

# INTRODUCTION

> The right of the people to be secure in their persons, houses, papers, and effects, against unreasonable searches and seizures, shall not be violated, and no Warrants shall issue, but upon probable cause, supported by Oath or affirmation, and particularly describing the place to be searched, and the persons or things to be seized.

Few decisions of the United States Supreme Court have generated as much powerful controversy over the past few decades as those dealing with issues raised under the Fourth Amendment. Since the provisions of the amendment cover some of the most crucial areas of criminal investigation—arrest, search and seizure, and even, in some circumstances, interrogation[1]—the issues bring into sharp focus the classic dilemma of order vs. liberty in the democratic state. The Court has come under heavy fire from opposing directions. According to some critics, it has often proved heedless of the community interest in eradicating crime and has gone too far in the direction of protecting individual liberty. In the view of others, the Court has sometimes been too accommodating to the claims of law enforcement and insufficiently vigilant in safeguarding the principles on which the Fourth Amendment is based. No matter which attitude the Court takes to the problems, it cannot avoid being at the center of controversy.

What accounts for the fact that the amendment has in recent years become one of the most litigated provisions of the Bill of Rights in the Supreme Court? A number of factors are responsible for this development, first and foremost among which is the question of enforceability. The amendment is not self-enforcing; on the face of it, it can be construed as a mere admonition to good conduct on the part of the police. But if the police refuse to heed the admonition, are there any means by which the amendment can be saved from becoming a dead letter?

There is a significant difference, it should be observed, between the effect of a violation of the Fourth Amendment and that of a violation of other procedural protections in the Bill of Rights. If, for example, a defendant is denied the right to counsel, or his con-

1. *Wong Sun* v. *United States*, 371 U.S. 471, 484–86 (1963).

fession is obtained by "third-degree" methods and is received in evidence, any resulting conviction, once the claim is proved, will automatically be reversed on appeal. The conviction is reversed precisely for the reason that guilt *has not been fairly established* if the required procedural safeguards are not observed at trial. Such is not the case, however, of convictions obtained from evidence seized in an unconstitutional search. Evidence seized in this manner is just as reliable as evidence seized under a valid warrant. The objection here is not to the trustworthiness of the evidence, or to the adequacy of the trial procedure, but to *the manner* in which the evidence was acquired. Yet unless such evidence is ordered excluded from trial, in a departure from common-law practice, the Fourth Amendment runs the risk of being reduced to the status of a mere scrap of paper. It was to save the amendment as a living constitutional guarantee that the Court in 1914 endowed it with an enforcement feature, when it ordered the exclusion from trial of evidence obtained through illegal search.[2] Many of the search decisions since then have been concerned with defining the scope of this exclusionary rule. The rule is by far the most controversial feature of Supreme Court doctrine in this area.

Since 1949 the problem of searches by state officers has been a second area that has engaged a considerable amount of the Court's attention. There exist numerous well-documented accounts of flagrant abuses of individual rights in searches by state policemen, far beyond anything with which federal officers can be charged. State action is not within the purview of the Bill of Rights, and searches by state officers are therefore not subject to the direct control of the Fourth Amendment. But the flexible due process clause of the Fourteenth Amendment has served to accomplish that which the Fourth Amendment could not, by placing state searches under federal constitutional restrictions. Ever since the nineteen twenties the due process clause has undergone a great deal of resourceful judicial development designed to require that the states provide for their defendants some of the safeguards provided by the Bill of Rights for defendants in federal cases. In 1949 the Court recognized that the "core" of the Fourth Amendment's freedom from unreasonable searches was embodied in the Fourteenth Amendment as a restriction on state searches, but it held that its enforcement feature, the exclusionary rule, was not.[3] In the series of cases which followed, the Court sought to lay down guidelines to make more precise the

2. *Weeks* v. *United States*, 232 U.S. 383 (1914).
3. *Wolf* v. *Colorado,* 338 U.S. 25 (1949).

nature of the safeguards against state searches which the due process clause provided, but with a conspicuous lack of success. Decision followed decision and dissenting opinion followed dissenting opinion, generating as much heat as light. This series of cases culminated in 1961 with a decision requiring the states to exclude from trial unconstitutionally seized evidence.[4] The Court has since made it clear, moreover, that the protection of the Fourteenth Amendment against unreasonable searches is coextensive with that of the Fourth Amendment.[5] This does not mean that all restrictions placed on federal officers now apply to state officers as well; to the extent that the federal rules go beyond constitutional requirements, they are not required of the states. The Court is now embarked on the formidable task of spelling out constitutional rules for the states to follow —a task that is likely to keep it busily engaged for a number of years.

Another pressing question concerns the *kind* of search to which the Fourth Amendment should be applied. The framers knew of only one type of search, where physical entry was made into a dwelling for the purpose of securing evidence of crime. It was to that sort of search that the constitutional restrictions were directed. But does the amendment protect against a more modern type of invasion of privacy—inspection of the home by health inspectors, housing inspectors, fire inspectors—where the purpose is not criminal investigation but the discovery and correction of conditions which pose a hazard to the community? The Supreme Court in a 1959 case held that inspections without warrant were not forbidden by the Constitution,[6] but in view of the close five-to-four decision the question cannot be regarded as closed.

The inspection involves physical entry, though not to seek evidence of crime. Wire tapping and certain electronic devices, on the other hand, do not require physical entry but are employed by the police to gather evidence of crime. When the wire tapping question first came before the Supreme Court in 1928, the Fourth Amendment was narrowly construed to apply to physical searches only, not to eavesdropping by means of scientific devices which did not require entry into the dwelling.[7] This decision met with much criticism, and Congress in 1934 enacted legislation which the Court has construed as forbidding wire tapping.[8] Since then, the Court has been engaged in interpreting the statute when dealing with the wire tapping problem.

4. *Mapp* v. *Ohio*, 367 U.S. 643 (1961).
5. *Ker* v. *California*, 374 U.S. 23 (1963).
6. *Frank* v. *Maryland*, 359 U.S. 360 (1959).
7. *Olmstead* v. *United States*, 277 U.S. 438 (1928).
8. 48 Stat. 1103, 47 U.S.C. sec. 605.

It is probable, however, that the Court will not for long be able to shelter behind the statute but will soon be required to reconsider the constitutional question. There are two reasons for making this assumption. First, long-standing congressional efforts to amend the statute so as to allow law enforcement officers some measure of freedom in wire tapping may be nearing fruition. Even if judicial safeguards were incorporated in such a bill, a significant constitutional question would be raised because the wire tap is by nature a dragnet, which picks up the voices of the innocent as well as the guilty. It is therefore problematical whether a warrant can be devised which will meet the Fourth Amendment's requirements of particularity. Second, the use of electronic devices that are not connected with the telephone wires is not regulated by statute, and such instruments are commonly used both in and out of government. In the few cases which the Court has considered in this area, it has simply fallen back on its old position that a search requires physical entry before the Constitution's protection can be invoked. As the development and use of these devices continues apace, however, it is unlikely that the Court can long avoid a thorough re-examination of the constitutional question.

What has been said in these paragraphs should be sufficient to give an indication of the importance and immediacy of some of the constitutional questions raised under the Fourth Amendment today. Hardly a term of court has passed in recent years without decisions in cases raising significant search and seizure questions. The Fourth Amendment promises to be an important area of judicial involvement and, if the past is any criterion, of judicial conflict in the years ahead. It is to an understanding of the course of the Supreme Court's search and seizure decisions thus far that this book is devoted.

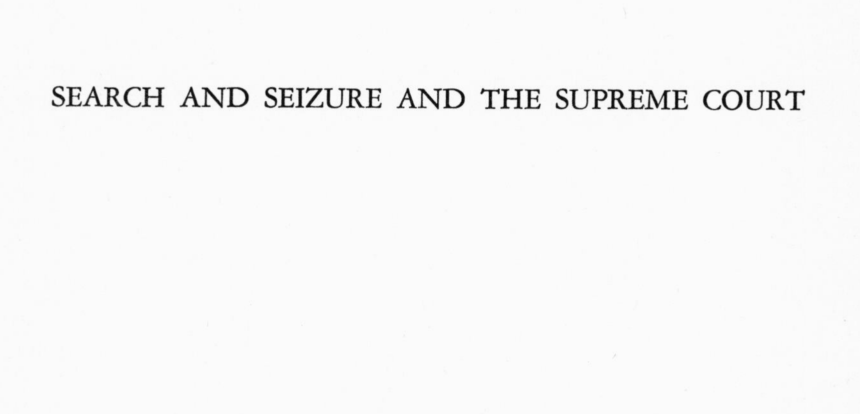

# SEARCH AND SEIZURE AND THE SUPREME COURT

## Chapter I

# THE FOURTH AMENDMENT: ITS ORIGINS AND SIGNIFICANCE

The provisions of the United States Constitution do not always furnish us with a gloss of history sufficiently rich to illuminate their meaning much beyond the bare words in which the provisions are stated. A few paragraphs in Farrand's *Records* or Elliot's *Debates* may be all that is available to demonstrate the framers' "intent" for legislators and judges called upon to construe a particular constitutional provision. Even the guarantees of the Bill of Rights are for the most part almost barren of meaningful historical background in terms of American, as distinguished from English, experience. Guarantees such as trial by jury, the privilege against forced incrimination, and that against double jeopardy were hallowed by the centuries; as part of the common law of England they became as firmly established in the American colonies as in the mother country itself. To understand why they were sufficiently prized to be placed in the Constitution, one must study English, rather than American, history. Such, however, is not the case with the Fourth Amendment. Alone among those constitutional provisions which set standards of fair conduct for the apprehension and trial of accused persons, the Fourth Amendment provides us with a rich historical background rooted in American, as well as English, experience; it is the one procedural safeguard in the Constitution that grew directly out of the events which immediately preceded the revolutionary struggle with England.

An understanding of the antecedent history of the Fourth Amendment is therefore important for an evaluation of the subsequent development of that amendment through judicial construction. History alone cannot, of course, provide the Supreme Court with clear guidance on all search and seizure questions up for decision, if only because the historical record is not always as clear as we should like it to be, and also because some issues raised under the Fourth Amendment—such as the constitutionality of wire tapping or compulsory blood tests in criminal cases—are of recent origin and could not have been anticipated by those who drafted the Bill of Rights. However, even concerning those questions—and they are many and important

—to which the words of the Fourth Amendment do not address themselves with a clarity sufficient to forestall constitutional controversy, history can shed a beam of light to illuminate the underlying purposes of the amendment and thereby provide some guidance for a selection from the possible interpretations of the one that would best realize those purposes. The Court's search and seizure opinions frequently invoke history as a basis for decision. Justice Frankfurter, for example, who was perhaps responsible for more memorable search and seizure opinions than any other member of the Court, strongly relied on his interpretation of the historical events that gave rise to the Fourth Amendment for his understanding of the amendment itself. Indeed, for Frankfurter, history was perhaps *the* determining factor in a number of his opinions, for he believed that the Fourth Amendment was designed to prevent the recurrence of a specific historical grievance and that its meaning therefore did not change with the ebb and flow of events, unlike such generic provisions of the Constitution as the First Amendment.

The Fourth Amendment was not a construct based on abstract considerations of political theory, but was drafted by the framers for the express purpose of providing enforceable safeguards against a recurrence of highhanded search measures which Americans, as well as the people of England, had recently experienced. These abuses, which in the American colonies took place largely in the fifteen years before the American Revolution and which extended over a much longer period of time in England, had done violence to the ancient maxim that "A man's house is his castle." It was to guard against a repetition of these experiences that six of the newly independent American states almost immediately wrote into their own constitutions provisions akin to those of the Fourth Amendment. The antecedent history of the Fourth Amendment, therefore, has two principal sources: the English and American experiences of virtually unrestrained and judicially unsupervised searches, and the action that had already been taken by some of the states to guard constitutionally against a recurrence of this abuse. From these tributaries flowed the Fourth Amendment.

A broad search and seizure power was first introduced into England by the Tudors. This power was continually exercised and expanded as an important instrument in the enforcement of the state licensing system for printed matter. The fight for freedom of the press waged in England for nearly three centuries was thus connected with the issue of the scope of the search power.[1]

Within fifty years of the introduction of printing into England in 1476, the control of seditious and nonconformist publications had become a matter of intense state concern. At first the Crown alone, by use of the royal prerogative, and later Parliament as well, by means of legislation, attempted to suppress undesirable publications. This control, in one form or another, lasted well into the final quarter of the eighteenth century.

A system of prior state censorship, making it mandatory for all publications to receive the nation's license, was introduced by Henry VIII in 1538.[2] With only brief interruptions the licensing system was continued until 1694, after which less direct methods of control were used for another hundred years.

To help enforce the licensing system, vast powers of search were conferred on those engaged in ferreting out violators and evidence. The Stationers' Company, a private guild organization, was incorporated under Mary in 1557 and, in return for monopoly privileges over printing granted to its members, was instructed "to make search wherever it shall please them in any place . . . within our kingdom of England . . . and to seize, take hold, burn . . . those books and things which are or shall be printed contrary to the form of any statute, act, or proclamation. . . ."[3] In delegating the search power to the printers themselves, the monarchy effectively silenced possible opposition by the printing trade to the enforcement of the licensing provisions. For nearly a century, until the decline and fall of the monarchy in the 1640's, the Company assumed the main responsibility of enforcement. Its zeal in making the licensing system effective was motivated solely by self-gain; in searching for non-licensed printing its members were, in effect, protecting their own monopoly rights. As was therefore to be expected, their effectiveness as official searchers over the years waxed and waned in proportion to the extent that their own interests were being served by the licensing system.

Three closely associated tribunals were responsible for suppression of seditious printing: the King's or Queen's (Privy) Council; its judicial offshoot, the Court of Star Chamber, created in 1487 but grown to new power and eminence under Elizabeth and her succes-

1. The restrictions on freedom of the press in England during this period and the utilization of the search power as an instrument of suppression are thoroughly and expertly discussed in Frederick Seaton Siebert, *Freedom of the Press in England: 1476–1776* (Urbana, Ill., 1952).

2. *Ibid.*, p. 48.

3. Edward Arber, *A Transcript of the Registers of the Company of Stationers of London, 1554–1640* (London, 1875), Vol. I, p. xxxi.

sors; and the ecclesiastical Court of High Commission, established by Elizabeth in 1558. These tribunals in the sixteenth and early seventeenth centuries developed into a fine art the search for forbidden materials; there is no evidence of its extensive use earlier.[4]

An Order in Council in 1566 expanded the authority of the Stationers' Company. In addition to confirming the power of the Company to search any premises on which it suspected that the printing laws were being violated, the order broadly empowered the wardens of the Company to open for inspection, and if necessary seize, all imported packages of papers and books. In 1576 the Company adopted regulations requiring that each printing house in London be searched weekly by a party of two printers. The size of the searching party was increased to three in 1585.[5]

In 1586 a Star Chamber decree, noting the widespread evasion of previous enactments, ordered even stricter censorship and severer penalties and reaffirmed the Company's virtually unlimited search powers. The decree even required that printers set up their presses in places that would be readily accessible to the searchers. Any press used for unlicensed printing was to be destroyed.[6]

Conditions in seventeenth-century England showed no improvement. James I directed the Court of High Commission "to inquire and search for . . . all heretical, schismatical and seditious books, libels and writings, and all other books, pamphlets and portraitures offensive to the state or set forth without sufficient and lawful authority"[7] and to seize the offending materials, together with the presses used to print them. It was in James's reign, apparently, that the writ of assistance (a general warrant for the search and seizure of smuggled goods, so called because it charged all officers of the Crown with assisting those executing the warrant) made its first appearance.[8] Charles I, smarting under Parliament's refusal to grant

4. The use of the search power prior to the Tudors seems to have been sporadic. The first parliamentary legislation on the subject did not appear until the fourteenth century. This legislation, passed in 1335 in the reign of Edward III, required innkeepers in the ports to search guests for imported counterfeit money. As a reward for their trouble they were given one quarter of the seizures. Nelson B. Lasson, *The History and Development of the Fourth Amendment to the United States Constitution* (Baltimore, 1937), p. 23. Lasson's book is a comprehensive and documented study of the origins of the Fourth Amendment and also contains a survey of the cases up to 1937. While still valuable, it must now be supplemented with more recent studies, such as Siebert's, cited in these pages.

5. Siebert, *Freedom of the Press*, pp. 83–84.

6. *Ibid.*, pp. 84–85.

7. Quoted in *ibid.*, p. 139.

8. Lasson, *Fourth Amendment*, p. 28. Historians generally attribute the appearance of this writ to the reign of Charles II, when it was first authorized by Parliament. Only Lasson, it seems, has established the fact of its existence as early as the reign of James I.

the "tonnage and poundage" duty he requested, authorized the collection of the duty on his own responsibility. In order to counteract widespread resistance to the enforcement of the measure, Privy Council messengers were empowered "to enter into any vessel, house, warehouse, or cellar, search in any trunk or chest and breach any bulk whatsoever. . . ."[9] The reign of Charles was also noteworthy for the general searches carried on for printed matter. Among those to suffer was the great luminary of the common law, Sir Edward Coke, then on his deathbed. Privy Council messengers searched his house and seized virtually all his manuscripts: "As Coke lay dying in the great curtained bed, they ransacked study and library, took away the manuscripts for all four parts of the Institutes, the manuscript notes for additional books of *Reports*,"[10] and some fifty additional manuscripts. In 1637, to aid enforcement of a still stricter censorship decree by the Star Chamber, the Stationers' Company was given express authority to "search at any time of the day or night they saw fit."[11]

But the days of the Star Chamber were drawing to a close. The decree of 1637 proved to be one of its dying gasps. The Long Parliament, which assembled in 1640, abolished the Courts of Star Chamber and High Commission and even ordered punishment for those who had executed general warrants against members of Parliament.[12]

However, these actions of Parliament proved to be episodic and did not put an end to highhanded search measures. The years 1641–43 were a licentious period. With the power of the monarchy in collapse, and the royal enforcement agencies gone, writers were for the first time able to give free rein to their opinions, and Parliament, as much as the King, was their target. The new Parliament was not long in acting. Once its authority was firmly consolidated, it passed much the same kind of censorship and search laws as had been previously decreed by Star Chamber.[13] It was in response to one such ordinance, passed in 1643, that Milton pleaded the cause of a free press in his famed *Areopagitica*.[14] The royal prerogative had now given way to the authority of Parliament, but the substance of the regulations remained unaltered. When Cromwell dispensed

9. *Ibid.*, p. 30.
10. Catherine Drinker Bowen, *The Lion and the Throne: The Life and Times of Sir Edward Coke, 1552–1634* (Boston, 1957), p. 533.
11. Lasson, *Fourth Amendment*, p. 32.
12. *Ibid.*, pp. 32–33.
13. Siebert, *Freedom of the Press*, pp. 173–76.
14. Lasson, *Fourth Amendment*, p. 33.

with Parliament during his Protectorate, he too issued orders strictly controlling the press, but he replaced the Stationers' Company with his Council of State as the chief enforcement agency.[15]

The Restoration Parliament proved to be no greater respecter of privacy. Its Regulation of Printing Act of 1662 "made provision for powers of search as broad as any ever granted by Star Chamber decree."[16] The secretaries of state were made responsible for enforcement of the regulations and were granted the broadest power to issue search warrants. The warrants issued ranged "all the way from complete particularization to the most general phrases."[17] An example of the latter is the warrant issued to Roger L'Estrange, named in 1663 to the newly created post of Surveyor of the Press, who was authorized to "seize all seditious books and libels and to apprehend the authors, contrivers, printers, publishers, and dispersers of them," and to "search any house, shop, printing room, chamber, warehouse, etc. for seditious, scandalous or unlicensed pictures, books or papers. . . ."[18]

After the Printing Act expired in 1679, Charles II summoned the judges of England, presided over by Chief Justice Scroggs of Star Chamber notoriety, to decide whether legislation was in fact necessary for the licensing of the press. Scroggs rendered an opinion that even without legislation, in conformity with the common law, no matter could be printed without the King's license, and he proceeded to issue general warrants to aid the King's independent efforts to suppress unlicensed printing.[19] Another important development under Charles II was the legislation authorizing issuance of writs of assistance in the search for smuggled goods.[20] However, as we have seen, this writ had already made its appearance, apparently without parliamentary authorization, under James I.

We have thus far witnessed a virtually uninterrupted growth of the search and seizure power in England over a period of a century and a half. When did limitations eventually come to be placed

15. The restrictions on freedom of the press during the Puritan Revolution, 1640–1660, are chronicled in Siebert, *Freedom of the Press*, pp. 165–233. Among those whose activity was restricted most by such ordinances were the Levellers, a democratic group well ahead of its time, which advocated such things as religious toleration, equitable parliamentary districts, and the suffrage without property qualifications for all males over twenty-one. The Levellers indulged extensively in unlicensed printing to spread their propaganda. See H. N. Brailsford, *The Levellers and the English Revolution* (Stanford, Calif., 1961), pp. 92, 470, 472.
16. Lasson, *Fourth Amendment*, p. 37.
17. Siebert, *Freedom of the Press*, p. 254.
18. Quoted in *ibid.*
19. Lasson, *Fourth Amendment*, p. 38.
20. 13 and 14 Car. II, c. 11.

on the exercise of this power? It seems that, with respect to Parliament's attitude, at least, the Revolution of 1688 marked a turning point of some moment. Even before the Revolution, in 1685, Chief Justice Scroggs was impeached, in part for his issuance of general warrants. This marked the first time that Parliament had granted recognition to "the idea that general warrants were an arbitrary exercise of governmental authority against which the public had a right to be safeguarded."[21] Strangely enough, the Printing Act was renewed in the very year in which Scroggs was impeached, and it continued in force for some time, even after the Revolution. When it expired in 1694, however, the Commons repeatedly refused to join the Lords in voting for another renewal.[22] The growth of a two-party system made it too risky a business for Parliament to entrust a government of one party with the enforcement of a licensing system that could be manipulated for political advantage.[23]

It was through efforts to control abusive enforcement of tax laws that limits were first placed on search and seizure. At the urging of the new king, William of Orange, one tax was abolished by Parliament specifically on the ground that the searches required in its enforcement constituted "a badge of slavery upon the whole people, exposing every man's house to be entered into, and searched by persons unknown to him."[24] In 1733 a tobacco and wine tax proposed by Walpole failed of parliamentary enactment because of its search provisions, though under its terms only warehouses would have been subject to search on a general warrant; a special warrant would have been required for the search of dwellings.[25] And in 1763 William Pitt proclaimed against the cider tax and its enforcement provisions. In words which have rung out through the centuries, he cried: "The poorest man may in his cottage bid defiance to all the force of the Crown. It may be frail—its roof may shake—the wind may blow through it—the storm may enter—the rain may enter—but the King of England cannot enter; all his force dares not cross the threshold of that ruined tenement!"[26]

Was there any deep-rooted principle in English law that could be set against the galloping search power, and which might be said to be the basis of our Fourth Amendment? Magna Carta (1215) has

21. Lasson, *Fourth Amendment*, pp. 38–39.
22. Siebert, *Freedom of the Press*, pp. 261–62, 306.
23. *Ibid.*, p. 263.
24. Quoted by Lasson, *Fourth Amendment*, p. 39, from the Preamble of the act.
25. *Ibid.*, pp. 40–41.
26. Quoted by Justice Douglas in *Frank* v. *Maryland*, 359 U.S. 360, 378–79 (1959) (dissenting opinion).

at least some relevance in this connection and was specifically cited in one of the judicial decisions,[27] to be discussed shortly, which placed limits on the search power. Among its provisions was the famous Chapter XXXIX, which denied to the sovereign the right to "go upon" or "send upon" any "freeman" except "by the law of the land." However, aside from the fact that the Great Charter was a feudal document which did not guarantee protection for all social classes, Chapter XXXIX was in any event not an early analogue to present-day search restrictions. It was merely intended to prevent the king from swooping down, as was his practice, on those who had offended him and arbitrarily meting out judgment without recourse to established legal procedures of the day (such as trial by combat).[28] Nevertheless, Magna Carta did set forth certain limiting principles of law enforcement which could later be extended to all subjects of the realm and expanded to cover new subject matter, as was indeed the case in the subsequent course of English history.

More important for our purposes than Magna Carta was the development of the common law. In disregard of the sweeping arrest and search authorizations by Star Chamber and Parliament, common-law jurists were busy formulating salutory rules of arrest, search, and seizure for everyday crimes either by judicial decision or by recommendation. Foremost among these jurists was Hale, who in his renowned *History of the Pleas of the Crown* charted legal rules,[29] some based on case precedents, which would later be elevated to constitutional principles in the United States.

Coke had gone so far as to declare that the common law gave no power "to break open any man's house to search for a felon or stolen goods either in the day or night."[30] Hale disagreed and authorized the use of search warrants on the ground of "necessity, especially in these times, where felonies and robberies are so fre-

27. *Huckle* v. *Money*, 2 Wilson 205, 207 (1763).

28. William Sharp McKechnie, *Magna Carta: A Commentary on the Great Charter of King John* (2d rev. ed.; New York, 1958), pp. 376–81. The full text of Chapter XXXIX is found on pp. 375–76.

29. Sir Matthew Hale, *The History of the Pleas of the Crown* (1st Am. ed.; Philadelphia, 1847), Vol. I, pp. 474ff.; Vol. II, pp. 105ff., 149r–52. Hale (1609–1676) was appointed to the bench by Cromwell. He at first refused Cromwell's offer of the appointment because "he was not satisfied with the lawfulness of his authority" and acquiesced only when Cromwell warned him that "if they would not permit him to govern by red gowns, he was resolved to govern by red coats." Emelyn's Preface, *ibid.*, Vol. I, pp. v, vi. Hale's will had directed that his manuscripts should not be published "lest they should undergo any expurgations or interpolations in the licensing. . . . [*H*]*e was resolved none of his writings should be at the mercy of the licensers.*" Emelyn's Preface, p. xx. Publication did not take place until 1736, after the licensing laws had been erased from the statute books.

30. Quoted in *ibid.*, Vol. II, p. 149r.

quent."[31] Nonetheless, in order to be valid the warrant had to meet certain standards. Hale declared general warrants void, though he admitted there was precedent for them even under common law. They "are not justifiable, for it makes the party to be in effect the judge; and therefore searches made by pretense of such general warrants give no more power to the officer or party, than what they may do by law without them."[32] Even specific warrants, which met the test of particularity in descriptions of persons and premises, were "judicial acts"[33] requiring judicial approval, and were not to be issued unless they followed an examination of the complainant under oath and a finding of probable cause. The following sentence sums up Hale's idea: "They [warrants] are not to be granted without oath made before the justice of a felony committed, and that the party complaining hath probable cause to suspect they are in such a house or place, and do shew his reasons of such suspicion."[34] It should be observed, finally, that the standards of probable cause required by Hale applied equally to arrest and to search warrants. Denouncing arrest on mere suspicion, Hale declared that "a justice cannot grant a warrant to apprehend all persons suspected, but must name their names. . . ." He admitted that the King's Bench had been known to order arrest on suspicion, but dismissed these deviations from common-law practice with the observation that "what is thus done in the highest court of ordinary justice, is not to be a pattern for particular justices or inferior jurisdictions."[35]

Such voices as Hale's had gone largely unheeded by King and Parliament. Now, with poetic justice, it was the judiciary which, in a series of important cases, provided the principal driving force for the abolition of the general warrant. Licensing of printing came to an end in England in 1694, but restraints on freedom of the press continued. Prosecution for seditious libel, which is to say punishment for offensive literature after publication, replaced prior restraint as the means of regulation.[36] To aid these prosecutions, the secretaries of state continued to issue general warrants, though their statutory authority to do so had lapsed with the Printing Act. Two such warrants led to a quartet of celebrated cases.

31. *Ibid.*
32. *Ibid.*, p. 150.
33. *Ibid.*
34. *Ibid.* Hale throughout uses the terms "probable cause" and "suspicion" interchangeably. At one point he refers to "the certainty of the crime" when speaking of probable cause. Vol. I, p. 577.
35. *Ibid.*, pp. 586–87.
36. Fox's Libel Act of 1792 changed the law of seditious libel and effectively put an end to such prosecutions.

In 1762 John Wilkes had begun publication of the *North Briton,* a pamphlet series violently attacking the government. Number 45 in the series, a particularly offensive document, aroused the government's ire. Lord Halifax, Secretary of State, issued a general warrant to four messengers, commanding the arrest of the perpetrators and the seizure of their papers. In a three-day period forty-nine persons were arrested, and from two of these, the printer and publisher of Number 45, the messengers learned of Wilkes's authorship of the pamphlet. Wilkes, denouncing the warrant as "a ridiculous warrant against the whole English nation," refused to accompany the messengers when they came to arrest him and had to be carried away, though his days in the Tower were limited because of his privilege as a member of Parliament. His bureau was thoroughly ransacked, and all his private papers were seized.[37] The printers brought suit against the messengers for false imprisonment and were awarded damages of three hundred pounds after Chief Justice Pratt told the jury that "to enter a man's house by virtue of a nameless warrant, in order to procure evidence, is worse than the *Spanish* Inquisition; a law under which no Englishman would wish to live an hour. . . ." Pratt admitted that the amount was excessive for six hours of imprisonment, but he refused to grant a new trial because, he said, it was not the slight injury done which excited the jury. Rather, "they saw a magistrate over all the king's subjects, exercising arbitrary power, violating *Magna Carta,* and attempting to destroy the liberty of the kingdom, by insisting upon the legality of this general warrant before them. . . . These are the ideas which struck the jury on the trial; and I think they have done right in giving exemplary damages."[38] Wilkes's own suit against the undersecretary in charge of the warrant's execution resulted in a verdict of one thousand pounds. (Years later he was awarded four thousand pounds against Lord Halifax himself.[39]) Pratt declared on that occasion that the question of the general warrant was "a point of the greatest consequence he had ever met with in his whole practice." "If such a power is truly invested in a secretary of state, and he can delegate this power, it certainly may affect the person and property of every man in this kingdom, and is totally subversive of the liberty of the subject."[40]

37. Thomas M. Cooley, *A Treatise on the Constitutional Limitations* (7th ed.; Boston, 1927), Vol. I, pp. 612–14, n. 1.
38. *Huckle* v. *Money*, 2 Wilson 205, 207 (1763).
39. 19 Howell's State Trials 1406.
40. *Wilkes* v. *Wood*, 19 Howell's State Trials 1153, 1167 (1763). Wilkes's immunity was, however, of short duration. He was soon successfully prosecuted for seditious libel and expelled from the Commons.

Pratt was the beneficiary of the nation's gratitude. He received the freedom of several cities, among them London and Dublin. The city of London commissioned Sir Joshua Reynolds to paint his portrait to be hung in the Guildhall, and Dr. Samuel Johnson supplied the inscription of "zealous supporter of English liberty by law."[41]

Pratt was not the only judge to speak out against the general warrant. In rejecting an appeal from a jury award of four hundred pounds to Leach, one of the printers seized in the Wilkes case, Chief Justice Mansfield of the Court of King's Bench proclaimed that the Secretary of State's issuance of general warrants, while admittedly of long usage and sanctioned by the Star Chamber, was nevertheless "contrary to the usage of all other justices and conservators of the peace." "Hale and all others hold such an uncertain warrant void: and there is no case or book to the contrary."[42] The other judges in the case delivered opinions denouncing the warrants as "illegal and void" and stated that "no degree of antiquity can give sanction to a usage bad in itself."[43]

The most famous case in the series was *Entick* v. *Carrington,*[44] decided in 1765, which, as we shall see later, exercised great influence on the subsequent course of search law in the United States as well as in England. Entick, the editor of a critical publication, the *Monitor,* was the victim, half a year before the Wilkes search, of a general search in which his papers were seized. Entick's association with the *Monitor* was well known, and the warrant was at least specific as to the person. Entick at first took no action, but was emboldened by Wilkes's success[45] and brought a suit for trespass which won a jury verdict of three hundred pounds. Pratt, now elevated to the peerage as Lord Camden, delivered the opinion of the Court of Common Pleas sustaining the verdict on appeal. "[I]f this point should be determined in favor of the jurisdiction," he declared, "the secret cabinets and bureaus of every subject in this kingdom will be thrown open to the search and inspection of a messenger, whenever the secretary of state shall think fit to charge, or even to suspect, a person to be the author, printer, or publisher of a seditious libel."[46] He rudely dismissed Star Chamber precedent as without authority in a common-law court. Such precedent "is null, and nothing but ignorance can excuse the judge that subscribed [to] it."[47]

41. Lasson, *Fourth Amendment*, p. 46.
42. *Leach* v. *Money*, 19 Howell's State Trials 1002, 1027 (1765).
43. *Ibid.*
44. 19 Howell's State Trials 1029 (1765).
45. Lasson, *Fourth Amendment*, p. 47.
46. 19 Howell's State Trials 1029, 1063.
47. *Ibid.*, p. 1071.

These judicial decisions, and the popular feeling they aroused, were influential in forcing Parliament to act. Beginning in 1764, an assault on general warrants was led in the House of Commons by Pitt, who admitted that in 1760, as Secretary of State, he too had authorized use of the warrants though he knew them to be illegal on the authority of Pratt, then Attorney General. He pleaded the exigencies of wartime emergencies to excuse his own misdeeds and denied any justification for continued use of the warrants. In 1766 the Commons denounced general search warrants as illegal except when their use might specifically be authorized by act of Parliament. The luster of this achievement was, however, somewhat dimmed by the failure of a proposal to abolish the general arrest warrant.[48] It must also be remembered that the power to issue writs of assistance to search for smuggled goods, previously authorized by Parliament, remained unimpaired.

While Englishmen were struggling to free themselves of the bane of indiscriminate searches, important developments concerning the search power were taking place across the Atlantic in England's American colonies. In defense of the mercantile system, Parliament had passed a number of navigation and trade acts which, through the imposition of prohibitive import duties, were designed to prevent the colonies from trading with areas outside the Empire. Before 1760 enforcement was lax and these laws were honored more in the breach than in the observance. Smuggling became rampant in the colonies and was engaged in even by the most respectable persons[49] in order to circumvent laws regarded as oppressive and unjustifiable. In 1760, however, with the French and Indian Wars successfully over, the effort to stamp out smuggling began in earnest. The principal enforcement weapon was the writ of assistance.

A difference may be noted between the effects of the writ of assistance in the colonies and in England. To be sure, the exercise of a broad search power to enforce the customs laws in England had not

48. Lasson, *Fourth Amendment*, pp. 48–49. And see Hargrave's note at the conclusion of the Entick case in the *Reports*.

49. Among the prominent men engaged in this profession was John Hancock. He was accused of smuggling in 1769 and was defended by John Adams. The case, together with Adams' argument, is reported in Quincy's *Massachusetts Reports, 1761–1772*, p. 457. Among other arguments, Adams used the familiar one of no taxation without representation. The law, said Adams, "was made without our Consent. My Clyent Mr. Hancock never consented to it. He never voted for it himself, and he never voted for any Man to make such a Law for him." For some unexplained reason the case was eventually dropped.

gone unchallenged; as we have seen, Parliament's rebuff to Walpole's tobacco and wine tax and Pitt's ringing declamation against the cider tax were occasioned by the search provisions of those acts. But, in general, the search for smuggled goods does not appear to have created a stir comparable to the one in America, perhaps because issuance of the writ of assistance in England was "an infrequent practice."[50] Opposition to arbitrary use of power is usually generated by the frequency and extent of its exercise.

The warrants of the Secretary of State in England, outlawed in the cases just discussed, were nevertheless an improvement on those authorized by the Star Chamber and the licensing acts. As in the Wilkes case, the Secretary's warrants, while general in nature, were at least directed at the perpetrators of a particular offense and were therefore limited as to both time and objective. The obnoxious feature of writs of assistance was their character as permanent search warrants placed in the hands of customs officials: they might be used with unlimited discretion and were valid for the duration of the life of the sovereign.[51]

In the colonies the writs of assistance, used more rigorously, caused profound resentment. Massachusetts furnishes us with most of the extant historical record concerning colonial writs of assistance, for it was in the Bay province that they were most frequently employed and there that most opposition to their enforcement was encountered. In Massachusetts, as elsewhere in the colonies, it was once the unopposed practice of customs officers to enter and search buildings with no more formal authority than that of their commissions as Crown officers.[52] When opposition to these searches was aroused, the Governor found it necessary to issue writs of assistance to the officers. This practice continued until objections to the propriety of the procedure led the Governor to advise the officers to apply for

50. Homer Carey Hockett, *The Constitutional History of the United States. 1776–1826* (New York, 1939), Vol. I, p. 74.

51. The texts of several writs are reproduced in Quincy's *Massachusetts Reports, 1761–1772*, App. I, pp. 395–540. This Appendix, which is the work of Horace Gray, Jr., later an Associate Justice of the United States Supreme Court, contains in its pages the outstanding study of writs of assistance in the colonies. (It is hereafter cited as Gray, in Quincy.) In addition to supplying Gray's own acute analysis and commentary, the Appendix is a virtual compendium of the important historical sources on the subject, upon which subsequent commentators have drawn generously. Gray's essay is for the most part concerned with the struggle over the writs in Massachusetts. For developments in the other colonies, it must now be supplemented with D. M. Dickerson's able study, "Writs of Assistance as a Cause of the American Revolution," in Richard B. Morris (ed.), *The Era of the American Revolution: Studies Inscribed to Evarts Boutell Greene* (New York, 1939), p. 40.

52. Lasson, *Fourth Amendment*, p. 55.

writs in the Superior Court.[53] Thereafter, the Superior Court took over the function of issuing writs. It granted the first writ in 1755 to Charles Paxton, who bore the ominous title of Surveyor and Searcher of the Port of Boston.[54]

The law respecting writs of assistance in the colonies was not at all clear. Two statutes were involved, and in each there was a grave obscurity. The first, dating from the reign of Charles II,[55] authorized the Court of Exchequer in England to issue writs of assistance but did not specify the standards which must be met for their issuance. It was at least arguable that only special writs were authorized.[56] The second statute, passed under William III,[57] simply applied the provisions of the earlier act to the colonies. But there was no Court of Exchequer in the colonies, and it was doubtful which court in each of the colonies best fulfilled the definition of an exchequer court.[58]

These gaps in the law had been filled by practice. For a century the Court of Exchequer had approved writs drawn up by the English customs authorities with none of the safeguards required for search warrants under the common law. And the Superior Court—the highest court in the province of Massachusetts—had since 1755 exercised the function of a court of exchequer there. The question of whether practice did indeed conform to legality was tested for the first time in 1761. It is truly remarkable that there had been no judicial comment on these statutes, either in England or in America, before that time.

53. Historians have invariably described the writ of assistance as a general search warrant, and a reading of the text of any of the warrants reproduced by Gray in Quincy's *Massachusetts Reports* appears to substantiate this view. However, Dickerson maintains that issuance of the writ was not at all a grant of the search power, since that power inhered in the officers in any event by virtue of their commissions. The writs, he says, were judicial orders which empowered the customs officials to summon the sheriff or constable (who was under the jurisdiction of the judges and not otherwise available) to keep the peace while the search was in progress. Dickerson, "Writs of Assistance," pp. 45–46. Lasson, on the other hand, is of the view that the earlier searches on the authority of the officials' commissions alone were "legally unjustified." Lasson, *Fourth Amendment*, p. 55. Whether or not the writs actually granted the search power, their importance—and the opposition aroused by their use—stemmed from the fact that the summoning of the peace officers to prevent frustration of the search made the general search an effective instrument of enforcement. Those opposed to the writs definitely regarded them as synonymous with the power to search itself.

54. Gray, in Quincy, pp. 401–5.

55. 13 and 14 Car. II, c. 11.

56. Yet another statute preceding these two had authorized the issuance of the writ only when preceded by the applicant's oath as to the facts. 12 Car. II, c. 19. If this statute had not been repealed by the later ones, the issuance of general writs was definitely illegal. Dickerson, "Writs of Assistance," p. 47.

57. 7 and 8 Wm. III, c. 22.

58. For discussion of these statutes, see Dickerson, "Writs of Assistance," pp. 43–47.

Two events which occurred in the year 1760 set the stage for the court test. The first was the death of George II in October. Since writs of assistance were valid only until six months after the demise of the sovereign in whose reign they were issued,[59] this meant that the writs then in force would expire early in 1761 and new ones would be needed. The second was the death of Chief Justice Sewall of the Superior Court—"a zealous Friend of Liberty," John Adams called him. Sewall had issued Paxton's writ but, according to Adams, was nevertheless troubled over "the Legality and Constitutionality of the Writ, and the Power of the Court to grant it."[60]

Sixty-three Boston merchants, opposed to the issuance of new writs, engaged James Otis, Jr., and Oxenbridge Thatcher to argue their cause. Otis had just resigned his lucrative Crown position as Advocate-General of Admiralty in order to avoid representing the government in this controversy. His father, James Otis, Sr., had been denied the hoped-for succession to the position of Chief Justice vacated by the death of Sewall, though he had twice been promised the first vacancy on the Superior Court. Governor Sir Francis Bernard, seeking a man pliable to the wishes of the monarchy, appointed instead Lieutenant Governor Thomas Hutchinson,[61] before whom the case came up for argument in February, 1761. Representing the provincial government was Attorney General Gridley, " 'father of the bar' in Boston, a man full of years and legal lore."[62] Once again the man seeking the writ was Paxton.[63] The questions at issue were whether the writs authorized by Parliament were indeed general rather than specific, and whether the Superior Court had the authority of a court of exchequer.

Gridley argued for the writs on the basis of the English statutes.[64] He even offered the argument that the writs were beneficial in

59. This feature, too, was merely a matter of legal practice rather than a legal requirement, according to Dickerson, "Writs of Assistance," p. 46.

60. L. H. Butterfield (ed.), *Diary and Autobiography of John Adams* (Cambridge, Mass., 1961), Vol. III, p. 275. (Hereafter cited as *Adams Diary*.)

61. Gray, in Quincy, pp. 410–11, n. 9.

62. Page Smith, *John Adams* (New York, 1962), Vol. I, p. 38.

63. In his later years John Adams, when writing of the case, confused Paxton with James Cockle, Collector at Salem, who, according to Adams, was the customs official making application for the writ. *Adams Diary*, Vol. III, p. 275. Adams' statement is accepted uncritically by the editor of his diary. *Adams Diary*, Vol. III, p. 329, n. 4. Page Smith, Adams' biographer, in apparent reliance on the diary, also gives Cockle as the applicant. *John Adams*, Vol. I, p. 51. There is no question, however, that the case was brought about by Paxton's application and that it was he who eventually received the writ.

64. No complete text of the arguments is available. What we have is based on the notes taken by John Adams, a youthful spectator in the courtroom, which were not made public until fifty years afterwards. See Charles Francis Adams, *The Life and Works of John Adams* (Boston, 1856), Vol. II, pp. 521–25. The arguments are re-

nature, providing "a check" on the exercise of arbitrary authority, since their execution required the presence of a sheriff who could be counted upon "to have an eye over" the customs officers.[65] He denied the right to privacy against the king: "Everybody knows that the subject has the privilege of house only against his fellow subjects, not vs. the King either in matters of crime or fine."[66]

Otis—"by far the most able, manly and commanding Character of his Age at the Bar,"[67] according to John Adams—might have confined himself to challenging the applicability of these statutes to writs of assistance in the colonies, as was indeed brilliantly done by Thatcher. Otis did argue along this line,[68] but he seized the opportunity to range broadly beyond these limited horizons and, in a stirring argument, on libertarian grounds asserted the principles of English constitutionalism. He denounced the writ as "the worst instrument of arbitrary power, the most destructive of English liberty and the fundamental principles of law, that was ever found in an English law-book."[69] "This writ is against the fundamental principles of law, the privilege of house. A man who is quiet is as secure in his house as a prince in his castle, notwithstanding all his debts and civil procedures of any kind."[70] Otis argued that statutory language said to authorize the writs be interpreted to apply to special warrants only. If this course were not feasible, and general writs were indeed authorized by act of Parliament, then such an act was unenforceable and void because it was in conflict with Magna Carta: "An Act against the Constitution is void; an Act against natural equity is void. And if an Act of Parliament should be made in the

---

produced by Gray, in Quincy, pp. 469–77, with annotations. However, the cause was reargued in November of the same year (see text), and partial notes on what was said were made by Quincy, the court reporter. Quincy, *Massachusetts Reports*, pp. 51ff. Since Gridley, Otis, and Thatcher were once again the protagonists, and the reargument covered the same ground as before, the discussion in the text combines both Adams' account of the argument (as reproduced in Quincy) and Quincy's account of the reargument. (Because notes of the arguments in this case are often expressed in disjointed phrases separated by dashes rather than in complete sentences, punctuation and capitalization in some of the quotations have been changed to conform to modern usage.)

65. Quincy, *Massachusetts Reports*, p. 57. Gridley stressed that the officers did not acquire greater authority through the writs than they already possessed by virtue of their commissions. This is also Dickerson's understanding of the matter. *Supra*, n. 53.

66. Gray, in Quincy, p. 477.

67. *Adams Diary*, Vol. III, p. 275. Adams attributed this estimate to his legal mentor, Putnam, but said it conformed to "the universal opinion."

68. The statutory arguments of Otis and Thatcher were along the lines of the points made above concerning the obscurities in the acts. Gray has a comprehensive discussion of the legality of the writs and arrives at the conclusion that there was at least "reasonable ground" for believing them to be legal. Gray, in Quincy, p. 540.

69. Adams, *Life and Works of John Adams*, Vol. II, p. 523.

70. *Ibid.*, p. 471.

very words of this petition, it would be void."[71] Here was an argument pregnant with promise, for it advocated judicial review of legislation, on the precedent of Dr. Bonham's case.[72] Thus the significance of Otis' speech went far beyond the immediate issue, important as that was, for it helped sow the seeds of later American constitutional practice.

So impressive was Otis' argument that, as Hutchinson later acknowledged, "the court seemed inclined to refuse to grant"[73] the writ. The Chief Justice, however, prevailed on his brethren not to render decision immediately but to continue the case while the question was referred to England. Hutchinson wrote for advice, not, as might be expected, to Pratt, who was then Attorney General, but to the provincial agent, who had once served as a Crown prosecutor in Massachusetts.[74] Upon his favorable reply, the court heard argument once again, in November, 1761, and proceeded to issue the first of the new writs—as it had the first of the old ones—to Surveyor and Searcher Paxton.[75]

The General Court (legislature) of Massachusetts struck back in 1762 with a bill outlawing general warrants and authorizing special writs only, but this was vetoed by the Governor.[76] Thereafter, the writs were executed without difficulty in Massachusetts until 1765. At least fourteen, in addition to Paxton's, appear to have been issued by the Superior Court.[77] Some agitation presumably continued to

71. *Ibid.*, p. 474.
72. 8 Coke's Rep. 107 (1609). Otis specifically referred to this case. Coke spoke in defense of the principle that no man may judge a cause in whose outcome he has a personal interest, and asserted by way of dictum that even Parliament could not by statute authorize violation of this principle: "And it appears in our books, that in many cases, the common law will controul [*sic*] acts of parliament, and sometimes adjudge them to be utterly void: for when an act of parliament is against common right and reason, or repugnant, or impossible to be performed, the common law will controul it, and adjudge such act to be void. . . ." *Ibid.*, p. 118. Coke's words were later echoed by other leading luminaries of the law in England. Lord Holt, for example, called the dictum "far from any extravagancy, for it is a very reasonable and true saying." For citations and discussion of this and similar statements see Gray, in Quincy, pp. 522–26. Nevertheless, Coke's views were not an accurate statement of the English law as of 1761. Coke himself later recanted and, after becoming the champion of Parliament in its struggle with the monarchy, held parliamentary power to be so "transcedent and absolute" that it "cannot be confined . . . within any bounds." Sir Edward Coke, *Institutes of the Laws of England* (London, 1804), Part 4, p. 36.
73. Quoted by Gray, in Quincy, p. 415n. John Adams recalled, in 1816, that Hutchinson had expressly announced from the bench that "the Court could not, at present, see any foundation for the writ of assistance. . . ." Adams, *Life and Works of John Adams*, Vol. X, p. 233.
74. Lasson, *Fourth Amendment*, pp. 62–63.
75. On this point Adams' memory failed him in later years. Writing in 1816, he stated that the case was never finally decided. Adams, *Life and Works of John Adams*, Vol. X, p. 233.
76. Gray, in Quincy, pp. 495–98.
77. *Ibid.*, pp. 422–34.

exist, for on July 24, 1765, the Governor and his Council found it expedient to appoint a committee to inquire into the legality of the writs. But the matter was considered so completely settled legally that the committee reported back only one week later, on July 31, that the power to issue the writs did exist. And among the members of the Council who voted to accept the report was none other than James Otis, Sr.[78]

This deceptive calm was shattered only a month later. The controversy flared up anew with the passage of the Stamp Act. Old animosities were revived, and in the riots on the night of August 26, which took their name from the act, the house of Chief Justice Hutchinson was "destroyed with a savageness unknown in a civilized country"[79] because of his judgment in the writs of assistance case. Before calling on Hutchinson, the mob went first to Paxton's house, which, in the colorful language of Horace Gray, Jr., "was saved by a present of a barrel of punch from the owner of the house."[80] Afterwards it became almost impossible to enforce the writs: the populace gathered to thwart the efforts of the customs officers whenever they appeared.[81] Despite passage of a new act of Parliament[82] in 1767, which removed all shadow of doubt about Parliament's intentions,[83] the writ of assistance was no longer a factor to be reckoned with in Massachusetts.

Until recently, historians uniformly treated the opposition to writs of assistance as almost entirely a Massachusetts affair. This estimate must be revised in the light of a study published in 1939.[84] Were it not for the fact that the other colonies shared in the opposition, it is not likely that the events in Massachusetts, important as they were, would in themselves have been responsible for the adoption of the Fourth Amendment. In Massachusetts resistance to the writs came from the people, elsewhere from the courts themselves. Only in Massachusetts and New Hampshire (which usually followed the practices of the Massachusetts courts) did the courts readily grant the writ; in the other colonies they appear to have refused it. The courts of Pennsylvania, Delaware, Virginia, Connecticut, Rhode Island, Georgia, and Maryland all either refused or ignored appli-

78. *Ibid.*, pp. 439–40.
79. Governor Bernard, quoted in *ibid.*, p. 416n.
80. *Ibid.*, p. 422n.
81. *Ibid.*, p. 445ff.
82. 7 Geo. III, c. 46.
83. Gray, in Quincy, p. 449.
84. Dickerson, "Writs of Assistance." This study supersedes Gray's rather thin discussion of writs of assistance in the other colonies, given in Quincy, pp. 500–11. See also Lasson, *Fourth Amendment*, pp. 73–76.

cation for the writ. Information is lacking on New Jersey and North Carolina, and no application appears to have been made in those colonies. Not until 1773, and then only under heavy pressure, was a writ granted in South Carolina, following previous refusals. New York granted a writ, but not in the form demanded. A new application for a writ in the customary form was handled in leisurely fashion and finally turned down five years later by a court headed by Robert R. Livingston.[85] This courageous action by the judges of most of the colonies in preserving the principles of the common law in the face of mounting pressures from the executive—which paid their salaries and could at any time remove them, or offer them preferment—was in no small part responsible for the later determination of Americans to secure an independent judiciary, free of political control.[86]

To Massachusetts and James Otis, Jr., nevertheless, belongs the credit for the first determined show of resistance to the writ of assistance. In the twilight of his life, John Adams, who was a youthful courtroom spectator during the arguments in the writs of assistance case and afterwards one of the fathers of independence, summed up his vivid impressions of Otis' scintillating oratory on that occasion: "Mr. Otis' oration . . . breathed into this nation the breath of life."[87] "[H]e was a flame of fire! . . . Every man of a crowded audience appeared to me to go away, as I did, ready to take arms against writs of assistance. . . . Then and there the Child Independence was born. In fifteen years, namely in 1776, he grew up to manhood, and declared himself free."[88] Again, years earlier, writing to his wife Abigail to inform her of the resolution for independence passed the day before by the Second Continental Congress, Adams had been pleased to recall the memorable argument by Otis and to designate it as first in "the Chain of Causes and Effects"[89] leading to independence.

The controversy over writs of assistance in the colonies continued all the way up to the Revolutionary War. Even after the outbreak of hostilities, the Continental Congress petitioned the King on October 26, 1774, for a redress of grievances, and among those listed

85. Dickerson, "Writs of Assistance," pp. 49–73.
86. *Ibid.*, pp. 74–75.
87. Adams, *Life and Works of John Adams*, Vol. X, p. 276.
88. *Ibid.*, pp. 247–48.
89. L. H. Butterfield (ed.), *Adams Family Correspondence* (Cambridge, Mass., 1963), Vol. II, p. 28.

was the abuse of the search power: "The officers of the customs are empowered to break open and enter houses, without the authority of any civil magistrate, founded on legal information."[90] It is therefore surprising that the Declaration of Independence, which in its main part consisted of a long list of grievances against the Crown, contained no specific mention of writs of assistance. But that subject may have been alluded to in the remonstrance: "He has . . . sent hither swarms of Officers to harass our people. . . ."[91] Even prior to the Declaration, in June of 1776, Virginia had already moved to provide a constitutional guarantee against recurrence of the abuse. Article X of its Declaration of Rights specifically denounced general warrants as "grievous and oppressive."[92] In the remaining months of 1776, Pennsylvania, Maryland, and North Carolina followed suit and adopted constitutional safeguards regulating searches.[93] North Carolina virtually copied the Virginia article, but Pennsylvania and Maryland went beyond a mere denunciation of the general search and set up standards to regulate all searches: Maryland required oath or affirmation in the application for a warrant, while Pennsylvania in addition set forth the concept of freedom from all unreasonable searches (though not in those words). Next to the last, and the most comprehensive, of the state declarations which antedated the Fourth Amendment was Article XIV of the Massachusetts Declaration of Rights,[94] adopted in 1780, and duplicated by New Hampshire[95] in 1784. Here is to be found for the first time in a constitution the phrase "unreasonable searches," and this article apparently served as the model for the Fourth Amendment:

90. Quoted in Lasson, *Fourth Amendment*, p. 75. The committee of twenty-one appointed by the inhabitants of Boston in Faneuil Hall on November 2, 1772, "to state the Rights of the Colonists—and . . . to Communicate and Publish the same . . . to the World" gave a lengthy explication on the subject of the writs: "Each of these petty officers . . . is entrusted with power more absolute and arbitrary than ought to be lodged in the hands of any Man or body of Men whatsoever. . . . Thus our Houses and even our Bed-Chambers are exposed to be ransacked . . . by Wretches, whom no prudent Man would venture to employ even as Menial Servants. . . ." Quoted by Gray, in Quincy, pp. 466–67.

91. The suggestion is Lasson's. *Fourth Amendment*, p. 80, n. 7.

92. Francis Newton Thorpe (ed.), *The Federal and State Constitutions* (Washington, 1909), Vol. VII, p. 3814.

93. Pennsylvania Declaration of Rights, Article X. Thorpe, *Constitutions*, Vol. V, p. 3083. Maryland Declaration of Rights, Article XXIII. *Ibid.*, Vol. III, p. 1688. North Carolina Declaration of Rights, Article XI. *Ibid.*, Vol. V, p. 2788. It is also proper to mention that Vermont—which was not one of the original colonies, and was not admitted to the Union until 1791—had already achieved a *de facto* independence by 1777, the year in which it adopted a constitutional search provision that duplicated the Pennsylvania article. Declaration of Rights, Article XI. *Ibid.*, Vol. VI, p. 3741.

94. *Ibid.*, Vol. III, p. 1891.

95. Bill of Rights, Section XIX. *Ibid.*, Vol. IV, p. 2456.

Every subject has a right to be secure from all unreasonable searches and seizures of his person, his house, his papers and all his possessions. All warrants, therefore, are contrary to this right, if the cause or foundation of them be not previously supported by oath or affirmation, and if the warrant to a civil officer, to make search in suspected places, or to arrest one or more suspected persons, or to seize their property, be not accompanied with a special designation of the person or objects of search, arrest, or seizure; and no warrant ought to be issued, but in cases, and with the formalities prescribed by the laws.

The Constitutional Convention which met in Philadelphia in 1787 did not include a bill of rights in its draft constitution. Astonishingly, the Convention does not seem to have considered the matter at all until five days before adjournment, and even then in a somewhat casual manner. George Mason, the principal author of the Virginia Declaration of Rights, interrupted a discussion in progress (on the need for providing trial by jury in civil cases) to press for the inclusion of a bill of rights in the proposed constitution. He thought that "with the aid of the State declarations, a bill might be prepared in a few hours."[96] A motion by Elbridge Gerry of Massachusetts, seconded by Mason, that a committee be set up to prepare a draft was unable to attract the support of even a single state delegation and went down to defeat.

Though the Convention, evidently in a hurry to adjourn, had sloughed off the bill of rights question as unimportant,[97] this opinion was not shared by the country as a whole, where the omission was resolutely protested. The absence of a bill of rights was largely responsible for the refusal of Mason and Gerry to sign the Constitution. Luther Martin of Maryland, who quit the Convention, also attacked the defect, while from France Jefferson made known his views, which were critical of the omission.[98] To be sure, the absence

96. Max Farrand (ed.), *The Records of the Federal Convention of 1787* (rev. ed.; New Haven, Conn., 1937), Vol. II, pp. 587–88. The vote was 10 to 0, with Massachusetts absent. The full story of the struggle over adoption of the Bill of Rights is contained in Robert Allen Rutland, *The Birth of the Bill of Rights 1776–1791* (Durham, N.C., 1955). Briefer accounts are in Lasson, *Fourth Amendment*, pp. 79–105; and Edward Dumbauld, *The Bill of Rights and What It Means Today* (Norman, Okla., 1957), pp. 3–56. Rutland's work also traces the historical origins of the rights enumerated and includes an analysis of the various state bills of rights.

97. James Wilson admitted as much in the Pennsylvania Convention. To a question about the absence of a bill of rights, he responded: "But the truth is, Sir, that this circumstance, which has since occasioned so much clamor and debate, never struck the mind of any member of the late convention till, I believe, within three days [*sic*] of the dissolution of that body, and even then of so little account was the idea that it passed off in a short conversation. . . ." Farrand, *Records*, Vol. III, p. 143.

98. For the views of Mason, Gerry, and Martin, see *ibid.*, pp. 136, 128–29, and 288–91, respectively. Jefferson's criticism was contained in letters written to friends on March 13 and March 18, 1789. Albert Ellery Bergh (ed.), *The Writings of Thomas Jefferson* (library ed.; Washington, 1903), Vol. VII, pp. 301, 323.

of a bill of rights was not the only feature of the Constitution to be severely criticized. But the bill of rights issue provided a convenient, and more respectable, ground for all the opponents of the Constitution. The chief reply to these critics, as articulated by Hamilton in *The Federalist,* No. LXXXIV, and James Wilson in the Pennsylvania Convention, was to the effect that a bill of rights was both unnecessary and risky—unnecessary because all rights not surrendered were retained, and risky because its inclusion would imply that rights not enumerated were surrendered.[99] This argument, the advocates of a bill of rights pointed out in reply, was contradicted by the fact that the Constitution did include some guarantees against oppression such as the *habeas corpus* provision, which, if the proposition were granted, should not have been necessary.[100]

Sharp debates followed in a number of the state ratifying conventions, with the upshot that ratification of the Constitution was for a time very much in doubt. In the pivotal state of Virginia, Patrick Henry forcefully urged rejection, and made the absence of a search provision a cardinal point in his argument:

> Any man may be seized, any property may be taken, in the most arbitrary manner, without any evidence or reason. Every thing the most sacred may be searched and ransacked by the strong hand of power. We have infinitely more reason to dread general warrants here than they have in England, because there, if a person be confined, liberty may be quickly obtained by the writ of *habeas corpus.* But here a man living many hundreds of miles from the judges may get in prison before he can get that writ.[101]

Virginia did eventually ratify the Constitution, but not before recommending the adoption of a bill of rights with a search provision even broader than the one in its own Declaration of Rights. New York, which also ratified after a struggle, did not include a bill of rights among its recommendations for amendment but prefaced these recommendations with a declaration enumerating a long list of rights, including "freedom from all unreasonable searches and seizures,"[102] in the understanding that they would be treated as inviolable by the federal government. North Carolina, like Virginia, proposed adoption of a bill of rights with a search provision, but did not ratify the Constitution and, together with Rhode Island,

99. Farrand, *Records*, Vol. III, pp. 161–62.

100. Jonathan Elliot (ed.), *The Debates in the Several State Conventions on the Adoption of the Federal Constitution* (Philadelphia, 1861), Vol. III, pp. 449, 461.

101. *Ibid.*, p. 588.

102. *Ibid.*, Vol. I, p. 328.

refused to join its sister states in union until the new government was already under way.[103]

In recognition of this national criticism, President Washington in his first inaugural address urged modifications in the Constitution to safeguard "the characteristic rights of freemen" but refused to make "particular recommendations."[104] James Madison, a leading light in the Convention, as in the struggle for ratification, committed his great prestige to the fight for a bill of rights and assumed the role of sponsor in pushing the amendments through Congress. He specifically adverted to the need for search safeguards in the light of the necessary and proper clause: "The General Government has a right to pass all laws which shall be necessary to collect its revenue; the means for enforcing the collection are within the discretion of the Legislature: may not general warrants be considered necessary for this purpose . . . ?"[105] Madison's solution to the problem was a clause to read as follows: "The rights of the people to be secure in their persons, their houses, their papers, and their other property, from all unreasonable searches and seizures, shall not be violated by warrants issued without probable cause, supported by oath or affirmation, or not particularly describing the places to be searched, or the persons or things to be seized."[106]

Madison's draft proposal for a bill of rights was referred to committee, where the search provision was altered to read: "The right of the people to be secured in their persons, houses, papers, and effects, shall not be violated by warrants issuing without probable cause, supported by oath or affirmation, and not particularly describing the place to be searched and the persons or things to be seized."[107]

After this version was reported to the House, two errors were noticed by Gerry and were corrected. The word "secured" was altered to read "secure," and the phrase "unreasonable searches and seizures," inadvertently omitted in the committee's draft, was inserted. Benson of New York, objecting to the words "by warrants

103. Six of the states—Delaware, Pennsylvania, New Jersey, Georgia, Connecticut, and Maryland—ratified without making recommendations for amendment, though in Pennsylvania and Maryland strong minority sentiment for recommending a bill of rights with a search provision was beaten down. In addition to Virginia and New York, Massachusetts, South Carolina, and New Hampshire all made recommendations for amendment, though these were for the most part concerned with the structure of government and not with individual rights. The proceedings in the state conventions may be traced in Elliot's *Debates*. Convenient summaries will be found in Rutland, *Birth of Bill*, chaps. vii–viii, and in Dumbauld, *Meaning of Bill*, chap. i.

104. *Inaugural Addresses of the Presidents* (Washington, 1961), p. 3.

105. Joseph Gales (comp.), *Annals of Congress* (Washington, 1834), 1st Cong., 1st Sess., p. 438.

106. *Ibid.*, pp. 434–35.

107. *Ibid.*, p. 754.

issuing" as not sufficiently strong, proposed to substitute the words "and no warrant shall issue," but this version was voted down by a substantial majority.[108] Why, might we ask, is Benson's version, the one which failed to carry, embodied today in the Fourth Amendment?[109] For the explanation we are indebted to Lasson. It is possible that Benson, as chairman of a committee to arrange the amendments as passed, instead reported his own version of the amendment as it had been rejected. No one apparently noticed the change. The authenticity of the Fourth Amendment as a constitutional provision is nevertheless beyond cavil. Whether or not Benson's alteration was noticed, the amendment *in its present form* was formally passed by the House and the Senate and ratified by the states.[110]

The amendments were submitted to the states by Congress in September, 1789. The approval of nine states was required, and the ratification process was not completed for over two years, until December, 1791, when Virginia—surprisingly laggard in view of her insistence on a federal bill of rights—became the ninth of the states to approve. The search and seizure provision, as the Fourth Amendment,[111] was now part of the Constitution. The long, drawn-out struggle for its inclusion had triumphed, but the difficult process of judicial interpretation still lay ahead.

The search and seizure provision, as finally drafted and adopted, had both the virtue of brevity and the vice of ambiguity. The amendment divides naturally into two parts, the first containing a general guarantee of freedom from "unreasonable" searches, the second specifying the conditions under which a warrant authorizing a search might be issued. Nowhere in the amendment is the term "unreasonable" defined or the relationship of the two parts clarified. Three possible interpretations emerge: (1) that the "reasonable" search

108. *Ibid.*

109. The right of the people to be secure in their persons, houses, papers, and effects, against unreasonable searches and seizures, shall not be violated, and no Warrants shall issue, but upon probable cause, supported by Oath or affirmation, and particularly describing the place to be searched, and the persons or things to be seized."

110. Lasson, *Fourth Amendment*, pp. 101–3. It should be noted that the Senate at that time deliberated in secret, and no account of the debate in that chamber is therefore available.

111. The Fourth Amendment was actually sixth in order of proposal. Congress submitted twelve amendments to the states, of which the first two—seeking to regulate the number of representatives and to prohibit changes in the salaries of members of Congress from going into effect before an intervening election—were not ratified. Thus the proposed Third Amendment became the ratified First Amendment, the Fourth became the Second, and so on. In the early case of *Ex parte Burford*, 3 Cranch 448, 451 (1806), Chief Justice Marshall referred to the Fourth Amendment as the "6th Article."

is one which meets the warrant requirements specified in the second clause; (2) that the first clause provides an additional restriction by implying that some searches may be "unreasonable" and therefore not permissible, even when made under warrant; or (3) that the first clause provides an additional search power, authorizing the judiciary to find some searches "reasonable" even when carried out *without* warrant.

From the foregoing historical account, the relationship of the two clauses seems clear enough. The first clause—"The right of the people to be secure . . . against unreasonable searches and seizures, shall not be violated"—recognized as already existing a right to freedom from arbitrary governmental invasion of privacy and did not seek to create or confer such a right. It was evidently meant to re-emphasize (and, in some undefined way, strengthen) the requirements for a valid warrant set forth in the second clause. The second clause, in turn, defines and interprets the first, telling us the kind of search that is *not* "unreasonable," and therefore not forbidden, namely, the one carried out under the safeguards there specified.

Either of the first two interpretations, therefore, is faithful to the intended meaning of the amendment (although the second is preferable). The third clearly is not. Until quite recently the Supreme Court apparently shared this view. In its decisions it generally interpreted the Fourth Amendment to make the "unreasonable" search synonymous with the warrantless search. It held, moreover, that the search for a person's private papers was unreasonable, and therefore forbidden, even when made pursuant to a warrant.[112] Since the late nineteen forties, however, and over the protest of Justice Frankfurter in particular, the Court has moved to the position that the first clause confers a search power of independent potency, one that is not restricted by the specific requirements of the second clause.[113] One exponent of this view is Justice Black.[114] He explains the amendment in this way: the warrant requirements in the second clause are "absolute" and not subject to modification, but the constitutionality of a search may nonetheless be determined by its "reasonableness," regardless of whether it was conducted under warrant. Black's view is not substantiated by history. It seems certain that the Fourth

112. *Boyd* v. *United States*, 116 U.S. 616 (1886); *Gouled* v. *United States*, 255 U.S. 298 (1921).

113. See in particular Justice Minton's opinion for the Court in *United States* v. *Rabinowitz*, 339 U.S. 56 (1950), discussed in Chapter IV.

114. Hugo L. Black, "The Bill of Rights," *New York University Law Review*, XXXV (April, 1960), 865, 873.

Amendment made no provision for the warrantless search[115] any more than it did for the general search warrant. The warrant requirement assures judicial determination of reasonableness *in advance* of the search; the warrantless search will be passed upon by a magistrate only retroactively, if at all. It would be strange, to say the least, for the amendment to specify stringent warrant requirements, after having in effect negated these by authorizing judicially unsupervised "reasonable" searches without warrant. To detach the first clause from the second is to run the risk of making the second virtually useless.

History also makes it clear that the searches to be controlled were of the kind which had constituted abuse of the asserted rights of the colonists—those carried out under public authority, in the name of the law, not those made by private persons not acting under color of law.[116] The private snooper might certainly be dealt with under statute or common law, but it was not to his actions that a constitutional provision was directed. Nor was the amendment directed toward all "unreasonable" governmental searches but only those made under the authority of the federal government. Like the rest of the Bill of Rights, which begins with the words "Congress shall make no law . . . ," the Fourth Amendment was not intended to apply to state action.[117] Several of the states had elaborate bills of rights, including search provisions, in their own constitutions, and it was not thought that any invasion of rights was likely to come from that quarter. Not until recently has the Constitution been interpreted to prohibit unreasonable state searches, through the agency of the due process clause of the Fourteenth Amendment, ratified in 1868.[118]

That the amendment was designed to protect against arbitrary arrests[119] as well as searches is evident from the history of the abuses

115. There are two historically defined "emergency" exceptions to this rule: search of moving vehicles, for the evident reason that the vehicle will disappear before a warrant can be obtained (*Carroll* v. *United States*, 267 U.S. 132 [1925]), and search of the person and the area under his control as incidental to a valid arrest, otherwise the suspect might reach for concealed weapons and make good his escape (*Weeks* v. *United States,* 232 U.S. 383 [1914]). For discussion, see Chapter IV.

116. *Burdeau* v. *McDowell*, 256 U.S. 465 (1921).

117. *Barron* v. *Baltimore*, 7 Peters 243 (1833); *Smith* v. *Maryland*, 18 Howard 71 (1855).

118. *Wolf* v. *Colorado*, 338 U.S. 25 (1949); *Mapp* v. *Ohio*, 367 U.S. 643 (1961).

119. This construction was given to the amendment by Chief Justice Marshall in the first Supreme Court case in which it figured. *Ex parte Burford*, 3 Cranch 448 (1806). He did not adduce any arguments in support of his position but simply assumed it to be self-evident. The state bills of rights were much more specific on this point: a ban on indiscriminate arrests was either clearly stated within the search article or was the subject of a separate article. See, e.g., the Massachusetts provision reproduced on p. 39, *supra.*

which gave rise to the amendment, and also from the amendment's coupling of the words "*persons and things* to be seized."[120] The problems of arrest and search are, of course, inextricably interwound: indiscriminate searches which result in the seizure of things will lead to the arrest of the person whom the evidence incriminates. Conversely, arrest usually leads to search. An important difference may nevertheless be noted in regard to the constitutional limitations placed on search and on arrest. In the latter case, the requirements of the Fourth Amendment are satisfied if the arrest is made on probable cause, regardless of whether or not a warrant has been obtained.[121] This distinction is based on common-law practice, which the Court has read into the amendment. While the common law had an overriding requirement of a warrant for the search of dwellings, no such restraint was placed on arrests, whether made outdoors or indoors.[122] A felon could be apprehended on probable cause alone; only in the case of a misdemeanor was a warrant required, and even there it might be dispensed with if the offense was committed in the presence of the arresting officer. The common law was ever more protective of property than of the person;[123] moreover, the danger that the felon might flee before a warrant was secured created an emergency situation justifying immediate action. The federal arrest laws[124] have followed common-law practice, and so, with minor variations, have the state statutes.[125] As might be expected, the arrest warrant is a rarity in this country today.

The Fourth Amendment does not prohibit all searches. In recognition of the social interest in solving crime, it does permit searches, but only when conducted with appropriate safeguards. Unlike the general warrant or writ of assistance, which allowed indiscriminate searches, the warrant authorized by the amendment requires, follow-

120. *Giordenello* v. *United States*, 357 U.S. 480, 485–86 (1958).

121. E.g., *Draper* v. *United States*, 358 U.S. 307 (1959). However, the Court has on one occasion noted that entry by force into the dwelling *during the nighttime* to make an arrest for felony "under circumstances where no reason appears why an arrest warrant could not have been sought" raised "a grave constitutional question." *Jones* v. *United States*, 357 U.S. 493, 499–500 (1958). Justice Douglas has taken the position that, where there is time to get a warrant, probable cause alone cannot justify an arrest without warrant. *Wong Sun* v. *United States*, 371 U.S. 471, 497 (1963) (concurring opinion).

122. For a discussion of the common-law rules of arrest which is more comprehensive than Hale's, see J. Chitty, *A Practical Treatise on the Criminal Law* (London, 1816), Vol. I, pp. 11–71.

123. So was Parliament. See p. 30, *supra*.

124. 18 U.S.C. sec. 3052.

125. Frank J. Remington, "The Law relating to 'on the Street' Detention, Questioning and Frisking of Suspected Persons . . .," in Claude R. Sowle (ed.), *Police Power and Individual Freedom: The Quest for Balance* (Chicago, 1962), pp. 11, 13–14.

ing an application made under oath or affirmation, particularity in the description of the persons, premises, and articles to be searched or seized. The degree of particularity required depends to some extent on the nature of the goods to be searched for. In the case of contraband liquor the Court has held that the description "cases of whiskey"[126] satisfies the requirement. However, where books were seized under a state antisubversive law, the Court ruled that the description "books, records, pamphlets . . . and other written instruments concerning the Communist Party of Texas . . ."[127] (which resulted in the seizure of some two thousand items) was insufficient. Particularity of "the most scrupulous exactitude," said the Court, was required in the case of books. "No less a standard could be faithful to First Amendment freedoms [of speech and press]."[128]

In the requirement of "probable cause" there is stated the principle that before a search warrant is issued there must exist reasonable grounds for believing that the dwelling contains the things to be searched for. In the case of arrest there must exist reasonable grounds for believing that the suspect has committed the offense. Probable cause is a flexible concept which does not lend itself to precise definition. There has been disagreement within the Supreme Court in a fairly large number of cases as to whether probable cause was indeed present. But this much is certain: there is no authority for the molestation of all those on whom the long shadow of suspicion falls in the hope that something damaging might turn up in the course of the search. The Court's most quoted definition of probable cause is "facts and circumstances . . . such as to warrant a man of prudence and caution in believing that the offense has been [or is being] committed. . . ."[129] In a 1932 case the Court said that only evidence which is admissible at trial could contribute to a showing of probable cause,[130] but this dictum seems never to have been followed in any of the succeeding cases. It was specifically repudiated in 1949[131] because, in the words of Justice Rutledge, "In dealing with probable cause . . . as the very name implies, we deal with probabilities. These are not technical; they are the factual and practical considerations of every-day life on which reasonable and prudent men, not legal technicians, act."[132]

126. *Steele* v. *United States* No. 1, 267 U.S. 498, 504 (1925).
127. *Stanford* v. *Texas*, 379 U.S. 476, 478–79 (1965).
128. *Ibid.*, p. 485. See also *Marcus* v. *Search Warrant*, 367 U.S. 717 (1961), and *A Quantity of Books* v. *Kansas*, 378 U.S. 205 (1964).
129. *Stacey* v. *Emery*, 97 U.S. 642, 645 (1878).
130. *Grau* v. *United States*, 287 U.S. 124, 128 (1932).
131. *Brinegar* v. *United States*, 338 U.S. 160, 174, n. 13 (1949).
132. *Ibid.*, p. 175.

Thus hearsay not within the personal knowledge of the officer is sufficient to supply probable cause if there is "a substantial basis for crediting the hearsay."[133] The word of an informer *who has supplied reliable information in the past* satisfies this requirement, at least where there is some corroboration from other sources.[134]

Above all, the warrant may be issued only by a judicial officer, who is interposed between the policeman and the citizen so that the policeman does not act as judge in his own cause. The amendment nowhere specifies that a warrant may be issued only by a judge, not by an executive official, but this fact has been assumed from the very beginning and is supported by its history. And it is not enough for the affiant to allege the crime: the affidavit must disclose the facts from which the officer has drawn his conclusions, so that the magistrate can make an independent determination.[135] It was in the disinterested magistrate that the Constitution placed its trust; it is he who, by judicious use of the warrant power, must attempt to strike the proper balance between the interests of society and the individual's right to privacy, so that one is not sacrificed for the benefit of the other.

In a very real sense, the Fourth Amendment embodies a spiritual concept: the belief that to value the privacy of home and person and to afford it constitutional protection against the long reach of government is no less than to value human dignity, and that this privacy must not be disturbed except in case of overriding social need, and then only under stringent procedural safeguards. As Justice Brandeis so eloquently summed up the essence of the amendment:

133. *Jones* v. *United States*, 362 U.S. 257, 269 (1960).

134. *Draper* v. *United States*, 358 U.S. 307 (1959); *Jones* v. *United States*, 362 U.S. 257 (1960). The identity of the informer need not be revealed by the police. Justice Douglas was the lone dissenter in both of these cases and protested the use of "faceless informers." 362 U.S. 257, 272. Douglas agreed that a showing of probable cause does not need to depend upon evidence which would be admissible at trial, but he felt that it should at least be obtained at first hand by the officer, as, for example, by "inferences from suspicious acts." 358 U.S. 307, 323. The refusal of the Court to require disclosure of the informant's identity is readily understandable; informers may be subject to reprisals, and the future effectiveness of undercover agents will be impaired. Nonetheless, abuses are possible. In *United States* v. *Pearce*, 275 F.2d 318 (7th cir. 1960), the nameless informer who supplied the information which resulted in the issuance of a warrant turned out to be a person whose reliability had *not* been established, despite the assertion to the contrary in the affidavit.

135. *Nathanson* v. *United States*, 290 U.S. 41 (1932); *Giordenello* v. *United States*, 357 U.S. 480 (1958); *Aguilar* v. *Texas*, 378 U.S. 108 (1964). However, affidavits "must be tested and interpreted by magistrates and courts in a commonsense and realistic fashion. They are normally drafted by nonlawyers in the midst and haste of a criminal investigation. Technical requirements of elaborate specificity . . . have no proper place in this area." *United States* v. *Ventresca,* 380 U.S. 102, 108 (1965).

The makers of our Constitution undertook to secure conditions favorable to the pursuit of happiness. They recognized the significance of man's spiritual nature, of his feelings and of his intellect. They knew that only a part of the pain, pleasure and satisfactions of life are to be found in material things. They sought to protect Americans in their beliefs, their thoughts, their emotions and their sensations. They conferred, as against the government, the right to be let alone—the most comprehensive of rights and the right most valued by civilized men.[136]

136. *Olmstead* v. *United States*, 277 U.S. 438, 478 (1928) (dissenting opinion).

# Chapter II

# THE BOYD CASE: THE FOURTH AMENDMENT BROADLY CONSTRUED

Like some other Bill of Rights provisions, the Fourth Amendment remained for almost a century a largely unexplored territory. One does not have to seek far to find the reasons. Until the latter part of the nineteenth century, the criminal jurisdiction of the federal government was seldom exercised by Congress. Moreover, the right of appeal to the Supreme Court in criminal cases was not granted until 1891.[1] These factors served to prevent any authoritative interpretations of the Fourth Amendment at the hands of the Court prior to the 1886 case of *Boyd* v. *United States.* [2] To be sure, one or two cases involving searches had been decided before,[3] but none of these was of great significance.

Not only was the Boyd case the first Fourth Amendment case of real consequence, but it remains to this day a landmark of constitutional interpretation. Though its judgment and sweeping dicta were to be much modified in subsequent cases, the ringing tones of its message and the grandeur of its passages assure it a prominent place among the Court's most historic pronouncements. With this case there properly begins the judicial definition of the Fourth Amendment, a task not yet ended and growing ever more complicated. Not only was the Boyd decision the Court's first authoritative utterance on searches, but the opinion was also the boldest pronouncement on the subject ever to come from our highest tribunal. It is, in the Court's own view, "the leading case on the subject of search and seizure. . . ."[4]

1. 26 Stat. 827.
2. 116 U.S. 616 (1886).
3. In the very first case which arose under the Fourth Amendment, *Ex parte Burford*, 3 Cranch 448 (1806), Chief Justice Marshall wrote the opinion holding that the amendment embraced arrest as well as search, and that an arrest warrant issued without probable cause was therefore invalid. Other cases were *Smith* v. *Maryland*, 18 Howard 71 (1855), which held that the amendment did not protect against searches conducted by state officers; *Murray* v. *Hoboken Land Co.*, 18 Howard 272 (1855), mentioned in this chapter (n. 13 *infra*, and accompanying text); and *In re Jackson*, 96 U.S. 727 (1878), perhaps the most significant of the pre-Boyd cases, where the Court said, in a dictum, that the Fourth Amendment prohibited the post office from opening sealed letters in the mails except when authorized by warrant.
4. *Carroll* v. *United States*, 267 U.S. 132, 147 (1925).

Like so many other important constitutional law cases, the Boyd case involved a relatively trifling offense. George and Edward Boyd, New York City merchants, had been accused in a federal forfeiture proceeding of importing thirty-five cases of plate glass into the port of New York in violation of the revenue laws. The alleged fraud was the result of a novel transaction. The government required a quantity of glass for the completion of the federal courthouse and post office building then under construction in Philadelphia and arranged to purchase the needed amount from the Boyds. Under the agreement the Boyds were to be permitted to import an equivalent quantity of glass, free of duty, in return for granting the government a discount from the domestic price equal to the duty rate. The government contended that the Boyds had fraudulently attempted to import a quantity of glass vastly exceeding that supplied to the government, and that, indeed, a previous duty-free importation by the Boyds of twenty-nine cases of glass had already exceeded the amount sold to the government. In short, the government alleged that the Boyds had taken advantage of the transaction to import the thirty-five cases on a duty-free basis to which they were not entitled.[5]

Were the government to prove its case, the glass in question would be confiscated under the provisions of the quaintly titled "Act to Amend the Customs Revenue Laws and to repeal Moieties,"[6] passed in 1874. This act made it an offense to defraud the government of import duties; violations were punishable by fine, imprisonment, and forfeiture of the imported goods. At the trial—which, it should be noted, was essentially a civil proceeding because the prosecutor did not seek the criminal penalties of the act but only the forfeiture of the glass—in order to prove the government's charge it was necessary to show the quantity and value of the twenty-nine cases of glass previously imported. Upon motion of government counsel, the district judge directed the Boyds to produce the invoice of that transaction. The Boyds complied under protest, and the jury found for the government. In the judgment given the thirty-five cases of glass were forfeited to the government.

Such are the facts of the case. The constitutional question arose out of the production of the Boyd records under compulsion. That Congress had clothed the trial judge with authority to order their production was not in doubt. Section 5 of the act specifically authorized this procedure in revenue cases which did not involve a criminal

5. Some of the facts in the case are taken from the Circuit Court's opinion, *United States* v. *Boyd*, 24 F. 692 (1885).
6. 18 Stat. 186.

prosecution, and required, moreover, that in the event of failure to comply the allegations were to be regarded as confessed.[7] It was the forced production, said the Court, which posed "a very grave question of constitutional law, involving the personal security and privileges and immunities of the citizen. . . ."[8]

Section 5 had replaced Section 2 of the act of March 2, 1867,[9] whose terms were even more drastic and which in turn was largely a restatement of a Civil War enactment of 1863.[10] These laws authorized the district judge to issue a warrant for the search and seizure of the papers and their production before the court for inspection by the Collector of Customs. The act of 1863, said the Court, "was the first legislation of the kind that ever appeared on the statute book of the United States, and, as seen from its date, was adopted at a period of great national excitement, when the powers of the Government were subjected to a severe strain to protect the national existence."[11] Thus the Court sought to belittle congressional approval of the original legislation by stamping it as a war measure conceived in haste and born of necessity but completely out of place in the more tranquil atmosphere of peace. Congress evidently agreed in some measure with this reasoning, for the act of 1874 modified the provisions of its predecessors to the extent that a search and seizure was no longer authorized; instead, the suspected party was required to produce the papers himself, and they were to remain in his custody "except pending their examination in court."[12]

Several serious obstacles stood in the way of making the Fourth Amendment, as it was then understood, serviceable in the Boyd situation. In the first place, no physical search of the Boyd premises had taken place. Secondly, even assuming that the forced production of private papers was a search within the meaning of the Fourth Amendment, there was, nevertheless, no search for evidence of

7. 18 Stat. 187:

In all suits and proceedings other than criminal arising under any of the revenue laws of the United States, the attorney representing the Government, whenever in his belief any business book, invoice or paper belonging to or under the control of the defendant or claimant will tend to prove any allegation made by the United States, may make a written motion, particularly describing such book, invoice or paper and setting forth the allegation which he expects to prove; and thereupon the court . . . may, at its discretion, issue a notice to the defendant or claimant to produce such book, invoice or paper in court . . . ; and if the defendant or claimant shall fail or refuse to produce such book, invoice or paper . . . the allegations in the said motion shall be taken as confessed. . . .

8. *Boyd* v. *United States*, 116 U.S. 616, 618.
9. 14 Stat. 547.
10. 12 Stat. 737.
11. 116 U.S. 616, 621.
12. 18 Stat. 187.

crime to be used in a prosecution. It should be observed that the Supreme Court had ruled in 1855 that the protection of the Fourth Amendment did not extend to a civil proceeding.[13] Lastly, even conceding that an unconstitutional search had taken place, under the common-law rule then in operation a trial court would not stop to inquire into the way in which competent evidence had been acquired: if the evidence was competent it would be received, regardless of the illegal manner of its acquisition. Clearly, if the Court was to find in favor of the Boyds on Fourth Amendment grounds, an extremely liberal construction of the amendment, going beyond its actual wording, would be required.

In his opinion for the Court, Justice Bradley said that a forfeiture proceeding qualified as a criminal action and therefore came under the protective umbrella of the Fourth Amendment. He gave the term "criminal"—not specifically used but possibly implied in the Fourth Amendment—a liberal rendering. He conceded that the procedure complained of did not apply to strictly criminal proceedings, but maintained that an action "instituted for the purpose of declaring the forfeiture of a man's property by reason of offenses committed by him, . . . though technically a civil proceeding, is in substance and effect a criminal one," and must therefore be classified as of a "quasi criminal nature."[14]

Turning to the definition of search, Justice Bradley once again interpreted the Constitution liberally. The fact that the act did not authorize a physical search for the records but merely required the owners to produce them upon request, said Bradley, was not sufficient to deprive the Boyds of the protection of the Fourth Amendment:

> It is true that certain aggravating incidents of actual search and seizure, such as forcible entry into a man's house and searching amongst his papers, are wanting . . . but it accomplishes the substantial object [of a search] . . . in forcing from a party evidence against himself. It is our opinion, therefore, that a compulsory production of a man's private papers to establish a criminal charge against him or to forfeit his property is within the scope of the Fourth Amendment to the Constitution, in all cases in which a search and seizure would be; because it . . . effects the sole object and purpose of search and seizure.[15]

In other words, the Fourth Amendment did not merely protect against actual searches, but also against other procedures, or figura-

13. *Murray* v. *Hoboken Land Co.*, 18 Howard 272 (1855).
14. 116 U.S. 616, 633–34.
15. *Ibid.*, p. 622.

tive searches, which sought to accomplish the objects of a search without affording the constitutional safeguards surrounding it.

Granted, then, that this was a search: was it, nevertheless, an *unreasonable* search falling within the Constitution's prohibition? Bradley replied in the affirmative for the reason that the Constitution permitted searches only for contraband articles—goods legally prohibited to the possessor and in which he therefore has no property interest—but not for mere evidence of crime. Issue of a warrant to secure private papers was not, therefore, within the power of the judiciary.[16] Even the writs of assistance, whose use and abuse had led to the drafting of the Fourth Amendment, merely authorized search and seizure of contraband, not of private papers to be used in evidence against their owner. The distinction between the two cases was evident: "In the one case [contraband], the Government is entitled to the possession of the property; in the other [private papers] it is not."[17] In the category of seizable items Bradley enumerated such things as smuggled goods, lottery tickets, and counterfeit coin. Here, however, the trial court attempted "to extort from the party his private books and papers to make him liable for a penalty or to forfeit his property."[18] It was this forced self-incrimination that made the procedure unreasonable and unconstitutional.

Justice Bradley had reached the most creative, and most controversial, feature of his opinion—the linking of the Fourth and Fifth Amendments so that one becomes definitive of the other, and one test of the reasonableness of a search becomes whether or not its object is to uncover incriminating evidence. In support of this view he analyzed at great length the famous opinion of Lord Camden in the celebrated English case of *Entick* v. *Carrington,* [19] decided in 1765, which was discussed briefly in the preceding chapter. Lord Camden's opinion in the Entick case was important, said Justice Bradley, because "the law as expounded by him has been regarded as settled from that time to this, and his great judgment on that occasion is considered as one of the landmarks of English liberty . . .

16. The Court evidently considered the judicial order enforcing production of the records as the equivalent of a search warrant; otherwise, if this were indeed a search, the absence of a warrant should alone have been sufficient for the Court to declare the procedure unreasonable.

17. 116 U.S. 616, 623.

18. *Ibid.*, p. 624.

19. 19 Howell's State Trials 1029 (1765). Lord Camden, not deeming his opinion to be "worthy of preservation," probably burnt the original. The one found in the reports was copied from the original by someone else. See Hargrave's prefatory note to the case in the English reports. For the reader's convenience, the citations given here for quotations from the Entick case correspond to the page numbers in the Boyd case where they appear.

one of the permanent monuments of the British Constitution. . . ."[20] Moreover, he continued, the framers were familiar with the Entick case, and since they "considered it as the true and ultimate expression of constitutional law, it may be confidently asserted that its propositions . . . were considered as sufficiently explanatory of what was meant by unreasonable searches and seizures."[21]

The Entick case was a civil suit, an action for trespass brought by John Entick, publisher of a political journal, the *Monitor,* against Crown messengers dispatched by the Secretary of State, the Earl of Halifax, to apprehend Entick and seize his private papers. The warrant with which the messengers were provided specifically charged Entick with seditious libel but did not specify the papers to be seized. It was therefore a general warrant with respect to the papers, though particular with respect to the person. The jury found against Carrington, one of the messengers, and awarded Entick three hundred pounds in damages.

The great issue before Lord Camden was whether the warrant had any justification in law. Asserting that the protection of property was the chief purpose of government, he could find no justification: "The great end for which men entered into society was to secure their property. That right is preserved sacred and incommunicable in all instances where it has not been taken away or abridged by some public law for the good of the whole. . . . By the laws of England, every invasion of private property, be it ever so minute, is a trespass. No man can set foot upon my ground without my license but he is liable to an action though the damage be nothing. . . ."[22]

Therefore, declared Lord Camden, a warrant was not legal except in the search for stolen goods (and presumably other contraband), though even this exception "crept into the law by imperceptible practice. No less a person than my Lord Coke denied its legality. . . ." As for the seizure of papers, they "are so far from enduring a seizure that they will hardly bear an inspection. . . ." Lord Camden admitted that warrants for the search of papers had once been in use, but said that this practice originated in the discredited Court of Star Chamber and had received no recognition by English legal thinkers outside of that tribunal. For the court to give legal sanction to such warrants "would be subversive of all the comforts of society."[23]

20. 116 U.S. 616, 626.
21. *Ibid.*, p. 627.
22. *Ibid.*
23. *Ibid.*, p. 628.

Lord Camden rejected the "argument of utility" that the authorization of such warrants would be of indispensable assistance in the apprehension of criminals. He pointed out that even in crimes such as murder, rape, and forgery, all more serious offenses than libel, "our law has provided no paper search in these cases to help forward the conviction." Why this was so he could not say, but he suggested that it proceeded either "from the gentleness of the law towards criminals, or from a consideration that such a power would be more pernicious to the innocent than useful to the public. . . ."[24]

The following passage of Lord Camden's was to provide the basis for the Court's opinion in the Boyd case: "It is very certain that the law obligeth no man to accuse himself; because the necessary means of compelling self accusation, falling upon the innocent as well as the guilty, would be both cruel and unjust; and it should seem that search for evidence is disallowed under the same principle. Then, too, the innocent would be confounded with the guilty."[25] Consequently, said Justice Bradley, the forced production of a man's private papers which may lead to his conviction or to a forfeiture of his property "is within the condemnation of that judgment. In this regard the Fourth and Fifth Amendments run almost into each other."[26]

There was no need for the Court to press the Fourth Amendment into service in order to protect the Boyds from the consequences of the forced production of their papers. The same result might have been reached in a different way by holding that since the Boyds were compelled to incriminate themselves under legal process, the procedure fell afoul of the Fifth Amendment. This view was taken by Chief Justice Waite and Justice Miller, who, in a concurring opinion by Miller, argued that the term "search" ought to be confined to its traditional meaning of physical entry. Here, said Miller, there was neither a search—for "the searches meant by the Constitution were such as led to seizure when the search was successful"[27]—nor a seizure, "because the party is not required at any time to part with the custody of the papers."[28]

The Court, however, felt that the act could be found unconstitutional on the basis of the Fourth Amendment as well as the Fifth. The Fifth Amendment, while doubtless also rendering the enforced production of papers unconstitutional, could be made to perform double duty here by serving as a guide to Fourth Amendment interpretation. Said Justice Bradley:

24. *Ibid.*, p. 629. 25. *Ibid.* 26. *Ibid.*, p. 630.
27. *Ibid.*, p. 641. 28. *Ibid.*, p. 640.

We have already noticed the intimate relation between the two Amendments. They throw great light on each other. For the "unreasonable searches and seizures" condemned in the Fourth Amendment are almost always made for the purpose of compelling a man to give evidence against himself, which in criminal cases is condemned in the Fifth Amendment; and compelling a man "in a criminal case to be a witness against himself," which is condemned in the Fifth Amendment, throws light on the question as to what is an "unreasonable search and seizure" within the meaning of the Fourth Amendment. And we have been unable to perceive that the seizure of a man's private books and papers to be used in evidence against him is substantially different from compelling him to be a witness against himself. We think it is within the clear intent and meaning of those terms.[29]

Therefore the search was illegal under the Fourth Amendment, and the admission of the records into evidence was prohibited by the Fifth Amendment. The judgment of forfeiture was accordingly reversed.

That the framers would have disapproved of the act, said Justice Bradley, did not "admit of a doubt." They would have considered procedures such as were authorized in the act "insidious disguises of the old grievance which they had so deeply abhorred"[30] and as better suited to "the purposes of despotic power" than to "the pure atmosphere of political liberty and personal freedom."[31] The principles at stake, in the Entick case as here, "affect the very essence of constitutional liberty and security."[32]

In closing, Justice Bradley wrote his most eloquent passage, often quoted by the Supreme Court in subsequent cases, which summed up the Court's philosophy in the Boyd case. After pointing out that "unconstitutional practices get their first footing . . . by silent approaches and slight deviations from legal modes of procedure," he went on to say: "This can only be obviated by adhering to the rule that constitutional provisions for the security of person and property should be liberally construed. A close and literal construction deprives them of half their efficacy and leads to gradual depreciation of the right, as if it consisted more in sound than in substance. It is the duty of courts to be watchful for the constitutional rights of the citizen, and against any stealthy encroachments thereon."[33]

The majority opinion in the Boyd case is one of those curious documents the whole of which is much superior to the sum of its parts.

29. *Ibid.*, p. 633. 30. *Ibid.*, p. 630. 31. *Ibid.*, p. 632.
32. *Ibid.*, p. 630. 33. *Ibid.*, p. 635.

While the decision has exerted an enormous influence on the entire subsequent course of Fourth Amendment interpretation, some of Bradley's reasoning fails to stand up under close scrutiny. Seldom has a Supreme Court decision been so variously esteemed by responsible commentators. The Supreme Court itself, in later years, even when departing from the letter, and occasionally the spirit, of the Boyd case, never failed to refer to it reverently. Rare indeed is the search opinion to which the Boyd case is relevant which does not cite it as precedent. Some critics, on the other hand, have heaped opprobrium on the decision, accusing the Court of "fundamental error,"[34] of sowing "the seeds of a dangerous heresy,"[35] and of having been "moved . . . by erroneous history."[36]

Some of the criticism has resulted from the fact that the Boyd decision served to protect proven smugglers—in the words of one scholar, "the decision protected practically nothing except the interests of smugglers in the profits of smuggling"[37]—though, ironically, it was, as we have seen, the unrestrained search for smuggled goods that brought the Fourth Amendment into being. More generally, however, whether the decision was praised or blamed depended largely on which side of the coin was being viewed at the time. The decision's detractors pointed to the weak spots in Bradley's reasoning, which was frequently much less than cogent; its supporters lauded the liberal spirit which animated the opinion and its end result, "which did much to chart the subsequent course of the federal law."[38]

A number of the Court's assumptions were clearly open to question. To begin with, the opinion treated the documents as private papers containing information to which the government was not entitled. On this point the Court's understanding of the act appears to have been faulty. The Constitution vests in Congress the authority to regulate foreign commerce. Congress may therefore prescribe the conditions under which imports are to be admitted. In order to guard against frauds on the government, Congress in this act required importers to furnish the government with a certified invoice of their

34. Knute Nelson, "Search and Seizure: Boyd v. United States," *American Bar Association Journal*, IX (December, 1923), 773, 775.
35. John Henry Wigmore, *A Treatise on the Anglo-American System of Evidence in Trials at Common Law* (3d ed.; Boston, 1940), Vol. VIII, Sec. 2264, p. 367.
36. *Ibid.*, Sec. 2184, p. 31.
37. Henry W. Edgerton, "The Incidence of Judicial Control over Congress," *Cornell Law Quarterly*, XXII (April, 1937), 299, 303.
38. Nelson B. Lasson, *The History and Development of the Fourth Amendment to the United States Constitution* (Baltimore, 1937), p. 107.

imports. This requirement the Boyds had failed to comply with. Yet the certified invoice was to contain essentially the same information as the original invoice, which the district court had ordered the Boyds to produce. Had the Boyds complied with the law, the production of the invoice by court order would not have been necessary. Therefore, when the Boyds produced the original invoice on the court's order, they were furnishing no more information than what the government was already entitled to under the commerce power.[39]

More fundamentally objectionable was the entire doctrine that private papers are constitutionally immune to seizure under legal process. Confronted with the vague first clause of the Fourth Amendment, the Court might have found that the unreasonable search was the one which failed to meet the warrant requirements specified in the amendment's second clause. Instead, the Court infused the first clause with independent potency and, with no guidelines for assistance other than the Entick case, made the term "unreasonable" relate to a search for noncontraband objects, such as private papers, of a mere evidentiary value. To accomplish this object, the Court linked the Fourth and Fifth Amendments in a mystical bond to accomplish a result which, the Court evidently felt, the Fourth Amendment was unable to achieve on its own strength. Dean Wigmore has conclusively demonstrated that the history of each of the two privileges—that against unreasonable searches and that against self-incrimination—is distinct, and that the Court was therefore "incorrect in its historical assertions."[40]

The general warrant, as we have seen, was prohibited in England following the Entick case in 1765, while the privilege against self-incrimination came into being a century earlier. John Lillburn, a "radical" opponent of the Stuarts, was ordered to prison by the Court of Star Chamber in 1637 on charges of printing or importing seditious literature. He did not object to answering the charges against him but refused to incriminate himself as to other crimes "because I see you go about by this examination to ensnare me; . . . and therefore, if you will not ask me about the thing laid to my charge, I shall answer no more. . . ." Lillburn was ordered whipped and pilloried, and the sentence was carried out in April, 1638. On his complaint to Parliament, the Commons, in May, 1641, declared the sentence "illegal and against the liberty of the subject." The Lords followed suit in 1645 by directing that the sentence "be totally

39. Nelson, "Search and Seizure," p. 773.

40. Wigmore, *Treatise*, Vol. VIII, Sec. 2184, p. 31. Wigmore's historical analysis was accepted by Zechariah Chafee, Jr., "The Progress of the Law, 1919–1922," *Harvard Law Review*, XXXV (April, 1922), 673, 697–98.

vacated . . . as illegal, and most unjust, against the liberty of the subject and law of the land and Magna Carta." In 1648 Lillburn was awarded three thousand pounds in reparation.[41] In July, 1641, two months after the Commons had acted on the Lillburn matter, the Court of Star Chamber was abolished by Parliament. Thereafter, according to Wigmore, "professional opinion apparently settled against the exaction of an answer under any form of procedure in matters of criminality or forfeiture,"[42] not only in informal, ex officio proceedings, as in Star Chamber, but also in formal legal proceedings.

The different historical origins of the two privileges demonstrate their different character. They are complementary, not duplicates. The Fourth Amendment protects the privacy of the home; the Fifth protects against legal inquisition. The Fifth, in the words of Professor Chafee, "is violated when a man is compelled to do something active, whereas he usually remains passive during an unreasonable search and seizure."[43]

Justice Bradley's reliance on Lord Camden's words in the Entick case to justify a doctrine of interrelationship between the two amendments was not well placed, for the Entick opinion proves nothing of the sort. In order to determine the existence of a trespass, it was necessary for Lord Camden to establish the illegality of the warrant authorizing the seizure of Entick's papers. Lord Camden found that since the general warrant had received no recognition in common law and Parliament had not authorized it, legal authority for its issuance did not exist. The thrust of his opinion was directed to the *generality* of the warrant, the fact that its issuance was grounded in mere suspicion and not based on probable cause. It was in this connection that Lord Camden stressed the self-incrimination analogy. Compulsory self-incrimination was not permitted by law because it would hurt "the innocent as well as the guilty. . . . [S]earch for evidence is disallowed upon the same principle. Then, too, the innocent would be confounded with the guilty. . . . [*I*]*f suspicion at large should be a ground of search . . . whose house would be safe?*"[44] The mere need to solve crimes, Lord Camden said in substance, did not allow

41. Wigmore, *Treatise*, Vol. VIII, Sec. 2250, p. 292.
42. *Ibid.*
43. Chafee, "Progress," pp. 697–98.
44. The last sentence was omitted by Justice Bradley and is at 19 Howell's State Trials 1029, 1074. (Emphasis supplied.) The preceding part of the quotation is at 116 U.S. 616, 629. For discussion see the Comment, "Search and Seizure in the Supreme Court: Shadows on the Fourth Amendment," *University of Chicago Law Review*, XXVIII (Summer, 1961), 664, 692–96.

the law to place its own enforcement above other values, as the privilege against self-incrimination demonstrated.

The judicial order for the Boyd papers was not a general warrant for a "fishing expedition," as in the Entick case, but a writ authorized by Congress ordering production of specific documents, so that there was no real analogy between the two cases. The protection of the Fourth Amendment is extended equally to "persons, houses, papers and effects"; the amendment does not appear to endow papers with any special sanctity.

That the proceedings against the Boyds were unconstitutional would have been assented to even by some of the Court's critics, but not for the reasons given in Justice Bradley's opinion. Rather, they would have agreed with the concurring justices that compulsory self-incrimination under legal process violated the Fifth Amendment.[45] The difference was fundamental. In assigning the wrong reason for the right decision—in holding the forced production of the papers to be an unreasonable search rather than an incrimination, and then requiring exclusion of the evidence—the Court was, in effect, discarding the common-law rule of admissibility and requiring exclusion of the fruits of illegal searches from *all* criminal trials.

A case in which the Supreme Court for the first time construes an important constitutional provision gives the Court the advantage of writing on a clean slate untouched by precedent. But for that very reason it is also likely to prove a "hard" case—and hard cases, as Justice Holmes once remarked, are apt to make bad law. Justice Bradley's opinion in the Boyd case was "bad" law in a technical sense and unlikely to commend itself to legal craftsmen; it was historically unsound and logically questionable. But it was much more than that. Relying on its own resources, with little in the way of guidance except an old English case, the Court might very well have limited the Fourth Amendment to protect against the abuse to which it was directed, the general warrant, and no more. Instead, looking to underlying principles rather than literal language, the Court construed the Fourth Amendment in such a way as to create a right of privacy not limited to the precise wording of the admendment. As Justice Bradley put it, the principles of the Fourth Amendment, as derived from the Entick case, "apply to all invasions, on the part of

45. Wigmore, for example, says that any form of testimonial compulsion, whether oral or documentary, can be refused. *Treatise*, Vol. VIII, Sec. 2264, pp. 363–64. Of course, the decision would still be subject to criticism on commerce clause grounds, a criticism that would apply equally to the concurring opinion. See pp. 57–58, *supra*.

the Government and its employees, of the sanctities of a man's home and the privacies of life."[46] It is this fact which is responsible for the fame of the opinion as a creative act of constitutional law. To be sure, subsequent cases would trim and modify the Boyd opinion, but it had set a tone and charted a path for the Supreme Court to follow in the future. As Justice Brennan said of the Boyd case seventy years later, "it was part of the process by which the Fourth Amendment . . . has become more than a dead letter in the federal courts."[47] In so saying he was re-echoing the words of that doughty warrior for civil liberties, Justice Brandeis, uttered forty years before: "*Boyd* v. *United States* . . . [is] a case which will be remembered as long as civil liberty lives in the United States."[48]

46. 116 U.S. 616, 630.
47. *Abel* v. *United States*, 362 U.S. 217, 255 (1960) (dissenting opinion).
48. *Olmstead* v. *United States*, 277 U.S. 438, 474 (1928) (dissenting opinion).

## Chapter III

# THE FEDERAL EXCLUSIONARY RULE

The rule implicit in *Boyd* v. *United States*,[1] that evidence secured by means of an unconstitutional search is inadmissible in federal court, was not destined to be followed immediately. The Boyd rule did eventually prevail, but only after it was "virtually repudiated,"[2] eighteen years after the Boyd case, in *Adams* v. *New York*.[3] This case arose in New York State, where Adams was convicted of possession of policy slips used in gambling. The policy slips had been taken under warrant, but private papers seized at the same time without benefit of a warrant were used at the trial, over Adams' objection, to identify his handwriting on the policy slips. Since the Adams case involved only state, not federal, officers, the Court could have disposed of it simply by applying the prevailing doctrine that the Constitution did not prohibit unreasonable searches carried out under state authority: this it did do a few years later in another state search case.[4] Instead, the Court went out of its way to stress its adherence to the common-law rule that a trial court must not create a collateral issue by stopping to inquire into the method by which otherwise competent evidence was acquired.

Delivering the opinion of the Court, Justice Day engaged in an exhaustive canvass of the precedents[5] favoring the common-law rule of admissibility, which, he said, was supported by "the weight of authority as well as reason."[6] In what seemed like an afterthought, Day added that the search in the Adams case was, in any event, not unconstitutional because a warrant existed for the seizure of the policy slips, if not of Adams' papers. Thus he likened the seizure of the papers to seizure of burglar's tools uncovered in the course of a lawful search for other things, and he went on to say that the purpose of the Fourth Amendment was "to punish [*sic*] wrongful invasion

1. 116 U.S. 616 (1886).
2. John Henry Wigmore, *A Treatise on the Anglo-American System of Evidence in Trials at Common Law* (3d ed.; Boston, 1940), Vol. VIII, Sec. 2184, p. 31.
3. 192 U.S. 585 (1904).
4. *National Safety Deposit Co.* v. *Stead*, 232 U.S. 58 (1914).
5. The leading case is *Commonwealth* v. *Dana*, 2 Met. (Mass.) 329 (1841).
6. 192 U.S. 585, 588.

of the home of the citizen."[7] But the tenor of the opinion indicated that even a search made without warrant would result in admission of the seized evidence. As for the troublesome precedent of the Boyd case, Day disclaimed any "wish to detract from its authority,"[8] and attempted to confine that case to its unique facts. The Boyds were "virtually compelled"[9] to testify against themselves, while Adams remained passive. The Boyd doctrine was thus limited to that rare situation where a positive act was required on the part of the defendant and was likely to be found only in a judicial proceeding, where he might be required to produce something. This was a misreading of the Boyd opinion, which had treated the compelled production of papers as a *search*. There is no satisfactory way of reconciling the Boyd and Adams cases, for still another reason. The Boyd decision was predicated on the belief that the use in a trial of a defendant's private papers—even when taken under warrant—violated the Fourth and Fifth Amendments.

But the Boyd doctrine was not to be discarded. If the Adams case had "virtually repudiated" the Boyd case, it, in turn, was soon to be virtually repudiated. In the case of *Weeks* v. *United States*,[10] decided in 1914, not only was the Boyd doctrine revived, but much that had been implicit in the Boyd case was now explicitly stated. In the opinion no indication was given of the factors which had occasioned the change in the Court's attitude. Indeed, the Court would not admit that any change had really taken place and attempted to reconcile the apparently conflicting decisions. No evidence was cited of an increase in illegal police behavior, which might have made desirable the adoption of a rule excluding illegally seized evidence as a means of curbing such activity. Moreover, both decisions were unanimous: the opinion in the Weeks case, as in the Adams case, was written by Justice Day, while several justices, including Holmes, joined in both decisions.

Weeks had been sentenced to jail for illegally using the federal mails to transmit lottery tickets. Evidence introduced against him at the trial had been obtained in a thorough ransacking of his home in Kansas City, Missouri. One day, while Weeks was away at work, the local police entered and searched his home without benefit of a warrant and seized various articles, which they turned over to the United States marshal. Later that day they returned, this time accompanied by the marshal, who was seeking further evidence, and more

7. *Ibid.*, p. 598.
8. 192 U.S. 585, 597.
9. *Ibid.*, p. 598.
10. 232 U.S. 383 (1914).

articles were seized, once again without a warrant. Most of the seized articles were later returned, but a number were not. In response to Weeks's petition in the district court, before the commencement of the trial, for the return of his property, the judge ordered the prosecution to return those articles which it did not need, but allowed it to retain those which it wished to introduce as evidence.

Without overruling the Adams case, the Court sought to limit its effect to situations where the defendant did not act promptly to have illegally seized evidence excluded, but waited until the trial was under way. In such circumstances, to allow a motion for the return of the seized items would unduly hamper the progress of the proceedings by requiring the trial court to stop and determine the source of the evidence. However, in situations where, as here, the motion was made before the trial and therefore independently of it, the court was bound to direct the return of the materials. The district court in this case conceded the illegality of the seizure when it ordered the return of those materials not required for evidence; it should therefore not have allowed the prosecution to retain the rest for use at the trial.

While the Adams ruling was thus differentiated and the two cases seemingly harmonized, the two opinions have little resemblance in their tenor. The Court in the Adams case approved the common-law rule of admitting illegally seized materials into evidence because the trial court has no business going beyond the issues of the trial and must confine itself to determining guilt or innocence. In the Weeks case, however, the Court broke with tradition and took the position that it is very much the business of the judiciary to inquire into the source of evidence to be used at trial and to order the return of such evidence as has come into the hands of the government illegally—provided that the motion for its return is "timely,"[11] that is to say, is made before the trial begins.

The articles seized by the marshal could not be used as evidence, said Justice Day, because the Fourth Amendment must not be construed as a mere admonition to good behaviour on the part of the police, the absence of which brings forth no attendant consequences. The amendment was one of a body of rights within whose framework law enforcement must operate. To allow evidence secured through its violation to be used at trial would serve to reduce the amendment to an unenforceable right: "If letters and private documents can thus be seized and held and used in evidence against a citizen accused of an offense, the protection of the Fourth Amend-

11. *Ibid.*, p. 393.

ment, declaring his right to be secure against such searches and seizures, is of no value, and, so far as those thus placed are concerned, might as well be stricken from the Constitution. . . . [Punishment of the guilty is] not to be aided by the sacrifice of these great principles established by years of endeavor and suffering which have resulted in their embodiment in the fundamental law of the land."[12]

It was not only the vitality of the Fourth Amendment that was at stake here, according to Day, but the integrity of the judicial process itself. When courts refuse to scrutinize the source of evidence, and permit the government to use the fruits of unconstitutional searches, they themselves become parties to the misdeeds of the police. The Fourth Amendment was a living principle to which the courts must pay more than lip service, by ensuring that the guilt of the erring policeman does not receive implied sanction in the courtroom. Courts were part of the law enforcement process and, as such, shared responsibility for preventing the invasion of constitutional rights: "To sanction such proceedings would be to affirm by judicial decision a manifest neglect, if not an open defiance, of the Constitution. . . ."[13]

Thus, in the Weeks case, the Court formulated and applied the exclusionary rule, the rule that materials seized in violation of the Fourth Amendment will not be admitted into evidence in a federal criminal trial. But it was more than a doctrine or a rule: it was a warning and a challenge to law enforcement to clean house or face public ignominy through the failure of its prosecutions, and it was also an affirmation of faith in the ability of law enforcement to achieve its objectives while acting within the limitations of constitutional morality.

To be sure, the exclusionary rule required amplification and delineation. For example, did evidence uncovered through an illegal search by state officers with whom federal officers co-operated fall within its scope? Again, what was the constitutional basis of the rule? On this matter the Weeks opinion was silent. Was it required by the privilege against self-incrimination, as suggested by the Boyd case? Or, while not an intrinsic part of the Fourth Amendment itself, was it nevertheless implied there? Or was the exclusionary rule nonconstitutional in origin and a rule of evidence only? In this event it could be negated by act of Congress. These and other questions would be dealt with in subsequent cases. Meanwhile, the Court, through the exclusionary rule, had infused life into the hitherto lifeless body of the Fourth Amendment. This process, begun without

12. *Ibid.*
13. *Ibid.*, p. 394.

clarity of exposition in the Boyd case, had achieved fruition and vigorous articulation in the Weeks case. There remained questions to be answered, but the most important answer had been given: the Fourth Amendment would not become a forgotten provision of the Bill of Rights.

The first case to test the scope of the exclusionary rule was that of *Silverthorne Lumber Company* v. *United States*,[14] which arose in 1920 and brought before the Court the question of whether copies of unlawfully seized papers might be introduced in evidence after the originals had been returned to their owners. A remarkable example of governmental subterfuge came to light in this case. The proprietors of the company, a father and son, were indicted by a federal grand jury and taken into custody. While they were under detention, federal officers, "without a shadow of authority," raided the company's offices "and made a clean sweep of all the books, papers, and documents found there."[15] While the records were in the government's possession, they were copied and photographed, and a new indictment was framed on the basis of the information revealed. The district court directed the return of the originals in response to the Silverthornes' motion but allowed the government to retain the copies and photographs. Subpoenas were then served on the Silverthornes, ordering them to produce the originals. When these were not forthcoming, the company was fined and the younger Silverthorne was imprisoned for contempt.

The Court, in an opinion by Justice Holmes, reversed the conviction.[16] Holmes asserted that the "outrage"[17] could not be allowed to work to the government's advantage. To grant the proposition that while the government may not search in violation of constitutional standards it may nevertheless avail itself of the fruits of the illegality would mean "only that two steps are required [to get the evidence] instead of one. In our opinion such is not the law. It reduces the 4th Amendment to a form of words." Holmes then added a sentence which has come to have great significance: "The essence of a provision forbidding the acquisition of evidence in a certain way is that not merely evidence so acquired shall not be used before the court, but that *it shall not be used at all*."[18] This prin-

14. 251 U.S. 385 (1920).
15. *Ibid.*, p. 390.
16. Chief Justice White and Justice Pitney dissented without opinion.
17. 251 U.S. 385, 391.
18. *Ibid.*, p. 392. (Emphasis supplied.)

ciple has since been applied by the Court in other Fourth Amendment situations. Thus, for example, an admission made by a suspect while he is under unlawful arrest cannot be used because it is directly derived from the unlawful act.[19] Had the Court not ruled as it did in the Silverthorne case, the exclusionary rule might have become meaningless, since the process of photographic reproduction could have made circumvention of the rule by prosecutors a commonplace.

The following year, in *Gouled* v. *United States*,[20] the Court closed to the government another possible avenue of escape from the consequences of the exclusionary rule. The search in question resulted from a suspicion that a man named Gouled was involved in a conspiracy to defraud the government on contracts for the purchase of equipment by the army. An army private who knew Gouled was assigned to call on him for the purpose of uncovering incriminating evidence. While "pretending to make a friendly call,"[21] Gouled's visitor removed several documents, one of which was later introduced in evidence at the trial, where the victim learned of the theft for the first time. Speaking for the Court, Justice Clarke rejected the contention that an unauthorized search becomes constitutionally reasonable when admission is "obtained by stealth instead of by force or coercion."[22] The decisive factor was not the manner of entry, but the absence of consent to the search by the victim. If the search was conducted "against his will," his constitutional rights were as much invaded "in the one case as in the other."[23]

Gouled had been unaware of the unlawful seizure of his papers until his trial was under way. In the Weeks case the Court had stressed that the motion to exclude unlawfully seized evidence must be made prior to trial in order to avoid the interruption of the trial for the raising of a collateral issue. The Court now modified this requirement to permit the motion to be made during the course of the trial, if that was the first appropriate time at which it could be made. The Court added, moreover, that even rejection before trial of a motion to suppress the evidence does not necessarily dispose of the matter finally. If the motion is renewed during the trial, and the circumstances indicate to the court that the defendant's cause may be just, it must *at that time* conduct a new inquiry into the manner of acquisition of the evidence. Said Justice Clarke: "While this [rule that a collateral issue must not be raised] is a rule of great practical

19. *Wong Sun* v. *United States*, 371 U.S. 471, 484–86 (1963).
20. 255 U.S. 298 (1921).
21. *Ibid.*, p. 304.
22. *Ibid.*, p. 305.
23. *Ibid.*, p. 306.

importance, yet, after all, it is only a rule of procedure, and therefore it is not to be applied as a hard-and-fast formula to every case, regardless of its special circumstances. We think, rather, that it is a rule to be used to secure the ends of justice. . . . A rule of practice must not be allowed for any technical reason to prevail over a constitutional right."[24]

Thus far the Supreme Court had found itself in a posture of virtual unanimity when applying the exclusionary rule.[25] Scarcely three months after the Gouled decision, however, the first open conflict appeared on the Court in *Burdeau* v. *McDowell*.[26] The facts of this case shed a harsh light on the business ethics of the day. McDowell, an officer in a business enterprise, was dismissed for fraud. Another officer of the business in question was dispatched to Pittsburgh, where McDowell was located, and took possession of his office. Almost all the furniture in the office, as well as one of the two safes there, was the property not of the business but of McDowell. This fact notwithstanding, McDowell's safe was blasted open by a private detective hired by his former employers, and his desk lock was forced. The contents of both, which contained much private material, were shipped to the head offices of the business in New York. The Department of Justice was informed by the company that McDowell had made fraudulent use of the mails, and a letter found in his desk was turned over to the government. The Department of Justice was also told that his employers would make available copies of the letters mailed illegally by McDowell, and even his private diary, if needed for indictment and prosecution. McDowell, charging that the government was making use of the stolen papers in an attempt to obtain an indictment, obtained an order in the district court restraining Burdeau, the government official in charge of the case, from presenting to the grand jury the papers seized.

The Supreme Court reversed the order. The majority felt that the application of the rule was uncalled for in a situation where the

24. 255 U.S. 298, 312–13. For other cases involving a belated motion to suppress the evidence, see *Amos* v. *United States*, 255 U.S. 313 (1921) (motion granted) and *Segurola* v. *United States*, 275 U.S. 106 (1927) (motion denied). Rule 41(e) of the federal Rules of Criminal Procedure, adopted since these cases were decided, provides: "The motion shall be made before trial or hearing unless opportunity therefor did not exist or the defendant was not aware of the grounds for the motion, but *the court in its discretion may entertain the motion at the trial or hearing*." (Emphasis supplied.)

A defendant whose pretrial motion to suppress evidence is denied cannot appeal that decision until the trial is completed. A court order suppressing evidence cannot be appealed by the government, save in narcotics cases, where the right of appeal was granted by Congress. *Di Bella* v. *United States*, 369 U.S. 121 (1962).

25. The only nonunanimous decision came in the Silverthorne case, where Chief Justice White and Justice Pitney dissented without opinion.

26. 256 U.S. 465 (1921).

Fourth Amendment, which is a restraint on government and not on private persons, had not been violated. The wrong done McDowell "was the act of individuals in taking the property of another,"[27] said Justice Day, an act in which the government did not share. He stressed that he knew of "no constitutional principle"[28] that required exclusion of the evidence in this case.

Justice Holmes's opinion in the Silverthorne case had included a sentence which seemed to sustain the majority view here. The evidence in that case, said Holmes, was not "acquired through the wrongful act of a stranger, but it must be assumed that the government planned or at all events ratified the whole performance."[29] The implication was clear that evidence "acquired through the wrongful act of a stranger" was admissible in court. Possibly in this sentence Holmes engaged in a mere rhetorical flourish, or possibly he had since undergone a change of heart, for in the Burdeau case he joined in Justice Brandeis' dissenting opinion. To Brandeis, the fact that the Fourth Amendment itself had not been violated was irrelevant. Taking a far more exalted view of the purpose of the exclusionary rule than did the majority, he could not agree that violation of the Fourth Amendment was the only occasion which called for the application of the rule. He urged the Court to treat the rule not merely as a shield in defense of constitutional rights, but also as a protector of constitutional morality. In the case before the Court, the government was the possessor of stolen property which it proposed to use to its own advantage. In the name of enforcing the law, the government would breed contempt for law. Moreover, procedural regularity, for Brandeis, was not determined solely by what had happened since the government had become involved in the case, but also by what had gone before: "At the foundation of our civil liberty lies the principle which denies to government officials an exceptional position before the law, and which subjects them to the same rules of conduct that are commands to the citizen. And in the development of our liberty insistence upon procedural regularity has been a large factor. Respect for law will not be advanced by resort, in its enforcement, to means which shock the common man's sense of decency and fair play."[30]

The Court's decision evoked some adverse comment. The ruling was thought by a number of critics to be inconsistent with the purpose of the exclusionary rule. Federal Judge Knox saw the case as giving rise to "inconsistency of law and morals," because the govern-

27. *Ibid.*, p. 475. 28. *Ibid.*, p. 476. 29. 251 U.S. 385, 391.
30. 256 U.S. 465, 477.

ment, though unwilling to "be a thief through the agency of one of its own officers, . . . has no compunction against acting as the '*fence*' for an unofficial thief."[31] A more intemperate attack came from a law professor, Forrest Revere Black, who referred to the case as "a judicial milepost on the road to absolutism." While conceding that the Court was "technically correct"[32] in holding that the Fourth Amendment served as a limitation on government officials only, he nevertheless felt that the decision "placed a premium on lawlessness."[33]

Since the Burdeau case involved no illegal seizure by government officials, it cannot properly be considered as having stated an exception to the exclusionary rule, even though Justices Holmes and Brandeis would have wished to *extend* the rule to cover that situation as well. In the Weeks case itself, however, even while it enunciated the rule and ordered the exclusion of evidence seized by the federal marshal, the Court at the same time left a wide crack in the exclusionary wall when it allowed the use of evidence seized by the local police before the marshal arrived on the scene. In other words, the rule was to apply only to evidence illegally seized by federal officials, not to evidence illegally seized by state officers which the federal government wished to use. In view of the exception for evidence illegally seized by state officers, the Burdeau decision, which also exempted evidence illegally seized by private persons, would seem to follow logically.

In two cases decided in 1927, however (*Byars* v. *United States*[34] and *Gambino* v. *United States*[35]), the Court appreciably limited this exception. The Court held, first, that *participation* by a federal officer in an illegal state search with an eye to obtaining evidence for federal use rendered the resulting seizure inadmissible in the federal courts, and, second, that even evidence illegally seized by state officers acting alone must be excluded from a federal trial if the search was made for the purpose of furthering a federal prosecution. In both cases the legality of the search was tested by federal rather than state standards. The Byars case involved a search for liquor conducted under a state warrant which was defective by federal stand-

31. Jno. C. Knox, "Self Incrimination," *University of Pennsylvania Law Review*, LXXIV (December, 1925), 139, 144.

32. Forrest Revere Black, "Burdeau v. McDowall [*sic*]—A Judicial Milepost on the Road to Absolutism," *Boston University Law Review*, XII (January, 1932), 32, 33.

33. *Ibid.*, p. 32. Black was particularly disturbed by the possibility that private vigilante groups, which during and immediately after the First World War had numbered their memberships in the hundreds of thousands, would at some time in the future be utilized by the federal government to do the illegal snooping which it was not permitted to do for itself.

34. 273 U.S. 28 (1927). 35. 275 U.S. 310 (1927).

ards. The state officers who made the search invited Adams, the local federal prohibition agent, to accompany them, and he too participated in the search. The searchers apparently uncovered no liquor but they did find counterfeit liquor stamps. Adams found some of the stamps and confiscated them, while the state officer who uncovered the rest immediately turned them over to Adams in the Byars home.

In reversing Byars' conviction, the Court, speaking through Justice Sutherland, affirmed "the right of the federal government to avail itself of evidence improperly seized by state officers operating entirely upon their own account." But the facts in this case went to show that Adams was an active participant in the search, interested in uncovering violations of federal law. Thus "the search in substance and effect was a joint operation of the local and federal officers."[36] In a later case Justice Frankfurter precisely stated the doctrine of the Byars case, which has since come to be known as "the silver platter doctrine," after Frankfurter's definition: "The crux of that doctrine is that a search is a search by a Federal official if he had a hand in it; *it is not a search by a federal official if evidence secured by state authorities is turned over to the federal authorities on a silver platter*."[37] The basis for the Court's decision in the Byars case, said Justice Sutherland, was the belief that the protection of the Fourth Amendment "is not to be impaired by judicial sanction of equivocal methods, which, regarded superficially, may seem to escape the challenge of illegality but which, in reality, strike at the substance of the constitutional right."[38]

Similar reasoning was employed by the Court to lead to an identical result in the Gambino case. Gambino was arrested and his auto searched near the Canadian border by New York State police, who had neither a warrant nor sufficient evidence to constitute probable cause. Illicit liquor found in the auto was turned over to federal officers, and Gambino's conviction followed. The facts demonstrated, said Justice Brandeis for the Court, that even though federal officers had not directed or participated in the acts of the troopers, "the wrongful arrest, search and seizure were made solely on behalf of the United States."[39] The Court sought to determine whether the search had been carried out in the enforcement of a state law, but no such law could be found. New York had no state prohibition law in 1924, at the time of the search; its own prohibition act had been repealed in 1923. However, the National Prohibition Act of

36. 273 U.S. 28, 33.
37. *Lustig* v. *United States*, 338 U.S. 74, 78–79 (1949). (Emphasis supplied.)
38. 273 U.S. 28, 33–34.
39. 275 U.S. 310, 316.

1919 did contemplate co-operation between federal and state agencies in its enforcement. Thus the act authorized state judges to issue search warrants for prohibition violations and permitted the states to hold violators at the expense of the nation. Moreover, the Governor of New York had told his state's officers that repeal of the state prohibition law "should make no difference in their action, except that thereafter the peace officers must take the offender to the Federal court for prosecution."[40] Therefore, the seized evidence was inadmissible in federal court, for the defendant's constitutional rights "may be invaded as effectively by such co-operation, as by the state officers acting under direction of the Federal officials."[41]

However, while the exception to the exclusionary rule made with respect to evidence seized in an unlawful state search had been significantly limited, the exception itself still stood and was to remain unchallenged in the Supreme Court for twenty-two years more. Then in 1949 there came a significant development on this question in *Lustig* v. *United States*.[42] Lustig was a counterfeiter. His case began one day in March, 1946, when the police in Camden, New Jersey, placed a call to a federal Secret Service agent, Greene, stating that in a hotel room in that city violations of the counterfeiting laws were probably taking place. Lustig was registered for the room under an assumed name. Greene hastened to the hotel and peeped through the keyhole of the room. He reported to the Camden police that he had found no evidence of counterfeiting but believed that something suspicious was taking place in the room. The police promptly obtained an arrest warrant against Lustig (made out in his assumed name) for violating a city ordinance requiring "known criminals" to register with the police within twenty-four hours of arrival in Camden. The warrant was, however, clearly invalid by federal standards.

Justice Frankfurter, in an opinion announcing the judgment of the Court, accepted the district court's finding that Greene did not initiate the search. "But search," he said, "is a functional, not merely a physical, process. Search is not completed until effective appropriation . . . is made of illicitly obtained objects for subsequent proof of an offense." It was in this connection that Greene's presence was helpful. Though he did not himself search, he facilitated the search by the police because "he did share in the actual examination of the uncovered articles as the physical search proceeded." Frankfurter continued: "It surely can make no difference whether a state officer turns up the evidence and hands it over to a federal agent for his critical inspection with the view to its use in a federal prosecution

40. *Ibid.*, p. 315. 41. *Ibid.*, p. 316. 42. 338 U.S. 74 (1949).

or the federal agent himself takes the articles out of a bag. . . . To differentiate between participation from the beginning of an illegal search and joining it before it had run its course, would be to draw too fine a line in the application of the prohibition of the Fourth Amendment. . . ."[43]

While the Lustig case may not on the surface appear to mark a turning point of moment in the fortunes of the "silver platter" doctrine, except to broaden the definition of federal participation to include searches in which federal officers took a part, no matter how minor or how late, in actuality this case marked the first serious challenge of the doctrine by members of the Court. Justice Frankfurter, who spoke for only four justices, found it unnecessary "to consider what would be the result if the search had been conducted entirely by State officers."[44] The three other justices who joined in his opinion, Murphy, Douglas, and Rutledge, in a separate concurring opinion by Murphy stated their conviction that *all* evidence illegally seized by state officers, even where not involving any federal participation, should be declared inadmissible in the federal courts.[45]

What were the factors responsible for the growing dissatisfaction on the Court with the "silver platter" doctrine? They were mainly two. First, on the very day on which the Lustig decision was announced, the Court for the first time found that unreasonable state searches violated the due process clause of the Fourteenth Amendment, though the state courts were not required to adopt the exclusionary rule.[46] It was inconsistent to find a state search in violation of the Constitution and yet to admit its fruits in federal court. In addition, a growing number of state courts had of their own volition adopted the exclusionary policy; to allow evidence excludable in the state courts to be admitted in federal court would frustrate the policies of obedience to the Constitution of these states. These were the reasons advanced by the Court for its action when the "silver platter" doctrine was finally repudiated in 1960,[47] a development which will be discussed at greater length in a later chapter.

Another, and less justifiable, exception to the exclusionary rule was the doctrine developed in the lower federal courts that evidence seized in violation of the constitutional rights of a third party—that

43. *Ibid.*, p 78. 44. *Ibid.*, p. 79.

45. Justice Black concurred separately. Justice Reed, joined by Chief Justice Vinson and Justices Jackson and Burton, dissented on the ground that "the search had ended before he [Greene] came into the room." *Ibid.*, p. 83. They stressed that Greene had not requested the search and that it had begun in his absence, which was sufficient to render it a state undertaking.

46. *Wolf* v. *Colorado*, 338 U.S. 25 (1949).

47. *Elkins* v. *United States*, 364 U.S. 206 (1960).

is, of a party other than the defendant—is admissible. Under this theory, only a person who had a property interest in either the home searched or the articles seized had the necessary "standing" to seek the protection of the rule. While Rule 41(e) of the federal Rules of Criminal Procedure, which became effective in 1946, authorized the suppression of evidence against any "person aggrieved by an unlawful search and seizure," the courts treated Rule 41(e) as a mere restatement of existing case law, which it probably was, and defined the "person aggrieved" as one whose property rights were violated. This raised all sorts of troublesome questions: for instance, what was the degree of property interest required? Did the house guest have "standing"? And if so, did he actually need to dwell on the premises, or was the occasional visitor protected as well? The federal courts were by no means uniform in their answers; hairsplitting distinctions and inconsistent decisions existed in profusion.[48] The Supreme Court, surprisingly, did not pass upon this limitation on the exclusionary rule until some three decades after its formulation.[49] When it finally did, however, the limitation, while retained, was drastically curtailed.

The first indication that the "property interest" (or "personal privilege") doctrine, as then applied, might be in for rough sledding came in 1948, in *McDonald* v. *United States*.[50] In this case the Court reversed not only McDonald's gambling conviction but that of his house guest as well, on the ground that the evidence used against McDonald had been illegally seized from him, and that if it had been properly suppressed against McDonald it would no longer have been available for use against the guest. The Court therefore found it unnecessary to decide whether the same decision would have resulted if the evidence seized had belonged to the guest, but this point was considered in Justice Jackson's concurring opinion. Joined by Justice Frankfurter, Jackson asserted that "even a guest may expect the shelter of the rooftree he is under against criminal intrusion."[51]

The views expressed by Jackson and Frankfurter in the McDonald case were adopted by the Court in 1950, in *United States* v. *Jeffers*.[52] This case involved the discovery of narcotics during an unlawful search of the hotel room occupied by the defendant's aunts, who permitted him to use the room but did not know that he stored narcotics

48. For a review of the cases see the Annotation in 96 L. ed. 66.

49. The limitation was formulated in *Haywood* v. *United States*, 268 F.795 (7th cir. 1920). In *Goldstein* v. *United States*, 316 U.S. 114, 121 (1942), it was mentioned with apparent approval.

50. 335 U.S. 451 (1948). 51. *Ibid.*, p. 461. 52. 342 U.S. 48 (1950).

there. The Court rejected the contention of government counsel that, because the search had not invaded Jeffers' own privacy, the seizure and its admission into evidence was justifiable. The seizure was "bound together" with the search and was not "isolable."[53] Moreover, even though the narcotics were contraband and Jeffers therefore had no legal property interest in them, they must nevertheless be considered *private* property for the purpose of exclusion; they need not be returned to the defendant, but they might not be used to convict him. In 1960, in *Jones* v. *United States*,[54] the Court carried this reasoning a step further. In the case of contraband, such as narcotics, possession alone constitutes the crime. In the seizure of contraband, therefore, the "property interest" doctrine required the defendant, in Judge Learned Hand's words, to "choose one horn of the dilemma,"[55] for if he asserted his innocence and denied possession he could not seek the protection of the exclusionary rule, while if he admitted possession he in effect admitted his own guilt, should the motion to suppress be denied. Jones was a guest in the apartment unlawfully searched, and he denied any connection with the narcotics found there. The Court nonetheless found that the exclusionary rule protected him too. The "person aggrieved by an unlawful search and seizure" as stated in Rule 41(e) was redefined to include "anyone legitimately on premises where a search occurs. . . ."[56]

While the exclusionary rule has been viewed with disfavor by some judges and scholars, even its supporters have been disturbed by the way in which the federal courts, including the Supreme Court,

53. *Ibid.*, p. 52. 54. 362 U.S. 257 (1960).
55. *Connolly* v. *Medalie*, 58 F.2d 629, 630 (2d cir. 1932).
56. 362 U.S. 257, 267. For discussion of these decisions, see Jerome C. Gorski's Note, "The Exclusionary Rule and the Question of Standing," *Georgetown Law Journal*, L (Spring, 1962), 585.

Another, and relatively unimportant, exception to the exclusionary rule was announced in the 1954 case of *Walder* v. *United States*, 347 U.S. 62, which permitted the admission of evidence illegally seized when the evidence was not used to gain a conviction but to impeach the credibility of the witness. At his trial for narcotics violations, Walder testified that he had never been in the narcotics business. Thereupon, the government sought and received permission to introduce evidence concerning a capsule of heroin seized illegally from Walder some years earlier.

Justice Frankfurter's opinion sustaining the conviction distinguished between application of the exclusionary rule to prohibit "an affirmative use of evidence unlawfully obtained"—that is, to get a conviction—and its proposed application in this case so that the defendant might "provide himself with a shield against contradiction of his untruths. Such an extension of the *Weeks* doctrine would be a perversion of the Fourth Amendment." *Ibid.*, p. 65. Justices Black and Douglas dissented without opinion.

for a long time failed to articulate the rule "so as to accord with its clear purpose . . . and . . . confused it too easily with unrelated doctrine."[57] Had the Court heeded its own admonition that the exclusionary rule was "to be used to secure the ends of justice,"[58] a greatly lacking symmetry in the rule's formulation might have been provided and much adverse criticism avoided.

The primary purpose of the exclusionary rule, of course, is to protect the vitality of the Fourth Amendment. When illegal searches are made unprofitable for the police because the number of convictions, upon which their professional reputation depends, is diminished, so the theory goes, they will lose the incentive to try to obtain convictions regardless of constitutional limitations. As a subordinate consideration, the rule also functions to protect the integrity of the judicial process by denying the trial court's implied sanction of violations of the citizen's rights.

Bearing in mind these considerations, it is difficult to reconcile the rule with its exceptions. If the purposes of the rule were to be realized, there would seem to be no reason for removing from its scope the fruits of unlawful searches conducted by state officers, a situation which has since been rectified by the overruling of the "silver platter" doctrine. The "property interest" doctrine, too, seems to have been formulated through a misconception of the exclusionary rule's function. The viewing of the rule as a personal privilege to be claimed only by the person whose privacy has been invaded serves to confuse property law doctrines with a sanction fashioned to deter violations of the Fourth Amendment. To be sure, there is a certain logic in viewing the exclusionary rule as a vindication of the individual's rights, and, concomitantly, in denying its protection to the individual whose own privacy is not invaded by the search. But the deterrent effect of the exclusionary rule is nevertheless weakened when the sanction is not applied to the fruits of unlawful searches made for the purpose of uncovering evidence against some person other than the victim. It might even be said that this sort of search is most destructive of individual privacy, since the victim might not himself be suspect of any wrongdoing, but only of having in his possession evidence usable in the prosecution of another person. And if the image of judicial integrity is indeed tarnished by the admission of unconstitutionally seized evidence, it

57. Comment, "Judicial Control of Illegal Search and Seizure," *Yale Law Journal*, LVIII (December, 1948), 144, 153.

58. *Gouled* v. *United States*, 255 U.S. 298, 312 (1921).

should make no difference whether the victim of the search was the defendant or some other person.

Some of the inconsistency in the application of the exclusionary rule may have stemmed from the Court's own lack of consistency in explaining the rule's derivation. The Boyd case joined the Fourth and Fifth Amendments in a mystical union to require exclusion. Since then, however, there have been fluctuating views on the part of the justices as to the derivation of the exclusionary rule. The Weeks case did not apply any specific constitutional provision, though the decision appears "to rest most heavily on the Fourth Amendment itself."[59] Following the Weeks case, and throughout the nineteen thirties, the Court retreated to the position of the Boyd case by advancing the Fifth Amendment as the basis for the exclusionary rule.[60] On the other hand, Justice Frankfurter's opinion for the Court in a 1949 case implied that the exclusionary rule is a judicially created rule of evidence, not required by the Constitution, and therefore subject to abrogation by Congress.[61] The Court's swaying back and forth in explaining the basis of the exclusionary rule is nowhere more evident than in an opinion by Chief Justice Taft in 1928: Taft managed the difficult feat of advancing on the same page first the Fifth Amendment, then the Fourth, as requiring the exclusion of evidence taken in violation of constitutional search standards.[62]

The use of the Fifth Amendment as the constitutional backbone of the exclusionary rule has led to inconsistent decisions. For one thing, corporations may not avail themselves of the protection of the Fifth Amendment, which is a personal privilege; yet the Court has

59. Justice Brennan dissenting in *Abel* v. *United States*, 322 U.S. 217, 255, n. 4 (1960).

60. E.g., Justice Clarke's opinion for the Court in *Amos* v. *United States*, 255 U.S. 313, 316 (1921); Justice Butler's opinion for the Court in *Agnello* v. *United States*, 269 U.S. 20, 33–34 (1925); Justice Stone's opinion for the Court in *McGuire* v. *United States*, 273 U.S. 95, 99 (1927); Justice Brandeis' dissenting opinion in *Olmstead* v. *United States*, 277 U.S. 438, 478–79 (1928); and Justice Holmes's dissenting opinion in the same case at p. 469.

61. *Wolf* v. *Colorado*, 338 U.S. 25, 28 (1949). In a later case Frankfurter was more specific and referred to the rule as having been made "under this Court's peculiarly comprehensive supervisory power." Dissenting opinion in *Elkins* v. *United States*, 364 U.S. 206, 240 (1960). In the same opinion, however, Frankfurter referred to the rule as meeting "a compelling public need implicit in" the Fourth Amendment. P. 235.

62. *Olmstead* v. *United States*, 277 U.S. 438, 462 (1928). "There is no room for applying the Fifth Amendment [to require exclusion] unless the Fourth Amendment was first violated." "[T]he Fourth Amendment, although not referring to or limiting the use of evidence in court really forbade its introduction if obtained by government officers through a violation of the Amendment."

held that they are protected by both the Fourth Amendment and the exclusionary rule.[63] Again, if the Fifth Amendment requires that illegally seized evidence be excluded because its use by the government would result in compulsory incrimination of the defendant, it should make no difference whether the evidence was seized by the government or by a private person. Even when seized by a private person, its use by the government still incriminates the defendant.[64]

More recently, despite an occasional reference to the Fifth Amendment in some opinions,[65] the Court has come around to the view that the Fourth Amendment does not need to depend for its enforcement upon any other constitutional provision. In 1961 the Court declared that "the exclusionary rule is an essential part of"[66] the Fourth Amendment. This is simply another way of saying that the Fourth Amendment, reasonably construed, allows the Court to apply the exclusionary rule if it is deemed necessary to ensure compliance with the provisions of the amendment.

There is an important difference between an exclusionary rule based on the search and seizure provision itself and one based on the self-incrimination clause of the Fifth Amendment. If the Fifth Amendment is the basis of the rule, the defendant possesses the personal privilege of not being convicted by the evidence seized from him unlawfully, and the question of whether exclusion does really serve to deter illegal searches is quite immaterial. If, on the other hand, exclusion is regarded as enforcing the Fourth Amendment because of its *deterrent* effect, it is not a vindication of the defendant's rights—for he has no right to exclusion—but an expression of the community's interest in maintaining constitutional standards of

63. This point is made by several commentators; e.g., Thomas E. Atkinson, "Admissibility of Evidence Obtained through Unreasonable Searches and Seizures," *Columbia Law Review*, XXV (January, 1925), 11, 27.

64. Comment, "Search, Seizure and the Fourth and Fifth Amendments," *Yale Law Journal*, XXXI (March, 1922), 518, 522.

65. E.g., Justice Black's concurring opinion in *Mapp* v. *Ohio*, 367 U.S. 643, 661–62 (1961).

66. Justice Clark's opinion for the Court in *Mapp* v. *Ohio*, 367 U.S. 643, 656 (1961), the case in which the Court applied the exclusionary rule to the states. In a very cloudy sentence, Clark described the exclusionary rule as "a clear, specific, and constitutionally required—even if judicially implied—deterrent safeguard. . . ." *Ibid.*, p. 648. However, in a later opinion for the Court, Clark interpreted his Mapp opinion as having "followed" the Boyd doctrine "that the Fourth Amendment implemented by the self-incrimination clause of the Fifth" required exclusion. *Ker* v. *California*, 374 U.S. 23, 30 (1963). It is true that the Boyd case was discussed in the Mapp opinion, but it is discussed as a matter of ritual in almost every search case to which it has some relevance. A reading of the Mapp opinion does not reveal any reliance on the Fifth Amendment. Justice Black's concurring opinion in the Mapp case urged that the Fifth Amendment *should* have been used by the Court rather than "the Fourth Amendment, standing alone," as he understood the Court to have done. 367 U.S. 643, 661–62. In any event, the asserted reliance on the Fifth Amendment in the Mapp opinion does not square with Clark's language there, quoted above.

law enforcement. In this view, the exclusionary rule is "calculated to prevent, *not to repair*."[67] Should the Court find that standards of law enforcement had been elevated to the point where violations of the Fourth Amendment were rare, it would presumably be free to say that the need for the exclusionary rule no longer existed. Similarly, the Court could, if it wished, make a distinction, when applying the rule, between the honest mistake which resulted in an infraction of the law and the deliberate, calculated effort to violate the defendant's rights. One can, of course, take the position that exclusion is the concomitant of the Fourth Amendment's right to be let alone—that the amendment embraces not only a right to protection from arbitrary invasion by the police, but also the right not to have the fruits of the invasion used against him whose right to privacy has been violated. Such a reading of the Fourth Amendment finds support in the Weeks case, where, without reliance on the Fifth Amendment, the defendant's *right* to exclusion of the evidence was stressed —its use, said the Court, would constitute "a denial of the constitutional rights of the accused"[68]—but finds little support in the recent cases where the deterrent effect of the rule is emphasized.[69]

The application of the exclusionary rule is no longer limited to violations of constitutional proportion. In *Burdeau* v. *McDowell*, it will be recalled, the Court, over the dissent of Justices Holmes and Brandeis, refused to order exclusion of evidence unlawfully seized by private persons. Later, in *Olmstead* v. *United States*[70] and again over the dissent of Holmes and Brandeis, the Court held that violation of a state statute by federal officers did not require exclusion of the evidence. It was, moreover, made clear by the Court on this occasion that even violation of a federal statute would require the same result. From 1943 on, however, the Court has taken a different attitude. In *McNabb* v. *United States* it was announced that admissibility of evidence in the federal courts was not to be determined by "principles . . . derived solely from the Constitution."[71] Acting in its

67. *Elkins* v. *United States*, 364 U.S. 206, 217 (1960). (Emphasis supplied.)

68. *Weeks* v. *United States*, 232 U.S. 383, 398 (1914). This interpretation of the Weeks decision is supported by the fact that the Court expressly declined to consider what "other remedies," short of exclusion, might be available to the defendant for the infringement of his rights. *Ibid.* The question of alternative remedies was surely an important one if the exclusionary policy was intended to serve as a deterrent rather than as a vindication of the victim's constitutional rights.

69. E.g., *Linkletter* v. *Walker*, 381 U.S. 618, 636–37 (1965). There is nevertheless a good deal of semantic confusion in some of the opinions. Justice Clark, for example, pointed to the deterrent effect as the justification for the rule, and at the same time referred to the rule as the "most important *constitutional privilege*" granted by the Fourth Amendment. (Emphasis supplied.) *Mapp* v. *Ohio*, 367 U.S. 643, 656 (1961).

70. 277 U.S. 438 (1928).

71. 318 U.S. 332, 341 (1943).

supervisory role over the federal courts, the Supreme Court ordered exclusion of a confession obtained while the defendant was illegally held without having been promptly arraigned as required by the federal Rules of Criminal Procedure. Since the McNabb case any violation of the federal rules, or of a federal statute,[72] has rendered the resulting seizure inadmissible. Thus there are today two different exclusionary rules in force, one, required by the Constitution itself, for violations of the Constitution, and another, not constitutional in origin, for the violation of any federal law.

Another and much criticized feature of Fourth Amendment interpretation relates not to the scope of the exclusionary rule but to the limits placed on seizable goods: this is the doctrine that private papers (and other materials of a mere evidentiary nature), unlike contraband, may not be seized even under warrant because their use in evidence would result in a compulsory incrimination. This doctrine is a legacy of the Court's utilization, in the Boyd case, of the Fifth Amendment to determine the meaning of an unreasonable search. As originally enunciated in the Boyd case, the doctrine applied to all private documents; as modified in 1906, in *Hale* v. *Henkel*,[73] its application was confined to personal papers, not corporate records. In the Hale case the power of the courts to subpoena corporate records was upheld on the theory that "the corporation is a creature of the state," and the state reserves the right "to investigate its contracts and find out whether it has exceeded its powers."[74] Though it is the state, not the federal government, which grants the corporation's charter, the public character of the corporation was evidently thought sufficient to justify a federal inquiry as well. The Court agreed that the Fourth Amendment protected corporations, as well as individuals, against unreasonable searches but found that the term "unreasonable" meant something different for the corporation than for the person, and was limited to a situation where the subpoena was "too sweeping in its terms to be regarded as reasonable."[75] A "sweeping" subpoena was regarded as unreasonable, it appears, because compliance with its terms would unduly hamper the conduct of the business, not because the information contained in the records was beyond the scope of legitimate governmental inquiry. If so, the Court might well have used as its constitutional instrument, instead

72. *Miller* v. *United States*, 357 U.S. 301 (1958). Whether evidence seized unlawfully by private parties or by federal officials in violation of state law would today be held subject to the exclusionary rule is an open question.
73. 201 U.S. 43 (1906).
74. *Ibid.*, pp. 74, 75.
75. *Ibid.*, p. 76.

of the Fourth Amendment, the due process clause of the Fifth, with its protection of "property" rights.

Even this limitation does not seem to apply when it is only the copies of the records that are sought rather than the records themselves.[76] The Court has in fact held that to request from a corporation a long list of business records extending over a three-year period is not so excessive a demand as to be unreasonable.[77] Nor does a showing of probable cause need to be made; it is sufficient that the investigation be authorized by law.[78] It appears, indeed, that not once since the Hale case has the Supreme Court found that a compelled production of business records violated the Fourth Amendment, though such claims have often been made before the Court by the corporations affected. Had the Court not modified the Boyd ruling, government supervision of the economy would have been jeopardized, and the regulatory commissions, which were just springing into existence, would have been stillborn.

Even where the business is unincorporated, its records are subject to governmental inspection where the law requires that the records be kept. Two cases decided in 1946, *Davis* v. *United States*[79] and *Zap* v. *United States*,[80] demonstrate how far-reaching the power of the government to investigate the activities of business concerns now is. In the Davis case federal agents acting without warrant forced the defendant, whom they suspected of operating in the gasoline black market, to unlock the door to his office in the service station he owned and to turn over to them gasoline ration coupons, which were later admitted into evidence at the trial. Justice Douglas, for the Court, found that the legality of the search must be sustained because the coupons demanded were "not . . . *private* papers or documents but . . . *public* property in the custody of a citizen. . . . The officer's claim to the property was one of right."[81] While conceding that even government property could not be reclaimed in a lawless manner, he did not think such was the circumstance here. "The filling station was a place of business," he said, "not a private residence."[82] Justice Frankfurter, in a forceful dissent, replied that the coupons could be lawfully requested but not seized in a coercive manner upon peremptory demand: "Merely because there may be

76. *Isbrandtsen-Moller Co.* v. *United States*, 300 U.S. 139 (1937).
77. *Brown* v. *United States*, 276 U.S. 134 (1928).
78. For discussion see *Oklahoma Press Pub. Co.* v. *Walling,* 327 U.S. 186 (1946).
79. 328 U.S. 582 (1946).
80. 328 U.S. 624 (1946).
81. 328 U.S. 582, 589, 592. See also the later case of *Shapiro* v. *United States,* 335 U.S. 1 (1948).
82. *Ibid.*, p. 592.

the duty to make documents available for litigation does not mean that police officers may forcibly or fraudulently obtain them." To say that the Fourth Amendment affords less protection against searches of business places than of private homes "would constitute a sudden and drastic break with the whole history of the Fourth Amendment and its applications by this court."[83] At any rate, whatever the "public" nature of the filling station itself, it seems inappropriate to designate as a public place the private office where the search took place.

In the Zap case federal agents investigating frauds on the government requested and took a check, later used in evidence, from the defendant's bookkeeper. Zap was a government contractor and the inspection of his records was authorized by law, but the removal of the check was not. In other words, the search was legal, but not the seizure. Justice Douglas, again speaking for the Court, thought that, because a warrant for the seizure of the check was readily obtainable, "to require reversal here would be to exalt a technicality to constitutional levels."[84] Dissenting once again, Justice Frankfurter indignantly replied that "the fact that this evidence might have been secured by a lawful warrant seems a strange basis for approving seizure without a warrant."[85]

The doctrine limiting the warrant to the search for and seizure of contraband goods, but not evidentiary items, has thus been drastically curtailed with respect to business records, but it still retains a good deal of vitality in the case of personal papers.[86] As the Court summed up the doctrine in 1921: "Although search warrants have thus been used in many cases ever since the adoption of the Constitution, . . . nevertheless, it is clear that, at common-law and as the result of the *Boyd* and *Weeks Cases* . . . they may not be used as a

83. *Ibid.*, p. 596.
84. 328 U.S 624, 630.
85. *Ibid.*, p. 633.
86. The limitation was strongly disapproved of by Professor Corwin, who called it one of the "least defensible features of the court's system of doctrine in this field of constitutional law. . . ." Edward S. Corwin, "The Supreme Court's Construction of the Self Incrimination Clause," *Michigan Law Review*, XXIX (December, 1930), 191, 205. Similar criticism has been voiced by many other writers. See, however, Comment, "Limitations on Seizure of 'Evidentiary' Objects," *University of Chicago Law Review,* XX (Winter, 1953), 319, 327, where it is suggested that the doctrine prohibiting the seizure of private papers, while not properly resting on the Fifth Amendment, might be justified on the ground that "the drafters of the Constitution intended to protect further a man's privacy [in addition to requiring a search warrant] by immunizing from seizure certain of his personal property." In rebuttal, one writer argues: "The privacy of the individual, however, would be just as well served by a restriction on search to the even-numbered days of the month." John Kaplan, "Search and Seizure: A No-Man's Land in the Criminal Law," *California Law Review*, XLIX (August, 1961), 474, 478–79.

means of gaining access to a man's house or office and papers solely for the purpose of making search to secure evidence to be used against him in a criminal or penal proceeding, but that they may be resorted to . . . [when the law] renders possession of the property by the accused unlawful. . . ."[87]

Here too, however, the doctrine as originally enunciated was significantly recast when the Court added that where the papers sought have become "instruments or agencies"[88] of crime—that is, where they were helpful in facilitating the commission of the crime—they are, even though legally private property, as subject to seizure as contraband itself.[89] The Court did not explain how the constitutional objection to the seizure of private property was overcome merely because the property was used for criminal purposes. Apparently, the "instrument of crime" is subject to seizure for no better reason than that under "very ancient" common law "the tool or other object which killed a man was deodand and forfeit. . . ."[90] It is somewhat ironical that under this modification "the invoice whose forced production gave rise to the *Boyd* case would today be subject to seizure as the immediate instrument of the fraud upon the revenues. . . . [T]he *Boyd* case is today bad law."[91]

Thus the continuing legacy of the Boyd case, which relied on the Fifth Amendment to explain the meaning of the Fourth, and the Supreme Court's failure to enunciate clearly the basis of the exclusionary rule have led to some questionable Fourth Amendment interpretation and to inconsistency in the exclusionary rule's application. Most of the cases discussed in this chapter fail to shed much light on the operation of the inner recesses of the judicial mind in regard to this subject. The Weeks case itself, while it forthrightly announced adoption of the rule, explained neither its basis nor the policy considerations underlying its adoption. If that case seems to have been decided without full consideration of the rule's possible consequences, it should be remembered that at the time it probably affected

87. *Gouled* v. *United States*, 255 U.S. 298, 309 (1921).

88. *Ibid.*

89. For apparently inconsistent interpretations in later cases of what constitutes an "instrument of crime," see *Marron* v. *United States*, 275 U.S. 192, 199 (1927), and *United States* v. *Lefkowitz*, 285 U.S. 452, 464–66 (1932). See also the formulation in the Federal Rules of Criminal Procedure, Rule 41(b).

90. *United States* v. *Kirschenblatt*, 16 F.2d 202, 203 (2d cir. 1926); see also *People* v. *Chiagles*, 142 N.E. 583 (N.Y. 1923).

91. Corwin, "The Supreme Court's Construction of the Self Incrimination Clause," *Michigan Law Review*, XXIX (November, 1930), 1, 19. The Boyd case is bad law on another count. The information contained in the invoice which the Boyds were ordered to surrender should, under law, have been turned over to the government at the time of the importation. For discussion see pp. 57–58, *supra*.

only a handful of offenders. Organized crime syndicates nationwide in scope were unknown in those days, and the federal government exercised a much more limited criminal jurisdiction than it does today. The enforcement of the criminal law was almost exclusively a responsibility of the states, and they were not then subject to any constitutional search restrictions. Not until the late nineteen forties and afterwards—mainly in the cases on state searches—do we get the kind of judicial discussion on matters of exclusionary policy that gives us a clear insight into judicial thinking.

From the outset, the exclusionary rule met with the implacable opposition of some noted judges and legal scholars, among them Judge (later Justice) Cardozo and Dean Wigmore. While a member of New York's highest court, Cardozo wrote what became the most famous of state judicial opinions rejecting the exclusionary rule.[92] Wigmore, whose influence in legal circles was enormous, denounced the rule in vigorous language as violating "the spirit of our law" by attempting "to do justice incidentally."[93] Moreover, this "misguided sentimentality"[94] was destructive of law enforcement. Instead of punishing the overzealous policeman, said Wigmore in his famous parody of the courts, they say:

> Titus, you have been found guilty of conducting a lottery; Flavius, you have confessedly violated the Constitution. Titus ought to suffer imprisonment for crime, and Flavius for contempt. But no! We shall let you *both* go free. We shall not punish Flavius directly, but shall do so by reversing Titus' conviction. This is our way of teaching people like Flavius to behave, and of teaching people like Titus to behave, and incidentally of securing respect for the Constitution. Our way of upholding the Constitution is not to strike at the man who breaks it, but to let off somebody else who broke something else.[95]

Wigmore's strictures are powerful: the exclusionary rule does indeed try to do justice in a roundabout way. It sets a guilty man free so as to teach a lesson to the law officer who disregarded constitutional requirements in seizing his evidence. But the criticism implies the availability of an effective *direct* way of punishing those who regard their badge of office as a license to violate the Constitution while enforcing the laws. Such, unfortunately, is not the case.

92. *People* v. *Defore*, 150 N.E. 585 (N.Y. 1926).
93. Wigmore, *Treatise*, Vol. VIII, Sec. 2180, p. 4.
94. *Ibid.*, Sec. 2184, p. 36.
95. *Ibid.*, p. 40.

The other deterrents most often suggested—prosecution of offenders and civil suit for damages—are definitely inadequate, as experience has shown, for law enforcement officers are not in the habit of prosecuting one another, while the financial redress obtainable in a civil suit is usually negligible.[96]

There is, nevertheless, no conclusive evidence of the extent to which the exclusionary rule eliminates illegal searches. That they have not been eliminated entirely is clear from the many instances of illegal searches that still come before the federal courts. But that the rule does serve to reduce them in number may be reasonably assumed, for in order to make "an efficient record of criminal convictions," law enforcement agencies must "avoid conduct which imperils successful prosecution."[97] The supporters of the rule view it, therefore, not so much as an answer to the problem of unlawful searches, but as the best alternative of the several proposed; they feel that through its agency "concrete meaning"[98] has been given to the Fourth Amendment's guarantee.

The exclusionary rule, in the view of its advocates, is also important for another reason. Courts have a function that goes beyond the deciding of cases: they also teach by example. And the example they set in allowing the use of evidence obtained in disregard of the Constitution is not one calculated to engender respect for law. The advocates of the rule would reject as a distinction without merit Wigmore's assertion that when the courts receive into evidence unlawfully seized materials "the illegality is by no means condoned; it is merely ignored,"[99] for to ignore is to condone by implication. They regard the traditional refusal of the courts to exclude illegally seized evidence as stemming from a conscious desire to assist law enforcement. In the view of Professor Thomas E. Atkinson, "there is no inherent reason for admitting evidence already found through an unreasonable search and excluding it where the evidence will not be learned until a witness is compelled to testify or produce something [in violation of the self-incrimination provision]." He goes on to ask: "Should there be a double standard . . . nullifying violations in the courtroom and winking at violations that occur outside?"[100]

96. Full discussion of the various suggested alternative remedies to restrain illegal searches, as well as of the pros and cons of the exclusionary rule, is reserved for later chapters dealing with state searches, for the reason that the Court itself did not thrash out these topics in the cases considered thus far.

97. Francis A. Allen, "The Wolf Case: Search and Seizure, Federalism, and the Civil Liberties," *Illinois Law Review*, XLV (March-April, 1950), 1, 20.

98. Robert E. Cushman, *Civil Liberties in the United States: A Guide to Current Problems and Experience* (Ithaca, N.Y., 1956), p. 136.

99. Wigmore, *Treatise*, Vol. VIII, Sec. 2183, p. 4.

100. Atkinson, "Admissibility of Evidence," p. 17.

One thing is certain: the exclusionary rule is the most creative single act of the Supreme Court in this area of constitutional law. The Court's interpretation of the Fourth Amendment revolves around the exclusionary rule. In the appeals that come before it in this area, the Court is usually called upon to decide only one question: should evidence admitted at the trial have been excluded. But to do so it must first determine whether the search met constitutional standards, and it must therefore chart and define those standards. Without the exclusionary rule, the illegality of the search would be immaterial to the admission of the evidence, and the judicial *development* of the Fourth Amendment as we know it would have proved impossible.

## CHAPTER IV

# CONSTITUTIONAL SEARCHES WITHOUT WARRANT

The Fourth Amendment first forbids the federal government to engage in "unreasonable" searches and then goes on to prescribe the terms under which a search warrant may be issued. It must not be inferred, however, that the constitutional reasonableness of a search always depends on the existence of a properly issued and executed search warrant—that, given the warrant, the search is constitutional, and that without the warrant, it is unreasonable. Often, it is true, the presence or absence of a warrant will be determinative of the constitutionality of a search. Such is not always the case, however, as was first made clear in *Boyd* v. *United States*,[1] where it was held that even the existence of a warrant did not make constitutionally reasonable a search for private papers. Conversely, the Supreme Court has ruled that two types of search may be reasonable in the absence of a warrant: the search of a person (and the area under his control) as incidental to a valid arrest; and the search of a moving vehicle, such as an automobile, where there is probable cause to believe that the vehicle is being used to transport contraband. The right to search without a warrant as incidental to arrest was first recognized by the Supreme Court in 1914 in the case of *Weeks* v. *United States*,[2] though the concept was to be developed in later cases. The right to search an automobile without a warrant was recognized somewhat later, in *Carroll* v. *United States*,[3] decided in 1925. To the extent that these exceptions to the requirement of a warrant are broadened in scope, the potential protection afforded by the Fourth Amendment is narrowed. For this reason, the cases involving automobile searches and searches incidental to arrest have generated powerful judicial controversy.

Before the nineteen twenties very few Fourth Amendment cases of any significance had been decided by the Supreme Court. With the adoption of the Eighteenth (Prohibition) Amendment in 1919,

1. 116 U.S. 616 (1886).
2. 232 U.S. 383 (1914).
3. 267 U.S. 132 (1925).

however, such cases began to appear in profusion. Interpretation of the search and seizure provision, Professor Chafee wryly remarked, "received new life from the fact that infractions of the Fourth Amendment frequently interfere[d] with the consumption of liquor in violation of the Eighteenth Amendment."[4] The Carroll case was one of the first prohibition search cases to reach the Court.

Carroll was convicted of transporting liquor in an auto in violation of the National Prohibition Act of 1919,[5] which was passed to implement the Eighteenth Amendment. In September of 1921, Carroll had agreed to sell liquor to federal prohibition agents, of whose real identity he was at first evidently unaware, but for some reason the transaction never went through, possibly because he subsequently learned who the would-be purchasers really were. Nearly three months later, in December, 1921, while the agents were patrolling the road between Detroit and Grand Rapids, Michigan, they spotted Carroll's car coming toward Grand Rapids. After following Carroll for some distance in their own car, they ordered him to stop. They searched his car, seized the liquor which was secreted beneath the upholstery, and made the arrest.

Chief Justice Taft, speaking for the Court, delivered an opinion sustaining the conviction. His basic premise was that the warrant requirements of the Fourth Amendment might be dispensed with where considerations of time prevented the issuance of a warrant, as in the case of an automobile which "can be quickly moved out of the locality or jurisdiction in which the warrant must be sought."[6] He pointed out that, from the beginning, Congress had distinguished between the search of a private dwelling and the search of a moving vehicle. As early as 1789, the First Congress had authorized search without warrant by revenue officers of vessels suspected of carrying goods on which duty had been evaded, and like provisions were inserted in a number of bills enacted since that time, though Congress was always careful to require a warrant for the search of dwellings suspected of harboring such goods. Here, too, in the Prohibition Act, Congress, while specifically denying the right to search a dwelling without a warrant, had authorized federal agents who "discover any person in the act of transporting in violation of the law, intoxicating liquors in any wagon, buggy, automobile, water or air craft" to seize the liquor and arrest the person in charge.

4. Zechariah Chafee, Jr., "The Progress of the Law, 1919–1922," *Harvard Law Review*, XXXV (April, 1922), 673, 694.
5. 41 Stat. 305, 315.
6. 267 U.S. 132, 153.

This distinction between dwellings and moving vehicles did not mean, Taft went on to say, that law officers might stop vehicles with impunity in order to search for evidence of crime: "It would be intolerable and unreasonable . . . to . . . subject all persons lawfully using the highways to the inconvenience and indignity of such a search."[7] Even though the reasonableness of an automobile search did not depend on the existence of a warrant, the automobile was nevertheless a constitutionally protected area, and the Fourth Amendment did impose certain standards on law officers. These standards required that the search be based upon probable cause to believe that there was contraband aboard the vehicle. Whether the search was constitutionally reasonable would, in the case of moving vehicles, depend upon the existence of probable cause rather than upon the procurement of a warrant.

But was there, in fact, probable cause for the search of Carroll's car? Taft thought that the requirement had been met in this case because the ascertainment of probable cause depended not alone on the actions of the suspect but also on the geographical location in which the suspected offense was taking place. "We know," said Taft, ". . . that Grand Rapids is about 152 miles from Detroit, and that Detroit and its neighborhood along the Detroit river, which is the international boundary, is one of the most active centers for introducing illegally into this country spirituous liquors for distribution into the interior."[8] This state of affairs, coupled with the fact that the same officers had once been approached by Carroll with an offer to sell them liquor, was sufficient to establish probable cause for the search.

Justice McReynolds, with the concurrence of Justice Sutherland, dissented. He admonished his brethren: "The damnable character of the 'bootlegger's' business should not close our eyes to the mischief which will surely follow any attempt to destroy it by unwarranted methods."[9] He did not agree that Congress had authorized warrantless searches of automobiles, even upon probable cause. The Prohibition Act, said McReynolds, authorized search without legal process only when the officers did "discover" the culprit in the illegal act of transportation, and probable cause was not the same as discovery. Besides, in McReynolds' view, there was not probable cause in this case, but merely suspicion. Carroll was known to the agents only through his offer to sell them liquor, an offer made close to

7. *Ibid.*, pp. 153–54.
8. *Ibid.*, p. 160.
9. *Ibid.*, p. 163.

three months before the search and never fulfilled. "Has it come about," he asked, "that merely because a man once agreed to deliver whisky, but did not, he may be arrested whenever thereafter he ventures to drive an automobile on the road to Detroit?"[10]

McReynolds' criticism appeared to be well taken, for, as Professor Forrest R. Black pointed out in a devastating critique of the Carroll case, the geographical area of which the Court took note as a center of liquor smuggling had a population of eighteen million people and included eighteen large cities. To lower search standards over such a large area would mean that "a large portion of our motoring public will on slight suspicion be at the mercy of the law enforcement enthusiast."[11] It seems fair to say that the Carroll case not only authorized the search of moving vehicles without a warrant upon probable cause, but also drastically reduced probable cause standards for such searches.

Even aside from McReynolds' arguments, the majority opinion is subject to criticism. Taft's use of history was faulty and did not prove his point, for the reason that the long-standing congressional approval of search of vessels without warrant sanctioned only a hunt for goods entering the United States on which duty had not been paid, not for evidence to be seized domestically for use in a criminal prosecution. In the words of Professor Black, "Congress has the authority to require every vehicle to stop and be subjected to search at an international boundary when the occupant thereof is seeking admission into the country, even in the absence of any suspicion or probable cause."[12]

Instead of attempting to root the Carroll decision in doubtful historical justifications and congressional intentions, the Court might have made the decision seem more plausible had it merely stated an exception to the rule that searches and seizures must be authorized by a warrant. The Court might simply have said that the invention of the automobile, with its ability to move contraband goods outside the range of search warrants, made the full requirements of the

10. *Ibid.*, p. 174.

11. Forrest R. Black, "A Critique of the Carroll Case," *Columbia Law Review*, XXIX (November, 1929), 1068, 1087.

12. *Ibid.*, p. 1075. One act cited by the Court was passed in 1889 with respect to Alaska; it permitted the seizure of the vessels and merchandise. 30 Stat. 1253, 1280. However, Congress did not at that time regard Alaska as an integral part of the United States to which all provisions of the Constitution applied. This much is evident from the fact that in the following year Congress sanctioned a six-man jury for the trial of misdemeanors in the territory instead of the common-law twelve-man jury required by the Constitution. This legislation was struck down by the Supreme Court as unconstitutional in *Rasmussen* v. *United States*, 197 U.S. 516 (1905), on the ground that Alaska was then a fully "incorporated" territory of the United States to which the entire Constitution applied.

Fourth Amendment inapposite for searches of such vehicles. The amendment was intended principally to protect private dwellings; it need not be construed, in the presence of probable cause, to protect against searches of moving vehicles. Moreover, there is far less invasion of privacy in the search of an automobile, the interior of which is plainly visible, than in the search of a private dwelling, which, in theory, resembles the castle shielding its inmates from intruders. In this connection, it is pertinent that privately owned open fields do not enjoy the protection of the Fourth Amendment regardless of whether or not there is probable cause for the search.[13] If Congress might determine the reasonableness of a search, there was no reason why the Court could not have done so on its own account; indeed, in the first great search case[14] it did so with scant respect for the legislative finding.

The doctrine of the Carroll case remains good constitutional law to this day, though certain refinements (generally in the direction of granting officers even greater leeway in regard to automobile searches) have since been made. In the Carroll case the Court did appear to place one limitation on the warrantless search of automobiles when Chief Justice Taft observed that "where the securing of a warrant is reasonably practicable it must be used. . . ."[15] But it is difficult to see in what circumstances the Court would consider it reasonably practical to secure a warrant for the search of an automobile on the road. In *Husty* v. *United States*,[16] decided in 1931, the Court rejected a claim that the search without warrant of a parked car was unreasonable, on the ground that the officers could not know when the suspect would move the car. Even though several officers took part in the search, the Court did not think it was necessary for one of them to secure a warrant while leaving the car under the watchful eye of the others. The Court later ruled that where there is probable cause to justify a search while the automobile is moving on the road, the right to search is not lost when the automobile is subsequently parked in an open private garage, observable by the officers from outside. The officers may enter the garage and search the car there.[17] No reference was made to the feasibility of conducting the search while the car was on the road.

13. *Hester* v. *United States*, 265 U.S. 57 (1924). This limitation on the Fourth Amendment is based on common-law precedent.
14. *Boyd* v. *United States*, 116 U.S. 616 (1886).
15. 267 U.S. 132, 156.
16. 282 U.S. 694 (1931).
17. *Scher* v. *United States*, 305 U.S. 251 (1938). "Passage of the car into the open garage closely followed by the observing officer did not destroy this right." *Ibid.*, p. 255. The Court also appeared to justify the search on the ground of search

The Carroll case had left unresolved one important question: would the Court uphold automobile searches without warrant in the absence of congressional authorization? In the Carroll case the Court had read a congressional authorization for such searches into the National Prohibition Act, and the other cases thus far discussed had also involved violations of this act. In two cases, decided in 1948 and 1949 (*United States* v. *Di Re*[18] and *Brinegar* v. *United States*[19]), the Court was confronted with this question. In neither case was there statutory authorization for the search without warrant. In the Di Re case the Court implied a negative answer to the question; in the Brinegar case the answer was given in the affirmative.

The Di Re case began when government agents were told by an informer that a certain person in Buffalo, New York, was going to sell him counterfeit gasoline coupons. An agent followed the suspect's car until it parked at the arranged rendezvous. Three persons were found seated in the car. Two of these were the suspect and the informer, who clutched in his hand two coupons which were later shown to be counterfeit. The third person was Di Re. Together with the others, Di Re was taken into custody. He was ordered to turn out his pockets, and several more coupons were uncovered. Later he was searched and a large number of coupons was found in an envelope concealed in his clothing. Di Re's conviction was reversed by the Supreme Court in an opinion by Justice Jackson.

In this case there was actually no search of the automobile itself, only of its occupants. Whether the evidence against Di Re was admissible depended, in the first instance, on the right to search the automobile on probable cause to believe that it contained contraband, and, in the second instance, assuming the right to search the vehicle did exist, on whether that right could be extended to the search of Di Re's person. Concerning the first question, said Justice Jackson, the Carroll case was not in point as a precedent because that case involved a violation of the National Prohibition Act, in which Congress had authorized warrantless automobile searches

---

incidental to arrest, although the arrest followed rather than preceded the search. But it seems clear that the Court would have justified the search even in the absence of an arrest, as the passage just quoted shows. The Scher case used the Carroll case as precedent, and in that case the search was justified quite independently of the arrest which followed it. The Scher decision may, however, have been eroded by the recent case of *Preston* v. *United States*, which held that where the suspect has been arrested and his automobile is in police custody, the police may not at some later time return to search the automobile without a warrant. 376 U.S. 364 (1964). The opinion in the Preston case, significantly, makes no mention of the Scher decision despite its obvious relevance.

18. 332 U.S. 581 (1948).
19. 338 U.S. 160 (1949).

upon probable cause; the Court had therefore been loath to negate an act of Congress. In any event, there was no need to decide the matter. Even if the broad language of the Carroll case could be made to justify the warrantless search of the automobile regardless of congressional authorization, that case nevertheless could not be made to do double duty as a justification for the search of Di Re. The right to search the automobile did not confer an incidental right to search any passenger who happened to be aboard, just as the search of a dwelling conferred no incidental right to search all the persons in the house, a point government counsel had conceded. Yet the interests of law enforcement would be as much served by the search of house guests as of passengers in an automobile, for the house guest is able to conceal contraband on his person as easily as is the automobile passenger. Here Jackson stated an important limiting principle on the search power: a person who happens to be in the neighborhood when an offense is committed does not on that account become subject to search himself.

Justice Jackson's opinion, even if only by dictum, had gone far in the direction of trying to limit the Carroll decision to cases where statutory authority could be cited for the search of automobiles upon probable cause alone. Where no such authority existed, the Court would not of its own accord declare this type of search reasonable—at least, said Jackson, "this Court has never yet said so."[20] Just one year later, in the Brinegar case, it did say so. The personnel of the Court had not changed, but there was a major shift in alignment. Three members of the majority in the Di Re case, Justices Frankfurter, Murphy, and Jackson, became the dissenting minority in the Brinegar case, while the majority in the Brinegar case counted two members who had shifted over from dissent (without opinion) in the Di Re case, Chief Justice Vinson and Justice Black. Only four justices—Reed, Douglas, Rutledge, and Burton—agreed with both decisions. Speaking for the six-man majority in the Brinegar case was Justice Rutledge.

The search in the Brinegar case was in some respects very much like that in the Carroll case. In 1936 Congress had made it a federal offense to import liquor into any "dry" state. Brinegar was convicted of violating this law by importing liquor into Oklahoma from Missouri. The evidence against him was seized by federal agents in the search of his automobile. One of the agents had arrested Brinegar five months earlier on a similar charge. Based on this experience, and on Brinegar's reputation as a liquor runner, the agents gave

20. 332 U.S. 581, 585.

chase when they saw Brinegar's automobile, which appeared to be heavily loaded, pass theirs on an Oklahoma road one evening in March, 1947. They overtook Brinegar's automobile and forced it to the side of the road. Before the automobile was searched, Brinegar admitted to the officers that he was carrying liquor. The district court and the court of appeals were in agreement that probable cause had not been established when the chase began but upheld the search on the ground that Brinegar's admission furnished probable cause. The Supreme Court, however, disagreed with the lower courts and took the position that probable cause did exist before the officers gave pursuit.

Justice Rutledge devoted his opinion almost entirely to a discussion of probable cause. He did not even consider the question of whether the warrantless search of an automobile was constitutionally reasonable when not authorized by legislation; he simply assumed that it was. He cited the Carroll case as authority for allowing a search on probable cause alone, although there the Court had based the result on its understanding that the National Prohibition Act authorized the search. Rutledge emphasized that an automobile, unlike a home, was not a "place of privacy."[21]

The facts of this case, in regard to probable cause, were very much like those in the Carroll case, said Rutledge. Here, as there, the offending article was liquor; the officers were patrolling the road in the regular exercise of their duties; they recognized the driver and the vehicle; and they knew the driver as having previously engaged in the illegal liquor business. In the Carroll case the Court took note of the character of the Detroit area as a center of liquor distribution; Joplin, Missouri, was also such an area. The two cases differed only in a few details, and these were not sufficiently significant to justify a finding that probable cause did not exist in the Brinegar case.[22] Though the officers who searched Brinegar's car did not appear to have recognized the license number, as had the officers in the Carroll case, their identification of the car was otherwise complete. It was true that Joplin, unlike Detroit, was a *legal* source of supply, for the consumption of liquor was allowed in Missouri, whereas the Prohibition Act had blanketed the entire country, but that distinction was unimportant. The important fact was that "Joplin was a ready, con-

21. 338 U.S. 160, 176.

22. The facts known by the agents, taken cumulatively, said Rutledge, "constitute positive and convincing evidence that Brinegar was engaged in that activity, no less convincing than the evidence in *Carroll*. . . ." *Ibid.*, p. 170. There is a curiously contradictory sentence later on: "The question presented in the *Carroll* Case lay on the border between suspicion and probable cause." *Ibid.*, p. 177.

venient and probable . . . [source] for persons disposed to violate the Oklahoma and federal statutes."[23] The agents' knowledge of Brinegar as an illicit liquor dealer was not based on his local reputation alone; much more than mere hearsay was involved. Though Brinegar, unlike Carroll, had never offered to sell liquor to the agents, one of them had twice before seen Brinegar loading liquor in Joplin and had recently arrested him for violating the same law. The fact of Brinegar's previous arrest, to be sure, would be inadmissible in a trial, but a finding of probable cause did not need to be based on probative evidence.

Joined by Justices Frankfurter and Murphy, Justice Jackson dissented in what was perhaps the most eloquent opinion he ever wrote in a search case. In what constituted an appreciative essay on the meaning and significance of the Fourth Amendment, he castigated his colleagues for giving a "preferred position" to First Amendment rights and assigning other constitutional rights, including those in the Fourth Amendment, to a subordinate position. "We cannot," he declared, "give some constitutional rights a preferred position without relegating others to a deferred position; we can establish no firsts without thereby establishing seconds. Indications are not wanting that Fourth Amendment freedoms are tacitly marked as secondary rights, to be relegated to a deferred position."[24]

The Brinegar decision, in Jackson's view, amply justified these strictures. The Carroll case had sustained a warrantless search of an automobile for which there was said to be congressional authorization. No such authorization was present in the Brinegar case. The decision therefore had the result of extending the Carroll doctrine to permit warrantless searches of automobiles for all federal offenses, a result of which Jackson disapproved. Nor did he approve of the finding of probable cause. The evidence upon which the agents acted was almost all hearsay, based on Brinegar's reputation. In the Carroll case the agents had personally negotiated with Carroll; that element was missing here. It was true that the agents had previously arrested Brinegar for liquor running, but the previous arrest had not thus far resulted in a conviction and was inadmissible in evidence at a trial; inadmissible evidence might well contribute toward a finding of probable cause, but should scarcely be allowed to establish probable cause when standing virtually "alone" and when the "other facts give little indication of guilt."[25] Jackson made the sug-

23. *Ibid.*, p. 168.
24. *Ibid.*, p. 180.
25. *Ibid.*, p. 187.

gestion that, when dealing with automobile searches, the Court might at least take into account "the gravity of the offense." Where human life was concerned, as in a kidnapping case, he would sustain a search "executed fairly and in good faith" even where probable cause was lacking; in such circumstances the search could well be considered reasonable. But it was a different matter to require probable cause and then water down its standards in order "to salvage a few bottles of bourbon and catch a bootlegger."[26]

Justice Jackson warned his brethren of the serious consequences that might ensue as a result of broadening the exceptions to the warrant requirements and thereby placing control over the search power in the hands of law enforcement officers instead of the judiciary. Speaking also as a former Attorney General of the United States, he asserted: "Only occasional and more flagrant abuses come to the attention of the courts. . . . There may be, and I am convinced that there are, many unlawful searches of homes and automobiles of innocent people which turn up nothing incriminating, in which no arrest is made, about which the courts do nothing, and about which we never hear. . . . So a search against Brinegar's car must be regarded as a search of the car of Everyman."[27]

Justice Jackson might have stood on firmer ground had he simply said that, as to probable cause, the Carroll case was wrongly decided, and not attempted to draw distinctions of fact between the Brinegar and Carroll cases. The grounds for a finding of probable cause do not appear to have been substantially different in the two cases. True, Carroll had personally offered to make a sale of liquor to the agents, but that sale was never completed. Brinegar, on the other hand, had actually been arrested previously by the agents as a bootlegger and presumably was caught red-handed with the liquor. The real vice in each case was that an automobile was stopped and searched primarily because of the driver's *past* record, not because of any real evidence that the automobile was being used in the commission of a crime *at the time*. The justification given for the warrantless automobile search is that of necessity—that the vehicle can be moved and the search frustrated before a warrant is obtained—and this fact should require a finding of probable cause based on present rather than past illegal conduct.[28]

26. *Ibid.*, p. 183.
27. *Ibid.*, p. 181.
28. There have been one or two more recent cases of automobile searches, but these have involved search as incidental to the arrest of the occupant. See, e.g., *Henry* v. *United States*, 361 U.S. 98 (1959).

Is there any situation short of probable cause which would justify a policeman in stopping an automobile? There is no doubt that he may do so for the purpose of enforcing the traffic laws, as, for example, the checking of drivers' licenses. One who drives an automobile does so subject to certain regulations made in the interest of community safety, and these would be meaningless if they could not be enforced. But where the object in stopping the vehicle is either to arrest or to search, probable cause must first be established. Roadblocks set up to stop and search indiscriminately all automobiles seeking to pass in order to catch a few violators of the law are definitely in violation of the Fourth Amendment (although, as noted before, Justice Jackson said that he would consider such procedures reasonable where human life is at stake).

Probable cause must, of course, be established at the time the arrest or search is made; arrest and search cannot acquire retroactive legality by what is uncovered later on. But does the mere stopping of an automobile itself constitute an arrest where the object is investigation rather than the immediate apprehension of the driver or passengers? Suppose probable cause was lacking at the time the vehicle was stopped but did become evident during the course of the investigation because of something the driver (or passengers) said or did. If the halting of the vehicle was an arrest, the subsequent developments could not legalize it, and evidence uncovered as a result of a search made incidental to the arrest would be inadmissible.

This question has arisen in two recent cases, but the Court has not forthrightly decided the matter. In the first case, *Henry* v. *United States*,[29] decided in 1959, the Court found that the arrest did indeed take place at the time when the automobile was stopped and the freedom of movement of its occupants thereby restrained. But not too much can be inferred from the decision because the government conceded the point in that case (arguing, however, that probable cause had been established at the time the automobile was stopped, an argument that the Court rejected). The next year, in *Rios* v. *United States*,[30] the same question arose, and this time the Court evaded the issue. The case was remanded to the district court for a determination of whether the arrest took place when the officers approached the taxi in which Rio was driving when it stopped for a red light (and at which time probable cause had not been established), or whether the arrest took place *after* the taxi was stopped and Rios was seen to drop a package of narcotics to the floor. The

29. *Ibid.*
30. 364 U.S. 253 (1960).

fact that the Court did not simply rely on the earlier Henry case at least leaves open the possibility that the momentary halting of an automobile for investigation does not automatically constitute an arrest.[31]

The judicial controversy found in automobile search cases is present to an even greater extent in cases of search incidental to a valid arrest, which is the other common type of warrantless search. "There are not too many instances," write two competent observers, "where this ground [of probable cause] must be resorted to [in automobile searches] because if probable cause exists, it is usually sufficient to support arrest as well as search."[32] The search is then carried out as incidental to the arrest. In no other area of search law, perhaps in no other area of constitutional law, have judicial tempers become so ruffled as in this one. In two respects, however, the controversy over search incidental to arrest differs from that over automobile searches. First, the right to search as an incident of arrest is deeply rooted in the common law and is conceded; the controversy, therefore, is not over the right of the search itself but over its scope. Second, whereas the automobile search was justified on the ground that it is usually impractical to obtain a warrant before the vehicle is moved out of the officer's jurisdiction, the Supreme Court has on several occasions justified searches of great scope as incidental to arrest and specifically disclaimed the need to obtain a warrant even when it was clearly feasible to do so.

The right to search the person of the prisoner as incidental to an arrest had its origin in the English common law and was justified by necessity. A search of the person and, to some extent, of his property was permitted even in the absence of a search warrant in order to protect the lives of the arresting officers, to ensure that the fugitive would not escape, and to prevent him from destroying the evidence of his crime.[33] The early American state cases followed the

31. Two members of the Court in the Henry case took the definite position that it is permissible to halt an automobile for the purpose of investigation. See the dissenting opinion of Justice Clark, in which Chief Justice Warren joined. 361 U.S. 98, 104. Earlier, Justice Burton had come to the same conclusion in his concurring opinion in the Brinegar case: "Government agents are commissioned to represent the interests of the public in the enforcement of the law and this requires affirmative action not only when there is reasonable ground for an arrest or probable cause for a search but when there is reasonable ground for an investigation." 338 U.S. 160, 179.

32. Raymond A. Dahl and Howard H. Boyle, Jr., *Procedure and the Law of Arrest, Search and Seizure* (Milwaukee, Wis., 1961), p. 163.

33. *Abel* v. *United States*, 362 U.S. 217, 236 (1960); and see H. Frank Way, Jr., "Increasing Scope of Search Incidental to Arrest," *Washington University Law Quarterly*, Vol. 1959 (June, 1959), pp. 261, 263.

English rules and, in general, "strictly limited the scope of the search to the body of the prisoner and to goods which were subject to seizure and were visible to the arresting officer. In no case was a search allowed to go beyond the things actually in the possession of the prisoner."[34] In 1914 the Supreme Court, in a dictum, recognized this common-law right of search without warrant as meeting the requirements of the Fourth Amendment.[35] Since that time the allowable scope of search incidental to arrest has perceptibly increased step by step; this process culminated in a decision,[36] which may still have the support of a majority of the Court,[37] that allowed the extended search of the entire residence in which an arrest was made.

The first indication that search incidental to arrest need not be confined to the person of the prisoner came in 1925 in the Carroll case, where, in addition to finding reasonable the warrantless search of an automobile, the Court added, again in a dictum, that "whatever is found upon his person or *in his control* which it is unlawful for him to have, and which may be used to prove the offense, may be seized and held as evidence in the prosecution."[38] In the same year, in *Agnello* v. *United States*, the Court restated this new doctrine in these words: "The right without a search warrant contemporaneously to search persons lawfully arrested while committing crime, *and to search the place where the arrest is made* in order to find and seize things connected with the crime as its fruits, or as the means by which it was committed, as well as weapons and other things to effect an escape from custody, is not to be doubted."[39] The Court set one important limit in the Agnello case when it refused to give its sanction to the search of Agnello's house, located several blocks from the scene of his arrest, and, in so doing, confined the search to the area *under his physical control* at the time of arrest.

Thus far there was nothing to indicate that the extension of the scope of search incidental to arrest from the person of the prisoner to the area under his control represented any drastic change in the law.

34. Way, "Scope of Search," p. 263.

35. The right "of the government, [has] always [been] recognized under English and American law, to search the person of the accused when legally arrested, to discover and seize the fruits or evidences of crime." *Weeks* v. *United States*, 232 U.S. 383, 392 (1914).

36. *Harris* v. *United States*, 331 U.S. 145 (1947).

37. The Harris case (331 U.S. 145 [1947]) was cited with evident approval in *Ker* v. *California*, 374 U.S. 23, 42 (1963). However, this portion of the Ker opinion reflected the views of only four justices; the other justices did not reach the question of search incidental to arrest. The Harris case was conspicuously omitted from the list of precedents in *Preston* v. *United States*, 376 U.S. 364 (1964), but was again cited, somewhat obliquely, in *Beck* v. *Ohio*, 379 U.S. 89, 91 (1964).

38. 267 U.S. 132, 158. (Emphasis supplied.)

39. 269 U.S. 20 (1925). (Emphasis supplied.)

The Court had been careful to justify the more extensive scope for the same reasons which originally gave rise to the right to search the person: the securing of the prisoner, the protection of the officer, and the prevention of destruction of evidence. If a suspect could make good his escape by using a gun hidden in his pocket, it was reasonable to assume that he could do so by using a gun within easy reach, though not on his person. It seemed sensible to permit the officers to eliminate such a possibility. That the language of the Carroll and Agnello cases was not thought to presage any important change in the law is evident from an opinion of Judge Learned Hand, written after the Agnello case and before the Supreme Court spoke next on the subject, in which he gave expression to his views on the limitations placed on officers searching incidental to arrest. Said Judge Hand: "[I]t is broadly a totally different thing to search a man's pockets and use against him what they contain, from ransacking his house for everything which may incriminate him, once you have gained lawful entry. . . . After arresting a man in his house, to rummage at will among his papers in search of whatever will convict him, appears to us to be indistinguishable from what might be done under a general warrant; indeed, the warrant would give more protection, for presumably it must be issued by a magistrate."[40]

Insofar, then, as the aforementioned practical necessities governed the permissible scope of the search, its expansion to include the search and seizure of objects under the physical control of the prisoner could be justified by the same rationale used for the search of the prisoner himself. However, once the scope of the search was extended to include portions of the premises not within reach of the prisoner, this rationale would not offer any justification for so broad a search. It was probably inevitable that unless a new rationale were fashioned the Court would find it difficult to set any practical limits on the search short of search of the entire premises on which the arrest was made.

The case which extended the scope of search incidental to arrest to include portions of the premises not under the person's physical control was *Marron* v. *United States*,[41] decided in 1927. In this case, prohibition agents entered a "speak-easy" while it was in full operation. They placed the bartender under arrest and proceeded to search the premises. They did possess a warrant for the search, but the warrant authorized only the seizure of liquor. Nevertheless, construing their authority broadly, they seized a ledger from a closet and took

40. *United States* v. *Kirschenblatt*, 16 F.2d 202, 203 (2d cir. 1926).
41. 275 U.S. 192 (1927).

certain bills from the room. These implicated Marron as the proprietor of the illegal venture. The Court rejected the contention that the seizure was valid as incidental to the execution of the search warrant but agreed that it could be sustained as incidental to the bartender's arrest, emphasizing that a crime was being committed in the presence of the agents. "The authority of officers to search and seize the things by which the nuisance was being maintained," it said, "*extended to all parts of the premises used for the unlawful venture.*"[42]

The Marron case thus opened up a potential Pandora's box of judicial troubles by fashioning a new concept of search incidental to arrest without justifying the new rule in terms of a rationale. And in the future, when justifying extensive searches as reasonably incidental to arrest, the Court was often no more enlightening. The Marron case was invoked as precedent, as if precedent in itself furnished a rationale. For the time being, however, the effect of the Marron case was limited by two other prohibition cases decided shortly afterwards, *Go-Bart Importing Co.* v. *United States*[43] and *United States* v. *Lefkowitz*,[44] which, in Justice Frankfurter's words, drew "the sting of the *Marron* case"[45] and "effectually retract[ed] . . . the loose consideration of the problem"[46] there. In the Go-Bart case, prohibition agents entered the company office and arrested Gowen, the president, and Bartels, the secretary-treasurer, on charges of illicit liquor trafficking. They had neither arrest nor search warrants, but the arrests were nevertheless valid because based on probable cause. One of the agents falsely said that he had a search warrant and coerced Gowen, under threat of force, into opening a desk and a safe, from which a very large number of private papers were removed. The district court had refused to issue a restraining order directing the prosecution not to use this evidence, and this decision was now being appealed by Gowen and Bartels.

The Supreme Court ruled that the evidence should be suppressed and limited the Marron decision to the facts of that case. In the Marron case the seized articles "were visible and accessible and in the offender's immediate custody. There was no threat of force or

42. *Ibid.*, p. 199. (Emphasis supplied). Though the ledger and bills were private papers, the Court justified their seizure as instruments of crime, necessary for the maintenance of the establishment, and therefore not shielded by the immunity which normally protects private papers from seizure.
43. 282 U.S. 344 (1931).
44. 285 U.S. 452 (1932).
45. *Davis* v. *United States*, 328 U.S. 582, 609 (1946) (dissenting opinion).
46. *Harris* v. *United States*, 331 U.S. 145, 168 (1947) (dissenting opinion).

general search or rummaging of the place."[47] This statement overlooked the fact that the ledger was seized from a closet and was evidently not visible from the place of arrest. The Court added: "There is no formula for the determination of reasonableness. Each case is to be decided on its own facts and circumstances."[48] Of course, the old rule of search incidental to arrest did furnish a formula for determining reasonableness in this context: what was on the person of the prisoner or within his reach could be seized; what lay beyond his grasp could not.

The Lefkowitz case also involved trafficking in liquor. Lefkowitz was arrested in his office on a valid warrant. Two desks, a cabinet, and two wastebaskets were searched and the contents seized. The conduct of the officers, said the Court, "was unrestrained . . . numerous and varied were the things found and taken."[49] Since no offense had been committed in the presence of the officers, the search was unjustified. "An arrest may not be used as a pretext to search for evidence."[50] Beisel's comment on this series of cases is very much to the point. "For whatever worth as an insight into this particular shift of position by the Court," he writes, "we can note that each of these three cases dealt with enforcement of prohibition laws and then recall the changing enthusiasm of the public during this period toward the enforcement of these laws."[51] It should also be noted that the Marron, Go-Bart, and Lefkowitz cases, like the Agnello case, were unanimously decided by essentially the same justices, and that the opinions for all four cases were written by Justice Butler.

Following the Go-Bart and Lefkowitz cases, the issue was laid to rest for one and a half decades. The interval was long enough to permit a complete change in the personnel of the Court. Whereas the earlier cases, even when inconsistently decided, enjoyed the support of a unanimous bench, from 1947 onward judicial conflict came to be the rule. (In fact, since then only one decision involving search incidental to arrest has enlisted the support of a

47. 282 U.S. 344, 358.
48. *Ibid.*
49. 285 U.S. 452, 464.
50. *Ibid.*, p. 467. In both the Go-Bart and Lefkowitz cases, the Court pointed out that the search for private papers is prohibited even under warrant, and that consequently a search without warrant as incidental to arrest could not confer the right to seize that which was immune to seizure even under warrant. In the Marron case this limitation was evaded by the designation of the papers as instruments of crime necessary for the functioning of the business. No clear explanation is given in the Go-Bart and Lefkowitz cases as to why the papers there seized were less important in the running of the business than those seized in the Marron case.
51. Albert R. Beisel, Jr., *Control over Illegal Enforcement of the Criminal Law: Role of the Supreme Court* (Boston, 1955), p. 24.

unanimous Court.[52]) In *Harris* v. *United States*[53] the justices fell into two groups: Chief Justice Vinson and Justices Black, Reed, Douglas, and Burton, who, in this area, elevated the claims of law enforcement over the claims of individual liberties, opposed to Justices Frankfurter, Murphy, Jackson, and Rutledge.[54]

*Harris* v. *United States* involved the most extensive search without warrant ever to receive the Court's sanction. In this case, said one commentator, "the Supreme Court took the biggest step backward in the protection of privacy in the nearly 160 years of its history."[55] Harris was apprehended at home, on a charge of using the mails to transport a forged check, by agents of the Federal Bureau of Investigation who possessed a valid arrest warrant but no search warrant. He was handcuffed, and five agents undertook a search of the entire apartment. For five hours they ransacked the four rooms in an effort to recover stolen cancelled checks believed to have been used in preparing the forgery. They did not find the checks but did come across evidence of a totally unrelated crime, in the form of an envelope, marked "personal papers," which contained Selective Service documents, including classification cards, for the illegal possession of which Harris was subsequently convicted.

In his opinion sustaining the conviction, Chief Justice Vinson justified the search in a six-step syllogism. (1) The entry into the premises was made lawfully, in the execution of the arrest warrant. (2) Once lawfully inside, the agents could search without warrant as incidental to arrest. (3) Previous cases had recognized that the search could, on occasion, extend beyond the person of the arrestee to the premises under his control. Hence it could lawfully extend to the entire apartment, not merely to the living room in which the arrest was made, for the entire apartment, including the bedroom in which the evidence was uncovered, was in Harris' possession at the time of his arrest. (4) An extensive search was necessary because of the nature of the articles sought. Cancelled checks are so small that they are not likely to be readily visible and might easily be concealed in any part of the apartment. (5) The search was not exploratory but was undertaken to locate evidence connecting Harris with the particular crime for which he was arrested. (6) Both the articles

52. *Preston* v. *United States*, 376 U.S. 364 (1964), the most recent case on the subject, where the search took place long after the arrest had been made.
53. 331 U.S. 145 (1947).
54. These groupings first became evident the year before in *Davis* v. *United States*, 328 U.S. 582 (1946), and *Zap* v. *United States*, 328 U.S. 624 (1946), discussed in the preceding chapter. Though these were not cases of search incidental to arrest, they were nevertheless closely related to such cases.
55. Way, "Scope of Search," p. 271.

sought and those discovered were legally subject to seizure as contraband. It was not important that the items seized were not those sought. While engaged in a lawful search, the agents came across government property properly subject to seizure because its possession constituted a continuing offense committed in their presence.

Justice Frankfurter, who was joined by Justices Murphy and Rutledge in a dissenting opinion, masterfully dissected the weak links in Vinson's chain of reasoning. The crux of the matter, said Frankfurter, was that the reasonableness of a search of the home depended on the authority of a warrant, save only for the search of that which "is in such open and immediate physical relation to him [the arrestee] as to be, in a fair sense, a projection of his person."[56] This was the true test of "possession" for purposes of search incidental to arrest. "Possession" in the sense used by the Court was a property concept inappropriate to the interpretation of the Fourth Amendment: it was illogical to speak of the entire apartment as being in Harris' possession, since he was under arrest at the time the search was made.

An illegal search, said Frankfurter, does not acquire retroactive legality by what it uncovers: A search stands or falls, legally speaking, on the manner in which it is *begun.* The fact that instruments of crime were sought did not make a search of this scope lawful, and the fact that the articles uncovered were government property did not make the seizure lawful. Even a search under warrant would not confer authority to seize items other than those enumerated in the warrant. How, then, could a search without warrant confer a greater privilege? There was time enough in this case for the officers to obtain a warrant for the search and a second warrant for the seizure of the unrelated items uncovered in the search. Justice Frankfurter concluded that the fidelity of the Court majority to the Fourth Amendment was something less than wholehearted. In a revealing passage, he declared: "A principle may be accepted 'in principle,' but the impact of an immediate situation may lead to deviation from the principle. Or, while accepted 'in principle,' a competing principle may seem more important. Both these considerations have doubtless influenced the application of the search and seizure provisions of the Bill of Rights."[57]

Justice Murphy's dissenting opinion was written along similar lines. His views were best summed up in his opening paragraph:

56. 331 U.S. 145, 168.
57. *Ibid.*, p. 157.

The Court today has resurrected and approved in effect, the use of the odious general warrant or writ of assistance, presumably outlawed forever from our society by the Fourth Amendment. A warrant of arrest, without more, is now sufficient to justify an unlimited search of a man's home from cellar to garret for evidence of any crime, provided only that he is arrested in his home. Probable cause for the search need not be shown; an oath or affirmation is unnecessary; no description of the place to be searched or the things to be seized need be given; and the magistrate's judgment that these requirements have been satisfied is now dispensed with. In short, all the restrictions put upon the issuance and execution of search warrants by the Fourth Amendment are now dead letters as to those who are arrested in their homes.[58]

In a separate dissent, Justice Jackson attacked the decision as sanctioning the evasion of the search and seizure provision by officers making an arrest; henceforth they would be careful to select the place where the arrest was to be made in order to make maximum use of their new-found authority to search extensively without benefit of a warrant. But neither could he agree with his fellow dissenters, for he understood them to say that objects *in plain view* of the arresting officers might be seized, and that it was only the intensity of the search to which they objected. He would go further and say that the search must not "go beyond the person arrested and the objects upon him or in his *immediate physical control*. . . . The fair implication of the Constitution is that no search of premises, as such, is reasonable [unless authorized by a warrant]."[59]

Since in the decision on the Harris case the justices were divided five to four, a change in the position of only one member of the majority would be sufficient to make the minority position the dominant one. This shift occurred just one year later, when Justice Douglas, in a fundamental change from his expressed views on searches and seizures, joined the Harris dissenters to form the majority in *Trupiano* v. *United States*.[60] Trupiano and three others had leased a farm in New Jersey. The farm owner communicated to the government his suspicions that they intended to erect an illegal still on the property. A revenue agent posing as a farm hand was able to obtain employment at the still. He reported the progress of the illegal venture, and a raid was planned. Three agents arrived one night at the farm and were able to smell the fermenting mash. Looking through an open door, one of the agents plainly saw the still in operation. He walked in, arrested the man in charge, and

58. *Ibid.*, p. 183.
59. *Ibid.*, pp. 197–98. (Emphasis supplied.)
60. 334 U.S. 699 (1948).

took possession of the still. The other three, including Trupiano, were arrested shortly afterwards.

The dissenting opinions in the Harris case had stressed the fact that in that case there was time enough for the officers to obtain a warrant. It was this consideration which proved decisive in the Trupiano case. The arrest was perfectly valid, said Justice Murphy for the Court, since the man was committing a felony in the presence of an officer. But the seizure of the still was not. Every detail of the operation was known to the agents long in advance of the raid, and they should have applied for a warrant: "the property was not of a type that could have been dismantled and removed before the agents had time to secure a warrant. . . ."[61]

In the Harris case Justice Jackson had protested that even the other dissenters would sanction a warrantless search for objects in plain view of the arresting officers. Whatever the correctness of his understanding of their position, it is clear that the views he expressed there prevailed in the Trupiano case, for here the still was operating in plain view of the officer, yet the seizure was deemed illegal. After sanctioning an extensive ransacking without warrant for well-hidden objects in the Harris case, the Court now veered in the opposite direction and prohibited the seizure even of objects in plain view.

But where the contraband is in plain view and has already been spotted by an arresting officer lawfully on the premises, what contribution toward protection of privacy can a warrant make? This was the question posed by Chief Justice Vinson, speaking for the dissenters. He chided the majority for "confound[ing] confusion in a field already replete with complexities."[62] But Murphy thought that a warrant would help protect privacy even in such a case. "A search warrant must describe with particularity the place to be searched and the things to be seized. Without such a warrant, however, officers are free to determine for themselves the extent of their search and the precise objects to be seized."[63] To emphasize this point, Murphy showed that search in this case had indeed extended beyond objects in plain view; a truck, for instance, had been searched on the farm grounds. Suppose, said Murphy, that the arrestee at the time of his arrest had not been on the premises. Could the search have taken place without a warrant? The answer was clearly in the negative. There is no authority to enter a home without a warrant even to seize objects in plain view. Why then should the seizure be

61. *Ibid.*, p. 706.
62. *Ibid.*, p. 716.
63. *Ibid.*, p. 710.

permitted merely because of the "fortuitous circumstance"[64] that when arrested Trupiano happened to be on the premises rather than on the street?[65]

The Trupiano doctrine that the reasonableness of a search must be tested by the availability of a warrant where it is feasible to obtain one was followed in *McDonald* v. *United States*,[66] decided the same year. In this case, police officers gained access to a rooming house, where they believed an illegal lottery was being operated, by unlawfully climbing into the landlady's quarters. They posted themselves in a hallway and, peeping through the transom of McDonald's room, observed the lottery in operation. McDonald, who was a boarder, was arrested and the gambling paraphernalia was seized. The Court might have reversed the conviction on the ground that the search had been begun unlawfully by its invasion of the landlady's privacy, a position taken by Justice Jackson in a concurring opinion. Instead, the Court, speaking through Justice Douglas, insisted that regardless of whether or not the entry into the landlady's premises had also invaded McDonald's constitutional right of privacy, the search as incidental to the arrest was nevertheless not permissible because there was time in which to obtain a warrant. "Where, as here, officers are not responding to an emergency," said Justice Douglas, "there must be compelling reasons to justify the absence of a search warrant."[67] The dissenting opinion of Justice Burton restated the dissent in the Trupiano case: a warrant for the seizure of objects in plain view was unnecessary because the objects were visible and did not need to be searched for.

But the Trupiano doctrine, which was now more firmly entrenched[68] than the Harris doctrine ever had been, was soon to be discarded. Search and seizure cases in this area have tended to age quickly, and the Trupiano case was no exception. The cause of this development was the death of the two most ardent champions of civil liberties on the Court, Justices Murphy and Rutledge, and their replacement with Justices Clark and Minton, who allied themselves with the group which had dissented in the Trupiano case. Even the defection from that group of Justice Black was not sufficient to offset the votes of the new appointees. In the 1950 case of *United*

64. *Ibid.*, p. 707.
65. The Court did not specifically overrule the Harris case, but the decision, of course, had the effect of doing so.
66. 335 U.S. 451 (1948).
67. *Ibid.*, p. 454.
68. For another case of the Trupiano genre, though there the Court found that there was no valid arrest to justify an incidental search, see *Johnson* v. *United States*, 333 U.S. 10 (1948).

*States* v. *Rabinowitz*,[69] the new Court majority announced: "To the extent that *Trupiano* v. *United States* . . . requires a search warrant solely upon the basis of the practicability of procuring it rather than upon the reasonableness of the search after a lawful arrest, that case is overruled."[70] Only twice before, it appears, had the Court formally reversed itself within such a short period of time.[71]

Rabinowitz was a stamp dealer who had once served a sentence for forging overprints on United States postage stamps. When the government got word that Rabinowitz was plying his old trade, an agent was sent to make a purchase of some stamps bearing overprints. The overprints were later found to be forgeries. Officers armed with an arrest warrant but with no search warrant called on Rabinowitz, arrested him in his one-room office, and for an hour and a half searched the desk, safe, and cabinets, from which they recovered a substantial number of stamps bearing forged overprints. Rabinowitz was convicted on two counts, one related to the four stamps purchased by the agent, the other to the stamps seized during the search. The purchased stamps were clearly admissible in evidence; the admission of those seized in the search, however, was protested as being contrary to the Trupiano decision, since the agents had adequate time to procure a warrant.[72]

The search in the Rabinowitz case was obviously not as extensive as the one in the Harris case. Justice Minton, in his opinion for the Court, stressed the relatively limited scope of the search: "the room was small . . . [and] the search did not extend beyond the room used for unlawful purposes. . . ."[73] Nevertheless, the decision seemed to be in line with the Harris case, for the seized stamps were neither in Rabinowitz's physical custody nor in full view.

In large measure the majority and dissenting opinions in the case restated those in the Harris case and as such would not command detailed attention. But there was one important innovation. The Court attempted to justify the expanded scope of search incidental to arrest through a reinterpretation of the reasonableness require-

69. 339 U.S. 56 (1950).
70. *Ibid.*, p. 66.
71. The Legal Tender cases, 12 Wallace 457 (1871), which overruled *Hepburn* v. *Griswold*; 8 Wallace 603 (1870); and *Murdock* v. *Pennsylvania*, 319 U.S. 105 (1943), which overruled *Jones* v. *Opelika*, 316 U.S. 584 (1942). A more recent example of such a quick reversal occurred in *Reid* v. *Covert*, 354 U.S. 1 (1957), which overruled the case by the same name decided less than one year before, 351 U.S. 487 (1956).
72. Justice Frankfurter in his dissenting opinion said that "the Government had at least seven, and more accurately fifteen, days in which to procure a search warrant." 339 U.S. 56, 85.
73. *Ibid.*, p. 64.

ment of the Fourth Amendment, a development which "constituted a fundamental change in fourth amendment theory."[74] What had previously been implicit in the Harris case was now made explicit. Hitherto it had usually been assumed that a reasonable search was one conducted under a warrant and that, conversely, an unreasonable search was the warrantless search or one in which the warrant was so lacking in specificity, like the general warrant, as to amount to no warrant at all. Search incidental to arrest was justified on common-law grounds as a necessary and implied exception to the amendment's standards, as was the warrantless search of moving vehicles. The expanded scope of search incidental to arrest was also justified, however inaccurately, by this common-law rule. In other words, the amendment's condemnation of unreasonable searches was read not independently but in conjunction with the warrant requirements; indeed, the reasonableness clause was thought to place certain limits even on searches with warrant.[75]

In the Rabinowitz case, however, the Court for the first time undermined this edifice by detaching the reasonableness clause from the warrant requirements and permitting the reasonableness of a search to be determined independently, without reference to the rest of the amendment. Search incidental to arrest was justified as built into the reasonableness clause of the Fourth Amendment rather than as a historical exception to the general need for a search warrant. Said Justice Minton: "What is a reasonable search is not to be determined by any fixed formula. The Constitution does not define what are 'unreasonable' searches and, regrettably, in our discipline we have no ready litmus-paper test. The recurring questions of the reasonableness of searches must find resolution in the facts and circumstances of each case. . . . The relevant test is not whether it is reasonable to procure a search warrant, but whether the search was reasonable. That criterion in turn depends on the facts and circumstances—*the total atmosphere of the case*."[76] "It is fallacious," maintained Minton, "to judge events retrospectively and thus to determine, considering the time element alone, that there was time to procure a search warrant. . . . Some flexibility will be accorded to law officers engaged in daily battle with criminals."[77]

74. Comment, "Search and Seizure in the Supreme Court: Shadows on the Fourth Amendment," *University of Chicago Law Review*, XXVIII (Summer, 1961), 664, 684.
75. *Boyd* v. *United States*, 116 U.S. 616 (1886); *Gouled* v. *United States*, 255 U.S. 298 (1921).
76. 339 U.S. 56, 63, 66. (Emphasis supplied.)
77. *Ibid.*, p. 65.

It was precisely in order to obviate the need for retrospective judgment that the dissenters in the case would always require a warrant prior to the search if time permits its procurement, for it is then that a disinterested magistrate is best able to determine, under constitutional standards, whether justification exists for the proposed search. The decision, they thought, abdicated to the police the judicial prerogative of determining reasonableness, leaving the courts in a position to review *retrospectively*, and then only if the victim was ever brought to trial. For this reason Justice Frankfurter dissented, in an opinion joined by Justice Jackson. Justice Black in a separate dissent showed himself in philosophical sympathy with the decision —for he had been among the dissenters in the Trupiano case—but in view of the fact that nowhere else was "the law's uncertainty . . . more clearly manifested," he felt that the Court should have stayed with the Trupiano doctrine, "at least long enough to see how it works."[78]

Justice Frankfurter, however, was completely out of sympathy with the decision, and not merely on account of the confusion it might create. He placed great emphasis on the abuses which had given rise to the Fourth Amendment and accused the majority of disregarding the lessons of history. The words of the amendment, he chided, "are not just a literary composition. They are not to be read as they might be read by a man who knows English but has no knowledge of the history that gave rise to the words."[79] Frankfurter stressed that the right to search the arrested person and his physical environs was historically a narrow exception based on *necessity*. In robust language he accused the majority of watering down the requirements of the Fourth Amendment in the interest of law enforcement. "The short of it is," he concluded, "that the right to search the place of arrest is an innovation based on confusion, without historic foundation, and made in the teeth of a historic protection against it."[80]

As for the Court's innovating doctrine that reasonableness was something to be determined independently of the amendment's warrant requirements, Justice Frankfurter protested that this had the effect of "tear[ing] 'unreasonable' from the context and history and purpose of the Fourth Amendment. . . . It is to make the arrest an incident to an unwarranted search instead of a warrantless search

78. *Ibid.*, p. 67. Justice Douglas, who would almost certainly have been aligned with the dissenters, took no part in the case.
79. *Ibid.*, p. 69.
80. *Ibid.*, p. 79.

an incident to an arrest."[81] Finally, Frankfurter, like Black, pointed to the uncertainty which was bound to be introduced in the overruling of the Trupiano case, a decision only two years old. In a pointed allusion to the new justices, Clark and Minton, who had helped form the majority, Frankfurter declared that the requirement of a search warrant wherever practicable was "not a rule invented in *Trupiano* v. *United States* . . . [and] not a rule of those who came on this Court in recent years."[82] The Court must be careful not to leave the impression "that Law is the expression of chance—for instance, of unexpected changes in the Court's composition and the contingencies in the choice of successors."[83]

But the Rabinowitz decision was not the Supreme Court's final decision on the subject. More recent decisions have once again cast doubt on the scope of search incidental to arrest. In the 1957 case of *Kremen* v. *United States*[84] an intensive search was made of a house in which three suspects were apprehended; the entire contents of the dwelling were seized and removed two hundred miles to the F.B.I. office in San Francisco for inspection. In a *per curiam* opinion reflecting the views of six justices, the Court ruled that a seizure of this magnitude went "beyond the sanction of any of our cases"[85] and was therefore unlawful. The real implications of the Kremen case were not, however, clear. Hundreds of items had been seized; ten pages of the *United States Reports* were required to list the inventory of articles taken. Suppose the search alone had blanketed the entire house, but the seizure had been confined, as in the Harris case, to items connecting the arrestees with crime: would this be considered lawful?

*Abel* v. *United States*,[86] decided in 1960, answered this question. In this case, the Court held good the extensive search of the hotel room and the adjacent bathroom of Abel, later convicted as a Soviet spy, on the express authority of the Harris and Rabinowitz cases. What was surprising was the fact that Justice Frankfurter, the "great

81. *Ibid.*, p. 80.
82. *Ibid.*, p. 84.
83. *Ibid.*, p. 86.
84. 353 U.S. 346 (1957).
85. *Ibid.*, p. 347. Dissenting jointly, Justices Burton and Clark maintained that "validity of a seizure is not to be tested by the quantity of items seized. Validity depends on the circumstances of the seizure as to each of the items that is offered in evidence." *Ibid.*, p. 348. In other words, the lawless seizure of some items should not render inadmissible such other items as were properly seizable.
86. 362 U.S. 217 (1960). By this time five of the nine justices had taken their seats since the Rabinowitz case; of the majority in that case, only Justice Clark was still on the Court. Chief Justice Vinson and Justice Jackson had died, and Justices Reed, Minton, and Burton had retired. Their replacements were Chief Justice Warren and Justices Harlan, Whittaker, Brennan, and Stewart.

dissenter" in the Harris and Rabinowitz cases, wrote the opinion for the badly divided Court. (Frankfurter did say that Abel's counsel had not asked the Court to overrule the Harris and Rabinowitz cases, but this reason does not seem particularly persuasive; the Court is not obligated to reaffirm decisions of which it no longer approves merely because the appellant did not call for their reversal.) Still more surprising was the fact that Frankfurter's opinion apparently expanded on the permissive doctrine of the Harris case in one respect. There, the seizure of items not related to the crime for which the arrest was made was justified on the ground that they were contraband belonging to the government. In the Abel case, however, the seizure of unrelated items was sustained even though they were not contraband.[87] The Kremen decision, said Frankfurter, was based not on the scope of the search but on the magnitude of the seizure; that decision stood for the proposition that the government may not "seize, wholesale, the contents of a house *it might have searched*. . . ."[88] Chief Justice Warren and Justices Black, Douglas, and Brennan dissented on other grounds.

The "total atmosphere" approach of the Rabinowitz case concerning the reasonableness of a search also had serious implications in regard to searches other than those made incidental to arrest, for the Court appeared to suggest that reasonableness, in *any* search situation, need not be determined by the feasibility of procuring a warrant. Yet at no time in its history had the Court sanctioned the search of a dwelling on probable cause alone: except where the search was made incidental to an arrest, a warrant was always required.[89] In the 1961 case of *Chapman* v. *United States*[90] the Court made it clear that the broad dicta of the Rabinowitz case would not be construed as sanctioning a deviation from this principle. Chapman's dwelling was searched after the landlord reported his suspicions that the house was being used for the illegal manufacture of liquor because of the odor emanating from it. Entry was made through a window, with the landlord's permission. Justice Whittaker's opinion for the Court stressed the necessity of obtaining a

87. "When an article subject to lawful seizure properly comes into an officer's possession in the course of a lawful search it would be entirely without reason to say that he must return it because it was not one of the things it was his business to look for." 362 U.S. 217, 238. The arrest of Abel was for the purpose of deportation, while the seized objects implicated him in espionage. Other aspects of the Abel case are discussed in Chapter IX.

88. *Ibid.*, p. 235. (Emphasis supplied.)

89. *Taylor* v. *United States*, 286 U.S. 1 (1932); *Johnson* v. *United States*, 333 U.S. 10 (1948); *Jones* v. *United States*, 357 U.S. 493 (1958).

90. 365 U.S. 610 (1961).

warrant for a search of the dwelling. Justice Frankfurter regarded the decision as a repudiation of the Rabinowitz doctrine and chided the Court for failing to overrule that case. He concurred, he said, on the basis of his dissents in the Harris and Rabinowitz cases, and did not mention his opinion in the Abel case the previous year. Justice Clark, dissenting, summed up the situation as follows: "For some years now the field has been muddy, but today the Court makes it a quagmire."[91]

The "quagmire" of which Clark spoke remains a quagmire to this day. In the recent case of *Ker* v. *California*[92] a badly divided Court upheld an extensive search incidental to arrest on the authority of the Harris case. The Ker case involved a search by state officers, but the Court ruled in the same case that the constitutional standards governing federal searches would henceforth be applied to state searches as well.[93] What the Court said in the Ker case, therefore, was of as much significance for federal as for state searches incidental to arrest.

The officer who entered Ker's apartment to arrest him for narcotics violations searched the entire place, uncovering narcotics in the kitchen and the bedroom. The search seems to have been almost as extensive as the one in the Harris case. Speaking for four members of the Court, Justice Clark upheld the warrantless ransacking on the ground that the nature of the articles sought was such as to make their disposal possible before a warrant could be obtained. The four dissenters[94] did not even discuss the issue of search incidental to arrest. They were too busy detailing their objections to the decision on another ground, that the search violated constitutional standards because the officers had made a furtive entry with a passkey provided by the building superintendent, instead of announcing themselves prior to entry.

The full import of the Ker decision may become clearer when Justice Harlan has another opportunity to clarify his views on the subject. He cast the deciding vote in a separate concurring opinion but, like the dissenters, did not reach the issue of search incidental to arrest. He agreed with the decision because he believed that the full force of the Fourth Amendment should *not* be applied to state searches. Only standards of "fundamental fairness" were required of the states, and these had not been violated by the Ker search.

91. *Ibid.*, p. 622.
92. 374 U.S. 23 (1963).
93. For discussion, see Chapter VI.
94. Justice Brennan, joined by Chief Justice Warren and Justices Douglas and Goldberg.

Whether Harlan would have voted to sanction a search of similar scope made by federal officers was left undetermined.

The Court's inconsistency in cases of search incidental to arrest is of such proportions that no criticism could exceed the severity of the statements made by the justices themselves in this connection. The shifts of the Court as a whole, due to changing personnel, and of individual justices, such as Black, Douglas, and even Frankfurter, have all contributed to this development. Basically, the trouble stems from the fact that search incidental to arrest has only two logical points of termination—either the person of the prisoner and the objects within his reach (and possibly even those in plain sight), or the entire dwelling. There does not seem to be any logical midpoint between these limits. Once the search of even one room is permitted, there is no logical reason, rooted in a principle, why the search of the entire dwelling should not likewise be authorized. Justice Frankfurter summed it up pithily: "I am aware that most differences in the law depend on differences of degree. But differences though of degree must not be capricious; the differences must permit rational classification."[95]

The justices who voted for the Harris and Rabinowitz decisions argued, in effect, that when privacy has already been invaded by a policeman who is on the premises legitimately, to make an arrest, the accompanying search is, at worst, only a minor additional invasion of privacy. This is an inviting argument. But it ignores the fact, which the dissenters stressed, that the Fourth Amendment protects not only the person but also his effects. Arrest standards were never as stringent as search standards under the common law, of which the Fourth Amendment is largely a restatement, mostly because a suspect can easily flee the jurisdiction; a house and its contents cannot. The Harris-Rabinowitz doctrine has the effect of pulling search standards down below those of arrest whenever the wanted man is apprehended at home. An arrest requires, if not a warrant, at least probable cause; the search of the dwelling as incidental to arrest requires neither a warrant nor probable cause. The "total atmosphere of the case" which, in this view, determines the reasonableness of the search gives no guidance at all to police officers because it is impossible for the Court to categorize, in advance, the elements which add up to reasonableness in the "total atmosphere." The officers must use their own judgment, and the tendency will be

95. *United States* v. *Rabinowitz*, 339 U.S. 56, 79 (1950) (dissenting opinion).

to push the search to the outermost limits of legality, and even beyond. As Justice Jackson said, even while dissenting, in the Harris case: "I do not criticize the officers involved in this case because this Court's decisions afford them no clear guidance."[96]

Several limitations have been placed on the scope of search incidental to arrest, but these are of doubtful effectiveness. (1) The search must not be exploratory, but must be for articles connected with the crime for which the arrest is made. However, when evidence relating to some other crime is discovered, it is nevertheless seizable even when not contraband. It would be difficult to prove later on that the search was exploratory even if such was the case. Only the officers know what they were searching for, and they cannot always be relied upon to tell the truth when the truth will implicate them in unlawful conduct. (2) The intensity of the search must be proportionate to the nature of the object sought. It is not permissible to search in nooks and crannies for large objects. But instruments of crime and contraband goods that might be concealed in a house are often quite small. (3) The arrest must not be used as a pretext for the search. We do know, however, that many arrests are made only for the purpose of effecting a search incidental to the arrest.[97]

The need for quick, efficient enforcement of the law is certainly more pressing in the urbanized society of today, with its rapid means of transportation, than in the rural society in which the Fourth Amendment was written. The need for warrants understandably tends to be regarded as a hindrance by harassed and hard-pressed law enforcement officers. They prefer, of course, to make a search incidental to arrest rather than to secure a warrant for the search. Thus there is no need to establish probable cause that the wanted articles are actually on the premises, and there is no warrant to set limits to the seizure that may result.[98] Strange as it seems, the search

96. *Harris* v. *United States*, 331 U.S. 145, 195 (1947) (dissenting opinion).

97. Wayne R. LaFave, *Arrest: The Decision To Take a Suspect into Custody* (Boston, 1965), pp. 186–87; Frank J. Remington, "The Law Relating to . . . Detention, Questioning and Frisking of Suspected Persons . . . ," in Claude R. Sowle (ed.), *Police Power and Individual Freedom: The Quest for Balance* (Chicago, 1962), pp. 11, 19. This limitation applies, of course, to search of the person as well as of the dwelling. However, even the most minor of crimes (outside of some traffic offenses) are commonly dealt with by arrest instead of by summons (as in other civilized countries), and the reason often lies in the desire to effect a search. The vagrancy arrest is particularly popular as a means of effecting a search of a suspicious individual. Paul E. Wilson, "Perspectives of Mapp v. Ohio," *Kansas Law Review*, XI (May, 1963), 423, 435.

98. Another reason given for the practice is the growing list of crimes, as, for instance, liquor law violations, which do not involve violence or any other offense against the person, and to which no witness is likely to come forward. Comment, *Chicago Law Review*, p. 681.

made incidental to arrest grants officers leeway not given even under warrant. A seizure going beyond the authorization of the warrant will be inadmissible in evidence; a seizure resulting from an incidental search is admissible regardless of how unrelated to the crime for which the arrest was made it might be. It may be that, in the light of modern conditions, Fourth Amendment warrant requirements are too restrictive, but, as Justice Jackson said, the framers "may have overvalued privacy, but I am not disposed to set their command at nought."[99]

That the Court's permissive attitude has indeed resulted in the framers' command being "set at nought" is evident from current practice. In this area, as in so many others, the state courts have followed the Supreme Court's lead. Abundant evidence exists that, at least on the state level, "the search warrant is a rarity."[100] To give one example, in the thirty-year span between 1931 and 1962 the Los Angeles County Municipal Court issued exactly 538 search warrants. Yet during the same period this court disposed of half a million felony cases.[101] It is believed that a far larger percentage of searches conducted by federal officers are made pursuant to warrant than is the case with searches made by state officers. Nonetheless, nearly all of the search cases decided by the Supreme Court in the past twenty years involved searches made without warrant.[102] The widening scope of search incidental to arrest is a prime example of how a particular law enforcement practice has shaped the constitutional law on the subject, rather than vice versa. As the Court has become more permissive, it has been confronted with searches of ever-widening scope. Some of the lower federal courts have even extended the scope of the search to cover "constructive possession"—that is, searches where the person arrested was not even on the premises searched, but nearby, as, for instance, in the yard.[103] Given this permissiveness on the part of the courts, search itself has become an investigative technique rather than the culmination of an investigation that has established at least probable cause for the search.

Searches of broad scope carried out incidental to arrest are now so commonplace that what was once an exception has become the rule. The rationale which originally justified the warrantless search has

99. *Harris* v. *United States*, 331 U.S. 145, 198 (1947).

100. Rex A. Collings, Jr., "Toward Workable Rules of Search and Seizure: An Amicus Curiae Brief," *California Law Review*, L (August, 1962), 421, 456.

101. *Ibid.*, pp. 456–57.

102. Comment, *Chicago Law Review*, p. 684, n. 118.

103. For discussion of cases, see Way, "Scope of Search," pp. 278–79; Gregory U. Evans, "Search and Seizure Incidental to a Lawful Arrest," *William and Mary Law Review*, IV, No. 2 (1963), 121, 126–27.

been all but forgotten. The search is no longer properly incidental to the arrest, that is, made for the purpose of securing the arrest; instead, the arrest is incidental to the search. The warrantless search is no longer justified in the name of necessity but is regarded as reasonable in itself. Underlying the Harris-Rabinowitz doctrine is the belief that the police have a special competence in determining who is likely to be harboring illicit articles in his house. But this view is surely contrary to the assumption underlying the Fourth Amendment that the magistrate should make an independent determination of the facts necessary to establish probable cause. One scholar has even questioned whether the Court has not exceeded its own authority—whether its decisions are not "unconstitutional," in the sense that the Court has ignored the "dominant consideration" underlying adoption of the Fourth Amendment (subjection of the law enforcement process to judicial control through the warrant requirement) and has allowed the police to use their own discretion in determining where a search is to be made.[104]

It is true that the courts will eventually review the reasonableness of some searches carried out incidental to arrest. But many such searches never come before the courts: either no evidence is found or it is insufficient to justify a prosecution. Even when they do, retrospective judgment is likely to accord more weight to the officers' views as to the existence of probable cause where criminal evidence was actually uncovered than would have been the case in an application for a warrant *prior* to the search. The protection of the Fourth Amendment is dangerously diluted when the warrantless search becomes commonplace as incidental to arrest. In the words of Judge Learned Hand, "it is a small consolation to know that one's papers are safe only so long as one is not at home."[105]

104. Beisel, *Illegal Enforcement*, pp. 30–31. Professor Beisel had in mind *Erie* v. *Tompkins*, 304 U.S. 64 (1938), where the Court found that one of its previous cases had been unconstitutionally decided.

105. *United States* v. *Kirschenblatt*, 16 F.2d 202, 203 (2d cir. 1926).

## CHAPTER V

# THE PROCESS THAT IS DUE

The Bill of Rights of the United States Constitution was designed as a limitation on the federal government only; it had no application to state action. The first eight amendments, declared Chief Justice Marshall in 1833, "contain no expression indicating an intention to apply them to the State governments. This Court cannot so apply them."[1] Historically, of course, Marshall's position was unassailable. The opening words of the First Amendment are: "Congress shall make no law. . . ." The controversy surrounding the absence of a bill of rights in the Constitution as originally drafted centered around the lack of legal protections against arbitrary action by the proposed federal government. It is true that the Constitution did forbid Congress to pass ex post facto laws and bills of attainder and required that the writ of *habeas corpus* be suspended only in exceptional circumstances.[2] But these limited guarantees were not thought sufficient. This apprehension is understandable in a people who had just won a bloody war, fought because it believed that its rights had been denied, the more so since a number of the states had prefaced their own constitutions with elaborate bills of rights. Even the citizens of states like New York, which had no bill of rights, feared the absence of constitutional safeguards for the individual against the actions of a national government in which no one state would have a predominant voice.

Following the Civil War, three amendments to the Constitution, which became known as the Civil War amendments, were proposed by Congress and ratified by the states.[3] Though these provisions were designed primarily to protect the newly emancipated Negro race, some of the language used in the amendments, which were couched in broad terms, lent itself to application as general limitations on

1. *Barron* v. *Baltimore*, 7 Peters 243, 250 (1833). The principle of state immunity with particular reference to the Fourth Amendment was reaffirmed in 1855. The amendment, said Justice Curtis, "has no application to state process." *Smith* v. *Maryland*, 18 Howard 71, 76 (1855).

2. Art. I, sec. 9.

3. The Thirteenth Amendment (1865), the Fourteenth Amendment (1868), the Fifteenth Amendment (1870).

the powers of the states. The most important of these amendments was the Fourteenth, which in its first section provided that: "All persons born or naturalized in the United States, and subject to the jurisdiction thereof, are citizens of the United States and of the State wherein they reside. No State shall make or enforce any law which shall abridge the privileges or immunities of citizens of the United States; nor shall any State deprive any person of life, liberty, or property, without due process of law; nor deny to any person within its jurisdiction equal protection of the laws." This section, and particularly its due process clause (which was laden with potentialities hardly yet recognized), was eventually to provide the vehicle whereby fundamental liberties and fair trial procedures would be protected against state infringement.

The phrase "due process of law" in the Fourteenth Amendment was not new to the Constitution. A parallel provision limiting the federal government is to be found in the Fifth Amendment: "nor [shall any person] be deprived of life, liberty, or property, without due process of law. . . ." The phrase first appeared in 1354 in a statute of Edward III, which provided that no person should be subjected to punishment "without being brought in answer by due process of law."[4] This statute is believed to be derived from, and synonymous with, King John's promise in Chapter XXXIX of Magna Carta that he would not "go upon" or "send upon" any "freeman" except "by the law of the land," at least such was the interpretation placed on the matter by Coke in the *Institutes*—"the source from which the founders of the American Constitutional System derived their understanding of the matter."[5] There Coke defined due process as the "due proces[s] of the common law,"[6] that is, the rights guaranteed in Magna Carta.

Shortly before the Civil War, while discussing the due process clause of the Fifth Amendment, Justice Curtis suggested that in applying the clause the Court "must look to those *settled usages and modes of proceeding* existing in the common and statute law of England. . . ."[7] Speaking in a similar vein, in *Davidson* v. *New*

4. 28 Edw. III, c. 3.

5. Edward S. Corwin (ed.), *The Constitution of the United States of America: Analysis and Interpretation* (Washington, 1953), p. 845.

6. Sir Edward Coke, *Institutes of the Laws of England* (London, 1797), Part 2, p. 50. Writing in 1833, Justice Story defined the due process clause of the Fifth Amendment as "but an enlargement of the language of Magna Carta. . . . So that this clause confirms the right of trial according to the process and proceedings of the common law." Joseph Story, *Commentaries on the Constitution of the United States* (Boston, 1833), Vol. III, p. 661.

7. *Murray* v. *Hoboken Land Co.*, 18 Howard 272, 277 (1856). (Emphasis supplied.)

*Orleans,* decided in 1878, Justice Miller declared that "a full and fair hearing" in court satisfied the requirement. "If this be not due process of law, then the words can have no definite meaning as used in the Constitution."[8] Thus far, then, due process had not served to limit the power of government itself; the substantive power remained unimpaired so long as it was exercised in a procedurally acceptable manner.[9] But the rise of socialist doctrines and the widespread growth of regulation resulted in pressures that became reflected in the attitude of the Court. The principles of Social Darwinism—that the economy ought to be ruled by an aristocracy of wealth, that poverty is inevitable and is in part the fault of the poor themselves, and that the role of government ought to be confined to that of policeman—had been widely accepted by intellectuals as well as businessmen.[10] The Court grafted these ideas onto the law. Beginning around 1890 and continuing over several decades of expansive development, due process became the foremost legal instrument for the protection of property rights as against governmental regulation.[11] Meanwhile, failure followed failure in attempts to apply to state process some of the substantive and procedural guarantees of the Bill of Rights.[12] Plainly, such an illogical state of affairs could not long continue. Property could not forever take precedence over the liberty of the person and the right to life itself. In 1908 Justice Moody suggested: "It is possible that some of the personal rights safeguarded by the first eight amendments against national action may also be safeguarded against state action because a denial of them would be a denial of due process of law."[13] The development of such a safeguard began to become a reality in 1925.[14] "Due process," a phrase pregnant with possibilities, was now to be a bulwark of personal liberties. The protections of the First Amendment were, one after another, soon absorbed into the due process clause of the Fourteenth Amendment and in this manner were

8. *Davidson* v. *New Orleans*, 96 U.S. 97, 105–6 (1878). See also the Slaughter-house cases, 16 Wallace 36 (1873).

9. The one conspicuous exception to this statement was the discredited Dred Scott decision, which invalidated an act of Congress prohibiting slavery in federal territory. This act's restriction on the slaveowner's property rights, said Chief Justice Taney, "could hardly be dignified with the name of due process of law." *Dred Scott* v. *Sandford*, 19 Howard 393, 450 (1857).

10. See, generally, Richard Hofstadter, *Social Darwinism in American Thought* (rev. ed.; New York, 1959).

11. E.g., *Chicago, Milwaukee and St. Paul Railway* v. *Minnesota*, 134 U.S. 418 (1890); *Lochner* v. *New York*, 198 U.S. 45 (1905).

12. E.g., *Hurtado* v. *California*, 110 U.S. 516 (1884) (grand jury indictment); *Twining* v. *New Jersey*, 211 U.S. 78 (1908) (self-incrimination); *Maxwell* v. *Dow*, 176 U.S. 581 (1908) (trial by jury).

13. *Twining* v. *New Jersey*, 211 U.S. 78, 99 (1908).

14. *Gitlow* v. *New York*, 268 U.S. 652 (1925) (freedom of speech).

applied against the states.[15] In matters of criminal procedure, too, decision after decision required the states to provide defendants with a fair trial.[16] With the decline of substantive "due process" as a protection for property following the reconstitution of the Supreme Court in 1937, the protection of personal liberties and fair procedure was to become the main business of the Court.

This development has not, however, eliminated conflict on the Court; on the contrary, it has exacerbated dispute. The differences now are not over whether or not the due process clause should be construed to safeguard personal liberties and procedural rights against state action, but rather how far the Court ought to go in this direction. In fact, the question of the scope to be accorded the due process clause has provoked one of the bitterest disputes on the Court of the last two decades. It is a dispute that has waxed particularly hot in a number of search cases, to be discussed in this chapter. Justice Black has taken the position that the due process clause guarantees, as against the states, "the complete protection of the Bill of Rights."[17] This position is not a new one; the first Justice Harlan had asserted as much in a dissenting opinion.[18] But Black, unlike Harlan, has made converts to his cause, and at one time he was able to muster four votes in support of his views.[19] Justice Frankfurter, who was Black's main antagonist, until his retirement from the Court in 1962, took the less popular, but historically more accurate position that the due process clause does not have a fixed content. In essence, he rested his case on Justice Cardozo's interpretation—which at one time had the assent of Justice Black—that due process respects only rights "so rooted in the traditions and conscience of our people as to be ranked as fundamental"[20] and "of the very essence of a scheme of ordered liberty."[21] The decision as to whether or not a particular right is protected by due process against state action should depend, according to Frankfurter, on how fully it has met these criteria, not on whether it is protected by the Bill of Rights against federal encroachment.

The conflict over the scope of the due process clause has been fought in large measure under the banner of historical interpretation; that is, the dispute has centered around the framers' intentions—

15. *Near* v. *Minnesota*, 283 U.S. 697 (1931) (freedom of press); *De Jonge* v. *Oregon*, 299 U.S. 353 (1937) (freedom of assembly); *Cantwell* v. *Connecticut*, 319 U.S. 296 (1940) (freedom of religion).

16. E.g., *Powell* v. *Alabama*, 287 U.S. 45 (1932) (right to counsel); *Brown* v. *Mississippi*, 297 U.S. 278 (1936) (coerced confession).

17. *Adamson* v. *California*, 332 U.S. 46, 89 (1947) (dissenting opinion).

18. *Hurtado* v. *California*, 110 U.S. 516, 538 (1884) (dissenting opinion).

19. *Adamson* v. *California*, 332 U.S. 46, 68 (dissenting opinion).

20. *Snyder* v. *Massachusetts*, 291 U.S. 97, 105 (1934).

21. *Palko* v. *Connecticut*, 302 U.S. 319, 325 (1937).

what did they intend the due process clause to mean? Justice Frankfurter argued that due process is not a mere shorthand version of the specific provisions of the Bill of Rights; if this were so, he said, the due process clause of the Fifth Amendment would become a redundancy or would have a meaning different from that of the Fourteenth Amendment; this supposition Frankfurter considered "too frivolous to require elaborate rejection."[22] But it is clear that there are some underlying factors, factors other than historical, which figure importantly in this dispute. The fact that this nation is a federal union strongly influenced Frankfurter's view of due process. To impose uniform procedural rules, he contended, "would tear up by the roots much of the fabric of law in the several states."[23] The belief that society is basically progressive is perhaps the main philosophical assumption underlying Frankfurter's views on due process. "It is of the very nature of a free society," he stated, "to advance in its standards of what is deemed reasonable and right."[24] This being so, it would be unwise to limit due process to any neat and tidy formula which categorizes and catalogues rights as permanent fixtures in the constellation of constitutional guarantees. Justice Black, on the other hand, is distrustful of the traditional due process formula as tending to limit the protection for civil liberties against state action and is trying to get some certainty into what is presently a shifting concept.[25] Also, he is fearful that the Court might one day resurrect due process as a protection for property rights against social regulation and would therefore like to limit the scope of due process to the protection of the *specific* provisions of the Bill of Rights.[26]

In charting the guidelines which had influenced the Court in ap-

22. *Malinski* v. *New York*, 324 U.S. 401, 415 (1945). The "redundancy" argument seems open to challenge because some provisions of the Bill of Rights are now absorbed into Fourteenth Amendment due process even though they could not possibly be included in Fifth Amendment due process because they are separately enumerated. Clearly, Frankfurter would insist, in reply, that due process does not "absorb" any Bill of Rights provisions but has an independent meaning: the rights "absorbed" would, even in the absence of a Bill of Rights, be protected by "due process" because of their fundamental nature. The term "absorption," it should be noted, is not one invented by Black but was used by Cardozo himself in the Palko case. 302 U.S. 319, 326. He, of course, gave it a different meaning than has Black.

23. *Malinski* v. *New York*, 324 U.S. 401, 415 (1945).

24. *Wolf* v. *Colorado*, 338 U.S. 25, 27 (1949).

25. Even granting the Black thesis, it is not at all certain that the prevailing judicial conflict would be dispelled, for the recognition that due process is not an independent legal concept, but a synonym for the Bill of Rights, would serve the cause of certainty only so long as the justices were agreed in their understanding of the Bill of Rights.

26. See, for example, his dissenting opinion in *Griswold* v. *Connecticut*, 381 U.S. 479, 507 (1965). The historical evidence is contrary to the Black thesis, according to Charles Fairman. "Does the Fourteenth Amendment Incorporate the Bill of Rights? The Original Understanding," *Stanford Law Review*, II (December, 1949), 7.

plying the due process concept, Justice Cardozo in 1937 defined the "rationalizing principle" as one which took into account the question whether the rights claimed were, in the opinion of the justices, "of the very essence of a scheme of ordered liberty."[27] Such rights as freedom of speech and press and the free exercise of religion were sufficiently basic to be carried over into due process; the privileges against self-incrimination and double jeopardy (at least in the circumstances under which they had thus far been claimed) were not. Of the protection against unreasonable searches Cardozo made no mention; he did not say whether or not he considered the Fourth Amendment a basic right.

The need for protection against arbitrary searches is certainly not confined to the federal level of government. On the contrary, the problem is prevalent in its most aggravating forms on state and local levels. Underpaid and insufficiently trained and disciplined local officers frequently regard the warrantless search as a convenient means of solving crimes without the intervention of the bothersome hand of the magistrate. Reporting in 1931, the Wickersham Commission observed: "Some kinds of lawless enforcement of law like the 'third degree' or searches and seizures without the warrants required by law, appear to result from *a definite official policy favoring habitual disregard of particular legal rules.* The remedy for an abuse of this sort involves the serious difficulty of altering rooted official habits."[28]

Frequently, the lawless enforcement complained of is not the result of bad faith on the part of the police, but of overzealousness. The police misinterpret their function and see it as that of the apprehension of lawbreakers regardless of the methods employed to do so. The end all too often is regarded as justifying the means; the value of solving crimes is placed above other values, even to the extent of excusing the violation of law in order to accomplish this end. As one Buffalo, New York, police official explained: "My oath of office requires me to protect this community. If I have to violate that oath of office or violate the Constitution, I'll violate the Constitution. Nobody thinks of hedging a fireman about with a lot of laws that favor the fire. Crime is as dangerous as fire, and the policeman and the fireman should be equally free."[29]

27. *Palko* v. *Connecticut*, 302 U.S. 319, 325 (1937).
28. National Commission on Law Observance and Enforcement, *Report on Lawlessness in Law Enforcement* (Washington, 1931), p. 340 (Emphasis supplied.)
29. Quoted in Comment, "Judicial Control of Illegal Search and Seizure," *Yale Law Journal*, LVIII (December, 1948), 144, 145, n. 4.

The fatal flaw in this rationalization is, of course, the contention that in order to live up to his oath of office an officer may be required to violate the Constitution. The oath of office requires an officer to act only within the Constitution. This may indeed result in the escape of some criminals, but that is the price we expect to pay for the free society. The Constitution, which is as much a limitation on government as it is a source of governmental power, declares in its Preamble that these powers *and limitations* were designed to "insure domestic Tranquility"; the escape of a few criminals from their just deserts may be necessary for the "tranquility" of the many. Alan Barth stated this thesis concisely: "The restraints which any society must impose upon its police if it wishes to preserve private rights and safeguard the innocent operate inevitably, in some measure, to impair public safety and to afford protection for the guilty. Every society is obliged, therefore, to seek a rational balance between public safety and private rights—to choose between the exigencies of law and order on the one hand and the imperatives of freedom on the other."[30]

Whatever the justification the police may use to defend their actions, there is no question that the problem is one of national dimensions and is a proper cause of national concern. While no precise or even approximate figure of the number of illegal searches is available, Professor Jerome Hall has estimated that as far back as 1933 there were about three and one-half million illegal arrests in the nation.[31] Since every arrestee is normally searched for concealed weapons and for evidence of crime, it is safe to say that the number of illegal searches, when including those searches not involving arrests, was considerably higher than this figure. And the number, according to all accounts, has increased with the passage of time and the growth in the crime rate. This is not to suggest that the states have been insensitive, formally at least, to the question of warrantless searches. Throughout the life of the nation most of the states have had in their constitutions provisions akin to the Fourth Amendment, though differing in phrasing. When, in 1938, New York added a search provision to its constitution,[32] all forty-eight states then in the Union had adopted constitutional provisions designed to regulate police searches for evidence of crime.

30. Alan Barth, *The Price of Liberty* (New York, 1961), p. x.

31. Jerome Hall, "The Law of Arrest in Relation to Contemporary Social Problems," *University of Chicago Law Review*, III (April, 1936), 345, 362, n. 74.

32. New York State Constitution, Bill of Rights, Art. 1, sec. 12. New York had previously dealt with the matter by statute.

As we have seen, the Supreme Court in *Weeks* v. *United States*[33] ordered the suppression in federal court of evidence secured as the result of an illegal search by federal agents. The sanction was designed to give the Fourth Amendment the backbone it needed to perform its function; in the absence of such a sanction, the Court felt, the Fourth Amendment would become a dead letter, a mere admonition to the police to behave. In similar fashion, some state courts began to apply the same sanction against illegal searches conducted by state officers. Vermont was first,[34] in 1901, but the doctrine remained in effect only for four years and was then virtually discarded.[35] In 1903 Iowa adopted an exclusionary rule[36] which has endured to this day. The Iowa rule anticipated the federal rule and was the only state exclusionary rule in force when the Supreme Court directed the federal courts to exclude illegally seized evidence.

Possibly of equal or greater importance than the Supreme Court's function as judge is its role as guide and exhorter. Following the Weeks decision, the doctrine of excluding from evidence the fruits of illegal searches began to gather momentum in the state courts. Whereas prior to the Weeks case twenty-six of the twenty-seven state courts which had considered the problem (that is, every one but Iowa) had rejected the exclusionary rule, by 1949 forty-seven of the states had passed on the matter, and sixteen had joined Iowa in adopting the rule.[37] Indeed, it was thought by one observer that "if it were not for the Eighteenth [Prohibition] Amendment, the doctrine of the *Weeks* case might have been accepted in practically all of the state courts."[38]

But while the states had provided their own constitutional safeguards against arbitrary searches, and a number of state courts had imposed the exclusionary sanction to implement these guarantees, the Supreme Court had never held that the Constitution protected against the unreasonable search made under state authority. In 1914 —the year in which the Weeks case was decided—the Court had unequivocally declared that the Constitution did not protect against

33. 232 U.S. 383 (1914).
34. *State* v. *Slammon*, 50 A. 1097 (Vt. 1901).
35. *State* v. *Krinski*, 62 A. 37 (Vt. 1905).
36. *State* v. *Sheridan*, 96 N.W. 730 (Iowa 1903).
37. *Wolf* v. *Colorado*, 338 U.S. 25 (1949) (Appendix to the opinion of the Court). The sixteen states adopting the exclusionary rule were, in addition to Iowa: Florida, Idaho, Illinois, Indiana, Kentucky, Michigan, Mississippi, Missouri, Montana, Oklahoma, South Dakota, Tennessee, Washington, West Virginia, Wisconsin, and Wyoming. Ten of these states had previously rejected the rule but then reversed themselves. Rhode Island was the only state that had not passed on the question.
38. Thomas E. Atkinson, "Prohibition and the Doctrine of the Weeks Case," *Michigan Law Review*, XXIII (May, 1925), 748.

unreasonable searches by state officers.[39] But during the next thirty-five years the due process clause of the Fourteenth Amendment gradually acquired new potency, and when the Court once more considered the question in *Wolf* v. *Colorado*,[40] the result was different.

The case involved a Denver obstetrician, Julius A. Wolf. In 1944 the local district attorney came into possession of information that Dr. Wolf was performing abortions. Without troubling to get the warrant required by law, his men raided Wolf's office and seized the office records for the years 1943 and 1944. On the basis of the information uncovered, Wolf was tried on charges of conspiracy to commit abortions, found guilty, and sentenced to prison. He now appealed his conviction on the ground that the Constitution prohibited the search and that the seized documents should not have been received in evidence. A mere recognition by the Court that Wolf's constitutional rights had been invaded would not be sufficient to reverse the conviction unless the Court was also prepared to go further and to require the state court to exclude the seized materials.

The opinion of the Court was delivered by Justice Frankfurter. For some reason he departed from the usual judicial practice of stating the facts of the case, for which we must consult the pages of the *Colorado Reports* or those of the *Pacific Reporter*,[41] and proceeded immediately to discuss the constitutional issue. He restated his (and the Court's) position that the due process clause of the Fourteenth Amendment is not a "shorthand"[42] statement of the Bill of Rights and does not automatically absorb the Fourth Amendment, but that it is an index of the contemporary moral climate and therefore protects against state action only those rights deemed basic. Such a right was at stake here, he found. In a passage which Justice Douglas would later refer to as a "resounding phrase,"[43] Frankfurter declared:

> The security of one's privacy against arbitrary intrusion by the police—which is at the core of the Fourth Amendment—is basic to a free society. It is therefore implicit in "the concept of ordered liberty" and as such enforceable against the States through the Due Process Clause. The knock at the door, whether by day or by night, as a prelude to a search, without authority of law but solely on the authority of the police, did not need the commentary of recent history to be condemned as inconsistent with the conception of

39. *National Safety Deposit Co.* v. *Stead*, 232 U.S. 58 (1914).
40. 338 U.S. 25 (1949).
41. *Wolf* v. *People*, 187 P.2d 926 and 187 P.2d 928 (Col. 1947).
42. 338 U.S. 25, 26.
43. *Frank* v. *Maryland*, 359 U.S. 360, 374 (1959) (dissenting opinion).

human rights enshrined in the history and the basic constitutional documents of English-speaking peoples.

Accordingly, we have no hesitation in saying that were a State affirmatively to sanction police incursion into privacy it would run counter to the guaranty of the Fourteenth Amendment.[44]

Justice Frankfurter seemed a particularly appropriate choice to announce an opinion that would bring a basic feature of the Bill of Rights into the ambit of due process. Of all Frankfurter's constitutional law opinions, none are more noteworthy than those dealing with search and seizure. No member of the Court then sitting had taken a more exalted view of the Fourth Amendment nor been more scornful of those who viewed the amendment as "a serious impediment in the war against crime."[45] Back of each unlawful search he saw the haunting specter of the police state. The Fourth Amendment was, in his view, "central to enjoyment of the other guarantees in the Bill of Rights"[46] and must therefore be assigned "a place second to none in the Bill of Rights."[47]

In the light of the foregoing statement, one might reasonably have expected that Justice Frankfurter would proceed to require the exclusion of illegally seized evidence from state criminal trials. But after having added nothing less than a new chapter to American constitutional law, Frankfurter appeared to undermine the edifice which he had built by refusing to require exclusion of the tainted evidence. The decision was based on considerations of federalism, the same considerations that are largely responsible for the prevailing interpretation of the due process clause in a manner other than as a synonym for the Bill of Rights. The question, said Frankfurter, was "not to be so dogmatically answered as to preclude the varying solutions"[48] which the states may wish to choose in dealing with the problem of unlawful searches. He pointed out that most of the English-speaking world, including England itself and thirty of the American states, still followed the common-law rule that the public is entitled to the use of all reliable evidence, no matter how it has been obtained.[49] One could, therefore, scarcely speak of the exclu-

44. 338 U.S. 25, 27–28.
45. *Harris* v. *United States*, 331 U.S. 145, 157 (1947) (dissenting opinion).
46. *Ibid.*, p. 163.
47. *Ibid.*, p. 157.
48. 338 U.S. 25, 28.
49. For a review of the current practices of the courts in a number of foreign countries, both English-speaking and other, see the Symposium on "The Exclusionary Rule under Foreign Law," *Journal of Criminal Law*, LII (September–October, 1961), 271ff. Of the various jurisdictions surveyed, only France appears to have a general rule for the exclusion of illegally seized evidence, though some countries compromise by excluding when the violation is of a grave character, as, for instance, when brutality is involved.

sionary rule "as an essential ingredient of the right"[50] to privacy as against arbitrary invasion by the police. The right itself was basic, but exclusion of evidence obtained as a result of an invasion of the right was not.

Justice Frankfurter conceded that exclusion might serve as an effective deterrent to illegal searches by depriving the police of the opportunity to maintain good conviction records, but he was not prepared to say that it was the only solution to the problem of preventing illegal searches upon which reasonable men might agree. He implied that Congress, acting under the authority of the enforcement section of the Fourteenth Amendment, might impose the exclusionary rule on the states if it wished. Meanwhile, in the absence of Congressional action, he commended to the potential victims of illegal searches "other methods which, if consistently enforced, would be equally effective." These he spelled out as "the remedies of private action and such protection as the internal discipline of the police, under the eyes of an alert public opinion, may afford."[51] He thought that public opinion on the local level could be more effective in making its pressure felt on the local police, "directly responsible to the community itself,"[52] than it would be on the national level, where it is more diffuse. He thus justified the imposition of the exclusionary rule on the federal courts and the refusal to impose it on the state courts.

In the course of his argument, Justice Frankfurter noted that the exclusionary rule "was not derived from the explicit requirements of the Fourth Amendment . . . [but] was a matter of judicial implication."[53] This statement is somewhat ambiguous. It may mean that although the Constitution does not explicitly require exclusion, the Supreme Court nevertheless felt that the Fourth Amendment implies it as a reasonable means of enforcing the amendment. On the other hand, it may mean that exclusion is no more than a judicial rule of evidence, not constitutionally based, which Congress might negate at any time. In a different sentence Frankfurter seemed to endorse the first interpretation when he said that "we have interpreted *the Fourth Amendment* to forbid the admission"[54] of unlawfully seized evidence in federal court. In a later case, however, he appeared to take the view that the exclusionary rule was not constitutionally based: it was formulated, he said, under the Court's "peculiarly comprehensive

50. 338 U.S. 25, 29.
51. *Ibid.*, p. 31.
52. *Ibid.*, p. 32.
53. *Ibid.*, p. 28.
54. *Ibid.*, p. 33. (Emphasis supplied.)

supervisory power."[55] The matter was so understood by Justice Black as well. He reiterated his view that the due process clause absorbed the entire Bill of Rights, including the Fourth Amendment, but nevertheless agreed with the decision because he was convinced "that the federal exclusionary rule is not a command of the Fourth Amendment but is a judicially created rule of evidence which Congress might negate"[56] and took this to be "a plain implication of the Court's opinion. . . ."[57]

Justice Frankfurter had spoken of "other remedies" short of exclusion which might act as a brake on unlawful searches by state officers. But how effective were these other remedies? It was to this question that Justice Murphy addressed himself in a dissent joined by Justice Rutledge. Murphy gave expression to a profound disappointment. "It is disheartening," he wrote, "to find so much that is right in an opinion which seems to me so fundamentally wrong." To him there was only one effective preventive measure, and that was exclusion. The alternatives were more apparent than real—paper remedies rather than effective sanctions. "For there is but one alternative to the rule of exclusion," he said. "That is no sanction at all."[58]

Justice Murphy proceeded to analyze the alternatives. "Self-scrutiny," he asserted, "is a lofty ideal but its exaltation reaches new heights if we expect a District Attorney to prosecute himself or his associates for well-meaning violations of the search and seizure clause. . . ." As for civil action, that was an equally "illusory"[59] remedy. The extent of the damages that might be claimed in a trespass action, he pointed out, usually was directly related to the physical injury to property. A carefully executed search would result in little or no damage to property. Punitive damages were permitted in some states, but even then, malice on the part of the trespasser had to be proved; thus police officers who bear no personal malice toward their victims but are seeking to solve crimes would certainly be absolved. In some states the bad reputation of the defendant or the plea of reasonable grounds to believe that the violated home

55. *Elkins* v. *United States*, 364 U.S. 206, 240 (1960) (dissenting opinion).

56. 338 U.S. 25, 40. Black was later to recant and take the position that while the Fourth Amendment alone did not require exclusion, the Fourth and Fifth Amendments taken in conjunction did. *Mapp* v. *Ohio*, 367 U.S. 643, 661–62 (1961) (concurring opinion).

57. 338 U.S. 25, 39–40.

58. *Ibid.*, p. 41. Justices Rutledge and Douglas dissented separately, generally along the same lines. They, like Murphy, shared Black's view that the due process clause absorbed the Fourth Amendment together with the rest of the Bill of Rights but, unlike Black, thought that the exclusionary rule was constitutionally required.

59. *Ibid.*, p. 42.

contained criminal evidence might be accepted in mitigation of punitive damages.

But what did Murphy have to offer in the way of evidence that exclusion *was* an effective deterrent? Unfortunately, beyond reporting the results of a questionnaire completed by twenty-six of the thirty-eight police chiefs in large cities, whom he himself had polled in an attempt to elicit some factual material on the problem, he could offer little proof, because very little existed. It was surely unique in the annals of the Court for a justice to poll those who might be able to shed light on a problem in order to obtain criteria for judgment. Based on the limited evidence available, Murphy found that in those jurisdictions which excluded illegally seized evidence the police were especially well instructed in the law of search. St. Louis, Milwaukee, Jackson, Mississippi, San Antonio, Dallas, and Washington, D.C., all offered intensive instruction. This instruction Murphy ascribed to healthy self-interest, so that officers would not by their blunders lose cases they might otherwise win. New York City, he noted by contrast, while it gave each officer a copy of the law on the subject, merely kept its officers advised that illegally seized evidence was still admissible! Baltimore and Cleveland, too, while they offered some guidance to their officers, nevertheless stressed the fact that illegally obtained evidence was admissible. In view of the origin of this case, the situation in Denver was ironic: there police instruction was thoroughgoing, although the State of Colorado followed the common-law rule of admissibility.

One of the principal merits of the good judicial opinion is that it brings into focus the fundamental concerns with which it is dealing. This task Justice Frankfurter failed to perform in the Wolf case. In view of Justice Murphy's trenchant dissent, the Court could scarcely have rejected exclusion as a policy for the states because it felt that exclusion failed to restrain unlawful searches, or because the alternatives proposed might be really effective. As of 1948—the year before the Wolf decision—an exhaustive study of the subject failed to reveal even a single American case in which large damages had been awarded for illegal search.[60] Frankfurter did say that the "other remedies," to be effective, would need to be "consistently enforced," but past experience scarcely gave grounds for optimism that such enforcement was about to take place. Reliance on public opinion to effect a housecleaning in police practices was misplaced,

60. Comment, *Yale Law Journal*, p. 151, n. 35.

in view of the fact that it is public opinion itself that has been largely responsible for the development of these practices. As Dean Pound observed: "the need for 'getting results' puts pressure upon prosecutors to . . . indulge in that lawless enforcement of law which produces a vicious circle of disrespect for law."[61] While it is true, as Frankfurter maintained, that "the exclusion of evidence is a remedy which directly serves only to protect those upon whose person or premises something incriminating has been found,"[62] its importance derives from the fact that it is designed to protect a long-range value, the privacy required by law-abiding people for the enjoyment of other basic liberties. This was the sort of disparaging remark that could have been faithfully echoed by those of his colleagues who were engaged in undermining the potency of the rule by expanding the scope of the warrantless search made incidental to arrest, a development which Frankfurter himself had resolutely protested.[63]

The Supreme Court has the unquestionable power to lay down sanctions for the enforcement of basic liberties in order to protect the vitality of the constitutional process. The Court does not usually say that a certain procedure violates the Constitution and then refuse to take corrective action. The coerced confession cases are a good example of this. It is true that originally exclusion of coerced confessions from the state courts depended on the trustworthiness of the evidence: if it had been compelled, it might not be reliable. More recently, however, at least since 1944, when *Ashcraft* v. *Tennessee*[64] was decided, it has become clear that even completely reliable evidence will be ordered excluded from the state courts if *the manner in which it was secured* is considered to be in violation of due process standards. As Justice Frankfurter himself stated the matter in 1952: "Use of involuntary verbal confessions in State criminal trials is constitutionally obnoxious not only because of their unreliability. They are inadmissible . . . even though statements contained in them may be independently established as true. Coerced confessions offend the community's sense of fair play and decency."[65]

Since the Supreme Court agreed that due process prohibited unlawful searches as it did coerced confessions, it is difficult to see why the Court chose to treat the violation of due process in search cases

61. Roscoe Pound, *Criminal Justice in America* (New York, 1930), p. 186; quoted in Justice Murphy's opinion, 338 U.S. 25, 42, n. 1.
62. 338 U.S. 25, 30–31.
63. For discussion see the preceding chapter.
64. 322 U.S. 143 (1944).
65. *Rochin* v. *California*, 342 U.S. 165, 173 (1952). (Emphasis supplied.)

in a different manner than in confession cases. In a later case Justice Frankfurter explained that the federal courts had no right "to assume the same supervisory control over state officials as they have over federal officials, even if that control could be effective. . . . And the exertion of controlling pressures upon the police is admittedly the only justification for any exclusionary rule."[66] But surely "supervisory control over state officials" had been the intended result in the confession cases. In one sense, it is true, exclusion of a confession is less destructive of the federal principle granting a certain leeway to the states in matters of criminal procedure—a principle which provided the underpinning for the Wolf decision—than exclusion of unlawfully seized evidence, for the state courts themselves had a policy of excluding the former, while most of them continued to admit the latter. In another sense, however, there is more justification for the exclusion of illegally seized evidence than for the exclusion of illegally coerced evidence. In the confession cases the record is often cloudy and the facts are heatedly disputed, while in the search cases "the facts are much less complicated, the evidence much less conflicting."[67] Moreover, it might be said that to the extent that the state courts do themselves exclude coerced confessions even when reliable, this exclusion has in no small part been due to the pressures exerted by the Court in the confession cases.

It is true that coerced confessions typically involve more sensational misconduct than do illegal searches. But this factor might well have served as a valid reason why the guarantee against unreasonable searches should not have been considered a basic right enforceable against the states. It is, however, quite a different thing for the Court to hold that the right is basic and yet that its violation does not require exclusion of evidence obtained in violation of that right. Professor Francis A. Allen has aptly observed that "to label a right as one 'basic to a free society' is to say about as much as one can say of a constitutional protection."[68]

Justice Frankfurter's reliance in part on the practices of the British Commonwealth courts, which did not require exclusion of illegally seized evidence, was quite misplaced. The imposition of an exclusionary policy on the states must in large measure be related to the incidence of unlawful conduct which that policy would be designed

66. *Elkins* v. *United States*, 364 U.S. 206, 241 (1960) (dissenting opinion).

67. Yale Kamisar, "*Wolf* and *Lustig* Ten Years Later: Illegal State Evidence in State and Federal Courts," *Minnesota Law Review*, XLIII (May, 1959), 1083, 1092. In a number of federal search cases, including *Weeks* v. *United States*, 232 U.S. 383, 392 (1914), the Court compared the illegal search to the coerced confession.

68. Francis A. Allen, "The Exclusionary Rule in the American Law of Search and Seizure," *Journal of Criminal Law*, LII (September–October, 1961), 246, 252.

to deter. We know that the problem of illegal search is a serious one in this country. Justice Frankfurter, however, did not demonstrate that the problem is also a serious one in the foreign jurisdictions which did not have an exclusionary policy. In any event, the common-law policy of admissibility has come under increasing fire in England. The scholar Glanville Williams, pointing to the fact that under English law a confession induced by trickery is inadmissible, although evidence seized unlawfully can be used against the defendant, wonders whether the "law is fundamentally consistent with itself" and goes on to say that the "question . . . cannot be regarded as finally settled."[69] Speaking in the same vein, Lord Justice Devlin, one of England's most influential judges, has voiced doubts about the wisdom of the English practice and finds it "contrary to the spirit" of the Judges' Rules, which regulate police interrogation of suspects: "If the court is prepared to exclude admissions given in answer to improper questioning, however potent evidence they may be of the commission of a crime, and if it does so because the benefit to the law of fair interrogation outweighs the justice of the individual case, *ought it not to follow the same principle where documents are unlawfully seized?* Perhaps some day a Wilkes will arise who will get that question answered."[70]

The Wolf decision actually carried with it a double limitation. Not only were the states not required to adopt the exclusionary policy, they were not even required to accept all the obligations which the Fourth Amendment placed upon the federal government; only "the core" of the amendment's guarantee was made obligatory upon them. But the opinion nowhere defined the nature of this obligation, and in the absence of an exclusionary rule it was unlikely that it ever would be spelled out, for the evidence would always be admissible. What were the standards by which the states would be required to abide in regard to issuance of warrants, probable cause, and a host of other search law questions? If individuals were not to be informed of the scope of their constitutional rights, and state courts and officers of the nature of their constitutional obligations, to what purpose, one might ask, did the Court rule that the states were forbidden to search arbitrarily? In the absence of this clarification, the Wolf case merely stated a rule of hypothetical unconstitutionality. And in giving expression to a basic constitutional right, while at the same time refusing to apply the one sanction that might

69. Glanville L. Williams, "The Exclusionary Rule under Foreign Law: England," *Journal of Criminal Law*, LII (September–October, 1961), 272, 273.

70. Patrick Devlin, *The Criminal Prosecution in England* (New Haven, Conn., 1958), p. 53. (Emphasis supplied.)

make the right effective, the Court appeared to be riding a horse in two directions at the same time. The only specific obligation placed on the states was that they might not "affirmatively . . . sanction" a policy of arbitrary police invasion of privacy. But this was really not much more than a reaffirmation of the existing guarantees in state law. It must be recalled that the right to protection against police lawlessness already existed in each of the forty-eight state constitutions; it was the reality of the right that was so frequently lacking, and this ingredient the Supreme Court refused to supply.

While the Supreme Court's decision not to require the state courts to exclude the fruits of illegal searches might be subject to criticism, it did appear that the Court had sanctioned admission of all illegally seized evidence, regardless of the nature of the constitutional violation. Such an inference finds support both in logic and in a reading of the Wolf opinion. If reliability of the evidence is to serve as the criterion for admissibility in search cases, logic would seem to dictate that, regardless of the nature of the violation, the victim should be required to invoke the "other remedies" which were thought to be a satisfactory substitute for exclusion. Moreover, since no distinction was drawn in the Court's opinion between one type of illegal search and another (indeed, the facts of the Wolf search were not even mentioned in the Court's opinion), it appeared that the states were free to admit the seized materials into evidence. However, the Court had not said its last word on the subject, and in the next case of this series, decided in 1952, the due process clause was tailored to require the exclusion of evidence acquired through an illegal search.

The facts of *Rochin* v. *California*[71] are particularly outrageous. Upon receiving information that a man named Rochin was in the narcotics business, three Los Angeles deputy sheriffs, who had not bothered to obtain a search warrant, called at the Rochin home. They found the front door open and walked in, climbed to the second floor, forced open the bedroom door, and found Rochin on the bed. When the officers began to question him about two capsules which they noticed lying on a nightstand, Rochin seized the capsules and tried to swallow them. The officers pounced on Rochin and attempted to extract the capsules from his mouth by force. When their efforts proved unsuccessful, they handcuffed Rochin and took him to a hospital, where a doctor administered an emetic which induced vomiting, and the capsules were expelled. They were found

71. 342 U.S. 165 (1952).

to contain morphine, and their admission at the trial resulted in Rochin's conviction.

Once again, Justice Frankfurter delivered the opinion of the Court. Though Justices Murphy and Rutledge had died in the interim and had been replaced by Justices Clark and Minton (the latter was absent in the present case), the change in personnel did not affect the result. All eight of the participating justices favored reversal, though only six joined in Justice Frankfurter's opinion. In separate concurring opinions, Justices Black and Douglas maintained that the evidence was inadmissible because it had been obtained in violation of the self-incrimination privilege of the Fifth Amendment, which they deemed applicable to the states.

The majority, however, took a different view of the matter. Justice Frankfurter, who in the Wolf case had committed to the discretion of the state courts the question of admissibility of illegally seized evidence, engaged in a lengthy exposition of the flexible nature of the due process clause, the interpretation of which he termed "a function of the process of judgment." Due process was "the least specific and most comprehensive protection of liberties" found in the Constitution. As if in explanation of the contrast between the decision in this case and that in the Wolf case, Frankfurter averred that due process, by its very nature, made it inevitable that the judgment would "fall differently at different times and differently at the same time through different judges."[72] Due process could not be defined "more precisely than to say that convictions cannot be brought about by methods that offend 'a sense of justice.' "[73]

Applying this consideration, therefore, to the present case, the Court found its sense of justice offended: "This is conduct that shocks the conscience. Illegally breaking into the privacy of the petitioner, the struggle to open his mouth and remove what was there, the forcible extraction of his stomach's contents . . . is bound to offend even hardened sensibilities. They are methods too close to the rack and screw. . . ."[74] Here, said Frankfurter, the Court was confronted with evidence obtained by brutal methods; the fact that the confession was extracted from Rochin's stomach rather than from his mind was immaterial. It was not alone the unreliability of coerced confessions which require their exclusion from evidence; even when reliable, as in this case, the mere presence of coercion in obtaining the confession mandated its exclusion. "[T]o sanction

72. *Ibid.*, p. 170.
73. *Ibid.*, p. 173.
74. *Ibid.*, p. 172.

the brutal conduct . . . would be to afford brutality the cloak of law. Nothing would be more calculated to discredit law and thereby to brutalize the temper of a society."[75]

Since nowhere in his opinion did Justice Frankfurter refer to search and seizure, one might consider this a confession case. The result could thus be harmonized with the Wolf decision in view of the different nature of the subject matter. A coerced confession must be excluded from evidence; the fruits of an illegal search need not. However, the fact that Frankfurter chose to stress the element of coercion does not alter the fact that there was an element of unlawful search as well.[76] The Fourth Amendment, and presumably the due process clause as well, prohibits the unreasonable search not only of a dwelling but also of the person. We see illustrated here the dilemma into which the Court had been plunged by its refusal to require the exclusion of illegally seized evidence and its confrontation, shortly thereafter, with a case where even the federalism-conscious judicial conscience was shocked by the naked force involved in the abuse of the defendant. The evidence was thus ordered excluded as a product of coercion. But even when the decision is viewed from the standpoint of coercion, the question still arises, and it is not answered in the opinion, of why a coerced confession, even when reliable, requires exclusion, while the fruits of an illegal search do not. The lawlessness in this case was, of course, far graver than that in the Wolf case; brutality always evokes a stronger visceral reaction in the civilized person than does a violation of law which does not involve violence. But surely the justification given for exclusion—that the conduct complained of was "calculated to discredit law and thereby to brutalize the temper of a society"—could be applied with equal force to illegal searches. One commentator observed that "the effective reconciliation of the *Wolf* and *Rochin* cases in terms of constitutional theory seemed to require more than mortal insight. . . ."[77]

The Rochin case had not answered one question: were cases involving an assault on the person the only ones in which an exception would be made to the Wolf rule, or might the circumstances of a particular search be so repugnant, even in the absence of violence, as to require exclusion of the seized evidence? The Court answered

75. *Ibid.*, pp. 173–74.
76. Dissenting in *Irvine* v. *California*, 347 U.S. 128, 144 (1954), Frankfurter remarked that "there was in *Rochin*, an element of unreasonable search and seizure. . . ." It is not clear whether he was referring to the illegal entry into Rochin's home or to the pumping out of his stomach.
77. Paul G. Kauper, *Frontiers of Constitutional Liberty* (Ann Arbor, Mich., 1956), p. 173.

this question in 1954, in the case of *Irvine* v. *California*.[78] The Irvine case involved an episode which, said Justice Jackson in an opinion announcing the judgment of the Court, "would be almost incredible if it were not admitted. Few police measures have come to our attention that more flagrantly, deliberately, and persistently violated"[79] a citizen's rights. California police, seeking evidence of bookmaking activities against one Patrick Irvine, got a locksmith to make a doorkey to the Irvine home while Irvine and his wife were away. In the course of the next few weeks the police made repeated entries into Irvine's home: they concealed a microphone on the premises, punched a hole through the roof, and strung connecting wires to a nearby garage, where officers were waiting to monitor the conversations picked up in the home. For a three-week period the microphone was even secreted in the bedroom. The evidence uncovered led to Irvine's conviction.

The Court sustained the conviction by a five-to-four vote which did not, however, result in a majority opinion. Seven members of the Court that considered the Irvine case had also participated in the Rochin decision,[80] yet they differed markedly in their estimates of the significance of that decision. A blizzard of five opinions fell from the bench. Joining in Justice Jackson's opinion were Chief Justice Warren and Justices Reed and Minton. Justice Clark concurred separately, while Justices Frankfurter, Black, Douglas, and Burton dissented,[81] with all but Burton writing opinions. The tenuous nature of the decision becomes even more pronounced when we note that the Chief Justice, without whose vote the conviction could not have been upheld, is said to have afterwards regretted joining in the judgment of the Court.[82]

Justice Jackson said that this case must be governed by the decision in *Wolf* v. *Colorado*, and that exclusion of illegally seized evidence from a state proceeding was not required by due process of law, no matter how shocking the violation, so long as there was no element of physical coercion. The Rochin decision was held to have turned entirely on the element of brutality there involved; it was for that reason that the Wolf case was not mentioned in the Rochin opinion.

78. 347 U.S. 128 (1954).
79. *Ibid.*, p. 132.
80. The two exceptions were Chief Justice Warren, who had replaced the deceased Chief Justice Vinson, and Justice Minton, who had been absent when the Rochin case was decided.
81. Justice Black's dissenting opinion was not based on Fourth Amendment grounds.
82. This information comes from one of Chief Justice Warren's former law clerks.

The Court, said Jackson, should not distinguish between different degrees of violation of the same constitutional right and require the exclusion of the evidence in some cases but not in others. The Court should make no distinction, with respect to the question of exclusion, between those unconstitutional searches "which produce on our minds a mild shock" and those which produce a "shock [that] is more serious."[83] Jackson chided Justice Frankfurter for having written the opinion of the Court in the Wolf case "entirely in the abstract,"[84] without even referring to the facts of the violation, which indicated that the nature of the violation did not determine the question of admissibility of the evidence. A definite rule must be laid down for the guidance of the states, said Jackson, and "a distinction of the kind urged here would leave the [Wolf] rule so indefinite that no state court could know what it should rule in order to keep its processes on solid constitutional ground."[85] This statement seems somewhat ironical in view of the fact that the justices splintered in so many directions that they did not even produce a majority opinion of the Court.

Justice Jackson perhaps gave a firmer clue to the assumptions underlying the Court's judgment by engaging in some disparaging comment about the effectiveness of the federal exclusionary rule. A study of the cases in the federal courts and of the Court's own cases would show that the rule had not succeeded in putting an end to illegal searches by federal officers, nor was there any reliable evidence that those states which followed an exclusionary policy were freer of the bane of police lawlessness than those which did not: "That the rule of exclusion and reversal results in the escape of guilty persons is more capable of demonstration than that it deters invasions of right by the police."[86] (This attitude was a far cry indeed from the great dissent that Jackson had entered in the Brinegar case[87] in defense of the exclusionary rule.) Unlike Justice Frankfurter in the Wolf case, however, Jackson was under no illusion as to the probable effectiveness of alternative remedies for deterring unlawful police conduct; these remedies were "of no practical

83. *Ibid.*, pp. 133–34.
84. *Ibid.*, p. 133.
85. *Ibid.*, p. 134.
86. *Ibid.*, p. 136. Justice Douglas asserted the contrary in his dissenting opinion. "Exclusion," he said, "is indeed the only effective sanction." "If police officials know that evidence obtained by their lawless acts cannot be used in the courts, they will clean their own houses and put an end to this kind of action." *Ibid.*, pp. 151, 152.
87. *Brinegar* v. *United States*, 338 U.S. 160, 180 (1949), discussed in the preceding chapter.

avail."[88] In effect, Jackson was saying that there is no effective method known to the law for preventing its lawless enforcement.

Justice Clark wrote an unusual and portentous concurring opinion. He believed that the exclusionary rule should be applied to the states, and explained that had he been a member of the Court in 1949 when the Wolf case was decided, he would have so voted. However, the Court having chosen to reject the exclusionary rule for the states, he believed that the value of legal certainty permitted no deviations. Moreover, there was a practical reason for rigid adherence to the Wolf doctrine because that course might "produce needed converts for its extinction."[89]

Justice Frankfurter's dissenting opinion, which was in large measure another composition on the meaning of due process of law and in which Justice Burton joined, was an attempt to clarify his reasoning and to show why the conduct complained of in the case before the Court was of such a nature that the exclusionary rule must be applied. The Court, said Frankfurter, misconceived the essence of due process, which bore the hallmark of flexibility and was "the very antithesis of a Procrustean rule,"[90] if it thought that this concept could provide definiteness and certainty in the law. "The effort to imprison due process within tidy categories . . . is a futile endeavor to save the judicial function from the pains of judicial judgment."[91]

88. 347 U.S. 128, 137. Jackson closed his opinion with the unusual recommendation, for which he got support only from Chief Justice Warren, that because the conduct of the California officers probably violated federal law, the record of the case, together with a copy of his opinion, should be forwarded to the Justice Department with a view to prosecution of those guilty. The other members of the Court refused to join Jackson in this recommendation for the obvious reason, stressed by Justice Black in his dissenting opinion, that prosecution, or even a suggestion of it, is an executive, not a judicial function.

An inquiry by the author to the Justice Department with respect to the developments which followed Jackson's recommendation elicited the following reply, in a letter dated January 11, 1962, from Burke Marshall, then Assistant Attorney General in charge of the Civil Rights Division:

The Supreme Court did send to the Justice Department the transcript in this case. The Federal Bureau of Investigation conducted a full investigation which revealed some significant facts which did not appear in the records or the opinion of the Supreme Court and were apparently unknown to the Court at the time of its review of the case. One of these significant facts was that the police officers who placed the dectograph or microphone in the defendant Irvine's home were acting with the full knowledge of the local District Attorney. This fact, together with the provisions of Section 653(h) of the California Penal Code, expressly providing for such conduct, forced us to the conclusion that it would be both useless and inadvisable to present this matter to the Federal grand jury. Our decision was largely influenced by the belief that the Government in presenting all the facts would not be able to satisfy the rigid standard of intent imposed by the Supreme Court's interpretation of "wilfulness" in the *Screws* case, 325 U.S. 91.

89. 347 U.S. 128, 138.

90. *Ibid.*, p. 143.

91. *Ibid.*, p. 147.

The Rochin decision, said Frankfurter, was not based specifically on considerations of search and seizure or of self-incrimination: these were concepts appropriate only for the federal courts, confronted with the specific provisions of the Bill of Rights. Nor was that decision required solely by the physical assault on Rochin's person. In applying due process, he said, the Court must consider "the whole course of events by which a conviction was obtained. . . ."[92] Given this criterion, the "decisive" factor in both the Rochin and Irvine cases was not the element of search alone but the "*additional aggravating conduct*. . . . [T]he conduct of the police here went beyond a bare search and seizure. The police devised means to hear every word that was said in the Irvine household for more than a month."[93]

Justice Jackson's reasoning did leave a good deal to be desired. He made no real attempt to draw a meaningful distinction, in terms of constitutional theory, between the shocking conduct of the police in the Irvine and in the Rochine case. Is physical coercion, no matter how minor, always more constitutionally offensive than other types of police misconduct, no matter how major? For that matter, was the "shocking" conduct in the Rochin case really more offensive than the "incredible" conduct in the Irvine case? As for the need to lay down guidelines for the state courts, in other types of due process cases (for instance, confessions) the Court had built up workable rules while adjudicating on a case-by-case basis.

Jackson's reading of Frankfurter's opinion in the Wolf case as a rejection of the exclusionary rule for *all* unconstitutional state searches might have been justified had Frankfurter's opinion stood alone. However, it did not stand alone: it had been modified by the Rochin opinion. Jackson was unjustified in reading the Rochin opin-
furter had stressed the flexible nature of due process. But Frank-
ion as sanctioning exclusion only for cases involving violence; Frankfurter's failure to enunciate his views clearly did leave those opinions open to Jackson's interpretation. As Professor Allen has suggested, Frankfurter had "become entoiled in a semantic mesh of his own making."[94] Moreover, Frankfurter was not quite consistent in his reasoning. In the Wolf case he had stressed the demands of federalism as mitigating against the imposition of the exclusionary rule on the state courts and had placed great stock on the practice of other English-speaking countries, as well as of most of the American states; indeed, as he later explained, the practice of the states was

92. *Ibid.*, p. 144.
93. *Ibid.*, pp. 145–46. (Emphasis supplied.)
94. Allen, "Exclusionary Rule," p. 252.

the "controlling factor"[95] in the Wolf case. But in the Rochin and Irvine cases he failed to show that in the situations there before the Court exclusion of the evidence would have resulted in those same nonexclusionary jurisdictions. In the light of the Wolf reasoning it was surely important to demonstrate that the type of conduct revealed in the Irvine case would have rendered the evidence subject to exclusion in those jurisdictions (certainly it was admissible in California). And in the Rochin case, Justice Douglas had chided Frankfurter for favoring exclusion when Douglas was able to find only four states whose courts would have excluded evidence acquired in that manner.

The fragmentation to which the Court had shown itself prone in dealing with state search cases was somewhat ameliorated when the next case in the series, *Breithaupt* v. *Abram*,[96] was decided in 1957. Two distinct viewpoints emerged, and only three opinions were written. This case bore certain similarities to the Rochin case. Breithaupt was driving a pickup truck in New Mexico when it collided with an automobile, killing three people. An almost empty whiskey bottle was found in the truck's glove compartment. Later on, as Breithaupt lay unconscious in a hospital, it was noticed that his breath was giving off an odor of liquor. These facts prompted the police to ask a doctor to take a sample of Breithaupt's blood to test it for alcoholic content. The result of the blood test, which showed that Breithaupt had been intoxicated at the time of the accident, was introduced at the trial, and he was convicted of involuntary manslaughter.

Breithaupt's conviction was sustained by the Court in an opinion by Justice Clark. He stressed, as had Justice Frankfurter in the preceding cases, that due process forbade only such conduct as fell below standards considered morally acceptable by the community, and he drew attention to the fact that all but one of the states had sanctioned the use of blood tests or other chemical tests in cases where the defendant was suspected of driving while intoxicated. Unlike the stomach pumping which had led the Court to reverse Rochin's conviction, the extraction of a blood sample by a qualified physician and without the application of force was a procedure to which even delicate persons would not raise objection. "The blood

95. *Elkins* v. *United States*, 364 U.S. 206, 243 (1960) (dissenting opinion).

96. 352 U.S. 432 (1957). There had been two personnel changes on the Court since the Irvine case. Justice Jackson had died and Justice Minton had retired. They were replaced by Justices Harlan and Brennan. The newcomers voted with the majority, as Jackson and Minton would almost certainly have voted had they still been on the Court.

test procedure has become routine in our everyday life. It is a ritual for those going into the military service as well as those applying for marriage licenses."[97] While the test did involve a "slight . . . intrusion"[98] on bodily privacy, the taking of blood, when balanced against the need of the community to prevent highway fatalities, was a reasonable exercise of the state's power to promote safety on the highways. Clark did not specify whether the compulsory blood test or other chemical test may be employed in a search for evidence of crimes other than drunken driving.[99] The drunken driver presents a particularly difficult problem. He is a menace to other citizens using the highways, but without the use of a reliable scientific test there is very often no way of proving to the satisfaction of a jury that he really was intoxicated while driving.

In a biting dissent Chief Justice Warren, joined by Justices Black and Douglas, protested that the Court had sapped the Rochin decision of any vitality it possessed, leaving it as "no more than an instance of personal revulsion against particular police methods."[100] He thought that comparable techniques had been used in both cases. Each involved an operation performed by a physician; each involved the extraction of body fluids; each technique was in rather common use. At stake here was the right of bodily privacy, a right that could not be violated for law enforcement purposes. The skin, tissues, and fluids of the human body were beyond the pale of official intrusion. The absence of physical violence, the result of Breithaupt's inability to resist while in a state of unconsciousness, did not render the procedure more palatable: a person's constitutional rights did not depend on his ability to claim them. Justice Douglas, joined by Justice Black, dissented separately along the same general lines.[101]

The Breithaupt case differed from the earlier state search cases in one notable respect. That an unconstitutional search had taken place was not even in dispute in each of the other cases, the sole question before the Court being whether the evidence thus seized must be excluded from a criminal proceeding. Here, however, the Court held that, taking all the circumstances into consideration—the routineness and widespread use of the test, the interest of the state in curbing highway fatalities, and the authorization of similar tests by

97. *Ibid.*, p. 436.
98. *Ibid.*, p. 439.
99. For an exploration of the constitutional problems involved and an analysis of the state cases, see James R. Richardson, "Rochin and Breithaupt in Context," *Vanderbilt Law Review*, XIV (June, 1961), 879.
100. 352 U.S. 432, 440.
101. Douglas apparently treated this as a confession case, while Warren did not mention any specific constitutional ground.

most other states—no violation of the Constitution had in fact taken place. It is true that this was a due process case, not a Fourth Amendment case, and the majority did not regard the due process clause as applying the entire body of Fourth Amendment law to state action. Nevertheless, the opinion places such a degree of emphasis on the reasonableness of the procedure that one might fairly wonder whether blood test evidence is admissible also in federal court—whether the finding of "reasonableness" disposes also of the self-incrimination defense. On the other hand, if the extraction of blood is considered a search, it is difficult to see how it could be justified, even with a warrant, in view of the rule prohibiting the seizure of items other than contraband and instruments of crime.[102]

These cases illustrate the difficulties that the Supreme Court has encountered in many other search cases. Unlike some other areas of constitutional law, where precedents may acquire sanctity from old age, if from little else, many search and seizure problems are of fairly recent origin and not precedent-bound. Such precedents as do exist are frequently ambiguous and tend to age quickly. Opinions are befogged by a rhetoric that obscures basic judicial assumptions, and the justices responsible for the decisions may later disagree on what they meant in earlier decisions and may give differing reasons for their arrival at the same result. The result is that, taken collectively, the cases discussed in this chapter resemble a battle of constitutional conflict rather than a chapter of constitutional law. As one observer of the Court remarked: "due process with respect to personal rights, for all its definiteness at its core, became so indefinite at the periphery that no amount of eloquent and perceptive analysis provided much guidance for citizens or government officers or even members of the Supreme Court."[103] Ferment was brewing in the Court, though the direction the stirrings would take remained undetermined as the nineteen fifties drew to a close.

102. *Boyd* v. *United States*, 116 U.S. 616 (1886); *Gouled* v. *United States*, 255 U.S. 298 (1921). The same question might today also be posed with respect to state searches in view of the Court's decision in *Mapp* v. *Ohio*, 367 U.S. 643 (1961), that the exclusionary rule must be applied to the states, and its further decision in *Ker* v. *California*, 374 U.S. 23 (1963), that due process requires the states to obey all the constitutional commands of the Fourth Amendment as applied in the federal courts. These decisions may have had the effect of overruling the Breithaupt case. Justice Frankfurter apparently believed that the Breithaupt decision was valid on Fourth Amendment, as well as due process, grounds. See *Elkins* v. *United States*, 364 U.S. 206, 246 (1960) (dissenting opinion).

103. Carl Brent Swisher, *The Supreme Court in Modern Role* (New York, 1958), p. 57.

## Chapter VI

# THE EXCLUSIONARY RULE AND THE STATES

As we have seen in preceding chapters, our federal form of government resulted in a limitation on the protection of the individual against unreasonable searches in two respects. First, the Supreme Court had ruled in the 1949 case of *Wolf* v. *Colorado*[1] that while the "core" of the Fourth Amendment's guarantee against unreasonable searches applied also to the states by virtue of the due process clause, this protection did not extend to the exclusion from state trials of unconstitutionally seized evidence; to conduct an unreasonable search would violate due process of law, but to use the fruits of the lawless activity to gain a conviction would not. Second, under the older "silver platter" doctrine, even the federal courts, which must exclude the fruits of lawless searches by federal officers, might nevertheless permit the use of evidence illegally seized by state officers in searches which neither involved federal participation nor were made for a federal purpose.[2] While these limitations on the constitutional guarantee appeared to have become firmly established, in the space of one year, beginning in 1960, the silver platter doctrine

1. 338 U.S. 25 (1949).

2. *Weeks* v. *United States*, 232 U.S. 383 (1914); *Byars* v. *United States*, 273 U.S. 28 (1927); *Gambino* v. *United States*, 275 U.S. 310 (1927). It should be noted that our federal system also developed limitations on the effectiveness of the Fifth Amendment's guarantees against self-incrimination and double jeopardy. Under the "twin sovereignties" doctrine a witness in a federal case could not refuse to testify merely because his testimony would incriminate him in a violation of *state* law. *United States* v. *Murdock*, 284 U.S. 141 (1931). Conversely, a witness in a state case could not refuse to testify merely because his testimony would incriminate him in a violation of *federal* law. *Knapp* v. *Schweitzer*, 357 U.S. 371 (1958). Evidence thus compelled was admissible in federal court. *Feldman* v. *United States*, 322 U.S. 487 (1944). However, the Court reconsidered and reversed these decisions in *Murphy* v. *Waterfront Commission* (378 U.S. 52 [1964]), following the absorption of the self-incrimination provision into due process in *Malloy* v. *Hogan* (378 U.S. 1 [1964]). But the limitation on the double jeopardy prohibition remains. Thus the federal and state governments may each punish for the same conduct where such conduct is forbidden by the laws of both sovereigns. *Fox* v. *Ohio*, 8 Howard 410 (1847); *Abbate* v. *United States*, 359 U.S. 187 (1959). Even where the courts of one sovereign have already acquitted, the courts of the other may nevertheless convict. *Bartkus* v. *Illinois*, 359 U.S. 121 (1959). For critical discussion of the "twin sovereignties" doctrine, see Richard A. Watson, "Federalism v. Individual Rights: The Legal Squeeze on Self-Incrimination," *American Political Science Review*, LIV (December, 1960), 887; Walter T. Fisher, "Double Jeopardy, Two Sovereigns and the Intruding Constitution," *University of Chicago Law Review*, XXVIII (Summer, 1961), 591.

was discarded and the Wolf case overruled. These events and their consequences are the subject of this chapter.

Important by way of prelude to subsequent developments is the case of *Rea* v. *United States*,[3] decided in 1956. The case arose in New Mexico, where Rea was indicted in federal court on a charge of unlawful possession of narcotics. At a pre-trial hearing Rea claimed that the evidence had been seized unlawfully because the warrant under which the search was conducted had been issued to a federal narcotics agent in violation of the standards prescribed by the federal Rules of Criminal Procedure. His motion to suppress the evidence was granted by the district court and the indictment was quashed. The agent then proceeded to swear out a complaint before a state judge and caused Rea's arrest for violating the narcotics laws of New Mexico. Rea petitioned the district court to enjoin the agent from testifying against him and to reacquire the evidence, should it already be out of federal custody, but the district court refused to interfere with the state process and was sustained in its refusal by the court of appeals.[4] Rea now renewed his plea before the Supreme Court.

A formidable obstacle lay in the way of Rea's request for an injunction, for the Court had turned down a similar request in the 1951 case of *Stefanelli* v. *Minard*.[5] Stefanelli was the victim of a lawless search of his home by the police in Newark, New Jersey. Evidence was seized which implicated him in bookmaking activities, and Stefanelli petitioned a federal district court to enjoin the use of the evidence at his forthcoming trial, but he was unsuccessful. Though the recently decided Wolf case had found unreasonable searches conducted by state officers to be unconstitutional, and though Stefanelli pointed to a civil rights act[6] whose terms authorized redress for any person who, under color of state law, had been deprived of his constitutional rights, the Supreme Court held that the injunction should not issue. Justice Frankfurter, for the Court, declared that the granting of an injunction was discretionary and not mandatory on the part of the federal courts, and "the balance is against the wisdom of using their power" because intervention of the federal courts in state judicial proceedings constituted "perhaps the most sensitive source of friction between States and Nation."[7] Stefanelli, in the Court's opinion, was not threatened with "such

3. 350 U.S. 214 (1956).
4. *Rea* v. *United States*, 210 F.2d 237 (10th cir. 1954).
5. 342 U.S. 117 (1951).
6. 8 U.S.C., sec. 43.
7. *Ibid.*, p. 120.

irreparable injury, clear and imminent" as would justify federal interference with the state judicial process. "At worst, the evidence sought to be suppressed may provide the basis for conviction,"[8] but a conviction so obtained would not, in light of the Wolf doctrine, deprive Stefanelli of due process of law. This conclusion evoked a brief but sharp dissent from Justice Douglas. "To hold first," he contended, "that the evidence may be admitted and second that its use may not be enjoined is to make the Fourth Amendment an empty and hollow guarantee so far as state prosecutions are concerned."[9] But it is difficult to see how else the Court could have ruled without in effect discarding the Wolf decision. If Stefanelli's flanking attack on the Wolf rule had been successful, it would have had the effect of giving the states formal permission to use in evidence the fruits of illegal searches, while at the same time allowing the federal courts to enjoin their use.

Thus, when the court of appeals denied Rea's petition for an injunction, it did so on the strength of the Stefanelli case. It was true, said the court, that the search in the Rea case differed from that in the Stefanelli case in that it was conducted by a federal rather than a state officer. But the underlying principle of the Stefanelli case, that the federal courts should not interfere with the course of a state judicial proceeding, was sufficiently potent to cover this situation. "Say what you will," said Judge Huxman, "the effect of the relief sought would make impossible the prosecution by the state of its action against appellant. That's the purpose and the only purpose sought to be accomplished. . . ."[10]

The Supreme Court, however, rejected this reasoning. In an opinion by Justice Douglas, the majority "put all the constitutional questions to one side,"[11] in the belief that the case raised "not a constitutional question but one concerning our supervisory powers over federal law enforcement agencies."[12] The factual difference between the Rea and Stefanelli cases was the crucial factor upon which the decision was based. No injunction was sought against state officials, nor was any direct attempt made to interfere with the orderly processes of the state courts. "The only relief asked is against a federal agent, who obtained the property as a result of the abuse of process issued by a United States Commissioner."[13] Douglas likened this case to *McNabb* v. *United States*,[14] where the Court had reversed a

8. *Ibid.*, p. 122.
9. *Ibid.*, p. 125.
10. 210 F.2d 237, 240.
11. 350 U.S. 214, 216.
12. *Ibid.*, p. 217.
13. *Ibid.*, p. 216.
14. 318 U.S. 332 (1943).

conviction resulting from a confession obtained in violation of the federal Rules of Criminal Procedure. He observed that exercise of the Court's power was not limited by constitutional considerations but extended to situations involving the mandates of the federal Rules, where the Court's vigilance was required in order to assure compliance:

> The command of the federal Rules is in no way affected by anything that happens in a state court. . . . Federal courts sit to enforce federal law; and federal law extends to the process issuing from those courts. The obligation of the federal agent is to obey the Rules. . . . They prescribe standards for law enforcement. They are designed to protect the privacy of the citizen, unless the strict standards set for searches and seizures are satisfied. That policy is defeated if the federal agent can flout them and use the fruits of his unlawful act either in federal or state proceedings.[15]

Justice Harlan, dissenting with the concurrence of Justices Reed, Burton, and Minton, was unable to square the decision with either the Wolf or the Stefanelli case. The Wolf case had allowed the states to use unconstitutionally seized evidence, and it was insufficient to answer that the injunction was directed solely against federally acquired evidence. The only difference between the Wolf decision and the Weeks[16] decision, requiring the exclusionary rule for the federal courts, was "the difference between state and federal courts; in each case, the substance of the constitutional command is the same, but the nature of enforcement varies with the forum."[17] And since the state's case depended entirely on the agent's testimony, the injunction would have the same effect "as if it had been issued directly against New Mexico or its officials."[18] Harlan pointed disapprovingly to the Court's assumption of supervisory power over federal law enforcement agencies other than courts. The McNabb case, he asserted, merely set standards for evidence admissible in federal courts but did not operate directly on law enforcement officials. "So far as I know, this is the first time it has been suggested that the federal courts share with the executive branch of the Government responsibility for supervising law enforcement activities as such."[19]

Harlan's logic is difficult to rebut, and the decision does appear to represent a significant inroad on the Wolf doctrine (though there was no candid recognition of this fact on the part of the Court).[20]

15. 350 U.S. 214, 217–18.
16. *Weeks* v. *United States*, 232 U.S. 383 (1914).
17. 350 U.S. 214, 220.
18. *Ibid.*, p. 219.
19. *Ibid.*, p. 218.
20. A lawyer who clerked for another member of the Court when the Rea case was argued told this writer that he recalls that Justice Frankfurter emphatically stated at the time that in his view Rea's petition could not be granted consistently with the Wolf decision.

The Rea case served to expand the scope of the exclusionary rule by denying to the states (at least indirectly, through the victim's invocation of a federal injunction) the use of evidence illegally acquired by federal officers. But can it, in the light of subsequent events, be regarded as the beginning of a pincer movement designed to make exclusion the rule, rather than the exception, in the state courts? Certainly, it is difficult to picture Justice Frankfurter, by his acquiescence in the Rea case, participating in the infanticide of his "children," Wolf and Stefanelli. He may, however, have been fighting to save as much as he reasonably could of the Wolf doctrine—conceding a battle in order to win the war and to forestall the events that nevertheless eventually took place.

Whether or not the Rea case began to lay the groundwork for the eventual extension of the exclusionary rule to the states, it did help to undermine the foundation of the silver platter doctrine. Even though the Rea case dealt with an illegal search by a federal, not a state, officer, its underlying premise was the need to maintain the constitutional integrity of federal criminal justice. It was not, however, the Rea case alone which cast a shadow on the silver platter doctrine. The Wolf case, in which the Court had absorbed the "core" of the Fourth Amendment's guarantee into the due process clause, had undercut the premises of the doctrine, which had been formulated before the development of due process as a regulator of state criminal procedure. When, prior to the Wolf case, the federal courts accepted evidence seized by state officers in circumstances which would have rendered the search unreasonable if conducted by federal officers, the admission of the evidence did not represent an implied "overlooking" of a constitutional violation, since none had in fact occurred. Following the Wolf decision, however, an unreasonable state search violated the federal Constitution, and it would have been anomalous to continue to admit its fruits into evidence in the federal courts.[21]

21. Professor Allen argues that the premise underlying the silver platter doctrine as originally enunciated was not that an illegal state search did not violate the Constitution, but that federal law enforcement had not been debased by the acts of the state officers. Francis A. Allen, "Federalism and the Fourth Amendment: A Requiem for Wolf," *The Supreme Court Review* (1961), pp. 1, 17. Nevertheless, the integrity of the federal system of criminal justice would be impaired if the federal courts were to admit evidence obtained in violation of constitutional standards which federal officers were required to observe. Prior to the Wolf case, an illegal state search might have violated the state constitution (or a state statute), since all forty-eight states then in the Union had constitutional provisions regulating searches. As far as the federal courts are concerned, however, a violation of a state constitution is in a totally different category from a violation of the federal Constitution.

That the Wolf decision had made doubtful the continued viability of the silver platter doctrine was recognized on two occasions by members of the Court. Announcing the judgment of the Court in *Lustig* v. *United States,* decided on the same day as the Wolf case, Justice Frankfurter said: "Where there is participation on the part of federal officers [as there was in the Lustig case] . . . it is not necessary to consider *what would be the result if the search had been conducted entirely by State officers.*"[22] A concurring opinion in the same case by Justice Murphy, joined by Justices Douglas and Rutledge, forthrightly called for the overthrow of the doctrine. Later on, Chief Justice Warren's opinion for the Court in *Benanti* v. *United States* contained the observation that "it has remained an *open question* in this Court whether evidence obtained solely by state agents in an illegal search may be admissible in federal court despite the Fourth Amendment."[23] The results of silver platter cases decided in the lower federal courts, however, reflected a virtual unanimity in favor of the retention of the doctrine. The lone exception was *Hanna* v. *United States,*[24] decided in 1958, in which the Court of Appeals for the District of Columbia circuit reversed a federal conviction based on evidence unlawfully seized by Maryland officers. Speaking for that court, Judge Hastie reviewed, in addition to the Wolf case, relevant statements made by members of the Court in other cases. Boldly "counting noses" on the Court, he concluded that the silver platter doctrine was ripe for overthrow.

Such, then, was the background of the problem when the Supreme Court announced its decision on the silver platter doctrine on June 27, 1960, in *Elkins* v. *United States.*[25] Elkins was convicted in federal court in Oregon on wire tapping charges. The evidence against him was uncovered by Oregon police who were searching the home of another person for obscene motion pictures. They did not find what they were looking for but in the course of their search came upon the wire tapping apparatus. A state prosecution on wire tapping charges failed when two Oregon courts ordered the evidence suppressed on the ground that the warrant with which the searchers were armed was invalid. Federal officers then took possession of the evidence.

22. 338 U.S. 74, 79 (1949). (Emphasis supplied.)
23. 355 U.S. 96, 102, n. 10 (1957). (Emphasis supplied.)
24. 260 F.2d 723 (D.C. cir. 1958). Writing in 1959, Professor Kamisar found that of the over thirty silver platter cases decided by the lower federal courts since the Wolf decision, in only three was the Wolf case even cited. Yale Kamisar, "*Wolf* and *Lustig* Ten Years Later: Illegal State Evidence in State and Federal Courts," *Minnesota Law Review*, XLIII (May, 1959), 1083, 1140.
25. 364 U.S. 206 (1960).

In the four years which had elapsed since the Rea decision, Justices Brennan, Whittaker, and Stewart had replaced retiring Justices Minton, Reed, and Burton, and it was Stewart who delivered the opinion of the Court. Essentially, Stewart noted two changes which had occurred since the silver platter doctrine was formulated and which had undermined its authority. First, the Wolf case had extended the constitutional prohibition of unreasonable searches to the states; this meant that the federal courts were presently admitting evidence obtained in violation of the Constitution and threatening the principle of judicial integrity. Second, a large number of states had, of their own volition, adopted the exclusionary rule to deal with lawless law enforcement within their jurisdictions; to permit federal agents to use in federal court the fruits of illegal searches by state officers in exclusionary jurisdictions helped to defeat the disciplinary policies of those states. Stewart also adverted to the expanding scope of federal criminal jurisdiction; this made increasing co-operation in federal-state law enforcement necessary, with a resulting probable circumvention of the federal exclusionary policy, since state officers could be utilized to search for evidence of federal crimes.

"If resolution of the issue were to be dictated solely by principles of logic," continued Justice Stewart, "it is clear what our decision must be." The victim's constitutional right of privacy is violated with equal force whether the search is contrary to the Fourth or to the Fourteenth Amendment. To distinguish, with respect to admissibility, between evidence seized by federal officers in violation of the Fourth Amendment and that obtained by state officers in violation of the Fourteenth Amendment would be "arbitrary" and "would appear to reflect an indefensibly selective evaluation of the provisions of the Constitution."[26]

What Justice Stewart had thus far said would have been sufficient to justify his conclusion that the silver platter doctrine should be overturned. Significantly, however, Stewart was not content to rest on logic alone and made the resolution of the issue turn upon an assessment of the working of the exclusionary rule. Launching into an appraisal of the exclusionary policy—the first such full-scale discussion to be found in an opinion of the Court—Stewart noted that it "has for decades been the subject of ardent controversy" and that aligned against it were such eminent jurists as Wigmore and Cardozo: in the words of Cardozo, "the criminal is to go free because the constable has blundered." But such arguments, "however felicitous their phrasing," said Stewart, misconceived the nature of the rule,

26. *Ibid.*, p. 215.

whose "basic postulate" was not remedial but preventive. "Its purpose is to deter—to compel respect for the constitutional guaranty in the only effectively available way—by removing the incentive to disregard it."[27]

But did the exclusionary rule indeed deter? Did it indeed "compel respect" for the Constitution? Justice Stewart acknowledged that no statistical data were available to prove that persons living in states following the exclusionary rule were safer from illegal searches than those living in states which did not, nor could the effect of the exclusionary policy on efficient law enforcement be demonstrated. "Since as a practical matter it is never easy to prove a negative," he said, "it is hardly likely that conclusive factual data could ever be assembled."[28] In the absence of precise statistical evidence, however, he engaged in intellectual speculation to answer these questions. The federal government had operated under the exclusionary rule since 1914 with no apparent ill effect on the efficiency of the Federal Bureau of Investigation. Moreover, half the states had followed the federal policy of exclusion, in a "movement . . . halting but seemingly inexorable."[29] Since the Wolf decision four states—Delaware, California, North Carolina, and Rhode Island—had adopted an exclusionary policy either by court action or by legislation.[30] Governor Edmund Brown of California, who as State Attorney General had strongly criticized California's adoption of the exclusionary rule in 1955,[31] now publicly acknowledged its excellent effect in inducing a greater degree of professionalization among police officers; far from impairing efficient law enforcement in California, the exclusionary rule had actually enhanced it.

More important, however, than the trend toward exclusion in the states in discarding the silver platter doctrine was the principle of federalism. In stressing this consideration, Justice Stewart turned the tables on his dissenting brethren who criticized the decision as

27. *Ibid.*, p. 217. Justice Cardozo's observation was made in *People* v. *Defore*, 150 N.E. 585, 587 (N.Y. 1926).

28. *Ibid.*, p. 218.

29. *Ibid.*, p. 219.

30. In an Appendix to the opinion of the Court, Justice Stewart showed that twenty-six states had adopted the exclusionary rule. The trend appeared, however, to be something less than "inexorable," for the following reasons: (1) since the Wolf decision in 1949, Michigan and South Dakota had both moved from total exclusion to only partial exclusion, Michigan by constitutional amendment and South Dakota by legislative enactment; (2) the Maryland rule was limited to misdemeanors; (3) the Alabama rule was limited to liquor offenses; (4) Alaska and Hawaii were listed as exclusionary states although these two states had only recently attained statehood and had not yet reviewed the exclusionary policy, which they had, of course, followed as federal territories.

31. *People* v. *Cahan*, 282 P.2d 905 (Cal. 1955).

destructive of the federal principle. "The very essence of a healthy federalism," he said, "depends on the avoidance of needless conflict between state and federal courts." Exclusion from the federal courts of evidence illegally seized in nonexclusionary states would work no hardship on those states: they could, after all, use it in their own courts. With respect to states which did follow the exclusionary rule, it was virtually mandatory to discard the silver platter doctrine. To sanction the admission in federal court of evidence illegally seized in those states "not only frustrates state policy, but frustrates that policy in a particularly inappropriate and ironic way. For by admitting the unlawfully seized evidence the federal court serves to defeat the state's effort to assure obedience to the Federal Constitution."[32]

Finally, said Justice Stewart, "there is another consideration—the imperative of judicial integrity."[33] The federal courts must not allow themselves to become "accomplices in the willful disobedience of a Constitution they are sworn to uphold." And in determining the constitutionality of a state search whose fruits federal prosecutors sought to use, the federal courts would not be bound by the findings of the state courts but must determine for themselves whether the search, "if conducted by federal officers, would have violated the defendant's immunity from unreasonable searches and seizures under the Fourth Amendment. . . ."[34] If such proved to be the case, the evidence was inadmissible in federal court. The Court therefore sent the Elkins case back to the district court with instructions that a determination be made of the constitutionality of the search which uncovered the evidence used at the trial.

This last portion of the opinion was significant, for in requiring the federal courts to judge the constitutionality of a state search by reference to Fourth Amendment standards, the Court appeared to say that the "core" of the Fourth Amendment standards which the Wolf case had applied to the states amounted to nothing less than the full requirements of the amendment. If standards falling below Fourth Amendment requirements might be deemed constitutionally reasonable for state searches, why must Fourth Amendment standards determine whether their fruits are admissible in federal court? The Court, in effect, imperiled the Wolf doctrine of admissibility itself, for if the Fourteenth Amendment was now construed to impose the same constitutional standards on state officials as the Fourth

32. 364 U.S. 206, 221.
33. *Ibid.*, p. 222.
34. *Ibid.*, p. 223. While the opinion invoked the Court's supervisory power over the federal courts and did not mention constitutional grounds, the decision was later accorded constitutional status. See n. 72, *supra*.

Amendment did on federal officers, why not carry the analogy one step further and require the state courts, like the federal courts, to exclude unconstitutionally seized evidence? Though the Court did not take this step until the next year, the Elkins case marks the transitional point between the old doctrine and the new, yet to be born.

Justice Frankfurter, joined by Justices Clark, Harlan, and Whittaker, entered a vigorous dissent. He found no evidence of a "seemingly inexorable" movement toward exclusion in the states. The Court majority was impressed by the fact that roughly half the states now excluded illegally seized evidence; Frankfurter, on the contrary, was impressed by the fact that the other half did not. As for the Wolf case, it was "a complete misconception"[35] to assume that it equated the Fourth and Fourteenth Amendments with respect to standards for reasonable searches. The due process clause absorbed the Fourth Amendment's "core" only, not the entire amendment. He thought it a "fragile assumption" unverified by the facts to say that federal officers engaged in devious means of circumventing the exclusionary rule with the connivance of their state colleagues. "I would not so belittle this Court's authority,"[36] he asserted.

The new exclusionary rule, said Justice Frankfurter, "is pregnant with new disharmonies between federal and state authorities and between federal and state courts."[37] The difficulties were three. First, the federal rule required the exclusion of all illegally obtained evidence, whether in violation of the Constitution or of a statute. So all-embracing was the rule that the federal courts had never needed and never troubled to develop criteria to distinguish the unconstitutional from the merely illegal. In the absence of such criteria the federal courts would have great difficulty in determining the constitutionality of many state searches. Was, for example, the federal limitation on night search warrants required by the Constitution? Second, the new rule ignored considerations of comity. Since the criteria for determining the admissibility of evidence seized by a state were to be federally fashioned, it would be possible for evidence to be ruled inadmissible in the state courts and yet find its way into federal prosecutions because the federal courts would consider it constitutionally obtained. By way of illustration, he pointed out that the Court was remanding the Elkins case itself to the district court for a determination of the reasonableness of the search there involved, though the Oregon courts had found it to be illegal.

35. *Ibid.*, p. 238.
36. *Ibid.*, p. 243.
37. *Ibid.*

Third, even where federal and state standards were identical with respect to criteria of reasonableness, it was still possible for a federal court to find legal the same conduct that a state court did not; the state court might suppress the very evidence which the federal court would later admit. The concept of judicial integrity invoked by the Court in partial justification of the overthrow of the silver platter doctrine should be applied to show respect for the determination of state courts as to the legality of state searches.

If, said Justice Frankfurter, he were confronted with the choice, without alternative, of the old silver platter rule or the new rule excluding illegally seized state evidence from the federal courts, he would find the old rule "far more preferable."[38] But a third and compromise choice was available: he favored rejecting such evidence coming from states which had adopted an exclusionary policy[39] but continuing to admit it from those states which did not exclude. The three justices who had joined in the Frankfurter dissent, however, (Harlan, Clark, and Whittaker) refused to associate themselves with Frankfurter's solution. In a memorandum by Harlan, they expressed their preference for the old silver platter doctrine which they would have retained "intact" as "sound constitutional doctrine under our federal scheme of doing things. . . ."[40]

Obviously, a basic factor in the decision, though not sufficiently discussed, was the Court's conviction that the silver platter doctrine enabled federal officers to escape the consequences of the federal exclusionary rule by arranging for their state colleagues to search unlawfully in the aid of federal investigations. Whether such a subterfuge did in fact take place on any significant scale is impossible to determine, but the system contained the potential for enormous abuse by federal officers acting in co-operation with their state colleagues. "Theoretically, at least," wrote one scholar, "each could act wrongfully, turn the evidence over to the other and sit back and let the other prosecute its criminals and do its work for it."[41] The

38. *Ibid.*, p. 251.

39. State standards would determine the legality of the search. Frankfurter admitted that even with his solution certain difficulties would be encountered: (1) a motion to suppress granted in a lower court might not be a sound reflection of the state's judicial policy; (2) a state court might never have passed on the problem, and the federal judge would not know how to interpret state policy; (3) a state decision of inadmissibility might interfere with an important federal case. But these difficulties, he felt, were less consequential than those of the rule fashioned by the Court.

40. *Ibid.*, p. 252. Justice Harlan cited the Abbate and Bartkus cases in his support. See n. 2, *supra.*

41. Judson A. Parsons, "State-Federal Crossfire in Search and Seizure and Self-Incrimination," *Cornell Law Quarterly,* XLII (Spring, 1957), 346.

danger was especially great because the enormous overlap of federal and state crimes naturally led to a great deal of close co-operation, sometimes to the point of a virtual merging of facilities, between federal and state law enforcement officers dealing with common problems and hunting for criminals who had violated the laws of both jurisdictions.[42] The Federal Bureau of Investigation has referred to co-operation as "the backbone of effective law enforcement," and its director, J. Edgar Hoover, has commented that "[state] officers often have accompanied [F.B.I.] Agents on dangerous assignments when their aid was needed. Many cases which have been successfully investigated by the FBI originated from information supplied by city, county, state . . . officers."[43] "These men work shoulder to shoulder. . . ."[44] While such federal-state co-operation is, of course, both necessary and commendable, it probably led to abuses under the silver platter doctrine. In point is the statement of Thomas E. Dewey: "In dozens of cases in my own experience as a federal prosecutor we had to rely upon the evidence procured by the unhampered police of the State of New York or important criminals would have gone free."[45] This extensive collaboration by law enforcement officers of nation and state led Professor Kamisar to refer to the silver platter doctrine as "based largely on some metaphysics about separate and distinct federal and state law enforcement."[46] The Elkins decision thus probably demonstrated the Court majority's dissatisfaction with a doctrine which in reality barred only evidence showing overt federal participation because of "the extreme difficulty of proving joint participation [of a covert nature] in an unlawful seizure. . . ."[47] Justice Frankfurter's assertion that to suspect

42. The long catalogue of crimes common to both state and nation includes possession and sale of narcotics, certain types of embezzlement, the sending of threatening or exhortative communications through the mail, fleeing from justice, fraud, bank robbery, kidnapping, and illegal transportation of liquor, lottery tickets, obscene matter, stolen goods, and automobiles. Alan C. Kohn, "Admissibility in Federal Court of Evidence Illegally Seized by State Officers," *Washington University Law Quarterly*, Vol. 1959 (June, 1959), pp. 229, 253.

43. Federal Bureau of Investigation, *Cooperation: The Backbone of Effective Law Enforcement* (Washington, n.d.), Introduction.

44. John Edgar Hoover, "Cooperation: The Key to Effective Law Enforcement in America," *Syracuse Law Review*, XII (Fall, 1960), 1, 4.

45. Quoted in Gerald H. Galler, "The Exclusion of Illegal State Evidence in Federal Courts," *Journal of Criminal Law*, XLIX (January–February, 1955), 455, 457, n. 15, citing statement of Thomas E. Dewey, *N.Y. Constitutional Convention*, Revised Record 372 (1938).

46. Kamisar, "*Wolf* and *Lustig*," p. 1180.

47. Galler, "Exclusion," p. 458. On the question of improper federal-state law enforcement co-operation, see the debate in *Bartkus* v. *Illinois*, 359 U.S. 121 (1959), where, under the "twin sovereignties" principle of federalism, the Court upheld a conviction for bank robbery obtained in a state court following the defendant's acquittal on a similar charge in federal court. Despite a high degree of co-operation

subterfuge on the part of federal officers is to "belittle this Court's authority" is easily answered. The Constitution itself prohibits unreasonable searches, yet it was deemed necessary to devise and apply the exclusionary rule to deter federal officers from violating the prohibition.

It is not difficult to see why the Court majority rejected Justice Frankfurter's contention that federalism required the retention of the silver platter doctrine. They refused to accept the argument that the principle of federalism is undermined by the formulation of rules of procedure to govern a federal prosecution in a federal court. In fact, the opposite seems to be true: federalism does not require that the procedural rules of the nation's courts be determined by the policies of the states. That federal and state courts may disagree on the constitutionality of a search is, as Justice Frankfurter himself said in a different context, "a price to be paid for our federalism."[48] The Court did not recognize any impairment of the federal principle when, in construing a statute, it unanimously held that evidence acquired through an illegal state wire tap must be suppressed in the federal courts,[49] though a state court is not prevented from receiving it in evidence.[50]

Finally, Justice Frankfurter argued that the decision would burden the federal judiciary with the task of determining for the first time which federal search rules are constitutional in origin, and therefore relevant to the states as well, and which are of a mere statutory nature, applicable only to the federal government. But such a clarification was long overdue, especially if, as Frankfurter contended, the due process clause applied only the "core" of the Fourth Amendment's prohibition to the states. A constitutional principle which is not spelled out places no obligations on those whose exercise of power it is designed to limit.

---

between federal and state prosecutors (some of the evidence had even been gathered by federal agents *after* the federal acquittal), Justice Frankfurter, speaking for the Court, said that the facts did "not sustain a conclusion that the state prosecution was a show and a cover for a federal prosecution, and thereby in essential fact another federal prosecution." *Ibid.*, p. 124. Justice Brennan, dissenting, came to the conclusion that the degree of co-operation was such as to make the state trial "a second federal prosecution." *Ibid.*, pp. 165–66. The difficulty of proving the existence of co-operation and the ease with which the Supreme Court was misled in the Bartkus case is forcefully driven home by Professor Broeder, who writes: "I happened to be in the federal courtroom when the jury came in with the acquittal. Judge Perry, the presiding judge, flew into a rage . . . and personally directed the United States District Attorney to have a state criminal prosecution for robbing the same bank instituted immediately." Dale W. Broeder, "Wong Sun v. United States: A Study in Faith and Hope," *Nebraska Law Review*, XLII (April, 1963), 483, 619, n. 487.

48. *Knapp* v. *Schweitzer*, 357 U.S. 371, 380 (1958).
49. *Benanti* v. *United States*, 355 U.S. 96 (1957).
50. *Schwartz* v. *Texas*, 344 U.S. 199 (1952).

So in the Elkins case the Court was moving forward in two directions. Not only did it repudiate the silver platter doctrine, but it also appeared to be expanding the Fourteenth Amendment's protection against unreasonable searches from its previous "core of the Fourth Amendment" position to one coextensive with the Fourth Amendment in its entirety. In so doing, the Court took the last step on the road to *Mapp* v. *Ohio*,[51] decided in 1961, in which the Wolf doctrine was formally repudiated and the exclusionary rule was applied to the states.

At this point, however, the narrative must be interrupted to record an inconsistent decision in the interlude between the Elkins and Mapp cases. As the Court in the Elkins decision took one step forward and abandoned the silver platter doctrine, it almost simultaneously took a backward step in a "reverse silver platter" situation. While the silver platter doctrine permitted federal prosecutions to utilize evidence illegally seized by the states, the reverse silver platter permitted state prosecutions to introduce evidence illegally seized by federal officials. The reverse silver platter was not an officially formulated doctrine, but it followed from the fact that the states were permitted to use *all* illegally seized evidence, whether federal or state in origin. What the Elkins case had done to the silver platter doctrine, the Rea case, it was thought, did to the reverse silver platter, although indirectly. By requiring the federal courts, at the victim's request, to enjoin federal officers from turning over to the states unlawfully seized evidence, the Court was presumed to have struck down the reverse silver platter. That this belief was only partially justified became evident in *Wilson* v. *Schnettler*.[52] In this case, following an allegedly illegal search by federal narcotics agents in Illinois, the evidence was turned over to state officers to further a prosecution against Wilson in the state courts. Nevertheless, his plea for injunctive relief was denied by the Court. In an opinion by Justice Whittaker, the Rea case was differentiated as having involved a prior federal court proceeding where the evidence was ordered suppressed; therefore, in turning it over to the state, the federal agent would have violated the district court's directive. Here, however, no federal proceeding prior to the state trial had taken place. The Court said, in effect, that federal agents were free to use their unlawful seizures to assist state prosecutions so long as they did not first bring them into federal court!

51. 367 U.S. 643 (1961).
52. 365 U.S. 381 (1961).

It is small wonder that one scholar was led to characterize the decision as "one of the most unconvincing and hairsplitting . . . to come from the Court in decades. . . ."[53] Justice Douglas, author of the Court's opinion in the Rea case, was less charitable. In a dissenting opinion joined by Chief Justice Warren and Justice Brennan, he stated that he regarded the Wilson decision as repudiating "the very basis of the *Rea* decision"[54] and as "an invitation to lawlessness"[55] on the part of federal officers. The Wilson case illustrates perfectly Justice Frankfurter's observation that "the course of true law pertaining to searches and seizures, as enunciated here, has not—to put it mildly—run smooth."[56]

Less than four months after the Wilson case came the landmark decision of *Mapp* v. *Ohio*,[57] which completed the logic of the Elkins case and brought the states into alignment with the federal government in the constitutional law of search and seizure by directing that they too must exclude from trials evidence seized in violation of the Constitution. The decision was announced by Justice Clark, who had served notice seven years earlier that he would vote to overrule the Wolf decision as soon as "needed converts"[58] were available.

The facts in the case reflected no credit on the Cleveland police department. One day in 1957, three policemen appeared at the home of Miss Dollree Mapp in that city and demanded to be admitted. They wished, they said, to question her, but they refused to give any further information. They did not tell her that they had come in response to a tip that a suspect wanted in a bombing incident was hiding in the house and had in his possession a quantity of gambling paraphernalia. Miss Mapp telephoned her attorney, who advised her to deny entry to the officers unless they produced a search warrant. Frustrated, they took up a vigil outside the house for about three hours, after which they were joined by at least four more officers. The police then forced their way into the house and, upon the arrival of Miss Mapp's attorney, refused to let him see her. When Miss Mapp demanded that they produce a search warrant,

53. Broeder, "The Decline and Fall of *Wolf v. Colorado*," *Nebraska Law Review*, XLI (December, 1961), 185, 193.
54. 365 U.S. 381, 394.
55. *Ibid.*, p. 398.
56. *Chapman* v. *United States*, 365 U.S. 610, 618 (1961) (concurring opinion).
57. 367 U.S. 643 (1961).
58. *Irvine* v. *California*, 347 U.S. 128, 139 (1954) (concurring opinion).

one of the officers waved a piece of paper in front of her, which apparently was not a warrant, for it was not produced at the trial. Miss Mapp seized the "warrant," and concealed it on her person in the evident belief that at least her bodily privacy was safe from intrusion, but she was mistaken. Following a struggle, the officers retrieved the paper, handcuffed her, and imprisoned her in the bedroom. In the course of their subsequent search, during which they ransacked the house and even went through Miss Mapp's personal papers and a photograph album, they found neither the suspect nor the gambling equipment. In the basement, however, they did discover a trunk containing allegedly obscene material. Miss Mapp disclaimed ownership, saying the material had been left behind by a former boarder, but she was nevertheless convicted on an obscenity charge and sentenced to prison. The Ohio Supreme Court agreed that the search was lawless but held that the conviction must stand because Ohio followed the common-law rule of admissibility (oddly enough, four of the seven judges thought the obscenity statute under which Miss Mapp was convicted to be unconstitutional, but they could not reverse the conviction because under Ohio law a finding of unconstitutionality requires the assent of at least six of the seven members of the state supreme court).

One remarkable feature of the case was the fact that at no time did Miss Mapp's counsel ask the Court to overrule *Wolf* v. *Colorado,* nor did he so much as cite it in his brief. In oral argument, in fact, when questioned from the bench as to whether he was seeking to have the Wolf case overruled, "counsel expressly disavowed any such purpose."[59] The American Civil Liberties Union alone, in a concluding paragraph of its *amicus curiae* brief, urged the Court to overrule the Wolf case. All this lends credence to the charge of Justice Harlan in dissent that the majority of the Court "simply 'reached out' to overrule"[60] the Wolf case. To this charge, however, Justice Clark replied that Miss Mapp "chose to urge what may have appeared to be the surer ground for favorable disposition"[61] of her case. Much the same reply was made by Justice Douglas in a concurring opinion. "It is true," he said, "that argument was mostly directed to another issue in the case, but that is often the fact."[62] Nonetheless, and granting that the issue had been canvassed in previous cases, there is no reason why the Court could not, and every reason why it should, have called for reargument on the ex-

59. 367 U.S. 643, 673, n. 6 (dissenting opinion of Justice Harlan).
60. *Ibid.*, p. 674 (dissenting opinion of Justice Harlan).
61. *Ibid.*, p. 646, n. 3.
62. *Ibid.*, p. 671.

clusionary question. Justice Stewart, author of the Court's opinion in the Elkins case, was so disturbed by the *manner* in which the Court had decided the Mapp case that he submitted a memorandum associating himself "fully" with Harlan's strictures on this point and refused to express any "view as to the merits of the constitutional [search] issue."[63] He did, however, agree that the conviction must be reversed because the Ohio statute was unconstitutional on First Amendment grounds of free speech and press.

Justice Clark's opinion laid the basis for the decision by announcing that, in the Court's view, the federal exclusionary rule "is of constitutional origin" notwithstanding "some passing references" in some cases to the rule "as being one of evidence."[64] It would have proved difficult to justify an exclusionary rule for the states if the federal rule itself were not constitutionally required but merely a product of the Court's supervisory power over the federal courts, a power that does not extend to the state courts. Furthermore, said Clark, the exclusionary rule was as much part of the Fourteenth Amendment as of the Fourth, for it was "an essential part of the right to privacy. . . . To hold otherwise is to grant the right but in reality to withhold its privilege and enjoyment."[65] "[W]ithout that rule the freedom from state invasions of privacy would be so ephemeral and so nearly severed from its conceptual nexus with the freedom from all brutish means of coercing evidence as not to merit this Court's high regard as a freedom 'implicit in the concept of ordered liberty.' "[66]

The decision in the Wolf case not to impose the exclusionary rule on the states, said Clark, was based on two "factual considerations":[67] first, most of the state courts had rejected the rule, and second, remedies other than exclusion of the illegally seized evidence were available as deterrents against unlawful searches. These considerations were now undermined. A majority of the states as of 1961 had adopted the exclusionary rule in whole or in part, and, moreover, they had done so in the conviction that the other remedies urged were useless. Clark regarded the decision as merely the logical culmination of the cases discussed earlier in this chapter. He pointed to the fact that there was no other constitutional right which the Court had enforced less strictly against the states than against the federal government. No such distinction between the nation and the

63. *Ibid.*, p. 686.
64. *Ibid.*, p. 649.
65. *Ibid.*, p. 656.
66. *Ibid.*, p. 655.
67. *Ibid.*, p. 653.

states had been made in the enforcement of First Amendment liberties or with respect to the requirements deemed necessary for a fair trial. The fact that evidence obtained in an illegal search was trustworthy was quite irrelevant to the exclusionary question. Only that year the Court had served notice in *Rogers* v. *Richmond*[68] that a coerced confession, however reliable, was inadmissible in a state proceeding. "Why should not the same rule apply to what is tantamount to coerced testimony by way of unconstitutional seizure . . . ?"[69]

As for the issue of federalism, Justice Clark said that the decision, far from promoting conflict between federal and state courts, would actually foster amity. Hereafter, "there would be no need to reconcile such cases as *Rea* and [*Wilson* v.] *Schnettler*, each pointing up hazardous uncertainties of our heretofore ambivalent approach."[70] Justice Clark, a former United States Attorney General who presumably knew whereof he spoke, asserted that the lack of an exclusionary policy in many of the states served to "encourage disobedience"[71] to constitutional standards on the part of federal officers and that a "double standard" had arisen, with federal officers "step[ping] across the street" to deliver unconstitutionally seized evidence to state authorities. The decision would promote federal-state cooperation in law enforcement activities, "if only by recognition of their now mutual obligation to respect the same fundamental criteria in their approach."[72] The exclusionary rule was not likely to impair effective law enforcement in the states, and, in any event, there was a more important consideration—the maintenance of constitutional standards. "Nothing can destroy a government more quickly than its failure to observe its own laws, or worse, its disregard of the charter of its own existence."[73] In summation he said: "Our decision, founded on reason and truth, gives to the individual no more than that which the Constitution guarantees him, to the police officer no less than that to which honest law enforcement is entitled, and, to the courts, that judicial integrity so necessary in the true administration of justice."[74]

68. 365 U.S. 534 (1961).
69. 367 U.S. 643, 656.
70. *Ibid.*, p. 658. Justice Clark was himself a member of the majority in each of these "ambivalent" cases.
71. *Ibid.*, p. 657.
72. *Ibid.*, p. 658. Clark added that "the fruits of an unconstitutional search . . . [would henceforth be] inadmissible in both state and federal courts, . . . [and] inducement to evasion . . . eliminated." Thus the silver platter and reverse silver platter situations are constitutionally forbidden. There is one constitutional standard, protected by both the Fourth and Fourteenth Amendments, and a violation of either amendment renders the evidence inadmissible in both federal and state courts.
73. *Ibid.*, p. 659.
74. *Ibid.*, p. 660.

Justice Clark's grounding of the exclusionary rule in the search and seizure prohibition itself, as implicitly derived from its requirements, did not, however, win the assent of Justice Black, who concurred separately. He expressed the view that the Fourth Amendment, "considered together with the Fifth Amendment's ban against self-incrimination,"[75] gave the exclusionary rule constitutional standing. In so saying, he repudiated the view he previously took in the Wolf case that the exclusionary rule was not required by the Constitution.[76] Black thought the Court's action "dissipates the doubt and uncertainty in this field of constitutional law."[77] In another concurring opinion, Justice Douglas also took the view that "a storm of constitutional controversy . . . today finds its end,"[78] and assailed the Wolf decision as not representing "the voice of reason or principle."[79]

Justice Harlan, speaking also for Justices Frankfurter and Whittaker, entered a blistering dissent. He expressed disapproval of the way in which the Court had turned a case raising a First Amendment issue into one raising a search and seizure question, and he hinted broadly that reversal of the conviction on First Amendment grounds would have enlisted the support of a unanimous Court. Turning to the constitutional question, Harlan entertained "considerable doubt"[80] that the federal exclusionary rule was required by the Constitution. But even assuming that it was required, it did not follow that the exclusionary rule should be imposed on the states, for the Wolf case had not made "the Fourth Amendment *as such* . . . enforceable against the States,"[81] but merely its core. The decision was destructive of the federal principle; the different states, with varying problems of crime control, should be allowed to deal with the unlawful search problem as they saw fit. The direct impact of previous extensions of the exclusionary rule, such as the overthrow of the silver platter doctrine, fell on federal courts and officials, whatever its indirect effects on the state courts. The coerced confession doctrine, said Harlan, was not in point. In fact, it "works strongly *against*"[82] the Court's decision. In excluding involuntary confessions the Court was concerned "not with an appropriate remedy for what the police

75. *Ibid.*, p. 662.
76. *Wolf* v. *Colorado*, 338 U.S. 25, 39–40 (1949).
77. 367 U.S. 643, 666.
78. *Ibid.*, p. 670.
79. *Ibid.*, p. 669.
80. *Ibid.*, p. 678.
81. *Ibid.*, p. 679.
82. *Ibid.*, p. 685.

have done"[83] but with preserving the vitality of the accusatorial system of justice. This system requires that a defendant not be convicted with the use of statements wrung from him unwillingly. "[T]his is a *procedural right* and . . . its violation occurs at the time his improperly obtained statement is admitted at trial. . . ."[84] Harlan considered the decision to be one "not likely to promote respect either for the Court's adjudication process or for the stability of its decisions"[85] and sharply admonished his colleagues of the majority for having handed down a decision "so unwise in principle . . . that our voice becomes only a voice of power, not of reason."[86]

Neither the majority opinion nor the dissent in the Mapp case is wholly free of ambiguity. To take the majority opinion first, the fact that a bare majority of the states had adopted the exclusionary rule could scarcely be considered as undermining the premise (assuming one accepts this as a valid premise) that the practices of the states are important guidelines for determining the content of due process. Nearly half of the states had not adopted the exclusionary rule, and among those that had were several which followed a policy of only partial exclusion. Furthermore, Clark stressed the importance of judicial integrity as a consideration in requiring the exclusionary rule for the state courts. This is a consideration which may have considerable potency when the Court is acting in its supervisory role over the federal courts, as it did in the Elkins case, but it is difficult to see where the Constitution empowers the Court to supervise the judicial integrity of the state courts. On the other hand, Harlan's elucidation of the coerced confessions doctrine is at variance with the plain import of a number of decisions over the last two decades[87] which have had as an important purpose the prevention of unfair procedures by the states in the acquisition of evidence. These decisions were designed quite as much to deter improper police conduct prior to trial as to ensure that the accusatorial system not be impaired through the use of such evidence in the courtroom. Moreover, as Professor Francis A. Allen notes, the "reasons for wishing to preserve the 'accusatorial' system of justice must surely include a desire that citizens be spared improper official aggressions before trial."[88]

83. *Ibid.*, p. 684.
84. *Ibid.*, p. 685.
85. *Ibid.*, p. 677.
86. *Ibid.*, p. 686.
87. At least since *Ashcraft* v. *Tennessee*, 322 U.S. 143 (1944).
88. Allen, "Federalism and the Fourth Amendment," p. 31.

There appears to be no sound reason why the exclusionary rule should not be required of the states if that is the best practical way to secure freedom from unreasonable searches for those to whom such freedom is guaranteed. Since Justice Frankfurter described the freedom from unreasonable searches as "central to enjoyment of the other guarantees in the Bill of Rights,"[89] it seems impossible to justify lower standards of enforcement against the states in this sphere than for the protection of other constitutional rights. As Professor Paulsen wrote, "the other freedoms, freedom of speech, of assembly, of religion, of political action, presuppose that arbitrary and capricious police action has been restrained. Security in one's home and person is the fundamental without which there can be no liberty."[90] With its decision to exclude from state prosecutions evidence seized in violation of the Constitution, the Court finally reconciled constitutional practice with constitutional theory and sought to give to the right to privacy the substance which might make it viable.

The most important question raised in the aftermath of the Mapp case was only lightly touched upon in Justice Clark's opinion. Did the decision mean that the Court would continue to apply the doctrine of *Wolf* v. *Colorado* that only protections at the "core" of the Fourth Amendment were safeguarded against state action, with the difference that seizures made in violation of these "core" rights would no longer be admissible? Or did the decision mean that the due process clause imposed the full force of the Fourth Amendment's standards of "reasonableness" on the states? If only the "core" protections were to apply, the states would retain a great deal of latitude in fashioning search and seizure rules; so long as they adhered to canons of "fundamental fairness," their discretion as to the content of the rules would presumably be complete. If, however, the Fourth Amendment's standard was taken over intact into due process, the area of state discretion would, of course, be considerably narrowed.

The Elkins case, as we have seen, indicated that the Court had made the due process protection coextensive with that of the Fourth Amendment. In his opinion in the Mapp case, Justice Clark included a cryptic phrase which appeared to confirm this belief. Henceforth, said Clark, federal and state officers would be obligated to respect

89. *Harris* v. *United States*, 331 U.S. 145, 163 (1947) (dissenting opinion).
90. Monrad G. Paulsen, "The Exclusionary Rule and Misconduct by the Police," *Journal of Criminal Law*, LII (September–October, 1961), 255, 264.

"the *same* fundamental criteria"[91] when conducting search and seizure. The following year a dictum in an opinion of the Court by Justice Stewart added strength to this conclusion. After citing the provisions of the Fourth Amendment, Stewart went on to say: "We may take it as settled that the Fourteenth Amendment gives to the people *like protection* against the conduct of the officials of any State."[92] Nevertheless, the Court had not spoken clearly on the matter; suggestion and backhanded comment are no substitute for forthright discussion.[93] In the 1963 case of *Ker* v. *California*,[94] whatever doubt that remained was finally dispelled.

A number of questions were before the Court for resolution in this case, but only two of these need concern us here.[95] The first, which has been discussed above, was that of whether the states were now required to abide by Fourth Amendment standards in search and seizure. In the event that this question was answered in the affirmative, the further question arose of whether those standards had been violated in this case.

The first question was quickly disposed of. In an impressive display of near-unanimity, the Court, speaking through Justice Clark, held that "the standard of reasonableness is the same under the Fourth and Fourteenth Amendments. . . ."[96] Only Justice Harlan disagreed. He would have preferred to stay with the old rule that only state searches which violated principles of "fundamental fairness"[97] were forbidden by the due process clause. Among the reasons he advanced for this view was the belief that to subject the states to federal constitutional standards would place them "in an atmosphere of uncertainty since this Court's decisions in the realm of search and seizure are hardly noted for their predictability."[98]

As if to provide forceful corroboration for Harlan's comment, the eight justices who had agreed that the requirements of the Fourth Amendment set the standards for state searches promptly proceeded to divide equally in seeking to apply those standards to the search in

91. 367 U.S. 643, 658 (1961). (Emphasis supplied.)
92. *Lanza* v. *New York*, 370 U.S. 139, 142 (1962). (Emphasis supplied.)
93. A number of commentators were not convinced that the straws in the wind cited above could be regarded as conclusive evidence that the Court intended to equate Fourth Amendment and due process standards. See, e.g., Roger J. Traynor, "Mapp v. Ohio at Large in the Fifty States," *Duke Law Journal*, Vol. 1962 (Summer, 1962), p. 319; Rex A. Collings, Jr., "Toward Workable Rules of Search and Seizure—An Amicus Curiae Brief," *California Law Review*, L (August, 1962), 421.
94. 374 U.S. 23 (1963).
95. One of the other questions raised in this case—whether the search made incidental to the arrest exceeded constitutional limits—is discussed in Chapter IV.
96. 374 U.S. 23, 33.
97. *Ibid.*, p. 46.
98. *Ibid.*, p. 45.

the Ker case. The case involved a furtive entry into Ker's apartment by California policemen, who had come to arrest him for a violation of state narcotics law. They obtained a passkey from the building superintendent and, stealing in quietly to avoid destruction of evidence, surprised Ker, who was sitting in the living room reading a newspaper. In the kitchen, in plain view of the officers, was a "brick" of marijuana, which was seized and which provided the evidence for Ker's subsequent conviction. Four of the justices thought that the furtive entry by the officers was in violation of Fourth Amendment standards; the other four disagreed. Justice Harlan, without passing on this question at all, cast the deciding vote to sustain the conviction on the ground that the facts of the case showed no violation of "fundamental fairness" by the police.

Germane to the Ker case was a previous decision, *Miller* v. *United States*.[99] In the Miller case the Court held invalid the arrest of a defendant and the subsequent search of his dwelling in the District of Columbia because the federal officers who had come to arrest him broke down his door without first properly identifying themselves and stating their purpose. No constitutional grounds were mentioned in Justice Brennan's opinion for the Court. Instead, the opinion emphasized that announcement of authority and statement of purpose were required by District of Columbia law,[100] and the evidence was ordered suppressed.

In the Ker case Justice Clark, speaking also for Justices Black, Stewart, and White, announced the decision of the Court sustaining the conviction. The furtive entry into Ker's dwelling was legal under California law, said Clark, and the nonconstitutional ground on which the Miller decision was based indicated that the federal requirement of announcement was not of constitutional dimension. Clark did, however, limit the decision to "the particular circumstances of this case."[101] Past experience of the police with narcotics offenders had shown that modern plumbing can quickly and easily dispose of evidence; in Ker's case the fear of destruction of evidence was even greater than usual because there "was ground for the belief that he might well have been expecting the police."[102]

Justice Brennan, whose dissenting opinion was joined by Chief Justice Warren and Justices Douglas and Goldberg, engaged in a

99. 357 U.S. 301 (1958).
100. There is no such requirement in the federal Rules of Criminal Procedure. The decision, in the light of the Ker case, is therefore limited to federal arrests made in the District of Columbia.
101. 374 U.S. 23, 40–41.
102. *Ibid.*, p. 40.

lengthy historical explication of the announcement requirement. It was deeply rooted in English and American law. He could not find a single English case which had dispensed with it. Some early American state cases did recognize exceptions, but only where there was no longer any reason for making announcement, as in the case of a felon in flight from arresting officers, who obviously knows their purpose when they invade the dwelling in which he has taken refuge.[103]

Failure by the police officers to announce themselves should, said Brennan, render any resulting arrest and search constitutionally "unreasonable." "Innocent citizens should not suffer the shock, fright or embarrassment attendant upon an unannounced police intrusion.[104] The requirement also serves to protect the police, who might otherwise be mistaken for prowlers and shot. His majority opinion in the Miller case was not based on constitutional grounds, said Brennan, only because of the "usual practice of the Court not to decide constitutional questions when a nonconstitutional basis for decision is available."[105]

The Ker case presents a classical example of the difficulty of determining "reasonableness" in some search and seizure situations. The arguments on both sides can be compelling. Modern plumbing does provide a ready means of disposing of evidence; on the other hand, furtive entry into the dwelling seems contrary to the principles of a civilized society, especially in view of the fact that the individual who is arrested or whose home is searched might prove to be innocent. The furtive entry into the Ker house took place after dark, and, as Justice Brennan noted, "such timing appears to be a common police practice, at least in California."[106]

The Ker case is merely suggestive of the problems related to state searches which the Court will have to deal with in order to give effect to the decision in the Mapp case. As might be expected, the lower federal courts have been responsible for much of the development of federal search law, with the Supreme Court offering guidelines in the occasional search cases which it decides. An incredible variety of search and seizure problems has been faced by the lower federal courts and by the courts of the exclusionary states, to which the Supreme Court has not yet directed its attention.

103. Brennan's historical analysis is subjected to strong criticism in G. Robert Blakey, "The Rule of Announcement and Unlawful Entry: Miller v. United States and Ker v. California," *University of Pennsylvania Law Review*, CXII (February, 1964), 499.

104. 374 U.S. 23, 57.

105. *Ibid.*, p. 53.

106. *Ibid.*, p. 52.

It appears that the great majority of Supreme Court decisions relating to federal searches were based on constitutional considerations and therefore now apply to state searches as well. Nearly all of the cases dealing with "standing," probable cause, the rule forbidding the seizure of "mere evidence," search incidental to arrest, and search of automobiles have been decided on constitutional grounds. Even so, huge gaps in the law remain. The "mere evidence" rule, for instance, is in need of a good deal of clarification; the Court has never clearly specified the nature of an "instrument of crime," which, unlike "mere evidence," is seizable. Again, how "fresh" do the facts necessary to establish probable cause have to be? In automobile search cases the Court has allowed a finding of probable cause on facts that were months old, but the automobile presents a peculiar problem, and it is virtually certain that similar leniency would not prevail in the search of a dwelling.[107] Another problem requiring particular attention is that of "consent." When the householder consents to a warrantless search by the police, he in effect waives his constitutional rights and cannot later object to the use in court of any incriminating evidence uncovered. But whether consent was indeed granted in any particular case is often a matter of the policeman's word against that of the defendant. Even where the facts are not in dispute, the "consent" may not have been truly voluntary: the householder may be overawed by the sight of the uniformed policeman at the door and perhaps even be unaware that he has a right to refuse admission. The effect of the Mapp decision would be vitiated if "consents" that were possibly coerced were not

107. In *Sgro* v. *United States*, 287 U.S. 206 (1932), the Court ruled that a United States Commissioner could not revalidate an old warrant which had expired without being served during the allowable limit of ten days simply by redating it on the basis of the old affidavit. Justices Stone and Cardozo dissented. While the decision appears to have been based on statutory grounds, the Court added, "it is manifest that the proof must be of facts so closely related to the time of the issue of the warrant as to justify a finding of probable cause at that time." *Ibid*., p. 210.

A number of other probable cause questions need clarification: for instance, is it permissible to arrest for a particular crime two persons, against each of whom probable cause has been established, when it is certain that the crime was not committed by more than one individual? Are the standards for probable cause the same for all crimes, or can a distinction be drawn between more and less serious crimes, as suggested by Justice Jackson? *Brinegar* v. *United States*, 338 U.S. 160, 183 (1949) (dissenting opinion). Similarly, can a distinction be drawn between high crime and low crime neighborhoods, as the Court did in the automobile cases? Is flight from an officer sufficient to establish probable cause? In *Wong Sun* v. *United States* (371 U.S. 471, 482 [1963], it was held that the defendant's flight was "ambiguous conduct" insufficient to establish probable cause. But there the decision was limited to the particular circumstances of the case: the officer identified himself as a federal narcotics agent only after telling the defendant (a laundry owner) that he was calling to collect his laundry. Must probable cause focus on a particular individual before police officers can enter a dwelling to make an arrest, or is it sufficient for them to know that someone inside is committing a crime? In *Johnson* v. *United States* (333 U.S. 10 [1948]),

given careful scrutiny.[108] The Court has ruled that a "consent" granted by a hotel clerk to search a room occupied by a guest is worthless,[109] as is the consent of a landlord to search a building he has let to someone else even though under local law the landlord has a right of entry for certain purposes.[110] In one case, decided as far back as 1921, the Court rejected, as coerced, a "consent" granted to officers who simply announced that they had come to make a search, but it did not reach the crucial question of whether a wife can consent to a search of the dwelling and, in effect, waive her husband's constitutional rights.[111]

Another area in need of clarification is that of arrest law. The Ker decision specifically imposed Fourth Amendment standards on arrests, as well as searches, made by state officers. It seems safe to say, therefore, that for a felony arrest to meet constitutional standards a showing of probable cause is required. But does a misdemeanor arrest (for a crime not committed in the presence of the officer) require a warrant, in line with common-law precedent? Since the classification of crimes as felonies and misdemeanors is a legislative prerogative, it would seem foolhardy to read into the Constitution a requirement that could be circumvented by simple legislative reclassification of the crime. Most states require prompt arraignment following an arrest, yet it is common police practice to disregard this requirement and detain the suspect for interrogation. Is the federal McNabb-Mallory Rule,[112] requiring the exclusion of a confession

---

it was held that an officer who smelled opium fumes coming from a hotel room had not established probable cause to enter and arrest the occupant because at the time of entry he did not know whether it was the occupant or someone else who was smoking the opium. This case was decided during a period when the Court construed the Fourth Amendment's protection very broadly (e.g., *Trupiano* v. *United States*, 334 U.S. 699 [1948]), and it might no longer be valid. It is common police practice to enter and arrest in such circumstances. Probable cause is the most flexible of the Fourth Amendment's standards, and the Court might decide to allow the states more latitude here than in any other Fourth Amendment requirement.

108. Professor Weinstein writes that in New York, following the Mapp case, policemen "politely knocked on doors and suggested that they would welcome an invitation to enter instead of forcing their way in as they had been known to do in the past. Addicts, for their part, welcomed police visitors as honored guests instead of fleeing to the roofs through fire escapes." Jack B. Weinstein, "Local Responsibility for Improvement of Search and Seizure Practices," *Rocky Mountain Law Review*, XXXIV (Winter, 1962), 150, 169, n. 101.

109. *Stoner* v. *California*, 376 U.S. 483 (1964).

110. *Chapman* v. *United States*, 365 U.S. 610 (1961).

111. *Amos* v. *United States*, 255 U.S. 313 (1921). Another case in which the Court found that a "consent" had been coerced is *Johnson* v. *United States*, 333 U.S. 10 (1948).

112. *McNabb* v. *United States*, 318 U.S. 332 (1943); *Mallory* v. *United States*, 354 U.S. 449 (1957). These decisions implemented Rule 5(a) of the federal Rules of Criminal Procedure, which requires prompt arraignment before a magistrate.

obtained while the suspect was held without prompt arraignment, constitutional in origin?[113] Does the stopping of a suspect on the street briefly and the request that he identify himself constitute an arrest for which probable cause must first be established? The law of arrest is one of the largest uncharted areas of the Fourth Amendment.[114] Very few arrest cases have been decided by the Supreme Court because of "the fact that an unlawful arrest does not deprive the court of jurisdiction to try an offender, so that there has been no occasion comparable to that created by the exclusionary rule to probe the constitutional limits of the arrest power."[115] Almost the only occasions on which the Court has decided on the legality of an arrest have been in some cases of search incidental to arrest,[116] for while an invalid arrest does not free the defendant, evidence seized in a search incidental to such an arrest must be excluded. Where the status of the arrest is in doubt, therefore, that question must be decided in order to determine the legality of the search.

113. Dean Edward L. Barrett, Jr., writes (letter to the author dated February 15, 1965):

> Personally, I would regard it as catastrophic to have a rule which purported to require that every arrested person be taken immediately to a court and charged with an offense. Effective screening of the innocent from the guilty is now performed primarily by police and prosecutors. I have very little confidence in magistrates being equipped to assume this function—especially since the only information available to them at this immediate point would be that presented by the police or by the defendant himself. In fact, I predict that as counsel are made available to defendants earlier in the process there will be a pressure from the defense side to delay this first judicial appearance in order to give the defense lawyer a chance to consult with the prosecutor and have some influence upon the charges to be filed, if any. Certainly that is our experience in California where defense lawyers, particularly public defenders, often are brought in contact with their clients shortly after arrest. . . . The best way that I know to feel better about the performance of police is to watch the performance of a magistrate in an arraignment court in a large metropolitan area. A case could certainly be made that the individual rights and dignity of the accused are accorded far greater respect while in police custody than they are in the context of this routine initial judicial appearance.

For the view that the McNabb-Mallory rule should be accorded constitutional status, see Weinstein, "Local Responsibility," pp. 162–63, and Broeder, "Wong Sun," pp. 564ff.

114. An excellent article on the subject is by Richard M. Leagre, "The Fourth Amendment and the Law of Arrest," *Journal of Criminal Law*, LIV (December, 1963), 393. Since 1789, state law has determined the legality of a federal arrest where there is no controlling federal statute. See *United States* v. *Di Re*, 332 U.S. 581, 589–91 (1948).

115. Caleb Foote, "Law and Police Practice: Safeguards in the Law of Arrest," *Northwestern University Law Review*, LII (March–April, 1957), 16, 40. The Supreme Court has on a number of occasions stated that where the suspect himself rather than the evidence was illegally seized the federal courts need not go beyond the question of guilt or innocence. *Ker* v. *Illinois*, 119 U.S. 436 (1886); *Mahon* v. *Justice*, 127 U.S. 700 (1888); *Frisbie* v. *Collins*, 342 U.S. 519 (1952). The explanation for the difference between illegal arrest and illegal search in this connection probably lies in the fact that exclusion of illegally seized evidence does not close off the possibility of prosecution for the crime charged: other, legally obtained, evidence might come to light at a later date. In the case of illegal arrest, however, the freeing of the defendant would confer immunity to prosecution.

116. E.g., *Henry* v. *United States*, 361 U.S. 98 (1959).

In all of the state search cases on which the Court has ruled since the Ker case, strict Fourth Amendment standards were applied. Thus it was held that the standards of particularity which the warrant must meet are the same under both the Fourth and Fourteenth Amendments;[117] that while "an affidavit . . . need not reflect the direct personal observations of the affiant . . . the magistrate must be informed of . . . some of the underlying circumstances from which the officer concluded that the informant . . . was 'credible' or his information 'reliable' ";[118] that the unsupported word of an informer who has not previously proved his reliability is insufficient to establish probable cause;[119] that the search of a room cannot be justified as incidental to arrest when the occupant was not in the room at the time the police called and no arrest in fact took place;[120] and that the exclusionary rule may be invoked not only in criminal proceedings but also in forfeiture cases.[121] The trend of decisions thus far encourages the hope that Justice Harlan's fear that the Mapp and Ker decisions would lead to "derogation of law enforcement standards in the federal system"[122] because of the pressure on the Court "to avoid unduly fettering the States"[123] will prove groundless. Nevertheless, the fear is not altogether fanciful, and the Court should not have neglected to explain why it had imposed Fourth Amendment standards of reasonableness on the states. Justice Clark's assertion in the Ker case that the Wolf case itself had required the states to obey Fourth Amendment standards, even though it did not require them to adopt the exclusionary rule, draws no support from the language of Justice Frankfurter's opinion in the Wolf case.

One question which became uppermost in the minds of state law enforcement officials in the aftermath of the Mapp case was whether the decision would be given retroactive effect by the Court, thus al-

117. *Stanford* v. *Texas*, 379 U.S. 476 (1965).
118. *Aguilar* v. *Texas*, 378 U.S. 108, 114 (1964).
119. *Beck* v. *Ohio*, 379 U.S. 89 (1964).
120. *Stoner* v. *California*, 376 U.S. 483 (1964).
121. *One 1958 Plymouth Sedan* v. *Pennsylvania*, 380 U.S. 693 (1965). See also *Fahy* v. *Connecticut*, 375 U.S. 85 (1963) (disallowed use of illegally seized evidence, even where other, legal, evidence, possibly sufficient to sustain the conviction, was also employed), and *Clinton* v. *Virginia*, 377 U.S. 158 (1964) (disallowed use of evidence obtained by penetration of eavesdropping apparatus into the wall of the dwelling). But see *Cleary* v. *Bolger*, 371 U.S. 392 (1963), in which the Court refused to enjoin a state officer from testifying at a state trial concerning evidence allegedly taken illegally by federal officers, to which act the state officer was a witness. The Court applied the principle of the Stefanelli case and differentiated the Rea decision as having operated directly on a federal, not a state, officer. It was pointed out that, in any event, following the Mapp case the defendant was entitled to have unconstitutionally seized evidence excluded in his state trial, and that if it were not excluded, there existed the right of appeal to the federal courts.
122. *Ker* v. *California*, 374 U.S. 23, 46.
123. *Ibid.*, p. 45.

lowing a defendant convicted prior to the Mapp decision with the aid of unconstitutionally seized evidence to seek release or a new trial. The retroactivity question was not answered by the Court until the last day of the 1964–65 term of court,[124] four years after the Mapp decision. The long delay may have been strategic; it can perhaps be explained by a desire on the part of the Court not to foreclose a retroactive interpretation by such state courts as might choose to follow this course, coupled with its own intention not to require a retroactive ruling. By the time that the Court ruled on the subject, most defendants convicted with the use of illegally seized evidence had probably completed their jail terms.

In his opinion Justice Clark stressed that the purpose of the exclusionary rule was to prevent future illegal police conduct, not to punish conduct which can no longer be affected. Therefore the Mapp decision would be given prospective effect only. Clark said, in effect, that the exclusionary rule was not designed to protect the obviously guilty defendant but was a practical remedy designed to protect society. He also pointed out that when, prior to the Mapp case, the state courts allowed the use of illegally seized evidence at trial, they did so with the specific assent of the Court in *Wolf* v. *Colorado*. Justice Black, dissenting with the concurrence of Justice Douglas, protested that the Court's decision meant "that the rule is not a right or privilege . . . but is a sort of punishment against officers in order to keep them from depriving people of their constitutional rights. . . ."[125] He argued that the exclusionary rule is required by the Fifth Amendment (without regard to its deterrent effects) and should, therefore, be given retroactive effect.[126]

These pages have merely outlined in the briefest form a few of the problems with which the Court will be confronted in the coming years. The Mapp and Ker decisions assure a great deal of involvement of the Supreme Court in search and seizure issues in the years to come.

124. *Linkletter* v. *Walker*, 381 U.S. 618 (1965).
125. *Ibid*., p. 649.
126. The issues in this case transcend Fourth Amendment considerations. For wide-ranging discussions, see Paul J. Mishkin, "The High Court, the Great Writ, and the Due Process of Time and Law," *Harvard Law Review*, LXXIX (November, 1965), 56; and Paul Bender, "The Retroactive Effect of an Overruling Constitutional Decision: Mapp v. Ohio," *University of Pennsylvania Law Review*, CX (March, 1962), 650.

## CHAPTER VII

# THE EXCLUSIONARY RULE AND THE PROBLEM OF ILLEGAL SEARCH

The Supreme Court's adoption of the exclusionary rule for the states in *Mapp* v. *Ohio*[1] raises important questions of judicial policy. Therefore, it might be appropriate to discuss the problem of illegal search and seizure in this country today and to review some of the considerations which were probably influential in persuading the Court to follow the course it did.

"Of all the two-faced problems in the law," wrote Justice Traynor of California, "there is none more tormenting than the admissibility of illegally obtained evidence. Whichever face one turns to the wall, the question of admissibility remains a haunting one."[2] Since the Supreme Court does not do its work in an intellectual vacuum, the justices, before announcing their decision, doubtless viewed the probable effects of an exclusionary policy in the context of the high incidence of crime in the nation and the difficulties faced by the police in their task of enforcing the law. As Justice Stewart noted on one occasion: "It can fairly be said that in applying the Fourth Amendment this Court has seldom shown itself unaware of the practical demands of effective criminal investigation and law enforcement. Indeed, there are those who think that some of the Court's decisions have tipped the balance too heavily against the protection of that individual privacy which it was the purpose of the Fourth Amendment to guarantee."[3]

Police work is often a frustrating, hazardous, and thankless task. The incidence of crime in the United States has been rising steadily over the years and shows no signs of leveling off. Each year has shown a spectacular increase in the crime rate over the preceding year. The nation's population increased by 10 per cent between 1958 and 1964, but the number of "serious crimes" committed during the same period increased by fully 58 per cent. Put differently,

1. 367 U.S. 643 (1961).
2. Roger J. Traynor, "Mapp v. Ohio at Large in the Fifty States," *Duke Law Journal*, Vol. 1962 (Summer, 1962), p. 319.
3. *Elkins* v. *United States*, 364 U.S. 206, 222 (1960).

the crime rate—that is, the number of offenses committed per hundred thousand population—increased by 44 per cent during these six years. In 1964, fewer than 25 per cent of crimes were "cleared by arrest." During the same year, fifty-seven policemen were murdered, and one out of every ten was assaulted.[4] It is small wonder that law enforcement officials groan under the burden they are expected to carry.

Given this grim picture, the temptation is great to blame the courts, and especially the most influential tribunal of all, the Supreme Court, as being partly responsible for the crime wave. The courts, it is said, are "coddling" criminals and removing the fear of punishment. Criminals take advantage of judicial leniency to act with impunity and prove that crime does pay.

While much of this criticism is found in the popular press and magazines,[5] it is increasingly heard from law enforcement officials[6]

4. Federal Bureau of Investigation, *Crime in the United States: Uniform Crime Reports—1964* (Washington, 1965), pp. 4, 95, 147, 148. The *Uniform Crime Reports*, issued annually, are our most accurate guide to the nation's crime picture, but they have been subject to a good deal of criticism by criminologists and sociologists. The most obvious deficiency arises from the fact that these statistics are collated by the F.B.I. from figures submitted by state and local law enforcement agencies throughout the country, and the standards of accuracy of these agencies are likely to vary greatly. Some agencies will try to protect their own reputation or that of their cities by underreporting the real incidence of crime within their jurisdictions. By way of illustration, the F.B.I. refused to accept New York City's figures, because of underreporting, between 1949 and 1952. The subsequent figures showed a spectacular "rise" in the crime rate, caused almost entirely by improved reporting. Between 1948 and 1952 burglary figures in New York rose from 2,726 to 42,491 and larceny figures from 7,713 to 70,949. In Philadelphia, when a new police commissioner took office in 1952, he discovered downright falsifications in the reporting system. Marvin E. Wolfgang, "Uniform Crime Reports: A Critical Appraisal," *University of Pennsylvania Law Review*, CXI (April, 1963), 708, 715–16. In Buffalo, New York, a state investigation showed that in 1960 "crimes reported by private citizens were 'buried' in the precincts where received and never reported to Headquarters as required. This was a regular practice in almost every precinct in the city." *Summary of the Activities during 1960 of the Temporary Commission of Investigation of the State of New York* (New York, 1961), p. 33.

The crime statistics are also vulnerable on two other grounds. First, the proportion of young persons aged fifteen to twenty-four, a particularly crime-prone group, is constantly increasing and this fact is bound to be reflected in the crime rates. Second, the figures pertain only to "serious" crime, officially defined as murder, forcible rape, robbery, aggravated assault, burglary, automobile theft, and larceny of fifty dollars and over. It is extremely doubtful whether the last two categories of crime should be classified as "serious," since the money value of things stolen rises as the national prosperity grows, while most "stolen" automobiles are not stolen at all but merely "borrowed" for brief joyrides, as indicated by the fact that nearly all of them are later recovered, in sharp contrast to the low recovery rate for other types of stolen goods. See *The New York Times*, March 22, 1965, pp. 1, 28.

5. A particularly pungent article is Virgil W. Peterson, "The Crooks Get All the Breaks," *Saturday Evening Post*, September 23, 1961, p. 10.

6. E.g., Edward S. Silver (then district attorney of Kings County, New York), "Is the Public Getting 'Due Process'?", address before a general session of the American Bar Association, Section on Criminal Law, August 9, 1961, St. Louis, Missouri. "I submit that the right to due process—in its real sense though extra-legal,

and even judges.[7] In 1964 the Republican presidential candidate contributed to it.[8] Some of it has come from well-informed scholars.[9] Individual justices of the Supreme Court have occasionally joined in this criticism; ironically, the author of the Court's opinion in the Mapp case, Justice Clark, just four months earlier admonished his brethren: "We hear much these days of an increasing crime rate and a breakdown in law enforcement. Some place the blame on police officers. I say there are others that must shoulder much of that responsibility."[10]

A good deal of this criticism is moderate, or at least well-meaning. There is an understandable bias in favor of law enforcement on the part of some of these critics, and they tend to view with alarm any restrictions placed on searches that will make it more difficult for police officers to do their job. Some of the criticism, however, amounts to nothing short of an attack on the Fourth Amendment itself. One police official told a California legislative committee that no warrants should be required in narcotics and gambling cases. "[T]hey say to us, 'If you want to search a place, get a search warrant.' That is practical only if you know what you are after, the actual objects."[11] It is, of course, the purpose of a search warrant to

---

and as a precept in the administration of criminal justice, must admit of due process for the People as well. In the face of the grave menace of mounting criminality today, it is fair to say that society itself—no less than any individual member—is entitled to the equal protection of the laws." A less temperate view was taken by William J. Parker, Los Angeles chief of police, whose department's conduct with respect to illegal searches was largely responsible for California's adoption of the exclusionary rule: "Our ability to prevent the commission of crimes has been greatly diminished . . . it affects our ability to protect you against the criminal army." Quoted in Yale Kamisar, "*Wolf* and *Lustig* Ten Years Later: Illegal State Evidence in State and Federal Courts," *Minnesota Law Review*, XLIII (May, 1959), 1083, 1153.

7. An able New York City judge told this writer: "The judges in Washington have no experience in law enforcement. They're removed from the actuality of day to day problems." A United States Court of Appeals judge confirmed this estimate: "They won't accept facts; they prefer to use their own imagination. They regard it as the duty of federal courts to run the country as beneficient despots and tyrants. They get a glory complex as soon as they're appointed to the bench."

8. Barry Goldwater, *The New York Times Magazine*, November 1, 1964, p. 23: "[O]ur highest court has been steadily taking away from local law enforcement agencies the powers needed to control law and order. The freedom and rights of law-abiding citizens have been jeopardized by excessive concern for the criminal defendant."

9. For example, Professor Fred E. Inbau of Northwestern University, who has been tireless in presenting the law enforcement point of view. One of his best contributions is " 'Fair Play' in Criminal Investigations and Prosecutions," *Northwestern University Tri-Quarterly*, III, No. 2 (1961), 3. The federal appellate judge referred to in note 7, *supra*, said about Inbau's writings, "It's refreshing to hear the practical point of view as opposed to all the theoreticians who've never had a gun pointed at them or had to face problems of crime in a metropolitan area."

10. *Chapman* v. *United States*, 365 U.S. 610, 623 (1961).

11. Joint Judiciary Committee on the Administration of Justice, Third and Final Report, *Crime and Criminal Courts in California* (1959), pp. 41–42.

limit the search to "the actual objects"; otherwise, the search would be even less restricted than that conducted under the general warrant.

Again, the prosecuting attorney of Cuyahoga County, Ohio, in a petition for rehearing of the Mapp case, told the Supreme Court with downright impertinence:

> Since crime wants discovery, there is no reason to castigate police officers because they discover criminal evidence without a search warrant. . . . The police, from a local level of law enforcement experience in this county, knew with whom they were dealing in this case. Further, *the sole function of a search warrant is to protect the police officer against a suit for trespass or against an action in tort.* . . . The right of privacy is guaranteed to law abiding citizens, not to those who use it as a protective shield for the commission of crime.
>
> The general object of the search and seizure provision is to protect the right of privacy as exercised by law abiding citizens, and to whatever degree and in whatever connection the right of privacy is unlawfully used for criminal activity, to that extent the protection of the Constitution should not apply.[12]

This position must be regarded either as licensing lawlessness on the part of the police or as a claim to infallibility, for unless a police officer can establish, in advance of entry, probable cause to believe that a dwelling contains contraband or instruments of crime, he may invade the privacy of citizens who are law-abiding; if he can show probable cause, there is no reason why he should not procure a warrant.

It must not be presumed, however, that this attitude is typical of all or even a majority of law enforcement officers. In a poll of Colorado police chiefs and sheriffs, Professor Jack B. Weinstein asked whether they approved of the lawless search in the Mapp case. Of the thirty respondents, only two thought the police conduct was proper, seven found it improper but justifiable, and the remaining twenty-one condemned it.[13]

Nonetheless, a great deal of illegal searching goes on, despite the fact that the constitution of every state in the Union has a provision patterned on the Fourth Amendment.[14] While the judicial reports show that the exclusionary rule has not succeeded in putting an end to unlawful searches by federal officers, the problem of illegal search is, without question, most serious on the state and local levels because

12. Petition for Rehearing, *Mapp* v. *Ohio.* Reprinted in *Journal of Criminal Law,* LII (November–December, 1961), 437, 442–43. (Emphasis supplied.)

13. Jack B. Weinstein, "Local Responsibility for Improvement of Search and Seizure Practices," *Rocky Mountain Law Review,* XXXIV (Winter, 1962), 150, 176.

14. The citations are collected in Joseph A. Varon, *Searches, Seizures and Immunities* (Indianapolis, Ind., 1961), Vol. I, pp. 5–6, n. 2.

of lower professional standards, poorer training, and the fact that the great bulk of law enforcement is carried on at those levels of government. Illegal search must be viewed in the context of the total criminal law process—arrest, search and seizure, interrogation, arraignment. Poor police performance in one of these areas is likely to mean poor performance in all. Illegal searches are therefore only part of the general problem of police lawlessness, which includes illegal arrest, brutality toward suspects, subtler forms of coercion, and illegal detention without arraignment. These illegal acts tend to be interrelated. Many of the illegal searches take place in conjunction with unauthorized arrests, which, in turn, are made for the purpose of keeping the suspect in confinement and, if possible, extracting a confession from him. By way of garish illustration, let us take the case of James Monroe and his wife, considered by the Supreme Court in 1961. Thirteen Chicago police officers, possessing neither arrest nor search warrants, broke into the Monroe home early one morning, "routed them from bed, made them stand naked in the living room, and ransacked every room, emptying drawers and ripping mattress covers."[15] Monroe was then removed to a police station, where he was questioned in connection with an unsolved murder. During his ten hours of detention he was not allowed to get in touch with either his family or his attorney, nor was he brought before a magistrate. He was released without any criminal charges having been brought against him.

Enormous difficulties stand in the way of obtaining even an approximately accurate statistical picture of the extent of illegal search prior to the Mapp case. In those states which followed an exclusionary policy of their own volition, a check of court records can sometimes be made, but in order to put together a picture of nationwide significance, an exhaustive state-by-state and city-by-city survey would be required. Such a survey remains to be made, although the forthcoming volume *Detection of Crime*,[16] in the American Bar Foundation's Series on the Administration of Criminal Justice in the United States, may help to close some of the gaps in our knowledge. In those states which did not adopt the exclusionary rule, the court records are largely useless because the evidence was admissible regardless of the legality of the search, and defense attorneys often

15. *Monroe* v. *Pape*, 365 U.S. 167, 169 (1961).
16. This volume will have a section on search and seizure written by Daniel M. McIntyre, Jr. The only volume in this pioneering series (under the general editorship of Professor Frank J. Remington of the University of Wisconsin) to be published thus far is Wayne R. LaFave, *Arrest: The Decision To Take a Suspect into Custody* (Boston, 1965).

did not even contest the admission of illegally seized evidence. It is doubtful whether a single police force in the nation keeps meaningful records of illegal searches conducted by its officers. Moreover, there is usually no record at all of searches which did not result in prosecutions.[17]

While the full extent of illegal searches prior to the Mapp decision is thus unknown, whatever fragmentary evidence we have suggests that it was sufficiently substantial to warrant Professor Fellman's conclusion, in 1958, that "perhaps no other constitutional right is breached so often, and with such an absence of popular resentment."[18] The New York City Deputy Police Commissioner for Legal Affairs admitted that before the Mapp decision "nobody bothered to take out search warrants." Since the evidence was admissible anyway, "the feeling was, why bother?"[19]

A number of very useful empirical surveys conducted in recent years, while admittedly limited in scope, point to very widespread illegal police activity in connection with arrests. These studies are important to us for two reasons. First, the Fourth Amendment's standard of probable cause applies to arrest as well as search.[20] Second, since an illegal arrest is usually accompanied by an equally illegal search of the person, and of the dwelling, if the arrest is made indoors, these studies shed much light on the extent of illegal search as well as arrest.

A survey of Philadelphia police procedures made in 1952 found it to be a common practice of the police to make random arrests or "spot checks" in crime-infested areas and to "round up" for interrogation numerous suspects in the hope of discovering incriminating information concerning either a particular crime or crime in general. "One reason the police arrest everybody caught in their net is the feeling among members of the force that the greater the number of arrests, the more likely their superiors and the public will think they are doing an efficient job."[21] It was found that 80 per cent of gambling arrests and 75 per per cent of disorderly conduct arrests were illegal.

17. These observations are based on discussions by the author with police officials in a number of cities.

18. David Fellman, *The Defendant's Rights* (New York, 1958), p. 153.

19. Deputy Commissioner Leonard Reisman, quoted in *The New York Times*, April 28, 1965, p. 50. A group of Colorado law enforcement officials estimated that as a result of the Mapp case their need for warrants would multiply more than threefold. The group used (approximately) 167 warrants a year prior to the Mapp case and estimated that it would now require 524 warrants annually. Weinstein, "Local Responsibility," p. 177.

20. *Ex parte Burford*, 3 Cranch 448 (1806); *Henry* v. *United States*, 361 U.S. 98 (1959).

21. Note, "Philadelphia Police Practice and the Law of Arrest," *University of Pennsylvania Law Review*, C (June, 1952), 1182, 1202.

Studies of police practices in other cities yield comparable results. In Detroit, of the 67,301 arrests made in 1956 (for all offenses except traffic violations), 26,696 were arrests for "investigation."[22] In Washington, D.C., a federal jurisdiction, at least 28 per cent of all felony arrests made in 1961 were made for the purpose of "investigation."[23] Alan Barth reports that while investigating four murders in a recent year the Washington police detained 6,170 persons, while in 1958, 90 suspects were rounded up in the course of a robbery investigation. "Sixty-seven of the arrested persons were held overnight at headquarters. None of the ninety was ever charged with the crime."[24] For the nation as a whole, 102,106 arrests on "suspicion" were recorded in 1964,[25] although statistics of this kind have been criticized as "virtually meaningless"[26] because the police often do not regard detentions for investigation as arrests and hence do not record them as such. In Los Angeles County in 1955, "41 per cent of all felony arrests were released without charge and in only 31 per cent of felony arrests were felony complaints actually filed."[27] The crime of vagrancy, a relic of the common law, is, like the arrest for investigation, a prime weapon for harassing indigents whom the police consider "undesirable" or for keeping suspects in custody while an investigation is under way.[28] Indicative of the misuse of the vagrancy statutes is the fact that in 1953 the conviction rate for vagrancy in San Francisco was only 26 per cent of those arrested. Many of those arrested were probably released for lack of evidence and never brought to court.[29] In 1964, 132,955 arrests for vagrancy[30]

22. *Hearings before the United States Commission on Civil Rights, Hearings Held in Detroit, Michigan, December 14 and 15, 1960*, p. 484.
23. *Report and Recommendations of the Commissioners' Committee on Police Arrests for Investigation* (District of Columbia, July, 1962), pp. 8–9. A ban on arrests for investigation in the District of Columbia effective as of March 15, 1963, was announced by the district commissioners on January 10, 1963. *Washington Post*, January 11, 1963, p. A1.
24. Alan Barth, *The Price of Liberty* (New York, 1961), p. 47.
25. *Uniform Crime Reports—1964*, p. 108, Table 19. Of course, even persons legitimately arrested on probable cause may later be released when further investigation shows them to be innocent. When, however, the percentage of those released goes as high as one-third or more, it is reasonable to believe that many of the arrests were illegal.
26. Caleb Foote, "Law and Police Practice: Safeguards in the Law of Arrest," *Northwestern University Law Review*, LII (March–April, 1957), 16, 20.
27. *Ibid.*, p. 22.
28. For discussion see William O. Douglas, "Vagrancy and Arrest on Suspicion," *Yale Law Journal*, LXX (November, 1960), 1; Foote, "Law and Police Practice," pp. 22ff.; LaFave, *Arrest*, pp. 307–8. A hilarious example of the misuse of this power occurred in New York City on June 3, 1964, when Frank Costello, reputed to be a king of the underworld, was arrested as a "vagrant" while dining in an expensive restaurant. *The New York Times*, June 4, 1964, p. 1.
29. Foote, "Law and Police Practice," p. 22.
30. *Uniform Crime Reports—1964*, p. 108.

were recorded in the nation, though here again the figures may be unreliable. The arrest for investigation and the misuse of the vagrancy laws make a mockery of the national belief, embedded in the Bill of Rights, that it is possible to reconcile law with order, and order with constitutional safeguards.

While ignorance and laziness are factors contributing to illegal police conduct, one scholar wrote, "by all odds the greatest cause . . . is to be located in the whole fabric of motivations that characterize our present-day police and prosecutive establishments. The stamp of success for American police and prosecutive officials . . . is conviction of suspected offenders."[31] Professor Inbau, a sharp critic of the exclusionary rule, admits that while an officer observing a person whom he deems a suspicious character is not authorized, in the absence of probable cause, to effect an arrest and search, "[a]s a practical matter, however, the officer will take further action. He will approach the man, with gun drawn; he will ask some questions and he may also effect a search. . . . But in doing so the officer is acting without legal authorization." The reason, according to Inbau, is that, should the suspicious-looking person later commit a crime, "in all probability his [the policeman's] commanding officer would transfer him to another assignment for *the purpose of placating the complaining public*."[32] Thus the police often seek the "easy way" of satisfying the public clamor for convictions.

Relevant to the problem of lawless law enforcement are a number of basic police problems which can be only briefly discussed here. These are interwound in a vicious circle of poor pay, political influence, and lack of high professional standards. Poor pay is in large measure responsible for a lack of morale, and without morale there can be no effective discipline. Poor pay is by no means universal,[33] but it is common. "The beginning salary for patrolmen in some of our cities having more than 500,000 population is barely $90 a week. In a number of smaller communities with less than 25,000 people, the beginning pay drops to approximately $50 per week."[34] The

31. Albert R. Beisel, Jr., *Control over Illegal Enforcement of the Criminal Law: Role of the Supreme Court* (Boston, 1955), p. 7.

32. Inbau, " 'Fair Play,' " pp. 4–5. (Emphasis supplied.)

33. The current starting salary for New York City policemen is $7,032 per year, exclusive of uniform allowance and fringe benefits.

34. John Edgar Hoover, "Message from the Director," *FBI Law Enforcement Bulletin*, XXXIII, No. 9 (September, 1964), 3, 4. The difficulty of attracting competent personnel is strikingly portrayed in a professional study evaluating the Chicago police department. While the study gave high marks to the department and its superintendent for their reform efforts in general (see n. 86 *infra*), it was nevertheless critical of the fact that "some recruits are now being certified who have less than normal intelligence." Field Service Division, International Association of Chiefs of Police, *Chicago Police Department: Policy Evaluation* (Washington, D.C., 1964), p. 60.

situation is often nearly as bad in the district attorneys' offices. As recently as 1954, District Attorney Frank Hogan of New York County was able to make the claim that in prohibiting his legal staff members from engaging in outside employment to supplement their incomes, he was unique: "No comparable [state] office in . . . the nation, as far as is known, enforces such a rule. . . ."[35] Police departments in our large cities are consistently undermanned because of inability, under present salary schedules, to recruit enough men to bring them up to authorized operating strength; there are simply not enough policemen on the beat. Inadequate budgeting for law enforcement also results in inadequate training: "The vast majority of law enforcement officers have no police academy or other facilities suitable for instruction, and no money in the police budget to provide for systematic and extended training in the law by the instructors available."[36] The over-all cost of law enforcement, despite the huge burdens which the police are expected to carry, has in recent years amounted to only 3 per cent of federal expenditures; for the states, the figure is 5 per cent, and for local government, 9 per cent.[37] The most ramshackle and run-down building in town is, as likely as not, the police station. The simple lesson which the nation still needs to learn is that cheap law enforcement is poor law enforcement.

In this state of affairs, the temptation for wrongdoing is, of course, great. While police scandals which have shaken the nation in recent years (sometimes involving nothing less than police gangs of safecrackers and burglars[38]) cannot be explained away solely by the financial problem, if only because most officers do not engage in such activities, it is clearly relevant. The temptation is enhanced by the ready availability of "graft payments" furnished by gambling and vice interests, such as recently corrupted the police forces of several New York cities.[39] The New York State Crime Commission found three causes for the breakdown of law enforcement in certain areas of that state—corruption, political influence, and incompetence.[40] "[T]here are probably not many prosecutor's offices in

35. *Report of the District Attorney, County of New York: 1949–1954* (New York, n.d.), p. 11.
36. Dwight J. Dalbey, "Taking Inventory," *FBI Law Enforcement Bulletin*, XXXIV, No. 7 (July, 1965), 12, 17.
37. James Willard Hurst, *Law and Social Progress in United States History* (Ann Arbor, Mich., 1960), p. 294.
38. Among the cities involved were Chicago, Des Moines, Denver, and Burlington, Vermont.
39. See Temporary Commission of Investigation of the State of New York, *Second Annual Report*, Legislative Document No. 103 (1960).
40. New York State Crime Commission, *First Report*, Legislative Document No. 23 (1953), pp. 20–24.

major cities in this country," writes a federal official, "in which the criminal organization swings no weight at all. . . . [T]here is every reason to believe that the trial courts of some of our large cities are liberally sprinkled with judges who are indebted in one way or another to the predominant local criminal organization. . . . There is strong evidence to support the conclusion that the long black hand of organized crime reaches into the legislative chambers of some of our larger states."[41] It is clearly in the interest of those politicians beholden to criminal interests that law enforcement be kept weak and subservient to those interests. It was in response to these conditions and the scandals they have produced that J. Edgar Hoover, Director of the Federal Bureau of Investigation, was moved to remark: "Good law enforcement is not possible without comprehensive background investigations of applicants, outstanding training programs, penetrative self-inspection, realistic pay scales, and promotions based on merit."[42]

Law enforcement is also plagued by a number of other problems. One is the multitude of criminal laws, to which new ones are constantly being added in line with the national belief that any social problem is capable of solution if only "there's a law" to deal with it. Not all of these laws can be enforced, and this leads to excessive law enforcement "discretion" as to which are to be enforced and which are not.[43] Such discretion, unless properly controlled in the public interest by administrative means, is obviously susceptible to corruption and, what can be just as bad, inefficiency. Thus vital manpower is often diverted to nonessential tasks, such as the harassment of harmless drunks.[44] According to a leading federal official, "more than three-fourths of the men and women . . . in local jails are

41. Earl Johnson, Jr., "Organized Crime: Challenge to the American Legal System," *Journal of Criminal Law*, LIII (December, 1962), 399, 420–21.

42. Quoted in the *Christian Science Monitor*, February 27, 1962, p. 10.

43. See LaFave, *Arrest*, pp. 63ff. There are also several outstanding articles on the subject. See Charles D. Breitel, "Controls in Criminal Law Enforcement," *University of Chicago Law Review*, XXVII (Spring, 1960), 427; Herman Goldstein, "Police Discretion: The Ideal versus the Real," *Public Administration Review*, XXIII (September, 1963), 140: Joseph Goldstein, "Police Discretion Not To Invoke the Criminal Process: Low Visibility Decisions in the Administration of Justice," *Yale Law Journal*, LXIX (March, 1960), 543.

44. John M. Murtagh (then Chief Justice, Court of Special Sessions, New York City), "Alcohol and the Law," address delivered at the University of California School of Medicine Symposium on Alcohol and Civilization, San Francisco, November 19, 1961. This speech contains an excellent discussion of the problem. The author is indebted to Judge Murtagh for a copy of the text. On the general problem of proper use of police manpower, see Herman Goldstein, "Guidelines for Effective Use of Police Manpower," *Public Management*, XLV (October, 1963), 218.

drunks, vagrants, mentally ill or defective, or social misfits of other kinds."[45]

Very little is done about the high rate of recidivism among criminals; few rehabilitation programs worthy of the name have been developed. States such as North Carolina, which have pioneered excellent rehabilitation programs, have sharply decreased the rate of recidivism,[46] but their example has not been followed by the nation as a whole. The prime weapon in crimes of violence, the firearm, is freely merchandized in almost every part of the country, with virtually no restrictions placed on its sale.[47]

While co-operation between law enforcement agencies has come a long way in recent decades (it was almost nonexistent as recently as 1930[48]), there is still far too much fragmentation of effort. No state-wide, let alone nation-wide, standards exist; within a single metropolitan area there may be literally dozens of different police departments with widely varying standards of integrity and professionalization. For example, "co-operation in New York State among the sixty-two district attorneys and the more than 600 separate local agencies is entirely voluntary; there is no state-wide supervision of

45. James V. Bennett, "A Cool Look at 'the Crime Crisis,'" *Harper's*, April, 1964, pp. 123, 124. Mr. Bennett was, at the time of writing, director of the Federal Bureau of Prisons. The multiplicity of laws to regulate crime is itself responsible for the breeding of more crime. A prime example is the narcotics laws. It was at one time perfectly legal to purchase narcotics without prescription. The historian Harry Elmer Barnes remembers an aged relative who "stopped on his way to bed every night and took a dose of laudanum, mixed with sugar and water, containing probably enough opium to last an addict of our time several days." He adds: "When I was in college, from 1909 to 1913, I met most of my living expenses by working in a drug store where I dispensed heroin as casually and freely as I would today aspirin or Vick's nasal drops." The repressive approach, says Barnes, is responsible for "the undermining of our courts and judicial procedure; the demoralization of police systems . . .; the distraction of police and public attention from more serious forms and causes of criminality; the marked increase of neighborhood thievery and robbery by addicts needing money to pay for ever-more-costly narcotics. . . . Yet legalizing drugs would wipe out the drug racket overnight." Book Review, *Saturday Review*, March 6, 1965, pp. 25, 57. Professor Packer agrees: "With the disappearance of controls, the price of narcotics would plummet and the financial ruin of the present illegal suppliers would quickly ensue." When use of a commodity is restricted by law, "what we are in effect doing is . . . increasing the risk to the seller, thereby driving up the price of what he sells." Sale of the commodity thus becomes a monopoly of the criminal element. Herbert L. Packer, "The Crime Tariff," *The American Scholar*, XXXIII (Autumn, 1964), 551, 553, 552.

46. *The New York Times*, August 23, 1965, pp. 33, 52.

47. Of the 225 police officers killed in the line of duty between 1960 and 1964, 96 per cent were slain with firearms. *Uniform Crime Reports—1964*, p. 2. A determined effort is currently being made in Congress, with the full backing of the administration, to place realistic controls on the interstate shipment of arms.

48. Hoover, "Cooperation: The Key to Effective Law Enforcement in America," *Syracuse Law Review*, XII (Fall, 1960), 1, 2.

any kind."[49] Even large police departments have not made the necessary adjustments for fighting crime in the mid-twentieth century. Not until 1962 did the biggest department in the country, that of New York City, begin to make provision for central planning on law enforcement problems instead of leaving them to be tackled, as a police official remarked, in the former "haphazard way."[50]

Equally important, law enforcement is hamperd by the related problems of public antagonism to the police,[51] public apathy to law enforcement problems, and widespread public indulgence toward such forms of proscribed conduct as gambling and vice. Failure to enforce law breeds corruption, yet it is the public which does not wish to have the law enforced. In New York City alone, according to *The New York Times*, half a million persons are daily engaged in illegal gambling.[52]

So long as these problems are not dealt with forcefully and the public is not aroused to the real needs of law enforcement, it would be folly to lay the blame for the high level of crime at the door of the courts. The roots of crime and of the failure of law enforcement lie deep in the fabric of American society and political life; they do not lie in the courtroom.

"The theory of our law," said Woodrow Wilson, "is that an officer is an officer only as long as he acts within his powers; that when he transcends his authority he ceases to be an officer and is only a private individual, subject to be sued and punished for his offense."[53] Such was, of course, the theory which justified the common-law rule of admissibility of illegally seized evidence. Whatever its validity once, the theory is surely discredited today, at a time when abundant evidence exists that the illegal searcher does not act on his own initiative but in response to orders from his superiors, who *as a matter of policy* persistently and brazenly defy the law they are charged with

49. J. Edward Lumbard, "The Administration of Criminal Justice: Some Problems and Their Resolution," *American Bar Association Journal*, XLIX (September, 1963), 840, 841–42. According to Judge George Edwards of the United States Court of Appeals for the Sixth Circuit, who served as police commissioner of Detroit, there are forty thousand *autonomous* police jurisdictions in the nation. *The New York Times*, December 7, 1965, p. 33.

50. *Christian Science Monitor*, January 22, 1962, p. 3.

51. Public antagonism was heavily felt by many law officers with whom this writer spoke. They speculated that this antagonism was two-fold in origin, stemming from exposure to traffic policemen, who are not always polite, and the fear of the police state in the light of recent European experiences.

52. *The New York Times*, June 26, 1964, pp. 1, 17.

53. Woodrow Wilson, *Constitutional Government in the United States* (New York, 1921), p. 19.

enforcing. In such a state of affairs the courts can no longer view an illegal search as a private act, but must consider it an act of government behind which stands the entire law enforcement machinery. This fact induced Justice Traynor of California, who had once written an opinion[54] rejecting the exclusionary rule for his state, to change his mind and vote for the rule in 1955, in the famous Cahan case.[55] As he later explained, "it was one thing to condone an occasional constable's blunder. . . . It was quite another to condone a steady course of illegal police procedures that deliberately and flagrantly violated the Constitution of the United States. . . ."[56] Left undisturbed, such conduct was likely to undermine all respect for law.

The fact that California, a state which had been plagued with the problem of unlawful searches,[57] had adopted the exclusionary rule to deal with this menace was an influential factor in the Mapp decision. Portions of Justice Traynor's Cahan opinion were quoted with approval in the Mapp case and in its progenitor, the Elkins case.[58] "The experience in California," said the Court in the Elkins case, "has been most illuminating."[59]

In the Cahan case Los Angeles policemen, acting on instructions of the chief of police, smashed their way into a number of private homes to obtain evidence of illegal bookmaking. The violations were freely admitted by the officers in court, a fact which led Justice Traynor to observe that "it is clearly apparent from their testimony that they casually regard such acts as nothing more than the performance of their ordinary duties for which the City employs and pays them."[60] The courts could not disclaim responsibility for such acts, he said, because "the success of the lawless venture depends entirely on the court's lending its aid by allowing the evidence to be introduced."[61] No other means had proved effective in deterring the police from lawless behavior. To the argument that law enforcement would be hampered by the exclusionary rule that California was that day adopting, Traynor sternly replied: "This contention is not properly directed at the exclusionary rule, but at the constitu-

54. *People* v. *Gonzales*, 124 P.2d 44 (Cal. 1942).
55. *People* v. *Cahan*, 282 P.2d 905 (Cal. 1955).
56. Traynor, "Mapp v. Ohio," p. 322.
57. Two of the Supreme Court's leading search cases in the nineteen fifties, in each instance involving a flagrant violation of the victim's constitutional rights, originated in that state. *Rochin* v. *California*, 342 U.S. 165 (1952); *Irvine* v. *California*, 347 U.S. 128 (1954). These cases are discussed in Chapter V.
58. *Elkins* v. *United States*, 364 U.S. 206 (1960).
59. *Ibid.*, p. 220.
60. 282 P.2d 905, 907.
61. *Ibid.*, p. 912.

tional provisions themselves. It was rejected when those provisions were adopted."[62]

Thus, in selecting the exclusionary rule as the appropriate instrument for deterring illegal state searches, the Supreme Court and the twenty-six states which of their own volition had previously adopted the rule came to the conclusion that no other effective legal deterrents were available. As a means of forcing changes in law enforcement procedures, public opinion is, as we have seen, a slender reed to lean upon. As Justice Jackson pointed out, "we rarely have a political issue made of any kind of invasion of civil liberty. On the contrary, district attorneys who have been rebuked by the courts are frequently promoted by the public. The attitude seems to be, leave it to the judges."[63]

That the fear of criminal prosecution or civil suit might serve to deter illegal searches was sufficiently contradicted by the facts. Only twenty-three states had any criminal provisions relating to illegal searches, and of these only eleven made searches without warrants punishable.[64] Prosecutions for violation of constitutional search provisions were "almost nonexistent."[65] A federal act[66] which had been on the statute books since 1921 made violations of search law by federal officers an indictable offense. Yet as of 1955 not a single prosecution had been attempted under its terms,[67] even though during the prohibition period "search and seizure litigation reached an unprecedented peak."[68] The federal civil rights act,[69] which makes it a criminal offense, punishable by one year in prison and a thousand-dollar fine, to deprive a person of his constitutional rights, is virtually unenforceable with respect to searches: the searcher is usually acting on the orders of his superiors, and so the requirement of the act that the offense be "willfully" committed is not met.[70] Even the enactment of state laws establishing stringent criminal sanctions would be unlikely to serve as effective deterrents because prosecution of violations would depend on district attorneys who themselves are sometimes implicated in these illegal activities and who, in any

62. *Ibid.*, p. 914.
63. Robert H. Jackson, *The Supreme Court in the American System of Government* (Cambridge, Mass., 1955), pp. 81–82.
64. *Mapp* v. *Ohio*, 367 U.S. 643, 652, n. 7 (1961).
65. Richard A. Edwards, "Criminal Liability for Unreasonable Searches and Seizures," *Virginia Law Review*, XLI (June, 1955), 621, 626. See also LaFave, *Arrest*, pp. 425–26.
66. 18 U.S.C., sec. 2236.
67. Foote, "Tort Remedies for Police Violations of Individual Rights," *Minnesota Law Review*, XXXIX (April, 1955), 493, 494.
68. Edwards, "Criminal Liability," p. 629.
69. 18 U.S.C., sec. 242.
70. See p. 139, n. 88.

event, cannot afford to jeopardize their close working relationship with the police.

As for civil suit, the situation has been no more promising. Professor Foote's exhaustive study of the subject finds this remedy to be "completely impotent."[71] The most important reason is that the persons injured usually do not belong to the "respectable" classes and would therefore be unable to convince a jury that their reputation had suffered. Attorneys are reluctant to take their cases because the chances of recovery are small. Some victims are simply ignorant of their rights, while others are afraid of police retribution. Many innocent victims, as Justice Jackson noted,[72] do not wish to draw public attention to the fact that they have been under police surveillance. The worthlessness of civil suit is suggested by the case of a Baltimore lawyer who was unlawfully searched, yet was awarded nominal damages of only one cent because he had shown no proof of pecuniary loss.[73] Only one year before the Mapp decision, the Court held that under another civil rights act the victim of an illegal search has a federal civil remedy available to him against the officers responsible —but not against the municipality which employs them.[74] The fact that the municipality is immune to suit will probably negate much of the potential value of the decision, since the officers are not likely to be men of means, against whom large sums can be awarded. Victims of unlawful searches will therefore be discouraged from filing suit.

Criminal sanctions and civil liability (or the lack of them) having failed to deter officers from illegal searches, a number of other approaches have been suggested as alternatives to exclusion of the seized evidence. Professor Foote has advocated statutes which provide for minimum liquidated damages without regard to the character of the plaintiff.[75] A California state bar committee recommended that the officer's employer—whether the state, a county, or a city—be held liable for damages. This proposal, said Dean Barrett, "gives promise of providing a more adequate solution than the exclusionary rule at a smaller social cost,"[76] especially since, unlike the exclusionary rule, the remedy would be available to the innocent as well as the guilty. Even tort liability for large sums, however, is not

71. Foote, "Tort Remedies," p. 498.
72. *Irvine* v. *California*, 347 U.S. 128, 137 (1954).
73. Foote, "Tort Remedies," p. 498.
74. *Monroe* v. *Pape*, 365 U.S. 167 (1960). For discussion see Thomas J. Klitgaard, "The Civil Rights Act and Mr. Monroe," *California Law Review*, XLIX (1961), 145. For the other civil rights act referred to, see 42 U.S.C., sec. 1983.
75. Foote, "Tort Remedies," p. 501.
76. Edward L. Barrett, Jr., "Exclusion of Evidence Obtained by Illegal Searches: A Comment on People v. Cahan," *California Law Review*, XLIII (October, 1955), 565, 595.

likely to prove an effective deterrent unless provision is made for trial before a judge without a jury because of the reluctance of juries to find against the police.[77] Others have advocated the establishment of an independent civil rights office in each jurisdiction with the sole function of eradicating lawlessness in law enforcement through the punishment of offenders.[78] The implementation of these suggestions would, however, require legislation, and the Supreme Court evidently did not believe that such action would be forthcoming in a significant number of states in the foreseeable future.

Granting that the threat of criminal prosecution or of civil suit is ineffective in putting an end to illegal searches, what evidence is there to show that the exclusionary rule is effective in achieving that objective? Unfortunately, no conclusive evidence is available. We have before us, of course, the example of the highly select F.B.I. organization, which operates with efficiency within constitutional limits. In sharp contrast to the low professional standards often prevailing in local law enforcement agencies, the F.B.I. stresses high standards, strict discipline, and promotion on merit. The morale of its agents is conceded to be high. Though the F.B.I. operates under exclusionary rule standards, in 1965 convictions were obtained in over 96 per cent of all prosecutions for which its investigative work was responsible.[79] It is not surprising, then, that, with the F.B.I. as an example, the Supreme Court thought that professionalized law

77. Comment, "Search and Seizure in Illinois: Enforcement of the Constitutional Right of Privacy," *Northwestern University Law Review*, XLVII (September–October, 1952), 493, 505.

78. E.g., Virgil W. Peterson, "Restrictions in the Law of Search and Seizure," *Northwestern University Law Review*, LII (March–April, 1957), 46, 62. The related and often-advocated proposal for civilian review boards to consider complaints against the police has met with virtually unanimous opposition from police officials. For an evaluation of the civilian boards functioning at present in Philadelphia and Rochester, N.Y., see Note, "The Administration of Complaints by Civilians against the Police," *Harvard Law Review*, LXXVII (January, 1964), 499.

79. These facts are drawn from the F.B.I. *Annual Report* for fiscal 1965 and from limited personal observation. Agents must be either graduates of a law school or of an accounting school. A constant check is kept on all the organization's agents, in both Washington and the branch offices, by the Inspection and Training Division. Agents are required to undergo periodical retraining, and some are assigned to specific cases for the sole purpose of learning the proper way to present evidence in court in such cases. Those agents with whom the author came into contact showed a keen understanding of, and a desire to live up to, the legal rules, qaulities which he sometimes found lacking in local police officials. An interesting comparison of F.B.I. and local police conduct in connection with brutality to the suspect is contained in Arnold Trebach, *The Rationing of Justice: Constitutional Rights and the Criminal Process* (New Brunswick, N.J., 1964), pp. 42–46. Of the twenty-four prisoners arrested by the F.B.I. whom Trebach interviewed, not one claimed that he had been subjected to violence or the threat of violence in order to extract a confession. By way of contrast, of the twenty-seven prisoners arrested by the Newark, New Jersey, police whom Trebach also interviewed, 78 per cent claimed to have been subjected to violence or the threat of violence.

enforcement could operate effectively under constitutional standards made enforceable by the exclusionary rule. It should be borne in mind, however, that the F.B.I. has experienced continuing readiness on the part of Congress to meet its financial needs and that its criminal jurisdiction is limited. It employs only fifteen thousand people, of whom only about half are agents. These agents are, in the main, specialized investigators and are not usually confronted with the split-second decisions sometimes required of officers on the beat. We also know that in California the rule has seemed to work well and to promote professionalization of law enforcement. According to the testimony of California's governor and former attorney general, Edmund G. Brown, "the police are doing better work. Their investigations are more thorough and within American constitutional concepts. . . . The over-all effects have been excellent. . . . I think there is more cooperation with the District Attorneys and this will make for better administration of justice."[80] Here again, a word of caution is in order. The California courts have construed the police search power much more liberally[81] than have the federal courts, and some of the California rulings may fall afoul of the Fourth Amendment. A much better example than either the F.B.I. or the California police would be the police in the District of Columbia, a densely populated urban area, who have managed to "live with" the exclusionary rule since 1914 without apparent harm to effective law enforcement.[82]

The burden of making an exclusionary rule work so as to conserve both public and individual interests rests on the judiciary. In Illinois (as of 1957) the exclusionary rule had had little effect in deterring illegal activity, partly because some judges applied it with political obligations in mind when freeing certain offenders and partly because the Chicago police seemed content to lose their cases in court so long as they could chalk up an imposing record of arrests with which to impress the public.[83] Thus a study of the Chicago Municipal Court branch known as the "Racket Court" for the year 1950 showed that in *two-thirds of all cases* the evidence was ordered suppressed as having been illegally obtained. However, the same study indicated that the rule was effective in deterring illegal searches where serious crimes were involved. In 19 per cent of narcotics cases and 25 per

80. Quoted in Kamisar, "*Wolf* and *Lustig*," p. 1158.

81. An authoritative article on the subject is David R. Manwaring, "California and the Fourth Amendment," *Stanford Law Review*, XVI (March, 1964), 318.

82. Washington has a clearance rate of major crimes that is twice the national average. Yale Kamisar, Book Review, *Harvard Law Review*, LXXVI (May, 1963), 1502, 1508, n. 22. Washington does have a high crime rate, but it is lower than that of some other major cities.

83. Peterson, "Restrictions," *passim*.

cent of concealed weapons cases the evidence was suppressed, in contrast to a record of 81 per cent suppression in gambling cases.[84] It is quite evident that where corruption and political influence exist, law enforcement officers will not be made to clean house under the influence of the exclusionary rule alone. Another study of the Chicago court system, made in 1951, showed that "raids are made to immunize the gamblers while at the same time satisfying the public that gamblers are being harassed by the police."[85] In such an environment the exclusionary rule itself becomes a tool of lawlessness, since the police can "arrest" the gamblers in the certain knowledge that they will be released following suppression of the evidence. As we have seen, however, even in Chicago the police were careful to obey the search law in most cases involving serious crime, that is, in cases where they really wished to obtain convictions.[86]

The exclusionary rule has been the subject of strong and frequent criticism.[87] The case against the rule can be simply stated and is, on the surface, a powerful one: a criminal is turned loose in order to teach a lesson to the policeman who collected the evidence and himself violated the law in so doing. The social cost is much too high. The proper way to deal with this situation would be to punish each directly for his own misdeeds. Under the exclusionary rule, however, the policeman is not disciplined, and society, upon which the criminal is now free to prey once again, is the ultimate loser. Moreover, the rule serves to recompense only the criminal, not the innocent victim of police misconduct whose case never comes before the court.

84. Comment, *Northwestern University Law Review*, pp. 497–98.

85. Samuel Dash, "Cracks in the Foundation of Criminal Justice," *University of Illinois Law Review*, XLVI (July–August, 1951), 385, 392.

86. Things have changed drastically for the better in Chicago since the appointment of a well-known criminologist, Orlando W. Wilson, as police superintendent in 1960, in the wake of a police burglary scandal. Mr. Wilson has completely energized his department, greatly improved its professional standing, and, for the most part, removed it from the political control which previously shackled it. This much was conceded by every expert on Chicago law enforcement, drawn from the police force and the local universities, whom the writer had the opportunity of interviewing in the fall of 1964 and the spring of 1965. See Virgil W. Peterson's annual *Report(s) on Chicago Crime*, issued by the Chicago Crime Commission, of which he is operating director, for details on the progress Chicago has made in recent years in obtaining honest and efficient law enforcement.

87. See, e.g., John Henry Wigmore, *A Treatise on the Anglo-American System of Evidence in Trials at Common Law* (3d ed.; Boston, 1940), Vol. VIII, Secs. 2183, 2184 (discussed on p. 84 *supra*); *People* v. *Defore,* 150 N.E. 585 (N.Y. 1926); Peterson, "Restrictions"; Frank J. McGarr, "The Exclusionary Rule: An Ill Conceived and Ineffective Remedy," *Journal of Criminal Law*, LII (September–October, 1961), 266.

The reply of the rule's proponents might be summarized[88] as follows: to advocate the punishment of search law offenders is to argue from logic, not experience. It is useless to talk of punishing offenders when such punishment does not in fact take place. Exclusion assists not only the guilty but the innocent as well, for in deterring unlawful searches it deters *all* unlawful searches, those of the innocent as well as of the guilty. To say that the rule has no effect in disciplining the offender is to ignore the fact that the conviction record upon which his professional reputation depends becomes tarnished when he does not obey the law. If the opponents of exclusion are sincere in their contention that illegal searches can be stopped by other means, why do they argue that exclusion hampers law enforcement? Does it make any difference whether it is the exclusionary rule or some other remedy which accomplishes that end? Law enforcement will suffer either way, and the criminal will go free in either case. In any event, there is no reason why law enforcement should suffer. The exclusionary rule might make it a little more difficult to catch criminals, but the Constitution never intended to make the policeman's lot an easy one. Finally, there are long-range interests of law to be preserved which go beyond the conviction of a particular criminal. These larger considerations require that the administration of justice not be sullied. If government is to be a teacher of good conduct, it cannot claim exemption from the same law which restrains both it and the individual.

It was amidst the interplay of these contending policy interests—the support of law enforcement lest society suffer through a more permissive attitude toward criminals, as against the support of individual security lest society suffer through a diminution of constitutional processes—that the Supreme Court chose in favor of the latter and imposed the exclusionary rule upon the states.[89] In so doing,

88. See e.g., Francis A. Allen, "The Wolf Case: Search and Seizure, Federalism, and the Civil Liberties," *Illinois Law Review*, XLV (March–April, 1950), 1; Monrad G. Paulsen, "The Exclusionary Rule and Misconduct by the Police," *Journal of Criminal Law*, LII (September–October, 1961), 255; the dissenting opinions of Justices Holmes and Brandeis in *Olmstead* v. *United States*, 277 U.S. 438 (1928); and *Youman* v. *Commonwealth*, 224 S.W. 860 (Ky. 1920).

89. Two alternative courses, short of total exclusion, remained to the Court. Neither of these was considered in the opinion. The Court could have imposed a selective exclusionary rule, by requiring the exclusion of evidence in the prosecution of most crimes, but not of the more serious ones, where the social cost of exclusion may outweigh the social benefits derived. Such an approach was tried in Michigan, which, operating under an exclusionary rule, nevertheless admitted in evidence firearms and narcotics illegally seized outside the home. "The consequences were predictable. The police, being of a pragmatic turn, tended to interpret the withdrawal of the rule in given offense categories as a license to proceed in those areas without legal restraint." Francis A. Allen, "Federalism and the Fourth Amendment: A Requiem for Wolf,"

the Court was being true to its own recent heritage and was bringing the freedom of privacy into line with other freedoms which it had protected from state interference with as much diligence as from federal interference. The fact that in the Mapp case the same decision could have been made on First Amendment grounds, and yet the case was decided on the search question, is an indication of the impatience which the Court evidently felt with the dilatory tactics of many of the states in not giving adequate protection to a federal guarantee.

The Mapp decision does not require the states to equate their search rules with the federal rules. So long as the states meet minimum constitutional standards (as yet largely undetermined), they will have freedom to develop search law consonant with their own particular needs. To be sure, there may be some initial confusion as state rules to meet constitutional standards are formulated, but even here the states, as a temporary expedient, may utilize the federal rules and decisions for guidance.[90] The Mapp decision affects not only the twenty-four states which followed the common-law rule of admissibility, but also the twenty-six which heretofore had adopted an exclusionary policy, since their standards must now conform to those of the Fourth Amendment. A number of exclusionary states, especially those which followed a policy of partial exclusion, clearly will have to revise their rules in the light of the Mapp decision. Many state courts and legislatures will be required to develop, for the first time, comprehensive rules regulating search and seizure. In those states which followed a policy of admissibility, little search law has been formulated because the evidence could be used in court regardless of the legality of its acquisition. Just as the federal exclusionary rule has forced the federal courts to develop the law of search and seizure, so the Mapp case will impose a similar task upon the state courts and legislatures with respect to state law. One of the most beneficial results of an exclusionary policy is that it

---

*The Supreme Court Review* (1961), pp. 1, 36. Or the Court might have adopted the policy of the Scottish courts that a deliberate violation of search law renders the seized evidence excludable, while an honest blunder on the part of the police allows its admission. Glanville L. Williams, "The Exclusionary Rule under Foreign Law: England," *Journal of Criminal Law*, LII (September–October, 1961), 272, 274–75. The Court may, however, have been apprehensive that this policy would result in a great deal of confusion in the state courts.

90. Some of the heretofore exclusionary states, for instance, Illinois and Missouri, had traditionally accorded the federal decisions a great deal of respect in their own courts.

requires constant education of police officers in the requirements of the law—a task that is usually neglected when the evidence, though illegally seized, is admissible. In jurisdictions which have adopted the exclusionary rule of their own volition, police departments have issued a large body of literature designed to acquaint their officers with restrictions placed on search and seizure.[91] Following the Mapp case, such literature may be expected to become even more plentiful.

Even the most enthusiastic advocate of the exclusionary rule would concede that the Mapp decision cannot be regarded as a cure-all for the problem of illegal searches. The decision does not, for instance, directly reach a large area of police misconduct in which unlawful search is carried on for the purpose of harassing the offender rather than prosecuting him. This misconduct is particularly rife in vice, gambling, and liquor cases, where evidence sufficient to justify a prosecution is difficult to acquire because there is little public co-operation, yet when nothing is done the police feel the lash of public resentment.[92]

The answer to the question of whether the letter and spirit of the Mapp decision will be implemented depends on the state judges. Not many cases, after all, get to the Supreme Court. One does not need the evidence of recent desegregation history to know that there is plenty of scope for judicial obstruction of Supreme Court decisions at the state level. A striking study by Professor David R. Manwaring of state court compliance with the Mapp decision shows that some state courts, such as those of New York, New Jersey, and Massachusetts, have moved with dispatch to implement the decision, while others, particularly Pennsylvania, have done everything possible to evade the consequences of the decision.[93] The problem is most pressing in the trial courts. Appellate judges are to some extent insulated; they do not have to see, in case after case, often sordid

91. Some of the titles are collected in Weinstein, "Local Responsibility," p. 170, n. 102. The volume currently authorized by the Milwaukee police force (Raymond A. Dahl and Howard H. Boyle, Jr., *Procedure and the Law of Arrest, Search and Seizure* [Milwaukee, Wis., 1961]) was written by a police inspector and a member of the bar and is as comprehensive a concise treatment of the subject as appears in the literature. An example of the kind of instruction offered in Washington, D.C., may be seen in the excellent series of lectures given to police officers on February 18, 1959, by the then United States Attorney, Oliver Gasch, and three assistants and later published under the title, *Application of Law on Search and Seizure to Police Procedures* (Washington, n.d.).

92. For discussion see LaFave, *Arrest*, pp. 300ff. Federal officers, too, engage in harassing tactics. The head of a federal narcotics unit told the author that his men do search unlawfully because they have an obligation "to get narcotics off the street" even if no prosecution results.

93. David R. Manwaring, "The Impact of *Mapp* v. *Ohio*," unpublished paper delivered at the 1964 Annual Meeting of the American Political Science Association, Chicago, Illinois, September 9–12, 1964.

defendants invoking the protection of the exclusionary rule and thereby escaping just punishment. Not only are trial judges confronted with obviously guilty defendants seeking their freedom via the exclusionary route, but also they tend to have close and frequent contacts with the police. Significantly, it is the appellate judges, not the trial judges, who are usually considered "enemies" of law enforcement by the police. A leading New York defense attorney writes that in the lower courts "great antipathy is directed to a defendant who asserts his fourth amendment rights."[94]

The warrant-issuing process will need to undergo some change. Magistrates, particularly in rural areas, often have no training in the law at all, while in urban areas they frequently handle their responsibilities in an extremely lackadaisical fashion. If warrants are to be used by the police more often than in the past, magistrates will have to be available on an around-the-clock basis, and they will need some knowledge of search law. Warrants that are issued on a *pro forma* basis are no more protective of the right to privacy than was the general warrant, yet abundant evidence exists that many overworked (and sometimes underworked)[95] judges do not scrutinize warrant requests.[96] They either sign without question or else delegate the warrant-issuing function to a clerk. Even on the federal level we do not know whether the warrant requirement is the protection for the citizen which the framers intended it to be. Many, if not most, warrants are issued by United States commissioners, who have standing as judicial officers. One-third of the commissioners were never trained in the law, and Chief Justice Warren has recently expressed his concern about their caliber.[97]

The Supreme Court can illuminate problems and bring them to public attention better than it can solve them. A concerted executive-legislative-judicial effort is required on both the federal and state level if the problem of unlawful searches (and of other forms of police misconduct) is to be solved. Courts need to know more in

94. Henry B. Rothblatt, "The Arrest: Probable Cause and Search without a Search Warrant," *Mississippi Law Journal*, XXXV (March, 1964), 252, 267.

95. Samuel Dash writes: "One day I clocked the speed at which cases were handled [in a Chicago court] and came out with an average of seven cases every few minutes, less than two minutes a case. The fastest judge I observed would arrive at 9:45 a.m. and be out at 10 a.m. having disposed of twenty cases." "Criminal Justice," p. 389.

96. E.g., LaFave, *Arrest*, p. 518; Frank W. Miller and Lawrence P. Tiffany, "Prosecutor Dominance of the Warrant Decision: A Study of Current Practices," *Washington University Law Quarterly*, Vol. 1964 (February, 1964), pp. 1, 5–6.

97. Address delivered by Earl Warren, Chief Justice of the United States, at the Annual Meeting of the American Law Institute, May 18, 1965. The author is indebted to Chief Justice Warren for a copy of the text.

the way of "hard facts" about law enforcement problems in solving crime; executive officials and legislatures must both do more to fulfill law enforcement needs. A couple of developments indicate that forceful leadership, at least on the national level, may be forthcoming. On August 10, 1964, the Justice Department created a new Office of Criminal Justice "to bridge the gulf between police and civil liberties advocates."[98] Then, on July 26, 1965, President Johnson announced the formation of a President's Commission on Law Enforcement and Administration of Justice, to be headed by the Attorney General. He charged the commission with a broad study of crime and its causes and of law enforcement problems in all their aspects and at all levels of government. The commission is to report to him in eighteen months with its recommendations.[99] One would hope that this commission will meet with more success in arousing the nation to its responsibilities than did its predecessor, the Wickersham Commission. The report of the Wickersham Commission in 1931[100] brought widespread police misconduct to the attention of the public, though it appears to have had less influence on Congress and the legislatures than on the Supreme Court. It is perhaps no coincidence that the Supreme Court's increased concern over the quality of criminal justice in this country began to manifest itself shortly after publication of the Wickersham Commission's report.

By no means all state police officials are antagonistic to the exclusionary rule. State law enforcement officers with whom this writer spoke were about evenly divided in their reception of the Mapp case. Many thought it a wholesome development which would result in a necessary clarification of search rules and would imbue state legislatures and city councils with a sense of the urgency of the need to overcome their apathy to law enforcement problems and to finance a thorough professionalization of police forces. In any event, the effect of the Mapp decision is not likely to cause a wholesale reduction in the number of convictions. The findings of Professor Weinstein's survey are pertinent. In a poll of Colorado law enforcement officials that he conducted, only four of the twenty-nine respondents thought that their ability to obtain convictions would be impaired in more than 10 per cent of their cases tried. Fourteen estimated that

98. *Washington Post*, August 11, 1964, p. 42.
99. *The New York Times*, July 27, 1965, p. 1.
100. *Report of the National Commission on Law Enforcement and Observance* (14 vols.; Washington, 1931).

they would be affected in fewer than 1 per cent of their cases.[101] The main burden is, of course, likely to fall on those police forces whose professional standards are lowest. A writer for a law enforcement journal asked, "Can law enforcement operate effectively within this limitation?" and then provided the answer: "The competent, intelligent and trained police officer can do so. The incompetent, unintelligent, untrained police officer cannot. The obvious solution to the search and seizure dilemma is professionalization of the police."[102] Perhaps state legislatures and police forces will heed the warning of F.B.I. Director J. Edgar Hoover, who said: "Civil Rights violations are all the more regrettable because they are so unnecessary. Professional standards in law enforcement provide for fighting crime with intelligence rather than force."[103]

The exasperation of prosecutors with the exclusionary rule is quite understandable. The prosecutor may develop the feeling that he has to fight courts as well as criminals, that the cards are "stacked" against him. Of course some criminals go free—there are no available statistics on the precise number, but it seems safe to say that on the whole it is small. (On the federal level 90 per cent of all defendants plead guilty.) In any event, it would be foolish to blame the high incidence of crime on the exclusionary rule: no criminal, when committing a crime, can safely assume that the evidence against him will be seized in an unlawful manner. If he *could* so assume, there would perhaps be even more reason for the rule, since it would be an indication that lawlessness in law enforcement was more rampant

101. Weinstein, "Local Responsibility," p. 176. Professor Nagel has done a limited but useful survey of the effects of the Mapp rule on law enforcement during the first two years of its operation. The results are encouraging. In the opinion of a clear majority of the 113 respondents to his questionnaire (who were drawn from the ranks of police chiefs, prosecutors, judges, defense lawyers, and American Civil Liberties Union officials across the country), police observance of law has increased and better education is being provided for police officers, both in states which had followed an exclusionary policy prior to the Mapp case and in those which initiated the policy in 1961. As for police effectiveness in searches, the states which had been exclusionary showed no change, but in the newly exclusionary states the respondents to the questionnaire were sharply divided: 39 per cent reported no change, 43 per cent reported a decrease, and 17 per cent actually noted an increase. Stuart S. Nagel, "Testing the Effects of Excluding Illegally Seized Evidence," *Wisconsin Law Review*, Vol. 1965 (Spring, 1965), pp. 283, 286.

The experience in Detroit is pertinent. Judge George Edwards of the United States Court of Appeals for the Sixth Circuit served as police commissioner of Detroit in 1962 and 1963; he required the police to adhere strictly to the rules of search and seizure (as well as to those relating to confessions, arraignment, and counsel) as formulated by the Supreme Court. "And the town did not fall apart. Murder and pillage did not run rampant," said Judge Edwards. On the contrary, law enforcement officers became more effective, and public confidence in the police was enhanced. *The New York Times*, December 7, 1965, p. 33.

102. Irving B. Zeichner. "This Is the Law," *Law and Order,* August, 1961, pp. 9, 81.

103. Quoted in *Elkins* v. *United States*, 364 U.S. 206, 218, n. 8 (1960).

than anyone had suspected. It should be emphasized that many violations of the search rules are quite needless: the requirements for the issuance of warrants can often be met, and warrants could be readily obtained, if only officers would take the trouble to apply for them.

The Fourth Amendment attempted to strike a balance between the community interest in order and the individual interest in liberty. The Mapp decision, in effect, constitutes a conscious judgment on the part of the Court that both law enforcement and the public can "live with" the constitutional search rules as presently formulated. The Court may be wrong. It is possible that the constitutional pendulum is swinging too far in the direction of individual liberty and that the community interest is no longer adequately protected (although when one considers the broad scope of search incidental to arrest and the Court's lenient attitude toward the standards needed to establish probable cause, one may legitimately question any such contention). If so, reinterpretation by the Court, and even constitutional amendment, might be in order. But we shall never know for certain unless a concerted effort is made to live within the confines of the Fourth Amendment. These may well prove to be sufficiently roomy to accommodate the interests of both the public and the individual. So far, this effort has not been made. With the Mapp decision on the record, perhaps it will be.

## CHAPTER VIII

## EAVESDROPPING AND THE CONSTITUTION

In one area involving Fourth Amendment problems, that of eavesdropping on conversations by means of mechanical devices, the problems are so intricate and the issues so controversial as to require separate discussion. The conditions of modern living, with close proximity of dwellings and people, rapid transportation, easy communication, and, not least, the developments of modern technology, have gravely accentuated the problem of retaining a reasonable area of privacy for the individual. The idealized house of the eighteenth and nineteenth century, castle-like in the privacy it afforded its inhabitants, has given way to the modern dwelling, which is subject to all sorts of intrusions never dreamt of by our forefathers. The modern eavesdropper is able not only to report on us, but with the assistance of science, can actually reproduce our very words as spoken with all their nuances, tones, and individual characteristics.

The problem of the eavesdropper who is ready to invade the privacy of others, either for his personal gain or out of a sense of public duty, has probably always been with us. Eavesdropping was made a crime by the common law. The great English jurist of the eighteenth century, Sir William Blackstone, defined the malaise, and its punishment, thus: "*Eaves-droppers*, or such as listen under walls or windows or eaves of a house, to hearken after discourse, and thereupon to frame slanderous and mischievous tales, are a common nuisance, and are presentable at the court-leet; or are indictable at the sessions, and punishable by finding sureties for their good behavior."[1]

The eavesdropper of old did not present a major problem to society, for it was possible to guard against his presence. With the invention of the telegraph and telephone and their quick acceptance as indispensable means of communication, however, the problem of the eavesdropper assumed new magnitude. No longer did the person spied upon need to be within listening distance. The devices of science could now be utilized to facilitate the task of the eavesdropper, who might be far removed from his victim physically and yet be able

1. Sir William Blackstone, *Commentaries on the Laws of England*, ed. William Draper Lewis (Philadelphia, 1900), Vol. IV, chap. xiii, sec. 168.

to maintain surveillance as efficiently as if he were hidden in the kitchen closet.

Eavesdroppers did not wait long to capitalize on the invention of the telegraph, and interception of transmitted messages became a prevalent practice. As a consequence, a number of state legislatures in the latter half of the nineteenth century enacted measures to deal with the menace. These laws, however, were "malicious injury" statutes, which had as their main purpose the protection of the telegraph company's property, not the safeguarding of the individual's privacy of communication.[2] When the interception of telephone communications—especially of news dispatches by competing newspapers—came into vogue, some of the states again acted. Thus, Illinois in 1895 prohibited interception of news dispatches, and California in 1905 forbade all telephone wire tapping.[3]

Inevitably, wire tapping did not long remain the preserve of private persons but was also resorted to by law enforcement officers as an aid in the solution of crimes. In New York City as early as 1895 the police had begun to tap wires with the co-operation of the telephone company. Following the disclosure of their tapping of the telephone of a Catholic priest in 1916, in an investigation of charity frauds, a clamor arose for federal action to outlaw wire tapping. Entry of the United States into the war forestalled immediate action, but in 1918 Congress did pass a law prohibiting all wire tapping.[4] "The motivation behind the adoption of the statute was apparently a congressional fear that the secrecy of governmental activities was being jeopardized by tapping."[5] This wartime law, however, was of limited duration; by its own terms it was to remain in effect only so long as the government operated the telephone system. With the war over and the telephone system again in the hands of private owners, the act expired.[6] Once more, there was no national policy for the control of wire tapping.

With the lapsing of this restrictive legislation, the federal government, which hitherto apparently had not engaged in wire tapping, began to do so. Attorney General A. Mitchell Palmer ordered the use of wire taps in connection with the antisubversive raids he was planning. In 1920 Treasury agents also began to utilize the wire tap

2. For an analysis of these laws see Margaret Lybolt Rozenzweig, "The Law of Wire Tapping," *Cornell Law Quarterly*, XXXIII (September, 1947), 73.
3. Samuel Dash, Robert E. Knowlton, and Richard F. Schwartz, *The Eavesdroppers* (New Brunswick, N.J., 1959), pp. 25–26.
4. 40 Stat. 1017.
5. Comment, "Wiretapping and the Congress," *Michigan Law Review*, LII (January, 1954), 430, 436.
6. *Ibid.*

to aid in enforcing the newly adopted Eighteenth Amendment. Protests were not long in coming, and in 1924 Attorney General Harlan F. Stone in unequivocal terms ordered the newly organized Federal Bureau of Investigation to make no use of wire tapping in its investigations. He branded wire tapping "unethical tactics" and declared that it would "not be tolerated" by the Justice Department.[7] This directive, however, had no effect on the Treasury Department, whose agents continued to tap wires as before; indeed, wire tapping was "the principal method used . . . to catch [prohibition] offenders."[8] It was one such Treasury wire tap that led to the case of *Olmstead* v. *United States*,[9] decided in 1928, where the Court for the first time dealt with the constitutional question raised by wire tapping. The Olmstead case is considered a landmark in constitutional law, perhaps not so much for the decision itself as for the quality of its oft-quoted dissenting opinions.

The term "search" is not self-defining, any more than is the term "unreasonable." Whether the Constitution permitted the interception of telephone communications for the gathering of criminal evidence—whether the wire tap was indeed a search within the terms of the Fourth Amendment—was the dilemma the Court was called upon to resolve in the Olmstead case. The men who wrote the Fourth Amendment knew of only one type of search, that involving physical entry into a dwelling. There was nothing in the way of precedent, and little in the way of analogy, to guide the Court. General principles derived from deeply felt moral values, rather than technical points based on precedent, would be decisive here.

The Olmstead case involved a gigantic conspiracy to violate the National Prohibition Act through the illegal importation, distribution, and sale of alcoholic beverages. Roy Olmstead, after whom the case takes its name, was merely one, though the most important, in a long list of persons convicted. No fewer than fifty persons were employed in the operation; two seagoing ships and a number of coastal vessels were involved. It was an amazingly lucrative enterprise: although capitalized at only twenty-one thousand dollars, sales exceeded two million dollars a year. Of the profits, Olmstead received half, and the remainder was divided equally among his eleven partners.

The evidence was uncovered through the use of taps placed on the conspirators' telephone wires. No trespass on private property was

7. William S. Fairfield and Charles Clift, "The Wiretappers," *Our Times: The Best from The Reporter*, ed. Max Ascoli (New York, 1960), pp. 50, 53–54.
8. Dash *et al.*, *The Eavesdroppers*, p. 28.
9. 277 U.S. 438 (1928).

involved because the taps were installed in the basement of the Seattle office building of Olmstead and his partners and in the streets near their residences. For five months their conversations on the telephone were overheard; the typed transcript of what they said filled 775 pages. Complete information on the operation, including details of the promise of graft to Seattle police officers, was obtained.

The novelty and difficulty of the case is suggested by the fact that the Court divided five to four, the first such close division in any search case. Chief Justice Taft, in his opinion for the Court, rejected the contention that wire tapping was a search under the Fourth Amendment. The Gouled case,[10] which equated the search by stealth with the search by force, at least involved physical entry into the home and was to be regarded as carrying "the inhibition against unreasonable searches and seizures to the extreme limit."[11] No analogy could be drawn between wire tapping and the opening of sealed letters in the mails, deemed by the Court to be in violation of the Fourth Amendment.[12] The government, which exercised a monopoly over the carrying of the mails, guaranteed their protection, but it bore no responsibility for the inviolability of the telephone wires. The Fourth Amendment covered only such searches as had given rise to its enactment. Viewed in this light, wire tapping did not run afoul of the Constitution. "There was no searching. . . . The evidence was secured by the use of . . . hearing and that only," said Taft. "There was no entry of the houses or offices of the defendants."[13] Nor could the interception of a conversation qualify as a seizure under the Fourth Amendment, for the amendment referred only to the seizure of tangible items. Moreover, one who uses a telephone

10. *Gouled* v. *United States*, 255 U.S. 298 (1921).

11. 277 U.S. 438, 463.

12. *In re Jackson*, 96 U.S. 727 (1878). In this case the Court, speaking through Justice Field, held that an act prohibiting the mailing of certain materials did not at the same time confer on the post office authority to search sealed letters for evidence of its violation. Such an authorization, said Field in a dictum, would not be consistent with the Fourth Amendment, which required a warrant for the search of correspondence no less than for that of dwellings. However, in another case, where the letters were opened not by the post office but by a prison warden in a routine censoring of the inmates' mail, the interception was deemed not violative of the Fourth Amendment. The letters, written by a prisoner who had killed a guard while in the penitentiary and used to convict him of the crime, "came," said Justice Day, "into the possession of the officials of the penitentiary under established practice, reasonably designed to promote the discipline of the institution." *Stroud* v. *United States*, 251 U.S. 15, 21 (1919).

13. 277 U.S. 438, 464. In a rather imperfect analogy, Taft cited *United States* v. *Lee,* where Justice Brandeis wrote the opinion of the Court holding that the use of a searchlight by Coast Guard officers for the purpose of spotting contraband aboard a vessel at sea did not violate the Fourth Amendment. "Such use of a searchlight," he said, "is comparable to the use of a marine glass or a field glass. It is not prohibited by the Constitution." 274 U.S. 559, 563 (1927).

is in communication with someone who is outside the house: "The language of the Amendment can not be extended and expanded to include telephone wires reaching to the whole world from the defendant's house or office. The intervening wires are not part of his house or office. . . ."[14]

Even if the Fourth Amendment did not render wire tapping a search in the constitutional sense, Olmstead contended that the evidence was nevertheless inadmissible as having been obtained in violation of Washington state law, which made wire tapping a criminal offense. The Chief Justice rejected this argument by limiting the application of the federal exclusionary rule to violations of the Constitution. This rule, he said, was derived from the terms of the Constitution itself and, as such, applied only to evidence gathered in violation of the Constitution, not of a statute. Congress, no doubt, could make such evidence inadmissible, but until this was done, it would be wrong for the Court to depart from the common-law rule that competent evidence was admissible at trial regardless of the manner of its acquisition. In a passage which revealingly summed up the majority's philosophy and its low esteem of the exclusionary rule (at least when its protection was invoked by bootleggers), he said: "A standard which would forbid the reception of evidence if obtained by other than nice ethical conduct by government officials would make society suffer and give criminals greater immunity than has been known heretofore."[15] He did not explain why, if this was so, the exclusionary rule was adopted for violations of the Fourth Amendment itself.

Justice Holmes's dissent is one of his best-known opinions because of his characterization of wire tapping as "dirty business."[16] Too much has been imputed to these words. Actually, Justice Holmes was referring not to wire tapping itself but to *illegal* wire tapping. Indeed, he was "not prepared to say that the penumbra of the 4th and 5th Amendments covers the defendant,"[17] and he addressed himself exclusively to the moral issue involved, that is, whether evidence secured in violation of law should be admissible. Justice Holmes thought not, for "the government should not itself foster and pay for other crimes, when they are the means by which the evidence is to be obtained. . . . We have to choose, and for my part I think it a less evil that some criminals should escape than that the govern-

14. *Ibid.*, p. 465.
15. *Ibid.*, p. 468.
16. *Ibid.*, p. 470.
17. *Ibid.*, p. 469.

ment should play an ignoble part."[18] If evidence obtained in violation of the Constitution was excludable from federal trials, evidence obtained in violation of statutory law, even state law, should also be excluded. The moral problem in each instance was the same and could be resolved only by forbidding the government to bring the evidence into court.

Justice Brandeis also had some strong words to say on the moral issue, but, unlike Holmes, he was unequivocal in his assertion that wire tapping was a search within the meaning of the Fourth Amendment. The Constitution was sufficiently flexible to deal with situations not envisaged when it was framed, and he therefore could not agree that a search was not a search merely because the method employed was of recent vintage and unknown to the eighteenth century: "Time works changes, brings into existence new conditions and purposes. Therefore a principle to be vital must be capable of wider application than the mischief which gave it birth."[19] It was situations such as this one that had prompted Chief Justice Marshall, in the great case of *McCulloch* v. *Maryland*, to declare: "we must never forget that it is *a Constitution* we are expounding."[20] Just as the Constitution had in numerous cases been interpreted so as to bring within the regulatory power of the federal government "objects of which the Fathers could not have dreamed,"[21] so must it also be interpreted to bring within the limitations placed on government other objects, destructive of individual liberty, equally unknown to the framers. The Court had previously construed the Fourth Amendment liberally, in terms of its underlying purpose rather than its exact wording. A number of cases, including *Boyd* v. *United States*,[22] bore testimony to that fact. The forced surrender of private papers to the government, with which the Boyd case was concerned, was hardly a search in the usual meaning of the word, yet it was deemed a violation of the Fourth Amendment. Nor was the opening of sealed letters in the mail forbidden by the Fourth Amendment, literally construed; once again the amendment was liberally interpreted, so as to protect against such a practice.

Justice Brandeis would have construed the Fourth Amendment not literally but liberally, placing the emphasis on underlying purpose rather than textual exegesis. In words that today seem to be almost prophetic, he painted a grim picture of the probable consequences to

18. *Ibid.*, p. 470.
19. *Ibid.*, pp. 472–73.
20. 4 Wheaton 316, 407 (1819).
21. 277 U.S. 438, 472.
22. 116 U.S. 616 (1886).

privacy of the new technology if the protection of the Constitution could not be invoked to cope with this development:

> Subtler and more far-reaching means of invading privacy have become available to the government. Discovery and invention have made it possible for the government, by means far more effective than stretching upon the rack, to obtain disclosure in court of what is whispered in the closet. . . . The progress of science in furnishing the government with means of espionage is not likely to stop with wire-tapping. Ways may some day be developed by which the government, without removing papers from secret drawers, can reproduce them in court, and by which it will be enabled to expose to a jury the most intimate occurrences of the home. Advances in the psychic and related sciences may bring means of exploring unexpressed beliefs, thoughts and emotions.[23]

Turning to the moral issue which had agitated Justice Holmes, Justice Brandeis agreed that, regardless of the constitutionality of wire tapping, evidence obtained by this method should be held inadmissible when obtained, as in this case, in violation of law. It was a fallacy, thought Brandeis, to regard the illegal act as one committed by private parties in which the government itself had no hand because of the theory that an officer of the law has no authority to violate it. This proposition is true only so long as the government does not put to use evidence so obtained. "When," however, "the government, having full knowledge, sought, through the Department of Justice, to avail itself of the fruits of these acts in order to accomplish its own ends, it assumed moral responsibility for the officers' crimes."[24] Brandeis drew an analogy to equity law, which denies relief to private parties coming to court with "unclean hands." "Where the government is the actor," he averred, "the reasons for applying it [the unclean hands doctrine] are even more persuasive. Where the remedies invoked are those of the criminal law, the reasons are compelling."[25]

For Brandeis, however, it was not logical symmetry alone that required the exclusion of evidence obtained by violation of statutory law no less than by violation of the Constitution. The exclusionary rule served not only as a deterrent of illegal conduct; it was also a powerful moral agency holding the government to the same standards of conduct as apply to the private citizen. "Our government is the potent, the omnipresent, teacher. For good or for ill, it teaches the whole people by its example. Crime is contagious. If the gov-

23. 277 U.S. 438, 473–74.
24. *Ibid.*, p. 483.
25. *Ibid.*, p. 484.

ernment becomes a law-breaker, it breeds contempt for law; it invites every man to become a law unto himself; it invites anarchy."[26]

Justices Butler and Stone, in separate opinions, agreed that wire tapping was unconstitutional. As Attorney General, Stone had prohibited the use of wire tapping by the Department of Justice, and he agreed with all that Holmes and Brandeis had said regarding the moral issue involved in the admission of evidence acquired through a violation of law. Butler, however, protested that the order granting *certiorari* had limited the arguments of counsel to the constitutional issue, and he therefore refused to say whether the violation of state law would alone have been sufficient to render the evidence inadmissible.[27]

Scholarly reaction to the Olmstead decision was varied. Most commentators agreed with the dissenters, though some thought the decision to be correct. Representative of the latter viewpoint was Dean Wigmore, who stressed the needs of law enforcement. "Ordinarily," he said, "no gentleman listens to another gentleman's private conversation. But we respectfully decline to agree that it is 'dirty business' for a gentleman to overhear deliberately a conversation held by a professed law-breaker in the process of doing his unlawful act."[28] To this contention one writer asked in rebuttal, "But is not this argument the age old fallacy of beginning with an assumption of guilt?"[29]

The Olmstead decision was unfavorably received in the country, and legislative efforts to nullify its effects were not long delayed. By 1932 eight bills had been introduced in Congress with the object of prohibiting wire tapping by federal officers, or at least of making evidence seized thereby inadmissible in federal court, but all these bills failed of enactment.[30] In 1933, however, these efforts were crowned with a limited degree of success when a rider to an appropriations bill prohibited the use of public funds for wire tapping in enforcement of the National Prohibition Act.[31] This act, however, became a dead letter the same year with the repeal of the Eighteenth Amendment.

26. *Ibid.*, p. 485.
27. Justice Stone replied that the Court had ample authority to treat any question necessary for the disposition of the case, regardless of the limitations placed on the arguments of counsel by the order granting *certiorari*.
28. John H. Wigmore, Comment, *Illinois Law Review*, XXIII (December, 1928), 377, 378.
29. Comment, "Wire Tapping," *Law Notes*, XXXII (January, 1929), 183.
30. Alan F. Westin, "The Wire-Tapping Problem: An Analysis and a Legislative Proposal," *Columbia Law Review*, LII (February, 1952), 165, 173–74.
31. 47 Stat. 1381.

In 1934 Congress passed the enabling act of the Federal Communications Commission. This act contained a provision, Section 605, which stated in part that "no person not being authorized by the sender shall intercept any communication and divulge or publish the existence, contents, substance, purport, effect or meaning of such intercepted communication to any person. . . ."[32] On the surface, Section 605 might appear to forbid unauthorized interception of telephone messages. But there is nothing in the legislative history of the act to indicate any such intention on the part of Congress. "On the contrary," write Professors Bradley and Hogan, "it is clear that the Federal Communications Act was chiefly designed to transfer jurisdiction over wire and radio communications [from the then-existing Radio Commission] to the newly-created Federal Communications Commission. The language of section 605 is almost identical in wording to the provisions of the old Radio Act of 1927, which was in effect when *Olmstead* was decided. . . . Certainly it is quite strange to style one who participates in a telephone conversation a 'sender.' "[33] Nevertheless, the Court was to take a different view of the matter.

The Olmstead case, in which the constitutional issue was decided, marked the first phase of Supreme Court decisions on wire tapping. The 1937 case of *Nardone* v. *United States*[34] marked the beginning of a new phase, dealing with the interpretation of Section 605. Nardone was convicted of alcohol smuggling. The evidence was obtained through the tapping of his telephone wires by federal agents. Nardone urged the Court to find that Section 605 applied to wire tapping and that, moreover, evidence so acquired was excludable from federal court. In an opinion by Justice Roberts, the Court agreed. While admitting that the legislative history did not demonstrate a congressional intent to apply Section 605 to wire tapping, Roberts nevertheless asserted that wire tapping was within the "plain mandate"[35] of the statute. The "plain words" of Section 605 prohibited interception and divulgence of telephone conversations. "To recite the contents of the message in testimony before a court is to

32. 48 Stat. 1103, 47 U.S.C., sec. 605. The penal provisions, authorizing imprisonment or fine or both for violations of Section 605, are in Section 501 of the same act. 48 Stat. 1100, 47 U.S.C., sec. 501.

33. Edwin J. Bradley and James E. Hogan, "Wiretapping from Nardone to Benanti and Rathbun," *Georgetown Law Journal*, XLVI (Spring, 1958), 418, 422.

34. *Nardone* v. *United States*, 302 U.S. 379 (1937).

35. *Ibid.*, p. 383.

divulge the message."[36] Roberts rejected the contention that, in any event, Section 605 was not intended to restrain wire tapping by law enforcement officers and that the word "person" in the act referred only to private persons. "Taken at face value," he replied, "the phrase 'no person' comprehends federal agents. . . ."[37] The reason why Congress had taken a position which might prove an impediment to law enforcement was "one of policy. Congress may have thought it less important that some offenders should go unwhipped of justice than that officers should resort to methods deemed inconsistent with ethical standards and destructive of personal liberty."[38]

Just as in the Olmstead case the Court had read the Fourth Amendment literally and found wire tapping permissible, so in the Nardone case the Court read Section 605 liberally and found wire tapping to be forbidden under its terms. "Assuming," say Professors Bradley and Hogan, "that there is any such 'mandate' in section 605, one can hardly speak of it as 'plain.' In fact the legislature could not have better obscured its 'mandate,' had it intended to send the Court looking for a needle in a legal haystack."[39] Evidently, it was the spirit of the Olmstead dissenters which animated Justice Roberts' opinion. Several important changes in the Court's personnel had taken place since the Olmstead decision. Gone from the Court were three members of the Olmstead majority—Chief Justice Taft and Justices Van Devanter and Sanford, who had been replaced by Chief Justice Hughes and Justices Roberts and Black—while three of the four Olmstead dissenters, Justices Brandeis, Butler, and Stone, still sat on the Court. (Justice Holmes had retired and had been replaced by Justice Cardozo.) It is of significance that the two survivors of the Olmstead majority, Justices Sutherland and McReynolds, were both to be found in dissent in the Nardone case.[40] The decision probably reflected an uneasiness on the part of the Court about the Olmstead decision, which it did not wish to overrule but which it instead circumvented by reading into Section 605 that which had been surrendered in the Olmstead case.

Despite the Nardone decision, federal law enforcement officers continued to search for loopholes in Section 605 to permit them to utilize wire tapping. It is worthy of note that from 1937 to 1942, and beginning with the Nardone case, only one conventional search

36. *Ibid.*, p. 382.
37. *Ibid.*, p. 381.
38. *Ibid.*, p. 383.
39. Bradley and Hogan, "Wiretapping," p. 422.
40. On the ground that Congress had intended to exempt law enforcement officers from the prohibition.

case reached the Court, as compared with five cases involving wire tapping or some other form of eavesdropping.[41] In *Weiss* v. *United States*,[42] decided in 1939, the Court closed two further loopholes in Section 605 by holding that the statutory prohibition of wire tapping extended to intrastate, as well as interstate, messages and that the consent of the sender obtained after the tapping by a promise of leniency was insufficient to render the intercepted message admissible in evidence. The Weiss decision was of far-reaching import. "Had the government been successful in its effort to confine section 605 to interstate calls, the prohibition would have been only a minor handicap to law enforcement officials. Instead, the *Nardone* doctrine now protected every telephone conversation in the United States."[43] However, as fast as the Supreme Court closed possible loopholes in Section 605, the Department of Justice diligently searched for and discovered new ones.

In the Nardone case, the Supreme Court had reversed the conviction as having been obtained through the use of evidence obtained by an illegal wire tap. However, the Court had no need on that occasion to rule on the question of whether evidence derivatively obtained through the use of wire taps is admissible at trial. In Fourth Amendment cases it is not only the illegally seized evidence itself that is inadmissible; equally inadmissible is other evidence obtained through leads provided by the illegal search. Thus, for example, a conviction obtained with the use of photostats made of documents illegally seized is as void as if the documents themselves were received in evidence because, in Justice Holmes's words, "the essence of a provision forbidding the acquisition of evidence in a certain way is that not merely evidence so acquired shall not be used before the court, but that it shall not be used at all."[44] Whether this doctrine applied also to wire tap evidence was the question at issue in the second Nardone case.[45]

Following the reversal of his conviction, Nardone was retried by the government and again convicted. At the trial his counsel sought to ascertain whether the government's evidence was obtained derivatively from the illegal wire taps but was denied permission by the

41. The only conventional search case decided in this five-year span was *Scher* v. *United States*, 305 U.S. 251 (1938), which is discussed in Chapter IV. The eavesdropping cases were, in addition to the Nardone case just discussed: *Weiss* v. *United States*, 308 U.S. 321 (1939); *Nardone* v. *United States*, 308 U.S. 338 (1939); *Goldstein* v. *United States*, 316 U.S. 114 (1942); and *Goldman* v. *United States*, 316 U.S. 129 (1942).

42. 308 U.S. 321 (1939).

43. Bradley and Hogan, "Wiretapping," p. 425.

44. *Silverthorne Lumber Co.* v. *United States*, 251 U.S. 385, 392 (1920).

45. *Nardone* v. *United States*, 308 U.S. 338 (1939).

trial judge to examine the prosecution for this purpose. This ruling, said Justice Frankfurter in his opinion for the Court, was erroneous. The burden of establishing wire tapping in the first place rests on the defense, but, once established (as it was in this case), the trial court must allow a determination of whether the government's case rests on leads furnished by the illegal wire taps. If this be so, the evidence, though derivatively obtained, is nevertheless inadmissible as "a fruit of the poisonous tree."[46] The first Nardone case, he remarked revealingly, "was not the product of a merely meticulous reading of technical language. It was the translation into practicality of broad considerations of morality and public well-being."[47]

What were the "broad considerations of morality and public well-being" which had animated the Court's reading of Section 605? By now it was clear that in construing the statute the Court was attempting to "reverse" the Olmstead case. The continuous analogies to search and seizure cases make this point obvious. In every issue arising under Section 605, that statutory provision was deemed to have no independent existence outside the framework of Fourth Amendment interpretation. No matter what the issue before the Court, it was decided with recourse to the analogous constitutional law of search and seizure. Regardless of the formal justifications offered for the decisions through ingenious readings of the statute, the Court simply imputed to Congress the intention to extend the protection of the Fourth Amendment to telephone messages. Thus Section 605 not only made wire tapping illegal after the manner of warrantless searches, but it also made evidence so obtained inadmissible, whether in its original or in a derivative form. The Supreme Court's constant recourse to the Fourth Amendment in order to ascertain the meaning of Section 605 is not surprising. "When the Supreme Court took an inappropriate rib from the Federal Communications Act and breathed into it a life-giving principle, it could not expect to be done with the matter. It had unleashed a statutory frankenstein to wander about the United States Code with little guide to its meaning."[48] The Fourth Amendment proved to be a handy device for the interpretation of Section 605.

To equate the meaning of Section 605 with the meaning of the Fourth Amendment might be both conducive to and destructive of individual privacy. As we have previously seen, a doctrine firmly entrenched in the lower courts, though never before considered by

46. *Ibid.*, p. 341.
47. *Ibid.*, p. 340.
48. Bradley and Hogan, "Wiretapping," p. 423.

the Supreme Court, held that the exclusionary rule could not be invoked by a defendant when the evidence against him was obtained in violation of the rights of a third party.[49] The Fourth Amendment was interpreted as a personal privilege, after the fashion of property rights. A house guest, for example, might be convicted on evidence illegally gathered from the dwelling of his host, for it was the host, and not the guest, whose property had been invaded. In the 1942 case of *Goldstein* v. *United States*,[50] the Court was called upon to decide whether Section 605 made an analogous doctrine mandatory for wire tapping evidence.

The Goldstein case was an aftermath of the Weiss case and dealt with some wire tap recordings suppressed when the protection of Section 605 was extended to intrastate messages. Goldstein, however, had not been a party to any of the intercepted calls, though what was said by others implicated him as well. If the Fourth Amendment was to be the guiding light in the interpretation of Section 605, the Goldstein conviction would have to stand, for the evidence had not been obtained in violation of Goldstein's personal rights. "The government in effect argued that what is sauce for the goose is sauce for the gander."[51] In his opinion for the Court, Justice Roberts agreed. Though he added that the statute itself made such a decision mandatory—"as the sender might make such divulgence lawful by his consent, none but he was intended to be protected against divulgence by the statute"—the main thrust of his opinion was directed at the Fourth Amendment analogy. "No court," he said, "has ever gone so far in applying the implied sanction for violation of the Fourth Amendment."[52] However, the opinion appeared to be more than a mere cementing together of Section 605 and Fourth Amendment doctrine and to represent a fundamental change of heart in the Court's attitude as evidenced in the Weiss and the two Nardone cases. Goldstein's counsel had argued that wire tap evidence was inadmissible even against a third party, since Section 605 forbade the "use"[53] of tapped messages. To divulge the evidence in court was therefore itself an illegal act. The government countered that only "use" for personal benefit was forbidden. The Court refused to decide the question but said that, in any event, the evidence was not thereby rendered inadmissible and that if federal

49. For discussion see Chapter III.
50. 316 U.S. 114 (1942).
51. Bradley and Hogan, "Wiretapping," p. 427.
52. 316 U.S. 114, 121.
53. "[N]o person having received such intercepted communication . . . shall . . . use the same or any information herein contained for his own benefit or for the benefit of another not entitled thereto. . . ." 48 Stat. 1103, 47 U.S.C., sec. 605.

officers had violated the statute, they could be punished directly. On this point the Court had recourse to the Olmstead doctrine that the exclusionary rule should apply only to constitutional, not to statutory, violations.

Dissenting, with the concurrence of Chief Justice Stone and Justice Frankfurter, Justice Murphy maintained that the statute prohibited the "use" made of the wire tap evidence in this trial and therefore rendered it inadmissible. The Court's decision would have the effect of emasculating Section 605 if use could be made of wire taps against defendants for the sole reason that they themselves had not uttered the intercepted words. The "personal privilege" doctrine did not, in Murphy's opinion, square with the inadmissibility of derivatively obtained evidence. If evidence illegally seized could not be used, it might not be used against *any* defendant, regardless of whether his own or somebody else's rights had been invaded in the illegal search or (as here) the wire tapping. It should be added that even though this doctrine served to limit the effectiveness of the exclusionary rule in search and seizure cases, its application to wire tapping cases would have a more destructive effect in that area. The chances of a person's being implicated in a crime through evidence illegally seized in another's home are presumably rare, whereas telephone conversations typically involve discussion of other people.

The Goldstein case properly marked a new phase of Supreme Court activity in the area of wire tapping. Just as the Court had previously retreated from the implications of the Olmstead case by utilizing Section 605 to forbid that which the Fourth Amendment assertedly did not, so now the Court was retreating from the implications of these intervening cases and returning to the Olmstead philosophy. We cannot, of course, know whether the Court was influenced by the fact that this was a wartime case and that wire tapping was then regarded as an important weapon in safeguarding the national security.[54] Whatever the reason, it was of no small significance that the Court had favorably cited the Olmstead decision, as it did again in another eavesdropping case decided the same day, *Goldman* v. *United States*.[55] There, federal agents placed a delicate listening device known as a detectaphone against a wall and picked up what was being said into the telephone by a suspect in the adjoining room. There had been no violation of the Fourth Amendment, said Justice Roberts (who by now qualified as the Court's leading writer of opinions in eavesdropping cases), for the reasons

54. See Fairfield and Clift, "The Wiretappers," pp. 58–60.
55. 316 U.S. 129 (1942).

given in the Olmstead decision, which required an actual invasion of the home to bring the protection of the amendment into play. Nor was Section 605 violated. Section 605, he said, contemplated only actual interference with the wire, not the interception of the message by other means: "The protection intended and afforded by the statute is of the means of communication and *not of the secrecy of the conversation*."[56] Chief Justice Stone and Justice Frankfurter jointly, and Justice Murphy separately, dissented and expressed their readiness to join in overruling the Olmstead case.

The Goldman decision meant that telephone messages were now legally interceptable by eavesdroppers so long as the eavesdroppers employed modern devices which did not interfere with the communications system. Ten years later, in *Schwartz* v. *Texas*,[57] the Court further limited the effectiveness of Section 605 by another Fourth Amendment analogy, this time to render illegal wire tap evidence admissible in state court. Since most law enforcement takes place at the state and local levels, as does most law enforcement wire tapping, the Court in effect cut the heart out of its own earlier reading of the statute.

The facts of the case are somewhat comical. Two thieves took part in a robbery in Texas and then quarreled. One, Jarrett, was taken into custody and was prevailed upon to telephone the other, Schwartz, who was responsible for Jarrett's apprehension because he had given the police a tip as to where Jarrett might be found. Jarrett consented to have the message recorded, with the result that evidence was obtained which led to Schwartz's conviction.

Speaking for the Court, Justice Minton announced that the conviction must stand. There was of course no specific language in Section 605 making wire tap evidence admissible in state court, any more than there was language to forbid its admission in federal court. Once again the Fourth Amendment was the beacon light. In 1949, fifteen years after the enactment of Section 605, the Court had decided that although the due process clause of the Fourteenth Amendment forbade the states to engage in "unreasonable" searches, it did not at the same time require them to exclude from the trial evidence so obtained.[58] In the Schwartz case Section 605 was given a similar rendering: although wire tapping was illegal, evidence so obtained might nevertheless be used to obtain convictions. The intention to require the exclusion of wire tap evidence from state trials

56. *Ibid.*, p. 133. (Emphasis supplied.)
57. 344 U.S. 199 (1952).
58. *Wolf* v. *Colorado*, 338 U.S. 25 (1949).

would not be imputed to the statute, said Justice Minton, for "if Congress is authorized to act in a field, it should manifest its intention clearly."[59] It need scarcely be added at this point that congressional intentions concerning Section 605 had been anything but "clear" in the preceding cases. It was the Fourth Amendment analogy that was decisive. Minton lightly glossed over a crucial distinction between illegal searches and illegal wire tapping with respect to admissibility of evidence: the illegal search is completed at the time of the seizure, whereas the introduction of wire tap evidence in court is itself a federal crime under Section 605, as constituting a divulgence of the intercepted message. This was "simply an additional factor"[60] which the state courts might wish to take into account when deciding whether to make wire tap evidence admissible; Section 605 itself did not require exclusion.[61] The language in this case sharply contrasted with the Court's statement, in the second Nardone case, that Section 605 was based on "broad considerations of morality and public well-being."[62] Given this yardstick, there was no reason why Congress should have demanded less of the states than of the federal government with respect to admissibility. Justice Douglas, who believed that wire tapping was a violation of the Fourth Amendment and that, moreover, the states were forbidden to make use at trial of illegal search evidence, was the sole dissenter.

The Supreme Court's interpretation of Section 605 had thus far produced a body of legal doctrine analogous to the constitutional law of search and seizure. It was the government's hope that the Court could be persuaded to push the analogy one step further. Since 1914, as we have seen in previous chapters, evidence obtained by federal officers in violation of the Fourth Amendment has been inadmissible in the federal courts.[63] Yet evidence uncovered in illegal searches by state officers without federal participation and then turned over to the federal authorities on a "silver platter" was admissible in federal prosecutions.[64] If the federal courts were allowed to receive in evidence the fruits of illegal state searches, the government, considering the trend of recent wire tapping decisions, was quite naturally encouraged in the belief that such would also be the case with respect to state-obtained wire taps. The Court itself, in

59. 344 U.S. 199, 202.
60. *Ibid.*, p. 201.
61. Justice Frankfurter, the author of the Court's opinion in *Wolf* v. *Colorado*, 338 U.S. 25 (1949), not requiring the exclusionary rule for the states in search cases, concurred in the result, as did Justice Black.
62. *Nardone* v. *United States*, 308 U.S. 338, 340 (1939).
63. *Weeks* v. *United States*, 232 U.S. 383 (1914).
64. *Ibid.*, and *Byars* v. *United States*, 273 U.S. 28 (1927).

the Goldstein case, had implied as much when it declared that Section 605 contained "no broader sanction"[65] against the admission of unlawfully obtained wire tap evidence than was to be found in the exclusionary rule required by the Fourth Amendment. It was on such a construction of the statute that federal law enforcement officers relied in their struggle to make use of wire tap evidence. If their contention were borne out by the Court, they would at least be able to use information gathered from the wire taps of their colleagues at the state level. The question came to the test in the case of *Benanti* v. *United States*,[66] decided in 1957, and in a surprising show of unanimity the Court refused to press the analogy between Section 605 and the Fourth Amendment any further.

Notwithstanding Section 605, New York State treated the wire tap like an ordinary search and authorized its law officers to tap wires pursuant to judicially obtained warrants. A tap on the phone used by Salvatore Benanti, installed in conformity with state law, led officers to believe that he was engaged in the narcotics traffic. A search, however, uncovered not narcotics but some five-gallon cans of alcohol which did not bear the required federal tax stamps, and for this crime Benanti was convicted in federal court.

In a significant retreat from recent doctrine as enunciated in the Goldstein and Goldman cases, the Court not only returned to the spirit of the Nardone and Weiss cases but for the first time explicitly rejected the analogy between Section 605 and the Fourth Amendment. Such an analogy, said Chief Justice Warren for the Court, was "neither necessary nor appropriate." As a result, Section 605 was given a construction which required a more stringent exclusionary rule in wire tapping cases than was required by the Fourth Amendment in search cases. "Section 605," said the Chief Justice, "contains an express, absolute prohibition against the divulgence of intercepted communications."[67] (It might be noted that Fourth Amendment doctrine did not for long remain out of alignment with the interpretation of Section 605. In the Benanti case the Chief Justice cast doubt on the continued viability of the silver platter doctrine in search cases by referring to the matter as "an open question."[68] This disparaging remark was approvingly quoted three years later in *Elkins* v. *United States*,[69] when the Court formally overruled the silver platter doctrine.)

65. *Goldstein* v. *United States*, 316 U.S. 114, 121 (1942).
66. 355 U.S. 96 (1957).
67. *Ibid.*, p. 102.
68. *Ibid.*, p. 102, n. 10.
69. 364 U.S. 206 (1960).

The Benanti decision was noteworthy for yet another reason. The government, in its argument to sustain the conviction, did not rely on the analogous law of search and seizure alone but went one step further and contended that Section 605 was never intended to outlaw wire tapping activities where specifically authorized by state law, as they were in New York, where the Benanti case originated. Congress, it was argued, had not intended to pre-empt control over wire tapping, and an affirmative state policy in favor of wire tapping was within the permissibility of Section 605. The Chief Justice rejected this interpretation of the statute in no uncertain terms. "The Federal Communications Act is a comprehensive scheme for the regulation of interstate communication,"[70] he said, and "had Congress intended to allow the States to make exceptions to [Section] 605, it would have said so."[71]

In the cases thus far discussed the Supreme Court had gone a long (if at times wandering) way toward establishing a coherent body of federal law with respect to wire tapping. Yet the Court had failed to define the nature of an illegal "interception" within the meaning of the statute. Section 605 forbids the interception of a message by any "person not . . . authorized by the sender. . . ." It is certain that the consent of both parties will make eavesdropping on the conversation legal. When, however, one party allows the eavesdropping without the knowledge of the other party, does this constitute an illegal "interception"? This question was important, for it is a common law enforcement practice to eavesdrop on threatening telephone calls with the consent of the intended victim and, obviously, without the knowledge of the person making the threat. The method of eavesdropping may vary: sometimes an extension telephone, either existing or specially installed, is used for the purpose; sometimes recording devices are attached to the extension phone or to the bell box or to the wire. A number of cases of this nature had been decided by the lower federal courts, with contradictory results.[72] Judge Learned Hand, for example, had ruled that in any telephone conversation neither of the parties is purely a "sender" or purely a receiver; each is alternately sender and receiver.[73] Consequently, the provision of Section 605 requiring the consent of the "sender" to the interception means, in effect, that the consent of both parties

70. 355 U.S. 96, 104.
71. *Ibid.*, p. 105.
72. The citations are collected in *Rathbun* v. *United States,* 355 U.S. 107, 109, nn. 4, 5 (1957).
73. *United States* v. *Polakoff*, 112 F.2d 888 (2d cir. 1940).

is necessary. In *Rathbun* v. *United States*,[74] decided on the same day as the Benanti case, the Court ruled on this question, and if the Benanti decision was an unexpected setback to law enforcement officers, the Rathbun case was a perhaps equally unexpected victory.

Rathbun had borrowed money from a man named Sparks and surrendered a stock certificate as collateral. Endeavoring to obtain the return of the certificate, Rathbun, then in New York, called Sparks in Pueblo, Colorado, and threatened his life should he not return the certificate. Sparks, anticipating another threatening call from Rathbun, invited the local police to eavesdrop on his phone conversations on an extension telephone. The expected threatening call was made and overheard and led to Rathbun's conviction in federal court.

In an opinion by Chief Justice Warren, the Court sustained the conviction. The number of extension instruments in use in homes and offices, he pointed out, was in the millions; such was the case even in 1934, when Section 605 became law. To require consent of both parties to the conversation before extension phones could be used would make criminals of business secretaries whose practice it was to listen in on the conversations of their principals and record them. Since it was conceded that there was nothing in the statute to prevent either party from recording the conversation and publishing it for all the world to read, it was unreasonable to say that the same party was prohibited from inviting a third person to listen in on an extension. The majority read the statute to mean that "one entitled to receive the communication may use it for his own benefit or have another use it for him. The communication itself is not privileged, and one party may not force the other to secrecy merely by using a telephone."[75] Though in this case the eavesdropping took place by means of an extension telephone not specially installed, it is reasonable to infer from the language of the opinion that, given the permission of one of the parties to the conversation, the eavesdropping would be legal regardless of the means employed.[76] To Justice Frankfurter, however, who dissented, joined by Justice Douglas, the majority's reading of the statute was defective. Any interception without the consent of the party who had initiated the call—the literal "sender"—was, he thought, forbidden.[77] This did not, how-

74. 355 U.S. 107 (1957).
75. *Ibid.*, p. 110.
76. For discussion, see Bradley and Hogan, "Wiretapping," pp. 438–41.
77. "Since this Court, in *Nardone*, read 'no person' to mean no person, it is even more incumbent to construe 'sender' to mean sender, as was the petitioner here, and not to read 'sender' to mean one of the parties to the communication, whether sender

ever, mean that it was illegal for a secretary to listen in on conversations, for "a secretary may fairly be called the employer's alter ego."[78]

The Benanti decision had come as a rude shock to New York law enforcement authorities, who were accustomed to tap the wires of suspects under court order and then use the evidence in court, fortified by the knowledge that this course was explicitly allowed by state law. The decision had the effect of transmuting such a court order into nothing more than a state license to commit a federal crime. In consequence, a few New York judges announced that they would no longer issue wire tap orders,[79] but the majority continued to give sanction to state wire tappers. A New York legislative report, issued in 1959, candidly noted: "The *Benanti* decision has been on the books since 1957, but it has never been implemented. Except as noted, law enforcement wiretapping has proceeded in New York as before."[80]

But if the state courts continued to accept wire tap evidence, might not the federal courts enjoin its use at the defendant's request? In other words, powerless to reverse a conviction obtained in state court through wire tap evidence as the federal courts were under Section 605 (so the Court has held in *Schwartz* v. *Texas*), might they not at least prevent the use of such evidence in the first place by means of the injunction? In a surprisingly brief *per curiam* opinion in the 1961 case of *Pugach* v. *Dollinger*,[81] the Court denied injunctive relief to a defendant threatened by the introduction of wire tap evidence in a New York court, "on the authority of *Schwartz* v. *Texas* . . . and *Stefanelli* v. *Minard*. . . ."[82] Thus the Court once more fell back on Fourth Amendment doctrine, for the Stefanelli decision[83] had held that a federal court should not stay the prosecution of a defendant in a state court the evidence against whom was obtained in an unconstitutional search by state officers. Justice Brennan agreed with the

---

or receiver." 355 U.S. 107, 113. This statement appears to mean that the authorization of the person placing the call is sufficient to render the interception legal. Frankfurter, however, went on to say that he agreed with Judge Hand's opinion in the Polakoff case, and there Hand had required the authorization of *both* parties to the call. See pp. 215–16, *supra.*

78. 355 U.S. 107, 114.

79. See e.g., the opinion of Justice Hofstadter in Application for an Order Permitting the Interception of Telephone Communications of Anonymous, 136 N.Y.S. 2d 612 (1955).

80. N.Y., Legislature, *Report of Joint Legislative Committee on Privacy of Communications and Licensure of Private Investigators,* Legislative Document No. 25 (1959), p. 18.

81. 365 U.S. 458 (1961). This case had an interesting history in the lower federal courts. See *Pugach* v. *Sullivan*, 180 F. Supp. 66 (S.D.N.Y. 1960); *Pugach* v. *Dollinger*, 275 F.2d 503 (2d cir. 1960); and 277 F.2d 739 (2d cir. 1960).

82. 365 U.S. 458.

83. 342 U.S. 117 (1951). This case is discussed in Chapter VI.

decision but would have relied on the Stefanelli precedent alone. Justice Douglas, who had dissented from both the Schwartz and Stefanelli decisions, dissented in the Pugach case as well, with the concurrence of Chief Justice Warren. He found it "incongruous" that the enforcement of Section 605 should be allowed "to make a detour around the precincts of a state court."[84]

As we have seen, the Supreme Court's interpretation of Section 605 and its interpretation of the search and seizure provision have tended to parallel each other. While never candidly acknowledging this reality, the Court has in fact usually read the statute as if Congress had simply directed that henceforth wire tapping be considered a search and seizure, in direct circumvention of the Olmstead decision. For the sake of convenience we might call this a doctrine of equivalent protection: the protection against wire tapping should carry the same force as the protection against unreasonable searches. Since interpretation of the Fourth Amendment (and of the due process clause of the Fourteenth Amendment insofar as it relates to the Fourth) has been a relatively unstable process, with the precedents of yesteryear frequently giving way to new constitutional interpretation, the interesting question arises of whether a reinterpretation of the constitutional law of search will influence the Court to make an equivalent change in an interpretation of Section 605 which was patterned after a discarded decision in a search case. In this instance, does the doctrine of equivalent protection retain its vitality and continue to stress the "equivalent" by taking into account the change that has taken place in the analogous law of search?

At the moment this question is quite important in the light of a significant recent reinterpretation of search law. Just as the federal courts exclude evidence obtained in unreasonable searches,[85] so must they exclude evidence gathered through wire tapping:[86] Section 605, said the Court, required no less. The state courts, on the other hand, the Court declared in *Wolf* v. *Colorado*,[87] were free to admit into evidence the fruits of illegal searches. When the question of state use of wire tapping evidence arose in *Schwartz* v. *Texas*, the parallel was not lost on the Court, which took its cue from the analogous search law. Section 605 was construed to exact no more obedience

84. 365 U.S. 458, 460.
85. *Weeks* v. *United States*, 232 U.S. 383 (1914).
86. *Nardone* v. *United States*, 302 U.S. 379 (1937).
87. 338 U.S. 25 (1949).

from the states than was exacted by the Constitution and not to require exclusion of wire tap evidence from the state courts. In 1961, however, in *Mapp* v. *Ohio*,[88] the Court overruled the Wolf case and ordered the states to exclude evidence acquired in unconstitutional searches. This decision leaves unanswered the question of whether the Schwartz case is still good constitutional law. Had the existence of the doctrine of equivalent protection been candidly acknowledged by the Court, the problem would scarcely arise, for the "intent" of Congress could logically be construed to require an equivalent protective function between Section 605 against wire tapping and the Fourth and Fourteenth Amendments against unreasonable searches. Reinterpretation of the Constitution would therefore require similar reinterpretation of Section 605.[89] However, since the doctrine has never received formal acknowledgment despite its use, it might prove embarrassing for the Court to overrule previous wire tapping decisions and to change retrospectively the congressional "intent" by judicial fiat.[90]

Another unanswered question of the same sort concerns the "personal privilege" doctrine, which states that only one whose personal rights have been infringed through wire tapping may seek the benefit of the exclusionary rule in federal court. This means that a person implicated in a crime who was not a party to the intercepted telephone call has no "standing" to object to the introduction of wire tap evidence at his trial. It is uncertain to what extent this doctrine, which in *Goldstein* v. *United States* was derived from the analogous law of search and seizure, still has vitality. In search cases proper the doctrine has since been substantially modified, so that now any person, including a guest, who has a right to be on the premises (even though he possesses no property rights in them) is regarded as having sufficient "standing" to object to the introduction of evidence seized there in an unreasonable search.[91] Whether this development

88. 367 U.S 643 (1961).

89. It could of course be argued that, even if Congress did intend Section 605 as an equivalent protection, this meant no more than an equivalent to the search law current at the time of its enactment, and not to future constitutional reinterpretations. In the Schwartz case, however, the Court implicitly rejected such an interpretation when it applied the analogous search law as expounded in 1949 in *Wolf* v. *Colorado*, though at the time Section 605 was enacted, in 1934, state searches were not subject to any constitutional limitations at all.

90. Subsequent to the Mapp decision, the Court has refused to review a New York conviction obtained with the use of wire tap evidence. *Dinan* v. *New York*, 371 U.S. 877 (1962). However, a denial of *certiorari*, into which many factors may have entered, is hardly determinative of how the Supreme Court may eventually decide the issue.

91. *United States* v. *Jeffers*, 342 U.S. 48 (1951); *Jones* v. *United States*, 362 U.S. 257 (1960). These cases are discussed in Chapter III.

foreshadows a similar modification of the "personal privilege" doctrine in wire tapping cases remains to be seen.[92]

The interpretation of Section 605 seems to be a classical case of judicial policy-making, which takes the form of statutory interpretation instead of the constitutional interpretation which is normally viewed as the Court's main task. The statute happily came to the Court's assistance at the very time when the Court's own thinking on the subject was changing. The Court was thus spared the pain of rethinking constitutional doctrine. Instead, Section 605 was usually construed in the very way that a Fourth Amendment ban on wire tapping would have been were it not necessary to overrule an embarrassing precedent.

Paradoxically, the Court may be coming to the end of its long road in construing Section 605 at the very time that the statute's continuing existence in its present form is subject to constant and ever-mounting challenge and is therefore very much in doubt. The opposition stems from a dissatisfaction on the part of law enforcement authorities with the meaning that Section 605 has acquired at the hands of the Court. To understand the controversy, we must briefly review the current state of wire tapping and public attitudes toward it.

Much has been written in recent years on the extent of wire tapping,[93] and the subject requires no elaboration here. Suffice it to say by way of summary that wire tapping is done on a flourishing scale throughout the nation. Professor Westin, in a carefully researched and documented study published in 1952, came to the conclusion that despite Section 605 and a profusion of state laws which prohibit wire tapping, this form of eavesdropping is nevertheless "carried on virtually unimpeded in the United States today."[94] Wire tapping has

92. One difficulty with any modification may be that there seems to be no logical point at which to stop, short of the complete abandonment of the doctrine and the granting of "standing" to object to anyone incriminated by the intercepted call. This observation stems from the different nature of the rights violated in searches and in wire tapping. In searches the rights violated are (according to the doctrine) of a property nature—the house has been trespassed—whereas in wire tapping the rights violated are those of a party to the call, a right conferred by statute regardless of property interest. A person calling from a public phone booth, for example, is as much a party to the call as one calling from his private phone. The nice distinctions, therefore, which can be drawn between, on the one hand, property owners and guests, who had every right to be on the searched premises, and, on the other hand, those who, like vagrants, had no such right, have no meaning in wire tapping cases, where one either was or was not a party to the call.

93. E.g., Dash *et al.*, *The Eavesdroppers, passim.*

94. Westin, "The Wire-Tapping Problem," p. 168.

been called "the freest of free enterprises."[95] "The truth," says Justice Douglas, "is that wiretapping is a plague on the nation."[96]

The lot of the wire tapper has been appreciably eased by mechanical refinements which have outmoded the crude equipment once used.[97] No longer need he himself, with pencil in hand and headphones clamped to his ears, listen to the conversation being intercepted; the more sophisticated equipment now in use permits the sounds to be amplified and recorded automatically on wire, tape, or wax for future reference. The modern eavesdropper is able to carry away the proof in his pocket and need not suffer the indignity of a challenge to his veracity. In recording a telephone conversation, he is now able not only to obtain the information sought but also a built-in proof that he is telling the truth. With the reproduction of the spoken word it is not so much the eavesdropper who reports on his victim as it is the victim who reports on himself.

Wire tapping knows no favorites, either among those who employ it or those whom it victimizes. Engaged in the wire tapping business are the Federal Bureau of Investigation (by the admission of its director),[98] other federal agencies,[99] state and city police, and private investigators. The information sought varies according to the source of the tapping. Federal officers seek evidence of major criminal activities, especially of a subversive nature. Though evidence so uncovered is inadmissible in federal court and hence useless for purposes of conviction, it is useful for keeping track of criminal activities and for removing subversive elements from government employment. The Commission on Government Security reported in 1957 that "a great deal of vital information on the subversive operations of both individuals and groups has been uncovered through the wiretapping technique."[100] Only recently, the disclosure that Treasury agents

95. Fairfield and Clift, "The Wiretappers," p. 50.

96. William O. Douglas, *The Right of the People* (New York, 1958), p. 151.

97. The most comprehensive description of the various wire tapping methods in use is in Dash *et al., The Eavesdroppers*, pp. 303ff. For a briefer description see Westin, "The Wire-Tapping Problem," pp. 197–200.

98. "It is no secret that the FBI does tap telephones in a very limited type of cases with the express approval in each instance of the Attorney General of the United States, but only in cases involving espionage, sabotage, grave risks to internal security, or when human lives are in jeopardy." J. Edgar Hoover, "A Comment on the Article 'Loyalty among Government Employees,' " *Yale Law Journal*, LVIII (February, 1949), 401, 405. Hoover is reported having said in 1950 that the F.B.I. was tapping about 170 telephones at the time. Fairfield and Clift, "The Wiretappers," p. 73. More recently Hoover put the number of F.B.I. wiretaps at about 80. Editorial, "Thirty Years," *Washington Post*, November 21, 1964, p. A8.

99. Fairfield and Clift, "The Wiretappers," p. 72.

100. *Report of the Commission on Government Security* (1957), p. 627. This wire tapping is presumably done by agencies other than the F.B.I., whose director has stated that wire tapping "is never done" by his agency "in the investigation of the loyalty of Federal employees." Hoover, "Comment," p. 405.

have been tapping the wires of suspected racketeers in order to uncover evidence of income tax frauds made front-page newspaper headlines.[101] City and state police seek evidence of crime in general, although in the case of state police the tapping may have "political overtones."[102] Samuel Dash, in a study he directed for the Pennsylvania Bar Association on wire tapping practices in a number of states and major cities, found that in only one city of all those surveyed, Boston, did the police not engage in wire tapping (but other law enforcement agencies in that city did).[103] Private wire tappers are employed by companies which seek information on labor union activities or business information about their rivals, and by husbands and wives who seek evidence that may be useful in establishing grounds for divorce. Private tapping may also have political overtones. In 1961 a federal grand jury in Louisiana indicted three men, one of them a state senator, for violating Section 605 by eavesdropping on the telephone conversations of three other men who advocated integration in the schools of Baton Rouge.[104] In the nineteen thirties a wire tap installation is said to have been discovered in Washington, D.C., with wires "connected to the telephone lines of justices of the Supreme Court." The wire tapping was assertedly "paid for by a major private business concern having an interest in matters pending before the Court."[105]

Because of the national problem that it has become, a brilliant spotlight has been focused in the past decade on wire tapping, principally through the medium of congressional hearings,[106] which have served as a forum for both advocates and opponents of the legalization of wire tapping through the amendment of Section 605. This protracted debate has served to clarify the issues involved and the values at stake. It has not, however, produced anything remotely resembling agreement on whether the gains for order to be achieved

101. *The New York Times*, July 14, 1965, p. 1.
102. Fairfield and Clift, "The Wiretappers," p. 80.
103. Dash *et al.*, *The Eavesdroppers*, pp. 146–47.
104. *The New York Times*, December 28, 1961, p. 1.
105. Dash *et al.*, *The Eavesdroppers*, p. 29.
106. U.S., Congress, House, *Hearings before Subcommittee No. 3, Committee on the Judiciary, on H.R. 408, H.R. 477, H.R. 3552, and H.R. 5149,* 83d Cong., 1st Sess., 1953; U.S., Congress, Senate, *Hearings before a Subcommittee of the Committee on the Judiciary, on S. 838, S. 2753, S. 3229, and H.R. 8649,* 83d Cong., 2d Sess., 1954; U.S. Congress, House, *Hearings before Subcommittee No. 5, Committee on the Judiciary, on H.R. 762, H.R. 867, H.R. 4513, H.R. 4728, and H.R. 5096* (*Ser. 2*), 84th Cong., 1st Sess., 1955; U.S., Congress, Senate, *Hearings before the Subcommittee on Constitutional Rights, Committee on the Judiciary; Wiretapping, Eavesdropping and the Bill of Rights,* Parts 1 and 2, 85th Cong., 2d Sess., 1958, Parts 3, 4 and 5, 86th Cong., 1st Sess., 1959; U.S., Congress, Senate, *Hearings before the Subcommitee on Constitutional Rights, Committee on the Judiciary, on S. 1086, S. 1221, S. 1495, and S. 1822,* 87th Cong., 1st Sess., 1961; U.S., Congress, Senate, *Hearings before the Committee on the Judiciary, on S. 2813 and S. 1495,* 87th Cong., 2d Sess., 1962. These hearings are hereafter cited by year of issue, e.g., *1961 Senate Hearings.*

through legalized wire tapping would outweigh the risks to freedom involved; there has not even been agreement as to the vital necessity of wire tapping for the solution of crime.

The telephone has so transformed our entire social and business relationships that it has now become an indispensable means of communication, often taking the place of the letter and the face-to-face meeting. But the telephone has also facilitated criminal organization and activities: the identities of the members of the top echelons of criminal organizations can now be kept largely secret because the need for them to consort with underlings—with the attendant risk of being seen in their presence—is greatly reduced. Consequently, these masterminds of organized crime are seldom arrested or convicted; their identity is often unknown to the very subordinates who carry out the crimes they plot and to whom they are often only voices on the telephone.

From these developments are derived the principal arguments both for and against legalized wire tapping.[107] Advocates of legalized wire tapping assert the need of it for the maintenance of effective public order. Those who are opposed assert that to allow wire tapping is to allow intrusions on life's most private relationships: those between husband and wife, minister and communicant, lawyer and client, doctor and patient.

The crimes for the solution of which wire tapping is most useful, it is generally agreed, are those of an organized nature, involving groups of criminals, usually operating as syndicates, rather than those which depend on individual initiative:

> Wiretapping is of very little use in connection with ordinary felonies and crimes of violence. There is lacking in this sporadic sort of crime the pattern of continuity necessary for effective wiretap operation by police officers. It is generally in the more sinister field of large scale, highly organized and more or less permanent types of criminal activity alone that wiretapping is worthwhile. Labor racketeering, gambling, narcotics and espionage are among the chief categories where it is most useful. Kidnapping and other extortion schemes, because of their dependence on telephone contacts, are also vulnerable to swift, intelligent employment of wiretaps.[108]

107. What follows is a synthesis of the views of advocates and opponents of legalized wire tapping as set forth in the congressional *Hearings* and supplemented with statements made by many judges, law enforcement officials, and others with an interest in the problem, in interviews with the author during 1961.

108. Peter Megaree Brown and Richard S. Peer, "The Wiretapping Entanglement: How To Strengthen Law Enforcement and Preserve Privacy," *Cornell Law Quarterly*, XLIV (Winter, 1959), 175, 183–84. Kidnapping, it should be added, is no longer one of the crimes for the solution of which legalized wire tapping is advocated, since under the doctrine of *Rathbun* v. *United States*, 355 U.S. 107 (1957), discussed earlier in this chapter, there is no violation of law when the eavesdropping takes place with the consent of a party to the conversation. Permission obtained from relatives, therefore, to listen in to calls from the kidnapper would make the eavesdropping legal.

Efforts of law enforcement officials to have Section 605 amended to allow a measure of wire tapping have been spearheaded by the Department of Justice. Wire tapping advocates contend that it is one of the most vital weapons in the arsenal of law enforcement and that the evasion of Section 605 proves this. Evidence against organized criminals, it is said, can seldom be uncovered by other means because victims will not talk out of fear of reprisals. To protect the privacy of telephone communications is therefore the equivalent of a grant of immunity to the leaders of organized crime. "It is only through wiretapping that we can establish the evidence," says one leading prosecutor. "I unhesitatingly state that legalized wiretapping has been a vitally necessary weapon in our efforts to combat organized crime."[109] He recounted convictions obtained by his office against notorious underworld figures through the use of wire tapping evidence and which, he said, could not have been obtained in any other way. Justice Frankfurter's revealing statement that, on the basis of his own experience in the United States Attorney's Office for the Southern District of New York, he felt that wire tapping was unnecessary and merely a substitute for good professional work[110] is disputed as based on the experience of a bygone era. A high official in that office stated that the nature of federal law enforcement has changed since Frankfurter was there. The Justice Department has moved from a preoccupation with "white-collar" crime, such as commercial fraud, where wire tapping is largely ineffectual, to new responsibilities in the tracking down of organized rackets, such as gambling and narcotics selling, where wire tapping can be most useful.[111] A state law enforcement official commented: "Forty years ago Frankfurter was right because then there were no big crime facilities, no use of planes across the continent; crime was local and the evidence could be followed locally. Today there are insufficient officers to follow national syndicates."[112] A nationally renowned state judge who once excelled as a prosecutor cautions that while the information yielded by wire tapping can be developed otherwise, the cost in manpower and money is usually prohibitive

109. Alfred T. Scotti, Chief of the Rackets Bureau, New York County District Attorney's Office, at Harvard Student Bar Association forum on October 8, 1958. The term "legalized wiretapping" refers to the New York State law permitting the practice under judicial safeguards.

110. *On Lee* v. *United States*, 343 U.S. 747, 761 (1952) (dissenting opinion).

111. Interview, summer, 1961. The official declined to be identified.

112. Interview, summer, 1961, with Isidore Dollinger, District Attorney of Bronx County, New York.

and that the economic factors of the problem have not received adequate consideration.[113]

Wire tapping advocates argue that when used under proper safeguards the method poses little if any danger to innocent persons; that other invasions of privacy in the interests of order are different in method but not in essence; and that what is yielded in the way of privacy is small in comparison to what we might suffer should we refuse to make this concession. "[A]uthorized wire tapping under careful restrictions in cases involving our national security is not a 'dirty business' at all," wrote Attorney General Brownell in 1954, "but a common sense solution by Congress which will protect the liberty and security of all the people. . . ."[114] The dishonest element among law enforcement officers who would use wire tapping for private gain does so already and is unlikely to be emboldened by the amendment of Section 605. On the contrary, a "more realistic" wire tapping law would result in more effective enforcement; the Department of Justice, no longer doubtful of the legality of its own wire tapping practices, would move vigorously against state officers to prosecute violations of law.

Those opposed to the liberalization of Section 605 admit that wire tapping can be a useful investigatory tool, but they are not prepared to concede that it is absolutely necessary. On this point they receive some support within law enforcement circles. In 1961 the attorneys general of Alabama, Oklahoma, Delaware, Missouri, and New Mexico were all either opposed to, or else saw no need for, federal legislation to legalize wire tapping.[115] The first chairman of the Senate Judiciary Committee's Subcommittee on Constitutional Rights, who was once prosecuting attorney for St. Louis, wrote: "During the course of our hearings on wiretapping I have been struck by the remarkable lack of *specific* information on a case-by-case basis, demonstrating the indispensability of wiretapping to the solution and prosecution of crime."[116]

The opposition to wire tapping, however, stems mainly from considerations wholly apart from that of its necessity. Unlike the search

113. Interview, summer, 1961, with Charles D. Breitel, Associate Judge, Appellate Division, First Department, New York State Supreme Court.

114. Herbert J. Brownell, "The Public Security and Wiretapping," *Cornell Law Quarterly*, XXXIX (Winter, 1954), 195, 205.

115. "Analysis of Survey Replies," *1961 Senate Hearings*, pp. 539, 542.

116. Thomas C. Hennings, Jr., "The Wiretapping-Eavesdropping Problem: A Legislator's View," *Minnesota Law Review*, XLIV (April, 1960), 813, 829. A Detroit police inspector is quoted as saying: "You can get the information you need if you just go out and develop it. But some of the boys would rather sit in an easy chair with the earphones on." Fairfield and Clift, "The Wiretappers," p. 76.

under warrant, which is limited to specified items, wire tapping, even under safeguards, assumes the character of the general search, and worse. It inevitably involves eavesdropping on intimate conversations unrelated to the reasons for which the tap was installed, and it involves prying on innocent parties because every conversation includes two persons, only one of whom is likely to be suspect. In the case of taps on public telephones the mischief is multiplied: hundreds of innocent persons will be eavesdropped upon in order to catch one suspected person known to use that telephone.[117] To grant recourse to the courts in the event of abuse by law enforcement authorities would be a futile right for, unlike the victim of an illegal search, which in most instances cannot be conducted in secrecy, the victim of wire tapping will not even know that the privacy of his home has been invaded.[118] Past experience, it is said, has shown that the police are not to be trusted in this regard. They have shown themselves contemptuous of wire tapping prohibitions already enacted into law and would be unlikely to act with greater restraint were wire tapping allowed. Wire tap information is a corrupting influence; it is always conducive to threats of blackmail when placed in the hands of unscrupulous officers, of whom there are always a few. Moreover, once the door is opened to legalized wire tapping, the safeguards originally provided will gradually be eaten away; further relaxation of the law will inevitably be requested and, in the name of necessity, granted. The safest way to protect privacy, therefore, is to keep the door to wire tapping shut tightly. Above all, the opposition to wire tapping is predicated on the belief that invasion of privacy in this manner is an assault on the dignity of the individual which is incompatible with a democratic society of ordered liberty. It has been argued that extorted confessions and the setting of children to spy on their parents might prove very effective in ferreting out crime, yet they receive no sanction because they are abhorrent to our principles of fair play. "I regard both [wiretapping and electronic eavesdropping] as contrary to our way of life," said the attorney general of New Mexico in 1961; "perhaps they are suitable in a police state. They are neither necessary nor desirable in the United States."[119]

117. That public telephones in New York are tapped is candidly admitted by state officials. See *1959 Senate Hearings*, Part 3, p. 540.

118. From the beginning of 1957 up to May 31, 1961, the Federal Communications Commission received only twenty-four complaints throughout the country alleging interception of telephone communications. *1961 Senate Hearings*, p. 505.

119. Earl E. Hartley, *ibid.*, p. 560.

The foregoing competing viewpoints represent the age-old conflict between order and liberty. Each side agrees on the necessity of maintaining a society of ordered liberty, but they differ on whether to place the stress on the first word or on the second. Each asserts that its own view best harmonizes the competing considerations of public order and individual freedom. Curiously, throughout the years the Department of Justice has embraced first one and then the other of these viewpoints.

Though Attorney General Harlan F. Stone prohibited wire tapping in his department in 1924,[120] every Attorney General since 1931, beginning with William D. Mitchell, has endorsed its use, at least in some types of cases.[121] This official policy in favor of wire tapping was reversed only temporarily by Robert H. Jackson, who, after the Justice Department lost three important wire tapping cases[122] in the Supreme Court, followed the example of Stone and in March, 1940, ordered the department to cease wire tapping. Jackson rescinded that order, however, "after receipt of a confidential Presidential directive of May 21, 1940," in which "President Roosevelt authorized the use of wire tapping in security cases provided in each case the Attorney General gave his specific approval."[123]

Shortly after he instituted his ban on wire tapping, Jackson announced that "the law on wiretapping is now clear and precise; and all future cases of wiretapping will be subject to prosecution in the Federal courts."[124] Now, however, the Department of Justice came up with a new, ingenious interpretation of Section 605 to justify the resumption of wire tapping. Stress was placed on the word "and" in the text of Section 605: "intercept . . . and divulge or publish. . . ." Only an interception *and* a divulgence, it was claimed, violated the law, and not an interception alone. "Any person," said Jackson, "with no risk of penalty, may tap telephone wires and eavesdrop on his competitor, employer, workman, or others, and act upon what he hears or make any use of it that does not involve divulging or publication."[125]

120. See p. 200, *supra.*

121. William P. Rogers, "The Case for Wire Tapping," *Yale Law Journal*, LXIII (April, 1954), 792, 794ff. The position of the Department of Justice has not changed since Mr. Rogers wrote his article.

122. *Nardone* v. *United States*, 302 U.S. 379 (1937); *Weiss* v. *United States*, 308 U.S. 321 (1939); *Nardone* v. *United States*, 308 U.S. 338 (1939).

123. Rogers, "The Case for Wire Tapping," p. 795 and n. 15. The directive "was never so much as mentioned until 1949 and . . . has still not been made public. . . . Why such a memo has never been publicly released is still a matter of conjecture. The best guess is that Roosevelt named specific suspected pro-Nazi Americans whose lines he wished to tap." Fairfield and Clift, "The Wiretappers," p. 58.

124. Quoted in Fairfield and Clift, "The Wiretappers," pp. 57–58.

125. Quoted in *ibid.*, p. 59.

Some further emendations, however, were required in order to complete the "reconstruction" of Section 605. Two problems remained. First, since wire tap information circulates among government officials (the eavesdropper obviously does not retain the information himself), does this then not constitute an unlawful divulgence? Second, since Section 605 forbids the "use" of wire tap information for anyone's "benefit," does not governmental use of the information violate the law? The department answered both questions in the negative. As a corollary to the new interpretation, the government was considered an organic entity for the purpose of divulgence; only an extragovernmental disclosure violated the law, it was claimed, not the passing of wire tap information from one federal official to another.[126] Similarly, "use" for public purposes was not the same as use for "benefit," which connoted only private gain.[127] (Jackson's statement that "any person" may intercept a telephone conversation so long as he does not divulge its contents is therefore certainly incorrect with respect to private wire tapping, since that would involve an illegal use for private gain.) This refurbishing of Section 605 provided a large area of immunity for wire tapping by the federal government.

This interpretation of Section 605 has never been directly ruled upon by the Supreme Court,[128] which has never needed to do so, since information yielded by wire tapping cannot be used to obtain convictions which might later be appealed. The interpretation has not, however, been accepted by either the Treasury Department or the Federal Communications Commission, both of which have taken the position that wire tapping itself is prohibited.[129] Most of those who oppose the liberalization of Section 605 nevertheless favor its redrafting to prohibit *all* wire tapping. Their view was summarized in 1961 by Thomas F. Eagleton, Attorney General of Missouri, when he said: "I would favor the strengthening of section 605 . . . so as

126. This view was announced by Attorney General Biddle in 1941. Richard C. Donnelly, "Comments and Caveats on the Wiretapping Controversy," *Yale Law Journal*, LXIII (April, 1954), 799, 801, n. 10.

127. Counsel for the government pressed this argument in *Goldstein* v. *United States*, 316 U.S. 114 (1942), discussed above. The Court found it unnecessary to pass on this construction, but Justice Murphy, joined by Chief Justice Stone and Justice Frankfurter in dissent, explicitly rejected it.

128. In *Benanti* v. *United States*, 355 U.S. 96, 100, n. 5. (1957), the Court specifically avoided a ruling on this point as unnecessary to the disposition of the case. In the first Nardone case, however, the Court apparently took the position that an interception alone constituted a violation of Section 605: "the plain words of [Section] 605 forbid anyone, unless authorized by the sender, to intercept a telephone message, and direct in equally clear language that '*no person*' shall divulge or publish the message or its substance to '*any person*.'" *Nardone* v. *United States*, 302 U.S. 379, 382 (1937).

129. Donnelly, "Comments and Caveats," p. 802.

to make the prohibition more explicit and clear up the ambiguity over 'intercept . . . AND divulge.' "[130]

The Department of Justice has consistently taken the position that Section 605 should be amended to allow some wire tapping under safeguards. Though this advocacy may reflect an uneasiness over its own interpretation of the law, the official attitude is that it is not wire tapping itself which needs be legalized but the admission of its fruits in court in order to obtain convictions.[131] Furthermore, it is claimed, the federal government cannot in good faith, under the present state of the law, prosecute state officials who engage in wire tapping pursuant to state law.[132] Why this should be so is unclear: regardless of the legality of an interception without a divulgence, there can be no question that divulgence of wire tap information in court does constitute, according to the Supreme Court, a federal crime. Here again, the Department of Justice may feel embarrassed to prosecute in view of its own wire tapping activities, carried out under an ambiguous interpretation of the law. This conclusion appears to be supported by the fact that although only a handful of states purport to authorize wire tapping by law enforcement officers,[133] there is no record of a single prosecution of a state officer anywhere for violation of the federal wire tapping law.[134]

In 1961 the Department of Justice asked Congress to enact the following legislation. 1. Authorize federal wire tapping and permit use in court of evidence so obtained in cases involving the national security, kidnapping, and other specified serious crimes: in national security and kidnapping cases authorization for the tapping would be granted by the Attorney General alone; in other criminal cases a court order following the pattern of a search warrant and fixing a time limit on the tapping must be obtained upon a showing of probable cause. 2. Allow the states to authorize wire tapping for any crime they wish, although a state court order upon a showing of probable cause would be required. 3. Specify that all unauthorized wire tapping is a criminal offense.[135]

130. *1961 Senate Hearings*, p. 554.

131. J. Edgar Hoover, "Rejoinder by Mr. Hoover," *Yale Law Journal*, LVIII (February, 1949), 422, 424.

132. Herbert J. Miller, Jr., Assistant Attorney General, Criminal Division, *1961 Senate Hearings*, p. 366.

133. As of 1961 only six states gave such authorization: Louisiana, Maryland, Massachusetts, Nevada, New York, and Oregon. *Ibid.*, p. 540.

134. Assistant Attorney General Miller in his testimony before the Senate subcommittee in 1961 was able to point to the prosecution of only fourteen *private* investigators since 1952. *Ibid.*, p. 364.

135. *Ibid.*, pp. 356ff.

These proposals evoked a storm of editorial criticism. The Department of Justice was condemned for its attempt to remove the Attorney General from judicial scrutiny in cases involving the national security—a nebulous term—and to allow the states to wire tap without federal restraint and without a time limit on the tapping, even in insignificant misdemeanor cases. "[W]hat the Department seeks," said one leading newspaper, "is permission for every police force, Federal, state and local, to listen in on telephone conversations at their own pleasure."[136] "[A]s to wiretapping by state and local police," added another, "the lid is off."[137] A cartoon by Herblock showed a citizen making a telephone call while glancing apprehensively at a photograph hanging on the wall—a picture of a sinister-looking Attorney General Robert F. Kennedy, on which was inscribed the words "LITTLE BROTHER." The cartoon was captioned, " 'Hello—ORwell 1984?' "[138]

Taken aback by such criticism, which developed both in and out of Congress, the department has shifted its stand with respect to state wire tapping. It now advocates that state wire tap orders be limited to forty-five days and restricted to several major crimes. However, the department continues to insist that the need for speed and secrecy precludes judicial review of wire tapping requests in national security cases and that the Attorney General be given a free hand to authorize wire taps in these cases.[139]

How such a law would work in practice must remain a matter for conjecture. The New York State experience might have proved instructive for test purposes if the factual situation there were not subject to dispute. New York authorizes wire tapping[140] in criminal investigations under safeguards akin to those required for search warrants. A showing of "reasonable grounds" (equivalent to probable cause) upon oath or affirmation before a judge is required. The court order limits the tapping to two months. Unauthorized

136. *Washington Post*, May 15, 1961, p. A12.

137. *The New York Times*, July 3, 1961, p. 14.

138. *Washington Post*, April 1, 1962, p. E4.

139. *1962 Senate Hearings*, pp. 11ff. For analysis of the proposed bill, see Donnelly, "Proposals for Meeting the Challenge of Interstate Organized Crime: Electronic Eavesdropping," *Notre Dame Lawyer*, XXXVIII, No. 6 (1963), pp. 667, 684ff. The crimes for which wire tapping would be authorized are murder, kidnapping, extortion, bribery, and narcotics selling, as well as conspiracy to commit any of these offenses.

140. In view of the decision in *Benanti* v. *United States*, 355 U.S. 96 (1957), which held the New York law to conflict with Section 605, a representative of District Attorney Frank Hogan of New York County announced that his office would no longer use wire tap evidence in court and asked that the indictments against seven narcotics defendants be dismissed. *The New York Times*, November 15, 1961, pp. 1, 31. Other district attorneys in the state have apparently not followed Mr. Hogan's lead, which was regarded as a move to exert pressure for a federal wire tap bill. *Ibid.*, November 19, 1961, p. 85.

wire tapping is a felony.[141] Wire tapping is permitted in the investigation of all crimes, on the theory that "the cumulative effects of illegal gambling"—a misdemeanor in law—"are far-reaching in providing a source of income for the underworld."[142]

Whether judicial scrutiny has indeed proved an effective means of restraint is, however, open to question. The experience of former United States Attorney General William P. Rogers, once an assistant district attorney in New York, was depressing. "The affidavits aren't very factual," he related. "They're just general in nature, and I don't recall any difficulty in getting the permission of the court. My own experience is that it's pretty easy."[143] A King's County grand jury presentment in 1950 roundly condemned the Brooklyn police for obtaining wire tap orders on false affidavits and strongly implied that blackmail was the intended result of the wire taps.[144] Such experiences, however, were said to be exceptional by a leading law enforcement official.[145]

The average number of law enforcement wire taps installed each year in New York State is also a matter of dispute. Figures supplied by the district attorneys show a total of 2,682 telephones tapped in the entire state during the five-year period 1950 to 1954—an average of about 500 telephones a year.[146] On the other hand, Westin and Dash both have charged that, at least on the police level (as distinct from the district attorneys' offices), a great deal of unauthorized tapping has taken place.[147] Dash places the figure for the New York City police at from 13,000 to 26,000. This figure is indignantly denied by law enforcement officers. At least New York State authorities, unlike the Justice Department, have initiated prosecutions against police officials engaging in unauthorized wire tapping.[148]

Ironically, efforts on the national level to authorize wire tapping have coincided with efforts on the state level to curtail the practice sharply or to prohibit it altogether. In 1952 one writer found that,

141. The New York laws became effective in 1957–1958. Less restrictive provisions had been in effect previously. For analysis, see Dash *et al.*, *The Eavesdroppers*, pp. 411–16.

142. Michael J. Murphy (then New York City Police Commissioner), *1961 Senate Hearings*, p. 347.

143. *1953 House Hearings*, p. 37.

144. Westin, "The Wire-Tapping Problem," pp. 195–96.

145. Edward S. Silver, "The Wiretapping-Eavesdropping Problem: A Prosecutor's View," *Minnesota Law Review*, XLIV (April, 1960), 835, 837–42.

146. Dash *et al.*, *The Eavesdroppers*, p. 106.

147. Westin, *1958 Senate Hearings*, Part 2, p. 206; Dash *et al.*, *The Eavesdroppers*, p. 68.

148. Three police officers, one a deputy inspector, were prosecuted in Kings County in 1959. Two pleaded guilty, while the inspector was the beneficiary of a hung jury. Aaron J. Koota, then assistant district attorney in charge of the Rackets Bureau, Kings County, in letter to the author dated December 14, 1961.

while legislation to prohibit wire tapping existed in two-thirds of the states, it was "badly drafted to handle wire-tapping problems. Disclosure is expressly forbidden by only two states: the rest allow wire-tap information to be used at will or in the courts, or exempt public officers."[149] Subsequent to 1953, however, "a civil liberties revolt had taken place in America over wiretapping and electronic eavesdropping."[150] Spurred on by wire tapping scandals—such as the one in New York, where in 1955 there was discovered a private wire tapping nest capable of tapping one hundred thousand telephone lines in the heart of Manhattan—state legislative committees have delved deeply into the problem, particularly in New York, California, New Jersey, and Maryland. By 1958 eighteen state legislatures had debated the eavesdropping situation, and a number of others have done so since then. Several states enacted controls over wire tapping or electronic eavesdropping, or both. Pennsylvania and Illinois prohibited wire tapping altogether, and Illinois, in addition, completely barred electronic eavesdropping.[151]

Despite what the chairman of the House Judiciary Committee calls "unceasing pressure for a bill to permit, with limitations, wire tapping,"[152] no federal legislation has yet been passed. That predictions about the immediacy of legislation authorizing wire tapping[153] have thus far not come true is due less, perhaps, to the potency of the opposition than to the fact that "no one approach has been able to satisfy a majority"[154] because of divisions among the advocates of such a bill with respect to the safeguards it should contain.[155] If a bill authorizing wire tapping should be passed, it will revive a constitutional issue largely dormant[156] since Section 605 was passed—the issue of whether wire tapping is a search within the meaning of the Fourth Amendment. Should the Supreme Court decide that it is, and overrule the Olmstead case[157] (a good possibility), this will

149. Westin, "The Wire-Tapping Problem," p. 183.

150. Westin, "Wiretapping: The Quiet Revolution," *Commentary*, XXIX (April, 1960), 333.

151. *Ibid.*, pp. 334–35; Westin, *1961 Senate Hearings*, pp. 196–97.

152. Emanuel Celler, letter to the author dated October 12, 1961.

153. E.g., "It is not unlikely . . . that legislation authorizing wire tapping will soon be enacted." Donnelly, "Comments and Caveats," p. 807. These words were written in 1954.

154. Celler, letter to the author.

155. In England wire tapping is done on a system of "direct lines from the central telephone offices" to a police office. Only "three or four carefully chosen officers" have access to the information. Dash *et al.*, *The Eavesdroppers*, p. 293. This system minimizes the possibility that wire tapping information may be used for blackmail purposes. Incriminating evidence is not used in court, but leads furnished by the wire tapping may be used to build a case.

156. Save in a few cases to be discussed in the pages that follow.

157. *Olmstead* v. *United States*, 277 U.S. 438 (1928).

in turn raise the question of whether a constitutionally adequate warrant can be devised to permit wire tapping. The difference between a search and a wire tap is crucial: a search is limited to designated objects; a wire tap has the character of a dragnet and inevitably involves listening to innocent parties and innocent conversations. The search, moreover, must be for contraband goods or instruments of crime only, not for evidence as such,[158] while wire tapping is done for the sole purpose of uncovering evidence. The Court might, however, take the view "that it is the nature of the telephone that requires the enlargement of the search. . . . It requires something of a different level of search."[159] The proscription of the search for evidence could therefore conceivably be modified to take into account this new method of communication.[160]

Wire tapping, however, is not an immediate constitutional problem. Whether it ever becomes one depends on the success of efforts to modify the ban of Section 605. Otherwise, the Court will continue to construe the statute, presumably with one eye cocked on analogous Fourth Amendment doctrine. Eavesdropping which does present a constitutional problem as of now is the sort being carried on with electronic gadgets not connected to telephone circuits and therefore not proscribed by Section 605 (or any other federal legislation).

This kind of eavesdropping, which may aptly be termed a magnification of wire tapping, poses a far more sinister threat to privacy because it can be carried on virtually anywhere. One can guard against the wire tap by not discussing confidential matters on the telephone, but there is no way to guard against instruments capable of picking up sounds through walls, save by remaining silent. Today,

158. *Boyd* v. *United States*, 116 U.S. 616 (1886); *Gouled* v. *United States*, 255 U.S. 298 (1921).

159. Westin, *1961 Senate Hearings*, p. 242.

160. Three members of the Court have discussed the subject of a warrant. Though they spoke in connection with electronic eavesdropping, not wire tapping, the problem is the same. Justice Douglas simply said that "a search . . . should be made, if at all, only on a warrant issued by a magistrate." *Silverman* v. *United States*, 365 U.S. 505, 513 (1961) (dissenting opinion). The controlling words are, of course, "if at all." Justice Brennan hinted broadly that it was possible to frame a warrant: "it is premature to conclude that no warrant for an electronic search can possibly be devised. The requirements of the Fourth Amendment are not inflexible, or obtusely unyielding to the legitimate needs of law enforcement." *Lopez* v. *United States*, 373 U.S. 427, 464 (1963) (dissenting opinion). Justice Murphy was unequivocal in his assertion that "a warrant can be devised" and pointed to the New York wire tapping warrant as an example. Murphy even went further and suggested that, as a substitute for a regular warrant, "some method of responsible administrative supervision could be evolved . . . which, like the valid search warrant, would adequately protect the privacy of the individual. . . ." *Goldman* v. *United States*, 316 U.S. 129, 140, n. 7 (1942) (dissenting opinion).

writes Edward Bennett Williams, there exist "devices which can pick up every sound in a room from without. Great success has been reported with contact microphones. These devices can be placed on the outside of a picture window or against any surface which acts as a sounding board. . . ." There even exist "devices which can pick up conversations hundreds of feet away."[161] Advertisements for such gadgets can be found with regularity even in leading newspapers. *The New York Times* has carried an advertisement offering a gadget which "you can poke . . . through the door crack, over the wall, under the rug, and even unreel it like a fishing line out the window down to the next story."[162] Another advertisement in the same paper announces "THE SNOOPER—Aim it at a group of friends a block away and hear every word!"[163] The price for this item was $18.95.

There is abundant evidence that the use of such instruments is common both in and out of government. A Senate subcommittee discovered that in a recent three-year period federal agencies purchased 397 electronic eavesdropping devices of one type alone, but it was unable to determine the use to which they were put.[164] The chief investigator for one congressional committee hired a hotel room next to the one occupied by a committee witness, Bernard Goldfine, and placed a listening device near the door separating the two rooms. "[H]e admitted that he overheard conversations even between Goldfine and his wife and between Goldfine and his counsel."[165] In New York State an electronic device was placed in a convict's cell and used to overhear conversations with a brother who visited him. The transcript was then placed in the hands of a legislative committee, which attempted to question him about what he had said.[166] The government has admitted that Internal Revenue Service conference rooms were fitted with electronic "bugs." These were used to overhear supposedly private conversations between taxpayers and their lawyers as they conferred in these rooms.[167]

161. Edward Bennett Williams, "The Wiretapping-Eavesdropping Problem: A Defense Counsel's View," *Minnesota Law Review*, XLIV (April, 1960), 855, 865.

162. *The New York Times*, March 21, 1965, p. 24S.

163. *Ibid.*, April 26, 1964, p. 24S.

164. *1960 Senate Hearings*, Part 5, pp. 1458–59. The years were 1957–1959, inclusive. The Department of the Army was the largest purchaser, buying 100. The Department of Justice purchased only 9. This particular type was meant to be concealed on the person.

165. Williams, "The Wiretapping-Eavesdropping Problem," p. 863. Williams was Goldfine's counsel. See also Williams, *One Man's Freedom* (New York, 1962), pp. 88–91.

166. *Lanza* v. *New York*, 370 U.S. 139 (1962).

167. *The New York Times*, July 14, 1965, pp. 1, 23.

Several times the Supreme Court has tackled this problem but never, it appears, with the sense of urgency which, as early as 1928, persuaded Justice Brandeis and his fellow dissenters in the Olmstead case[168] that the Fourth Amendment must be construed to guard against mechanical eavesdropping; otherwise, they feared, the amendment would become a dead letter once new scientific developments made the physical search unnecessary.

The Court ruled in the Goldman case,[169] it will be recalled, that law enforcement use of electronic devices capable of picking up conversations in a dwelling without interfering with the telephone wire violated neither Section 605 nor the Constitution. The device in the Goldman case was sufficiently powerful to pick up the conversation from an adjoining room without physically penetrating the suspect's constitutionally protected sanctuary. Suppose, however, that the device was brought into the dwelling through concealment on the person of a government agent who entered with consent: would the Goldman decision apply here too? It was this question that the Court was called upon to answer in 1952, in the case of *On Lee* v. *United States*.[170]

On Lee, a Hoboken, New Jersey, laundryman, was convicted of violating federal narcotics law. Chin Poy, a government undercover agent who was once an employee of On Lee's, obtained the evidence by entering On Lee's laundry and engaging him in a conversation, in the course of which On Lee incriminated himself. Unknown to On Lee, however, the conversation was not being conducted in privacy; concealed on Chin Poy's person, in his overcoat pocket, was a microphone which transmitted the sounds to a receiving set carried by another agent, Laurence Lee, who was stationed outside the place. Laurence Lee was able to overhear the entire conversation and later testified in court to what he had heard.

Justice Jackson wrote the opinion of the Court sustaining the conviction. The Goldman case was Jackson's guiding light and was held to be decisive of the issue. The fact that in the On Lee case the listening instrument was brought onto private premises he did not regard as a distinction of importance because Chin Poy came in with On Lee's consent and was not a trespasser. Nor did he think the eavesdropping procedure to have been so inconsistent with fair play as to require the Court to exercise its supervisory power over the federal courts and exclude the evidence, as it had done in *McNabb*

168. *Olmstead* v. *United States*, 277 U.S. 438 (1928).
169. *Goldman* v. *United States*, 316 U.S. 129 (1942).
170. 343 U.S. 747 (1952).

v. *United States.*[171] "Society," he said, in rebuttal to this contention, "can ill afford to throw away the evidence produced by the falling out, jealousies, and quarrels of those who live by outwitting the law." Lightly glossing over Chin Poy's conduct, he asserted that the government must not "be arbitrarily penalized for the low morals of its informers,"[172] whose use he compared to the "turning of state's evidence by denizens of the underworld."[173] a procedure no more palatable but nonetheless constitutionally and morally acceptable.

Justice Black dissented. He did not challenge the authority of the Goldman case, but he evidently felt that the low morals imputed to Chin Poy could not be disassociated from the conduct of his employer, the federal government, on whom they reflected adversely. Consequently, he would have required the exclusion of evidence acquired in this manner on the basis of the McNabb rule. Black did not explain why he regarded the official conduct in this case as less savory than that revealed in the Goldman case. Two explanations suggest themselves: either he regarded the conduct in the On Lee case as worse than an ordinary eavesdrop because it was directed toward eliciting a confession of guilt on the part of the suspect; or he felt that, even though there was no constitutional violation, the penetration of the transmitter onto the premises was morally repugnant.[174]

In a strongly worded dissent, Justice Frankfurter accused the majority of approving "legally what we disapprove morally" and of yielding "to a short-sighted view of practicality . . . [derived from] a preoccupation with what is episodic and a disregard of long-run consequences."[175] The effect of a decision approving the use of eavesdropping by electronic means would be destructive of public morality. "The contrast between morality professed by society and immorality practiced on its behalf," he asserted, "makes for contempt of law."[176] But even on practical grounds he thought the decision vulnerable. "My deepest feeling against giving legal sanction to such 'dirty business'," said Frankfurter, ". . . is that it makes for lazy and not alert law enforcement. It puts a premium on force and fraud, not on imagination and enterprise and professional training."[177]

171. 318 U.S. 332 (1943).
172. 343 U.S. 747, 756, 757.
173. *Ibid.*, p. 756.
174. Neverthless, in the fairly similar case of *Lopez* v. *United States*, 373 U.S. 427 (1963), which is discussed shortly, Black joined in the majority opinion sustaining the conviction and did not call for the invocation of the McNabb rule.
175. 343 U.S. 747, 758.
176. *Ibid.*, pp. 758–59.
177. *Ibid.*, p. 761.

Frankfurter's call for the overruling of the Olmstead case was echoed by Justice Douglas in his dissenting opinion. In a tribute to Brandeis' dissent there (Douglas remarked, "I cannot improve on it"[178]) Douglas' dissent consisted almost entirely of paragraph-length quotations from the Brandeis opinion. In a rare confession of error on the part of a member of the Court, Douglas said that he could no longer stand by his previous approval of the Goldman decision. "Reflection . . . has brought new insight to me. I now feel that I was wrong in the *Goldman* case."[179]

Justice Burton's separate dissenting opinion was written within the framework of the Olmstead and Goldman cases. Burton did not call for the overruling of the Olmstead decision, nor did he seek the invocation of the McNabb rule. Instead, he maintained that the On Lee decision went beyond the sanction of the Olmstead and Goldman cases for the reason that there was an illegal intrusion into the On Lee shop. There was a constitutional distinction between eavesdropping from within, and from without, the premises. While it was true that Chin Poy himself had consent to enter, the consent did not include the transmitter concealed on his person which "amounted to Chin Poy surreptitiously bringing [Laurence] Lee with him. . . . The presence of the transmitter . . . was the presence of Lee's ear."[180]

In the 1961 case of *Silverman* v. *United States*,[181] the Court for the first time reversed a conviction obtained with the assistance of electronic eavesdropping but did not re-examine the Olmstead doctrine, this time because it did not need to. The case concerned an eavesdrop by police on conversations in the headquarters of a Washington, D.C., gambling venture by means of a "spike mike"—a microphone with a foot-long spike attached. The pointed portion was pushed under the floor of the adjoining house (where the police were stationed with the co-operation of the owner) until it touched a heating duct in the gamblers' headquarters and converted the heating system into a conductor of sound. Justice Stewart, in his opinion for the Court, declared that it was the unauthorized intrusion of the eavesdropping apparatus onto the private premises which put this case beyond the pale of the Goldman and On Lee decisions. Even if there was no technical trespass under law, the searchers nevertheless usurped "an integral part of the premises"[182] when they in-

178. *Ibid.*, p. 763.
179. *Ibid.*, p. 762.
180. *Ibid.*, pp. 766–67. Burton pointed to *Gouled* v. *United States,* 255 U.S. 298 (1921), where the Court held that an unauthorized search conducted furtively is as constitutionally offensive as one made with force.
181. 365 U.S. 505 (1961).
182. *Ibid.*, p. 511.

serted their spike and used the gamblers' heating duct as a microphone.

The fact that the Court considered a mere physical intrusion, without a legal trespass, sufficient grounds for applying the Fourth Amendment represented an advance on the preceding eavesdropping cases but reflected no more than the Court's own recent efforts to disassociate the constitutional protection against unreasonable searches from the law of property with which it had hitherto been equated.[183] Privacy itself, however, as a concept to which the Constitution gave protection regardless of the means used to violate it, did not receive the blessing of the Court, and it was to this question that Justice Douglas addressed himself in a concurring opinion in which he chided his colleagues for "a matching of cases on irrelevant facts."[184] The physical intrusion—by which the majority sought to differentiate the Silverman and Goldman cases—was "beside the point. Was not the wrong in both cases done when the intimacies of the home were tapped, recorded, or revealed? The depth of the penetration of the electronic device . . . is not the measure of the injury." "[O]ur sole concern should be with whether the privacy of the house was invaded."[185]

The Court's most recent pronouncement on the subject of electronic eavesdropping came in *Lopez* v. *United States*,[186] decided in 1963. Lopez, a night club operator who was under investigation for evasion of excise taxes, attempted to bribe an Internal Revenue Service agent as an inducement to drop the case. When the agent reported the matter to his superiors, he was told to continue to feign an interest in the bribery scheme. He was outfitted with a miniature recording instrument for the purpose of recording further conversations with Lopez. The recordings were admitted into evidence and resulted in Lopez's conviction.

Justice Harlan's opinion for the Court sustained the conviction on the narrowest possible ground. A distinction was drawn between the use of electronic devices to eavesdrop on conversations which would otherwise be beyond the range of the government's ear and the mere recording of a conversation to whose contents the government is already privy by right. "The Government did not use an electronic device to listen in on conversations it could not otherwise have heard." The agent had Lopez's permission to be on the premises, and the device "neither saw nor heard more than the agent him-

183. See pp. 74–75, *supra.*
184. 365 U.S. 505, 512.
185. *Ibid.*, p. 513.
186. 373 U.S. 427 (1963).

self." It merely provided corroboration for the agent's own testimony, and there is no "constitutional right to rely on possible flaws in the agent's memory."[187] For this reason the Court found it unnecessary to reconsider the Olmstead and Goldman decisions, though the On Lee decision was apparently endorsed. Harlan drew an analogy to *Rathbun* v. *United States*,[188] where the Court had interpreted Section 605 of the Federal Communications Act to allow eavesdropping on the telephone lines with the consent of a party to the conversation. Finally, Harlan rejected the contention that, even lacking constitutional grounds, the Court should order exclusion of the evidence under its supervisory power over the federal courts. Only "manifestly improper conduct,"[189] such as the violation of a statute or of the Rules of Criminal Procedure, could, in the absence of a constitutional violation, justify the application of the exclusionary rule. "Improper conduct" was thus equated with "illegal conduct," a condition that was not met in this case.

Chief Justice Warren concurred in the result, but not in the Court's opinion, because he felt that the Court had renewed its imprimatur on the On Lee decision, with which he disagreed. Warren refused to assume that all electronic eavesdropping was either constitutionally prohibited or permissible: he preferred to distinguish among different situations. "One of the lines I would draw would be between this case and *On Lee*."[190] He differentiated the eavesdropping in the two cases on the basis of the difference in "purpose."[191] In this case the transmitter was employed solely for the purpose of protecting the credibility of the government agent. In the On Lee case, however, it was used in order to avoid putting the informer, apparently a person of weak credibility, on the witness stand. It thus became impossible for the defense to ascertain whether, for example, any psychological pressure had been placed on the informer to turn informer, or whether On Lee's confession had been induced by an appeal to friendship—courses of conduct which, he thought, might well not be permissible.[192] The major weakness in the Chief Justice's

187. *Ibid.*, p. 439.
188. 355 U.S. 107 (1957).
189. 373 U.S. 427, 440.
190. *Ibid.*, p. 441.
191. *Ibid.*, p. 443.
192. Warren recognized that the Court had not yet held that such conduct was not permissible, but he was of the view that "the [constitutional] issue is substantial," and he drew attention to two cases where the Court had ordered exclusion of confessions resulting from either psychological pressure or an appeal to friendship "under not totally dissimilar circumstances." *Ibid.*, p. 444. *Leyra* v. *Denno*, 347 U.S. 556 (1954); *Spano* v. *New York*, 360 U.S. 315 (1959). Actually, the circumstances were quite dissimilar. In the Leyra case, the psychological pressure had been placed on the confessor, not on the person (in this instance, a psychiatrist) who induced him to make the confession. The confession in the On Lee case would therefore seem to be untainted

position, as Justice Brennan pointed out in dissent, is that the considerations he advanced do not relate to the Fourth Amendment's guarantee of privacy. It is one thing to say that the Court should invoke its supervisory power to prevent unfairness to the defense; it is quite another to say that the scope of the right to privacy should be determined by the manner in which the evidence seized is used later on. If, in the On Lee case, the informer had been placed on the stand, the recording would presumably, according to Warren, have acquired retroactive constitutionality.[193]

Justice Brennan's dissenting opinion, in which he was joined by Justices Douglas and Goldberg, obviously represents a major effort to delineate a broad constitutional right of privacy and requires thoughtful consideration. Brennan thought that it was high time for the Court to reconsider the permissive doctrine of the Olmstead case, in view of the "terrifying"[194] problem which electronic eavesdropping had become. At times the recordings are not even accurate but "lend themselves to diabolical fakery"[195] through imaginative editing. The Court was confronted with an "intolerable situation" in that the protective value of the Court's decisions guarding against unreasonable conventional searches was now being circumvented by scientific devices posing "the greatest danger to the right of private freedom."[196] The Court's failure in the Olmstead and subsequent cases to bring wire tapping and electronic surveillance within the scope of the Fourth Amendment he laid at the door of two "unarticulated premise[s]." First, there was the fear that a warrant could not be framed to meet constitutional standards, and the Court was loath to deprive law enforcement officers of a useful investigative aid. This assumption, he said, if correct, "would be a compelling reason for forbidding them [electronic eavesdropping devices] altogether." In any event, though the question was as yet undecided, an

---

because it was not a direct result of pressure, even assuming that the government's conduct with respect to the informer was tainted. In the Spano case, a policeman friend who got Spano to confess falsely told him, on instructions, that Spano's earlier telephone call to him for help would result in his (the policeman's) losing his job unless a confession was forthcoming. The Court concluded that Spano's "will was overborne." 360 U.S. 315, 323. This is quite different from an appeal to friendship on the part of one whom the suspect has no reason to believe is in any way connected with government.

193. Warren's opinion is not, in fact, very clear on whether his distinction between the On Lee and Lopez cases is constitutionally based or not. He seems to mix up the Fourth Amendment with the Court's supervisory power: these cases, he said, "are quite dissimilar constitutionally *and* from the viewpoint of what this Court should permit under its supervisory powers. . . ." 373 U.S. 427, 441. (Emphasis supplied.)

194. *Ibid.*, p. 467.

195. *Ibid.*, p. 468.

196. *Ibid.*, p. 471.

"imaginative solution"[197] might be possible. Second, there was the fear that other investigative techniques involving deception, such as the use of undercover agents or plainclothesmen, might then prove equally susceptible to constitutional challenge. But, said Brennan, the two situations were qualitatively distinguishable. A person can guard against conventional deception and has only himself to blame if he does not, since the risk of being deceived "is probably inherent in the conditions of human society." But the use of electronic devices leaves one defenseless, without "even a residuum of true privacy."[198]

Justice Brennan agreed with the Chief Justice that the On Lee decision should be scrapped, but he could not agree that the difference in the situation confronting the Court in the Lopez case was of constitutional proportions: the two cases were "in principle indistinguishable."[199] On Lee's admissions were relayed, through a transmitter, to an agent listening on the outside, while Lopez's admissions were recorded. The fact that there was no human third party auditing Lopez's discussion with the agent was not a distinction of substance; the recording instrument itself was an outside auditor serving the same function as a human eavesdropper because it furnished "*independent* evidence of the statements"[200] made. Brennan refused to draw a constitutional distinction between "secrecy" and "privacy." The Fourth Amendment protected both equally. Even though Lopez did surrender his secrecy with respect to the admissions made to the agent, he did not at the same time surrender his right of privacy against third parties to whom he did not intend to communicate his thoughts. The admissions were therefore constitutionally privileged against any *outside* auditor. "If a person commits his secret thoughts to paper, that is no license for the police to seize the paper; if a person communicates his secret thoughts verbally to another, that is no license for the police to record the words."[201]

To create a broad right of privacy of discussion as against electronic intruders, Justice Brennan sought to link the First, Fourth, and Fifth Amendments. The right of privacy, he said, "embrace[s] a concept of the liberty of one's communications."[202] The free society could ill afford to tolerate the danger to uninhibited free speech which these instruments presented when placed in the hands of law

197. *Ibid.*, pp. 465, 464, 465.
198. *Ibid.*, pp. 465, 466.
199. *Ibid.*, p. 452.
200. *Ibid.*, p. 448.
201. *Ibid.*, p. 449.
202. *Ibid.*

enforcement officers. A party to a conversation is, of course, free to divulge what was said there. That is a risk which people normally take when speaking to others, but they can minimize the risk by carefully selecting those to whom they intend to reveal their innermost thoughts. This safeguard is not, however, available against uninvited electronic "ears." The real victim will be not the occasional violator of the law who is trapped into an admission of his misdeeds, but the free society itself: its continued existence and vitality is imperiled when free speech becomes muted out of fear. The Fourth Amendment, in its second clause, required that a search be conducted only under warrant, but in its first clause, forbidding unreasonable searches, it stated a broader principle which, allied with the Fifth Amendment's self-incrimination prohibition, amounts to "nothing less than a comprehensive right of personal liberty in the face of governmental invasion."[203] This did not mean, said Brennan, that all conversations were necessarily protected by the Constitution. "For example, a distinction might be drawn between surveillance of home or office on the one hand, and surveillance of public places, streets, and so forth, on the other hand."[204] The Rathbun case did not support the majority view; not only was the decision limited to statutory interpretation, but the extension phone there used was not installed for eavesdropping purposes, and the conversation was not electronically recorded.

Justice Brennan's argument for the recognition of a right to privacy as the concomitant of the right to free speech is a powerful one. Just as the Fourth Amendment protects one's physical possessions, so should it logically also protect one's oral communications. A person's thoughts are surely no less his "effects" than is his property. As Brennan said, "Our possessions are of little value compared to our personalities."[205] Yet the opinion leaves something to be desired. For one thing, it is difficult to see why Brennan chose to link not only the First and Fourth Amendments but the Fourth and Fifth Amendments as well. Surely the Fourth Amendment alone is powerful enough to accomplish the desired end, as the dissenters in the Olmstead case and its offspring evidently thought. The linking of the Fourth and Fifth Amendments might be of value if Brennan sought to prohibit electronic eavesdropping altogether, even when conducted under warrant, yet Brennan appeared to disavow this object. The Boyd case[206] had linked the two amendments to create a

203. *Ibid.*, p. 455.
204. *Ibid.*, p. 466, n. 12.
205. *Ibid.*, p. 469.
206. *Boyd* v. *United States*, 116 U.S. 616 (1886).

right to privacy of personal possessions (as distinct from contraband goods) which even a search warrant could not penetrate.[207]

But whatever the force of Brennan's argument with respect to eavesdropping by someone not a party to the conversation, it loses much of its power in the situation which the Lopez case presented. Even if we readily grant that a man's communications should normally be inviolate, why must this principle also follow when the communication has been made to one he *knows* to be an officer of the law? The Rathbun decision was based on no such narrow considerations as Justice Brennan would have it; the decision turned on the principle of the consent given by a party to the conversation, not on whether the eavesdropping apparatus was or was not specially installed or the conversation recorded.[208]

That the much criticized and only narrowly approved Olmstead doctrine, enunciated in 1928, should have survived—despite the Court's interpretation of Section 605—through the Goldman case in 1942, the On Lee case in 1952, the Silverman case in 1961, and the Lopez case in 1963 testifies to its extraordinary resiliency, for in each of these cases (with the exception of the last) most of the justices then sitting on the Court had not been appointed when the previous case in the series was decided. Perhaps it is more accurate to say that the doctrine has survived *because of* Section 605, which forbade wire tapping and therefore made a re-examination less urgent. The Court has more or less perfunctorily relied on the Olmstead case without ever engaging in a full-scale re-examination of its doctrine. Such a

207. Justice Brennan may have been using the occasion to construct a right to privacy for use in situations not involving a search for evidence. Thus, two years later, in *Griswold* v. *Connecticut*, 381 U.S. 479 (1965), the Court drew not only on the First, Fourth, and Fifth, but also on the Third and Ninth Amendments to establish a due process right to marital privacy as against the power of a state to forbid the use of contraceptives. Whether the Griswold case foreshadows any change in the Court's attitude twoard electronic eavesdropping remains to be seen. The two situations are not analogous; Justice Harlan, who wrote for the majority in the Lopez case, and Justice White, who joined in the opinion, both agreed with the Griswold decision (each concurring separately).

208. The Lopez and On Lee decisions may no longer be valid for a reason not connected with the Fourth Amendment: the suspect did not have the benefit of counsel, nor was he advised of his privilege against self-incrimination, when the admissions were elicited. See *Massiah* v. *United States*, 377 U.S. 201 (1964), and *Escobedo* v. *Illinois*, 378 U.S. 478 (1964). It should also be noted that one aspect of the Olmstead decision—that a nontangible item is not an "effect" within the meaning of the Fourth Amendment—has now been repudiated. In *Wong Sun* v. *United States*, a noneavesdropping case decided in 1964, the Court ruled that a verbal statement is an "effect" protected by the amendment and hence excludable from evidence when obtained from the suspect while he was under illegal arrest. 371 U.S. 471, 484–86.

re-examination, however, is increasingly likely to take place in the next few years, for the full measure of the menace to privacy posed by electronic devices is only now becoming appreciated. Brandeis' farsighted predictions in 1928 are now assuming the stature of reality, and the Court may finally have to heed his words. Congress could, of course, once again come to the Court's rescue by prohibiting electronic eavesdropping, but that is not at present in prospect and is, indeed, less likely than that Section 605 will be amended to allow a measure of wire tapping. The Department of Justice has recommended to the Congress that no legislation with respect to electronic eavesdropping be enacted at the present time.[209] This recommendation, if accepted, would have the effect of leaving the law of electronic eavesdropping where it stands today: all such eavesdropping not involving tampering with telephone wires and not requiring an encroachment on private property is legal, and the evidence thus obtained is admissible in court.

The Court cannot resolve the matter simply by holding that the Fourth Amendment provides protection against electronic eavesdropping. The difficulties which the Court may encounter are suggested by the variety of approaches in the several opinions which the Lopez case elicited. As new refinements for these eavesdropping techniques appear and they are used widely, the Court may be entering a new and perhaps continuing phase in its interpretation of the constitutional protection of privacy, one that will tax its ingenuity and wisdom as few other constitutional issues have done in recent years.

209. *1961 Senate Hearings*, p. 357.

## CHAPTER IX

# ADMINISTRATIVE INVASION OF PRIVACY

The warrantless search with which the framers were familiar and against which they directed the Fourth Amendment was composed of two elements: entry into the dwelling (1) for the purpose of securing evidence of crime (2). The preceding chapter was concerned with eavesdropping, which relates only to the second element—the search for evidence—and does not require entry into the dwelling. This chapter is concerned with the type of search, the administrative inspection, which contains only the first element, entry into the dwelling, and does not have as its purpose the securing of evidence of crime.

In the second half of the nineteenth century, and more particularly in the twentieth century, the development of industrial society gave rise to a multitude of social problems requiring for their solution the active intervention of government. Whole sectors of life once free of governmental scrutiny came under the supervision of administrative officials, both federal and state. Much of what had once been regarded as strictly private and properly outside the realm of governmental interest was brought by the law into the domain of publicly regulated activities because of abuses that demanded redress. In this manner wages and hours legislation, regulation of factory working conditions, and protective measures for the benefit of mine workers and women employees were enacted, which depended for their effectiveness upon a corps of efficient administrators and inspectors. Without inspection of the buildings, machinery, elevators, and fire escapes of factories and of other establishments, such as those engaged in the sale of food to the public, there could be no guarantee that the abuses legislated against would in fact be corrected. As regulation grew, so did the administrative quest for facts.[1]

The right of government inspectors to enter these establishments without a warrant in order to ensure compliance with regulations did

1. Administrative inspection of a different kind—the inspection of business records—is discussed in Chapter III.

not present legal questions difficult to resolve.[2] The premises inspected were, after all, not private dwellings, but of a public nature. Professor Ernst Freund's standard work on the "police power" of government—its power to protect public health, morals, and safety —sanctioned the warrantless inspection of public places on the grounds that "the power of inspection is distinguished from the power of search; the latter is exercised to look for property which is concealed, the former to look at property which is exposed to public view . . . and in nearly all cases accessible without violation of privacy."[3]

If the inspection of public places raises no serious constitutional problems, the same cannot be said of the inspection of private dwellings, for it was to prevent the warrantless search of the private dwelling that the Fourth Amendment was written. Today, however, state and city codes in profusion sanction the inspection of private dwellings by fire inspectors, health inspectors, building inspectors, and other such officials. While these enactments differ in detail, they are largely uniform in the kind of authority that they confer. A Wisconsin statute is typical: "The state fire marshal, his chief assistant and deputies, upon complaint of any person, or without any complaint previously entered, shall have a right at all reasonable hours, for the purpose of examination, to enter into and upon all buildings and premises within their jurisdiction."[4] Is it consistent with the Constitution, then, that a private home may be inspected by administrative officials who are not police officers, without a warrant and against the occupant's will, whenever they regard inspection as necessary for the safeguarding of the public health and safety?

This issue was raised before the Supreme Court in 1950 in *District of Columbia* v. *Little*.[5] A regulation of the district, which is a federal jurisdiction, required the owner or occupant of a dwelling to keep it clean. In case of failure to comply with the law, the person responsible was to be notified and instructed to correct the abuse; further neglect made him liable to punishment. For the purpose of enforcing the ordinance, the health officer was empowered to inspect

2. For the nature of the legal challenges to the right to inspect and the decisions of the courts around the turn of the century, see Andrew Alexander Bruce, "Arbitrary Searches and Seizures as Applied to Modern Industry," *The Green Bag*, XVIII (May, 1906), 273. This article apparently enjoys the distinction of being the first on search and seizure to appear in an American law review.

3. Ernst Freund, *The Police Power* (Chicago, 1904), p. 42. Even though there were no federal constitutional limitations on the state search power before 1949, most of the states throughout their history have had "little Fourth Amendments" in their own constitutions.

4. Wisconsin, *Statutes*, sec. 200.22.

5. *District of Columbia* v. *Little*, 339 U.S. 1 (1950).

any dwelling suspected of being in an unsanitary condition. Interference with an inspection was made punishable by a fine.

Geraldine Little, a resident of the district, refused to admit a public health official who, acting on a complaint of unsanitary conditions in her home, had come with a police officer to inspect the building. Someone named Allen came to the door and denied entry to the officers because the owner was not at home. Miss Little, who was across the street at the time, noticed the officers at her door and called to Allen to bar their entry. Returning home, she became aware for the first time of the nature of their mission but persisted in her refusal. For this she was arrested, convicted in the municipal court, and fined twenty-five dollars.

The court of appeals, however, found in favor of Miss Little.[6] Judge Prettyman, in an opinion of memorable eloquence, said that there was no basis "in semantics, in constitutional history, or in reason" for drawing any distinction between an inspection and a search. " 'Inspect' means to look at, and 'search' means to look for." It would be ascribing "a degree of irrationality"[7] to both the framers and ratifiers of the amendment to believe that they objected merely to officials who came into private homes to look for some object which they wished to take away, but not to those who came to pry for some other reason. A search was a search regardless of whether it had as its object a seizure.

Nor, said Judge Prettyman, did the Fourth Amendment permit a distinction between policemen and other law enforcement officials. The amendment applied to both alike because the right to privacy was a basic feature of democratic society, comparable to freedom of speech and religion. "If private homes are opened to the intrusion of government enforcement officials, at the wish of those officials, without the intervening mind and hand of a magistrate, one prop of the structure of our system is gone and an outstanding characteristic of another form of government will have been substituted."[8] He made short shrift of the suggestion that because the Fourth Amendment was designed as a protection against the general warrant, the use of which had been confined largely to criminal and forfeiture cases, it had no application in inspection cases. This reasoning was a "curious substitution of incident for basic principle."[9] The viola-

6. *District of Columbia* v. *Little*, 178 F.2d 13 (D.C. cir. 1949). The conviction had earlier been reversed on Fourth Amendment grounds by the district's municipal court of appeals. *Little* v. *District of Columbia*, 62 A.2d 874 (1948). It was this decision which the district appealed in the circuit court.

7. 178 F.2d 13, 18.

8. *Ibid.*, p. 16.

9. *Ibid.*, p. 19.

tion of the citizen's right to privacy, not the purpose for which the violation was accomplished, was the controlling criterion. The argument was also made that the protection of the Fourth Amendment extended only to searches for evidence of crime, not to inspections, because the amendment did not stand in isolation but had to be considered in conjunction with the Fifth Amendment's prohibition against compulsory self-incrimination. Where the possibility of self-incrimination does not arise, it was urged, the protection of the Fourth Amendment cannot be invoked. "The argument," said Judge Prettyman, "is wholly without merit, preposterous in fact."[10] The close relationship of the two amendments (according to the Boyd case, they "run almost into each other"[11]) obviously meant that the Fifth Amendment served to complement the Fourth, not to limit it. "The basic premise of the prohibition against searches was not protection against self-incrimination; it was the common-law right of a man to privacy in his home, a right which is one of the indispensable ultimate essentials of our concept of civilization."[12]

The Supreme Court, however, expressly chose to side-step the constitutional question and resorted to an ingenious but strained interpretation of the ordinance. Justice Black, speaking for six members of the Court, was of the opinion that "mere refusal to unlock the door accompanied by remonstrances on substantial constitutional grounds was [not] the kind of interference prohibited by the regulation."[13] Only Justices Burton and Reed, in a dissenting opinion by Burton, met the constitutional issue. They believed that the conduct complained of constituted a violation of the ordinance, and that, moreover, the "reasonable, general, routine, accepted and important character"[14] of the inspection fully squared with the requirements of the Constitution.

But the constitutional challenge could not long be avoided by the Court and was finally met in 1959, in *Frank* v. *Maryland*.[15] Only four members of the Court which had so ingeniously disposed of the Little case—Justices Black, Frankfurter, Douglas, and Clark—were still sitting. They were joined by five members appointed in the interim, Chief Justice Warren and Justices Harlan, Brennan, Whittaker, and Stewart. This time the case came from a state court and

10. *Ibid.*, p. 16.
11. *Boyd* v. *United States*, 116 U.S. 616, 630 (1886).
12. 178 F.2d 13, 16–17.
13. *District of Columbia* v. *Little*, 339 U.S. 1, 5–6 (1950).
14. *Ibid.*, p. 7.
15. 359 U.S. 360 (1959).

involved the due process clause of the Fourteenth Amendment rather than the Fourth Amendment itself.

The Baltimore City Code provides that the owner or occupant of a dwelling in which "the Commissioner of Health shall have cause to suspect that a nuisance exists"[16] is subject to a fine of twenty dollars for refusal to open his house for inspection. Failure to meet the standards of the health code does not itself render the offender liable to punishment. He is first contacted and told to correct the condition. Only if he fails to heed the warning does he become subject to prosecution.

The Baltimore Health Department received a complaint from a resident that rats were infesting her basement. A department inspector named Gentry was dispatched to inspect the houses in the neighborhood to locate the source of the trouble. When his knock on the door of Aaron D. Frank's detached house went unanswered, Gentry proceeded to inspect the exterior and discovered half a ton of trash in the yard. By this time Frank had made his appearance and demanded to know Gentry's business. Upon being told what it was, he refused Gentry permission to inspect the basement. The next day Gentry, this time accompanied by two policemen, returned to the scene, and once again his knock on the door of the Frank home was not answered. He then obtained a warrant of arrest for Frank, who was convicted and fined twenty dollars. The Maryland Court of Appeals denied *certiorari*, thus by implication upholding the statute. Since an interpretation of a state statute by that state's highest court is regarded as binding by the Supreme Court, no further temporizing by the Court on the constitutional issue was possible.

The Supreme Court, with Justice Frankfurter speaking for the majority, divided five to four in upholding the constitutionality of the inspection procedure. Since this was a state case to which not the Fourth Amendment but only its "core," as applied through the due process clause, was directly relevant, the inspection procedure could have been sustained simply on the grounds that no fundamental right was thereby placed in jeopardy. There was no need for Frankfurter to resort to the explicit requirements and the historical background of the Fourth Amendment. It is important to bear in mind that for Frankfurter due process was an independent concept and not a derivative of the provisions of the Bill of Rights, even when the right that was protected, as in the case of the Fourth Amendment's guarantee of privacy, lay in the same area. Nevertheless, Frankfurter appeared to go out of his way to give the inspection

16. Baltimore City Code, Art. 12, sec. 120.

procedure the sanction of the Fourth Amendment as well as of the due process clause.

Justice Frankfurter turned first to the historical background of the Fourth Amendment. After reviewing the landmark cases of *Entick* v. *Carrington*[17] and *Boyd* v. *United States*[18] and the memorable argument of James Otis, Jr., in the historic Writs of Assistance case,[19] he arrived at the conclusion that the Fourth Amendment placed no obstacles in the way of the inspection procedure. The searches which the framers had chiefly sought to proscribe were those for evidence of crime or for goods subject to confiscation. In a passage that constituted the heart of his opinion, he declared:

> [T]wo protections emerge from the broad constitutional proscription of official invasion. The first of these is the right to be secure from intrusion into personal privacy, the right to shut the door on officials of the state unless their entry is under proper authority of law. The second, and intimately related protection, is self-protection: the right to resist unauthorized entry which has as its design the securing of information to fortify the coercive power of the state against the individual, information which may be used to effect a further deprivation of life or liberty or property. . . . [*H*]*istory makes plain, that it was on the issue of the right to be secure from searches for evidence to be used in criminal prosecutions or for forfeitures that the great battle for fundamental liberty was fought.*[20]

But if history did not *require* the Court to find the inspection procedure unreasonable, neither did it require the Court to find the procedure permissible. The right to be free from all official intrusions into privacy, even where prosecution or forfeiture was not the intended result, was conceded by Frankfurter to be one of the concerns, even if not the primary concern, of the Fourth Amendment. Plainly, the Court would have to formulate policy in the guise of constitutional interpretation, to engage in the delicate "balancing" of public needs and individual rights. Since the Court, then, was free to choose between competing alternatives of public interest and individual privilege, Frankfurter addressed himself to the task of making explicit the bases for the decision. The Baltimore ordinance, he said, was a reasonable one, "hedged about with safeguards designed to make the least possible demand"[21] on the privacy of the homeowner. Inspection could take place only during the daytime; a showing of something like probable cause was required; the inspector had no

17. *Entick* v. *Carrington*, 19 Howell's State Trials 1029 (1765).
18. *Boyd* v. *United States*, 116 U.S. 616 (1886).
19. Quincy's *Massachusetts Reports, 1761–1772*, p. 469.
20. 359 U.S. 360, 365. (Emphasis supplied.)
21. *Ibid.*, p. 367.

authority to make a forcible entry and had not done so in this case. "Here was no midnight knock on the door, but an orderly visit in the middle of the afternoon with no suggestion that the hour was inconvenient."[22]

It was not, however, the reasonableness of the procedure alone that impressed Justice Frankfurter, but also the fact that the inspections were designed to protect vital community interests. The inspection device as used in Maryland was hallowed by long usage. For over two hundred years, dating from pre-Revolutionary days, Maryland had authorized inspections for general welfare purposes. Maryland's adoption, in 1776, of a constitutional provision analogous to the Fourth Amendment was followed not by a decrease but a notable increase in the number of such authorizations. The old enactments endured, and new ones were added.[23] The growth of cities, said Frankfurter, had aggravated the conditions that necessitated periodic inspection of dwellings in order to safeguard the health and well-being of the population. In the light of these needs, which "have multiplied manifold,"[24] even "giving the *fullest scope* to this constitutional right to privacy, its protection cannot here be invoked."[25]

One last question remained to be answered as Justice Frankfurter rounded out his opinion: why not require a warrant? An important policy consideration dictated otherwise, he answered. For inspections to accomplish their purpose, the standards for issuance of a warrant would have to be considerably reduced from those needed for a warrant in criminal cases, thus leading to "a synthetic search warrant. . . . [T]he requirement cannot be flexibly interpreted to dispense with the rigorous constitutional restrictions for its issue."[26]

Justice Douglas was joined by Chief Justice Warren and Justices Black and Brennan in dissent. His opening remarks were cast in somber tones: "The decision today greatly dilutes the right of privacy which every homeowner had the right to believe was part of our American heritage. We witness indeed an inquest over a substantial part of the Fourth Amendment."[27] Douglas went on to say that his reading of history did not correspond with Frankfurter's. The elder Pitt's eloquent remonstrance against official intrusions into the home concerned not entry to search for evidence of crime but for the pur-

22. *Ibid.*, p. 366.
23. A cursory review of the evidence cited by Frankfurter shows, however, that for the most part these statutes related to the inspection of private property other than homes, for example, business establishments and ships.
24. 359 U.S. 360, 371.
25. *Ibid.*, p. 366. (Emphasis supplied.)
26. *Ibid.*, p. 373.
27. *Ibid.*, p. 374.

pose of enforcing a tax on cider.[28] Similarly, the famous speech of James Otis was directed against all unreasonable intrusions on privacy, not against the search for evidence of crime exclusively. In any event, said Douglas, the Court was unjustified in drawing a distinction between criminal and civil in a case such as this one, where failure to abate a nuisance would indeed give rise to prosecution. "The knock on the door in any health inspection case may thus lay the groundwork for a criminal prosecution."[29] He cited the restraints placed by the Court on inspection of business records by the regulatory commissions[30] even where no criminal prosecutions were directly contemplated, but only cease and desist orders.

There were also practical considerations militating against the warrantless inspection, said Justice Douglas. Police officers may be encouraged to utilize health inspectors to make searches for evidence of crime in the guise of inspections. "In some States the health inspectors are none other than the police themselves,"[31] and it would be folly to expect them to be able to separate their functions and to forget that they are policemen when called upon to make health inspections. Douglas did not depreciate the importance of health inspections. "But they are hardly more important than the search for narcotics peddlers, rapists, kidnappers, murderers, and other criminal elements."[32] The requirement of a warrant when the householder objected to the inspection would scarcely imperil the public health program in view of the fact that refusals to co-operate were extremely rare; prosecutions in Baltimore for refusal to permit inspection had averaged one a year in recent years, although more than thirty-six thousand inspections were made in 1958 alone.

In conclusion, Douglas rejected Frankfurter's contention that the formulation of a warrant for inspection purposes would result in a "synthetic" search warrant. The admission that a different kind of warrant was required was not at all an admission that the Constitution did not consider an inspection without warrant to be an unreasonable search. The proof to be required would not be the same as for a warrant in criminal cases only because "the facts that would justify an inference of 'probable cause' to make an inspection are clearly different from those that justify such an inference where a criminal investigation has been undertaken. Experience may show

28. This example was poorly chosen because the discovery of goods that had evaded customs led to their forfeiture.
29. 359 U.S. 360, 375.
30. For discussion see Chapter III.
31. 359 U.S. 360, 375.
32. *Ibid.*, p. 382.

the need for periodic inspection of certain facilities without a further showing of cause. . . . The passage of a certain period without inspection might of itself be sufficient in a given situation to justify the issuance of a warrant. The test of 'probable cause' . . . can take into account the nature of the search that is being sought."[33] To emphasize this argument, Douglas pointed out that English law did require a warrant for health inspections where entry into the home was otherwise denied.[34]

The dissenters, though outvoted in the Frank case, were, however, determined to keep the issue of administrative inspections alive. Since, as in a grant of *certiorari*, the votes of only four justices are required to note probable jurisdiction, they soon forced a noting of probable jurisdiction in an Ohio case[35] which in some respects resembled the Frank case. There is evidence that this move was designed to embarrass the majority. In the first place, probable jurisdiction was noted only one month after the Frank decision. Furthermore, Justice Stewart would almost certainly absent himself from the consideration and decision of the case, since his father was a member of the Ohio Supreme Court at the time that it reviewed the case, and an evenly divided Court would be the probable result.

A *per curiam* opinion noted jurisdiction, but whereas this normally ends the matter, and the anonymity of the judicial alignments is preserved until the justices have voted on the merits, in this instance members of the Court took the unprecedented step of resorting to opinions to identify and explain their votes. In a joint memorandum opinion, Justices Frankfurter, Clark, Harlan, and Whittaker announced that they had voted against noting probable jurisdiction because they believed the Frank case "to be completely controlling upon the Ohio decision. . . ."[36] The hearing of the case "would manifest disrespect by the Court for its own process"[37] in

33. *Ibid.*, p. 383.

34. An English lawyer comments: "To the English reader of the dissenting judgment [*sic*] in *Frank* v. *Maryland* the notion that English law is 'conscious of civil liberties' in this respect can cause a wry smile." Even though the Public Health Act of 1936 did require a warrant, there is no uniform pattern concerning entry into the home by administrative officials. "Since 1946, for instance, at least seventeen statutes still in force have conferred rights of entry upon various public officials without requiring in any circumstances the necessity of a magistrate's warrant." D. W. M. Waters, "Rights of Entry in Administrative Officers," *University of Chicago Law Review*, XXVII (Autumn, 1959), 79, 83, 85.

35. *Ohio* ex rel. *Eaton* v. *Price*, 360 U.S. 246 (1959).

36. *Ibid.*, p. 248.

37. *Ibid.*, pp. 248–49. Justice Clark separately explained his own negative vote in a similar manner.

view of the very recent decision in the Maryland case. Justice Brennan, who voted to note probable jurisdiction, took to task those of his colleagues who had voted in the negative and then committed the indiscretion of identifying themselves. Anonymity should have been preserved, he lectured them, until after the case had been argued and decided, since "public expression of views on the merits of a case by a Justice before argument and decision may well be misunderstood. . . ."[38] Since the case was finally decided by an equally divided eight-man Court in a one-sentence *per curiam* opinion[39] which sustained the conviction, the facts must be gathered from the opinion of Justice Brennan, who spoke for the four dissenters, the others being, here as in the Frank case, Chief Justice Warren and Justices Black and Douglas.

The Ohio code closely resembled the Baltimore code previously sustained, but there was one important difference. Justice Frankfurter had stressed the reasonableness of the Baltimore code and the fact that something like probable cause was required as a prerequisite to inspection. The Ohio code, however, authorizes the Housing Inspector "to enter, examine and survey at any reasonable hour all dwellings. . . ."[40] A showing of probable cause, or anything resembling it, is not required. Refusal to permit entry for the purpose of inspection makes the occupant liable to fine and imprisonment.

Earl Taylor was a plumber living in Dayton, Ohio. Three housing inspectors appeared at his door one day and demanded to inspect the house. When Taylor protested their lack of a warrant, they replied that they did not need one. Taylor nevertheless refused to admit them. Two subsequent attempts at inspection were equally unsuccessful. When Taylor told the inspectors, "I have nothing in my house for inspection," they replied, "We have a right to come in your house, go through your house, inspect the whole inside of your house."[41] But they were not admitted. A summons from the Dayton city prosecutor, requiring Taylor to appear in his office and answer a complaint, was ignored. The upshot was that Taylor was committed to jail when he could not post bail. A lower Ohio court, finding the ordinance unconstitutional, freed him, but the Ohio Supreme Court declared the ordinance valid. Taylor flung his last legal challenge at the ordinance before the Supreme Court.

38. *Ibid.*, pp. 247–48. It was totally different, said Brennan, for a justice to identify himself as dissenting from a denial of *certiorari,* something that is quite common, for "such notations do not tend to foreclose or embarrass consideration of the case . . . since by definition it is not to be heard." *Ibid.*, p. 248, n. 2.

39. *Ohio* ex rel. *Eaton* v. *Price,* 364 U.S. 263 (1960).

40. Dayton, Ohio, Code of General Ordinances, Sec. 806–30 (a).

41. 364 U.S. 263, 266.

Justice Brennan's dissenting opinion was largely a strong reiteration of Justice Douglas' dissent in the Frank case, and as such does not require extensive comment. However, he took considerable pains to highlight the differences between the Maryland and Ohio cases. Without retreating from the dissenters' position that no inspection without a warrant meets constitutional standards, he nevertheless pointed out that in the Frank case there was a complaint concerning a health hazard and that the inspector had seen the trash in the rear of Frank's house. In this case, however, there was no cause for suspicion nor was there any evidence that the inspection was part of a systematic plan. Indeed, the inspectors might have been motivated by "personal or political spite. It hardly contradicts experience to suggest that the practical administration of local government in this country can be infected with such motives."[42]

The tenor of Justice Frankfurter's opinion in the Frank case and, in particular, his use of historical data had left little ground for believing that federal cases arising under the Fourth Amendment, with its more explicit terminology, would fare any differently than state cases arising under the Fourteenth. Whatever doubts remained, however, were dispelled in the case of *Abel* v. *United States*,[43] "a notorious case, with a notorious defendant,"[44] which also involved an administrative search, though of an unusual sort.

The Abel case began in 1957, when the Federal Bureau of Investigation came into possession of information, originating from a defected Soviet spy, that Soviet espionage in the New York area was being directed by Rudolph Ivanovich Abel, a colonel in the Soviet Army who had been living in New York City under various assumed names since 1948.[45] Following an investigation of the case, the F.B.I. was unable to collect sufficient evidence to justify an arrest on espionage charges and informed the Immigration and Naturalization Service that Abel was an alien illegally residing in the United States.

42. *Ibid.*, p. 271.
43. 362 U.S. 217 (1960).
44. *Ibid.*, p. 248 (Justice Brennan dissenting).
45. The factual information contained in the opinions regarding Abel's espionage activities and his subsequent apprehension and interrogation has been supplemented by reference to *The New York Times*, February 11, 1961, p. 40, and to Edward L. Barrett, Jr., "Personal Rights, Property Rights and the Fourth Amendment," *The Supreme Court Review* (1960), pp. 46, 56. The full story of Abel's apprehension, detention, trial, and appeals, as well as of the subsequent international exchange of Abel for Francis Gary Powers, the American U-2 pilot who was serving a prison sentence in the Soviet Union, is told by Abel's attorney. James B. Donovan, *Strangers on a Bridge: The Case of Colonel Abel* (New York, 1964).

Armed with an administrative arrest warrant issued by the district director of the I.N.S., which authorized them to apprehend Abel and hold him for deportation, two I.N.S. officers were directed to Abel's abode in a Manhattan hotel by several F.B.I. agents, who were promised the right to confer with Abel to solicit his co-operation. In the event that he would not co-operate, the I.N.S. men, who had repaired to an adjoining hotel room, were to step in and arrest Abel. The efforts of the F.B.I. agents proved fruitless, and the I.N.S. men made the arrest. An exhaustive search of Abel's person, his belongings, and his room followed, both before and after his removal to the local I.N.S. headquarters. The F.B.I. agents watched but did not participate. A number of incriminating objects were uncovered, including a forged birth certificate, a coded message, a hollow pencil filled with microfilms, and a cipher code hidden in a block of wood covered with sandpaper.

After several hours in the I.N.S. office, Abel was put on a plane and spirited to a detention camp over a thousand miles away. There he remained for five weeks ("as far as the world knew, he had vanished"[46]) before the federal government arraigned him on criminal charges and returned him to New York for trial. "Though grilled ceaselessly for five days without sleep, and then daily for three weeks, Abel gave no information concerning his activities."[47] His subsequent trial and conviction resulted in a thirty-year prison sentence, which he appealed to the Supreme Court.[48] At issue was whether the evidence secured by a search which is made incidental to an *administrative* arrest for deportation is admissible in federal court.

Speaking for the same five-man majority as in the Frank case, Justice Frankfurter sustained the conviction. He pointed out that as early as 1798 Congress had authorized the arrest of aliens for deportation on warrants issued by administrative officials. As for the search, the concept of search incidental to arrest applied not only to criminal arrests but to administrative arrests as well because the same rationale was valid; the fugitive must be secured, the lives of the arresting

46. 362 U.S. 217, 252 (Justice Douglas dissenting).

47. Professor Harold J. Berman of the Harvard University Law School, quoted in the *National Observer*, February 18, 1962, p. 13. Only after Abel had been in the detention camp for several days was he allowed access to counsel with respect to the deportation charges.

48. The Abel case had a long travail in the courts. That the Supreme Court must have experienced great difficulty with this unusual case is evidenced from the scheduling of the oral arguments. On March 23, 1959, less than one month after having heard two days of oral argument (February 24 and 25), the Court ordered the case restored to the docket for reargument. It was reargued in the following term of Court on November 9, and the decision was not announced until March 28, 1960.

officers must be protected, and the evidence must be safeguarded from destruction. "[T]he need for the proof is as great in one case as in the other, for deportation can be accomplished only after a hearing at which deportability is established."[49]

Granted that a search is permitted for the purpose of establishing deportability: was this not, however, a search for *evidence of crime* on a warrant issued by an administrative officer removed from judicial control, and did not the collaboration of the F.B.I. and the I.N.S. bear out the theory of collusion for this purpose? Justice Frankfurter answered in the negative. He agreed with the finding of the lower courts that the record did not disclose "bad faith."[50] In this sort of situation it was entirely proper for the two agencies to work together, each performing its own special task. It was the F.B.I.'s duty to bring Abel's illegal residence in this country to the attention of the I.N.S., and it was the duty of the I.N.S. to bring deportation proceedings. The F.B.I. was not barred from seeking Abel's cooperation prior to the administrative arrest nor from continuing its investigation of his espionage activities once the administrative arrest had been made.

It was precisely because the two agencies do usually work together in this type of situation that Justice Douglas, dissenting with the concurrence of Justice Black, believed that the conviction should not stand. He was certain that the search was the result of collusion between the F.B.I. and the I.N.S. He pointed out that F.B.I. agents had participated in Abel's interrogation while he was in the detention camp and thought that "the record plainly shows that F.B.I. agents were the moving force behind this arrest and search," and that the arrest was really for the purpose of criminal investigation and not deportation. Though the F.B.I. had ample time to get a search warrant, it did not, and the reason for the omission was clear. "The administrative warrant of arrest was chosen with care and calculation as the vehicle through which the arrest and search were to be made."[51] A magistrate might impose restrictions in compliance with the requirements of the Fourth Amendment. "How much more convenient it is for the police to find a way around . . . the Fourth Amendment!" He did not question the good faith of the F.B.I. but accused it rather of overzealousness. Douglas felt that the Court had

49. 362 U.S. 217, 236. The issue in this case of search incidental to arrest is discussed in Chapter IV.
50. *Ibid.*, p. 240.
51. *Ibid.*, p. 244.

been influenced by two factors. First, there was the influence of a bad precedent: "The opening wedge that broadened the power of administrative officers—as distinguished from police—to enter and search peoples' homes was *Frank* v. *Maryland*. . . ."[52] A second factor was the notoriety of the defendant, which, he thought, had adversely influenced the majority: "When guilt permeates a record, even judges sometimes relax and let the police take shortcuts not sanctioned by constitutional procedures."[53]

Justice Brennan, who spoke for all four dissenters (the same dissenting group as in the previous cases), did not advert to the subject of collusion but rested his argument on the belief that an administrative warrant is insufficient to sustain criminal charges. It would not do to justify the procedure by calling it civil and thereby to remove it from the protection of the Fourth Amendment. "The distinction [between criminal and civil] is rather hollow here, where the proofs that turn up are in fact given in evidence in a criminal prosecution."[54] The search power added to the arrest power "create[s] a complete concentration of power in executive officers over the person and effects of the individual."[55] The Fourth Amendment should properly be considered a barrier to the procedures employed in this case.

As these cases unfolded, the ramifications of *Frank* v. *Maryland* became evident. Both the Ohio inspection case and the Abel decision definitely broadened the Frank ruling. In the Ohio case there was no reason to believe that a nuisance detrimental to public safety existed on the premises—a factor which was present in the Frank case and was emphasized in Justice Frankfurter's opinion for the Court. Moreover, one could not say of the Abel search, as Frankfurter had said of the Frank inspection, that it made "the least possible demand on the individual . . . the slightest restriction on his claims of privacy."[56] A more exhaustive search is hardly to be found in the records of the Supreme Court.

So stands the matter today. The Court, by the narrowest possible majority, has placed its stamp of approval on the warrantless inspection as meeting constitutional standards. Here, as elsewhere,

52. *Ibid.*, p. 242.
53. *Ibid.*, p. 241.
54. *Ibid.*, p. 254.
55. *Ibid.*, p. 252.
56. 359 U.S. 360, 367.

we are confronted with the problem of constitutional vagueness. History can aid in interpretation, but there are limits to its usefulness. The same historical evidence cited by Justice Frankfurter to prove that the Fourth Amendment was intended primarily to place limits on searches for evidence of crime was employed by Justice Douglas, with equal effect, in rebuttal of Frankfurter's views. It is one thing to show that the events which gave rise to the amendment involved a particular type of abuse; it is quite another to demonstrate that the protection of the amendment does not apply against other forms of conduct equally offensive to the basic principle of the Fourth Amendment—that the privacy of the home must not be violated by a government official acting without prior judicial approval. Since historical evidence often proves insufficient, the Court can fall back on an examination of the contending and conflicting social interests involved and attempt to balance them, although "balancing" in constitutional law usually means not compromise but the elevation of one interest at the expense of another that is considered to be less important. This is precisely what Justice Frankfurter did in *Frank* v. *Maryland,* once he had come to the conclusion that history did not tie his hands and compel him to find that the administrative inspection without warrant violated the Fourth Amendment.

But did the Court properly balance the individual and public interests competing for judicial favor? Justice Frankfurter was quite right in pointing out the importance of municipal inspections; he found no disagreement there. It might even be said that in one respect unsanitary conditions pose a greater evil to the community than do the instruments of crime which the police wish to seize, for the unsanitary conditions are a continuing offense, whereas the crime has already been committed and may never be repeated. Yet if the necessity of inspections is granted, it by no means follows that they should be sanctioned without the intervening hand of a judicial officer.

It is true that the possibility of an inspection leading to a prosecution is remote whenever the householder is first given the opportunity to remedy the conditions uncovered.[57] But the opportunity for collusion between the police and inspectors exists and may well be

57. See, nevertheless, the Court's sanction of the refusal of a witness to answer certain questions before a grand jury. "Answers to the questions asked," said the Court, "would have furnished *a link in the chain of evidence* needed in a prosecution. . . ." *Blau* v. *United States*, 340 U.S. 159, 161 (1950). (Emphasis supplied.)

abused. Following the decision in the Frank case upholding the Baltimore inspection procedure, such an incident took place in that city. A policeman was assigned to the Sanitation Department for the purpose of spying out an illegal lottery while ostensibly making a health inspection, though in this instance the deception was uncovered and the evidence excluded.[58]

It was to be expected that Justice Frankfurter, the former Byrne Professor of Administrative Law at Harvard, would have a keen appreciation of the value of the administrative process and would find it difficult to associate the administrative official with the police officer. He was in the mainstream of progressive thought of twentieth-century America and had been associated with the sociological school of jurisprudence, whose views, broadly stated, are that law is a social instrument for the satisfaction of human needs. Control of disease is surely one of those needs. But much that is precious to the free society is lost if in satisfying community needs a basic right is vitiated. Welfare recipients are sometimes hounded at all hours of the day and night by investigating inspectors seeking to determine whether eligibility has been properly established or whether assistance payments have been fraudulently solicited.[59] Sometimes administrative inspections are carried out by policemen. (In both the Little and Frank cases the inspectors were *accompanied* by policemen.) Conversely, administrative officials are sometimes given authority to investigate for evidence of crime. Thus, in Ohio, fire marshals are authorized to investigate cases of arson.[60] It would be idle to expect Ohio fire inspectors to forget that they are also acting as policemen when inspecting homes. Multiple functions cannot easily be separated in the mind of the official involved.

Inspectors admittedly are seldom confronted with refusals to cooperate. Health hazards of serious magnitude due to frustration of health inspections are therefore unlikely to develop. There does not seem to be much merit to the contention that to sanction an inspection warrant with requirements different from those needed for a

58. The case is discussed by Justice Douglas in *Abel* v. *United States*, 362 U.S. 216, 242–43 (1960) (dissenting opinion).

59. For an illuminating discussion of the constitutional problem, see Charles A. Reich, "Midnight Welfare Searches and the Social Security Act," *Yale Law Journal*, LXXII (June, 1963), 1347.

60. See *In re Groban*, 352 U.S. 330 (1957). At least one state, Wisconsin, specifically authorizes inspections without warrant by fire marshals for the gathering of evidence of arson to be used in criminal prosecutions. Wisconsin, *Statutes*, sec. 200.21. This provision would seem to be clearly unconstitutional, even according to the Court's majority view.

search warrant would result in a "synthetic" document which would lead to a weakening of the Fourth Amendment's requirements in criminal cases. It is surely the duty, and within the capability, of the judiciary to make certain that this does not come about. The alternative of no judicial control at all over inspections seems a far more drastic choice.[61] In the Olmstead wire tapping case Justice Holmes wrote: "There is no body of precedents by which we are bound. . . . Therefore, we must consider the two objects of desire both of which we cannot have and make up our minds which to choose."[62] In the inspection cases the Court was confronted with no such drastic choice; a compromise was possible—along the lines of the warrant suggested by the dissenters—such that neither the community nor the private interest need be sacrificed.

It is possible to take the attitude, as one commentator did in writing on the Ohio case, that "laissez-faire concepts of government are relics of an age past. We live today in an era of positive government. . . ."[63] However, does not the surrender of so many aspects of our privacy because of the exigencies of modern life require that the last bastion of privacy, the home, remain inviolate? For half a century prior to the late nineteen thirties, the Court had placed the individual in a central role and had taken a jaundiced view of regulation designed to promote the public interest. The pendulum may now have swung too far in the opposite direction. The individual, far from being the central figure in the law that he once was, is now in danger of being swallowed up by society, completely losing his dignity and privacy and hence his very individuality. As matters now stand, the criminal whose home has been searched without a warrant may have the evidence excluded. The law-abiding householder faces a prison sentence or fine when he refuses to permit his privacy to be

61. A student Note argues that there are certain disadvantages to a warrant requirement. To cite one example, an inspector who has no warrant will probably leave and come back at another time if so requested, while if he possesses a warrant he is likely to demand immediate entry, regardless of the inconvenience to the householder. Moreover, in one respect a warrant would give the inspector greater powers because it would authorize entry by force, something which the inspection codes do not. Note, "Administrative Inspections and the Fourth Amendment—A Rationale," *Columbia Law Review*, LXV (February, 1965), 288. But such criticism misses the point. Surely it is for the householder to decide whether or not it is to his advantage to demand a warrant when confronted with a request to enter without one. Since refusals to co-operate are rare, it is highly unlikely that the inspector will come armed with a warrant *before* being denied entry.

62. *Olmstead* v. *United States,* 277 U.S. 438, 470 (1928) (dissenting opinion).

63. Lloyd T. Whittaker, "Is This Trip (to the Supreme Court) Necessary?", *Journal of Public Law*, IX (Spring, 1960), 260, 267.

invaded. It seems contradictory to construe the Fourth Amendment in such a manner as to make it a protection for the criminal suspect who misuses his privacy to shield the evidence of his guilt, and not for the honest citizen who values privacy for its own sake. In the words of Judge Prettyman, "to say that a man suspected of crime has a right to protection against search of his home without a warrant, but that a man not suspected of crime has no such protection, is a fantastic absurdity."[64]

64. *District of Columbia* v. *Little,* 178 F.2d 13, 17 (D.C. cir. 1949). This point is developed by Dean Barrett:

does it matter to any significant degree to the law-abiding person whether his house is searched by an administrative official such as an immigration officer or a health inspector or by a police officer seeking evidence . . . ? In each case, his privacy has been invaded by an official authority which he is powerless to resist. . . . One may be able to justify on grounds of history, if not policy, a constitutional doctrine which prefers property interests to personal liberty. But neither history nor policy can justify a doctrine which accords special protections to the privacy of lawbreakers which are not enjoyed by citizens generally.

Barrett, "Personal Rights," pp. 73–74.

## CHAPTER X

# THE SUPREME COURT AND THE FOURTH AMENDMENT

The work of the Supreme Court in formulating the constitutional law of search and seizure can be divided into four tolerably distinct periods. In the first period, which began with the Boyd case[1] in 1886 and lasted into the nineteen twenties, the Court, with only occasional deviations, heeded its own admonition "that constitutional provisions for the security of person and property should be liberally construed."[2] It was in this period that the exclusionary rule for the federal courts was fashioned and, in general, the freedom from unreasonable searches was interpreted so as to recognize a constitutional right of privacy not limited to the literal language of the Fourth Amendment. In 1924, for instance, Justice Holmes, in a bristling opinion for the Court, denounced any departure from "the spirit as well as the letter of the Fourth Amendment,"[3] and asserted that such a departure would "sweep all our traditions into the fire."[4]

Beginning in 1925, however—in the midst of the prohibition era, which brought a large number of search cases involving bootleggers before the Court—a new and more tolerant attitude toward law enforcement procedures became evident. The warrantless search of the automobile was deemed constitutional[5] (at least when authorized by Congress), the scope of search incidental to arrest was considerably expanded,[6] wire tapping was held not to be forbidden by the Constitution and wire tap evidence admissible even when obtained in violation of state law.[7]

The years following World War II and continuing into the late nineteen fifties were marked by notable inconsistency and, for the first time, invariable judicial disagreement. The Fourteenth Amendment was construed as requiring the states to meet constitutional search standards but at the same time as allowing them to use evi-

1. *Boyd* v. *United States*, 116 U.S. 616 (1886).
2. *Ibid.*, p. 635.
3. *Federal Trade Commission* v. *American Tobacco Co.*, 264 U.S. 298, 305 (1924).
4. *Ibid.*, p. 306.
5. *Carroll* v *United States*, 267 U.S. 132 (1925).
6. *Marron* v. *United States*, 275 U.S. 192 (1927).
7. *Olmstead* v. *United States*, 277 U.S. 438 (1928).

dence obtained in violation of those standards.[8] Search incidental to arrest was first expanded in scope,[9] then narrowed,[10] then expanded again.[11] The warrantless search of automobiles even in the absence of specific congressional approval was held constitutional[12] only one year after the Court had implied the opposite.[13] Writing in 1950, Professor Francis A. Allen found that "among the civil liberties cases . . . the battle has nowhere waxed hotter than in those involving the constitutional protections against unreasonable searches and seizures."[14]

More recently, since about 1960, the Court has given some indication of a return to the broad libertarian principles which animated Fourth Amendment interpretation up to 1925. The silver platter doctrine has been overruled.[15] The exclusionary rule has been required for the state courts,[16] and the protection against unreasonable searches afforded by the Fourteenth Amendment is now coextensive with that of the Fourth.[17] Furthermore, the tenor of the Court's most recent opinions on the subject of electronic eavesdropping indicates that it may be reconsidering its position that an invasion of privacy by such means does not violate the Constitution.[18]

Nevertheless, whatever the relative consistency which may be credited to the Court in recent years, search and seizure remains a subject fraught with judicial controversy. In other words, while we may be witnessing the beginning of a certain coherence and order in the Court's work which have long been missing, we are still far from seeing any real agreement among the justices on the principles which should govern constitutional interpretation in this area. Why this is so was perhaps best explained by Professor Allen when he wrote of the considerations competing for judicial favor and the difficulty of making a choice among them:

In the application of few other constitutional guarantees is the Court apparently confronted with so difficult a choice of competing social values, each of the highest and most obvious importance. Few could gainsay the vital role

8. *Wolf* v. *Colorado*, 338 U.S. 25 (1949).
9. *Harris* v. *United States*, 331 U.S. 145 (1947).
10. *Trupiano* v. *United States*, 334 U.S. 699 (1948).
11. *United States* v. *Rabinowitz*, 339 U.S. 56 (1950).
12. *Brinegar* v. *United States*, 338 U.S. 160 (1949).
13. *United States* v. *Di Re*, 332 U.S. 581 (1948).
14. Francis A. Allen, "The Wolf Case: Search and Seizure, Federalism, and the Civil Liberties," *Illinois Law Review*, XLV (March–April, 1950), 1, 3.
15. *Elkins* v. *United States*, 364 U.S. 206 (1960).
16. *Mapp* v. *Ohio*, 367 U.S. 643 (1961).
17. *Ker* v. *California*, 374 U.S. 23 (1963).
18. *Silverman* v. *United States*, 365 U.S. 505 (1961); *Lopez* v. *United States*, 373 U.S. 427 (1963).

of the protections of the Fourth Amendment in a free society, especially as they may guard against invasions of privacy of those suspected of unorthodoxy in matters of political belief and conscience. . . . On the other hand, the interest of the community in effective enforcement of the criminal law is hardly less obvious. . . ."[19]

While the dilemma of choosing between competing individual and community interests also confronts the justices in the interpretation of other personal rights guaranteed by the Constitution, the Fourth Amendment differs markedly from those rights in a couple of important respects. First, as Justice Jackson put it:

> We must remember . . . that freedom from unreasonable search differs from some of the other rights of the Constitution in that there is no way in which the innocent citizen can invoke advance protection. For example, any effective interference with freedom of press, or free speech, or religion, usually requires a course of suppressions against which the citizen can and often does go to the court and obtain an injunction. Other rights, such as that to an impartial jury or the aid of counsel, are within the supervisory power of the courts themselves. . . .
>
> But an illegal search and seizure usually is a single incident, perpetrated by surprise, conducted in haste, kept purposely beyond the court's supervision and limited only by the judgment and moderation of officers whose own interests and records are often at stake in the search. There is no opportunity for injunction or appeal to disinterested intervention. The citizen's choice is quietly to submit to whatever the officers undertake or to resist at risk of arrest or immediate violence.[20]

That is why, in the words of Justice Douglas, "under the Fourth Amendment, the judiciary has a special duty of protecting the right of the people to be let alone. . . ."[21] "[T]he command of the Fourth Amendment implies a continuous supervision by the judiciary over law enforcement officers, quite different from the passive role which courts play in some spheres."[22]

On the other hand, this right, which more than any other requires the judiciary to stay on guard against its violation, is the very one which will be claimed in the courts by those least worthy of it, for the Fourth Amendment is almost always invoked by those guilty of crime. For this reason, the Court, when sustaining convictions in cases raising search and seizure issues, has sometimes been accused by dissenting justices of being influenced more by the obvious guilt of the defendant than by the commands of the Constitution. Speak-

19. Allen, "The Wolf Case," p. 3.
20. *Brinegar* v. *United States,* 338 U.S. 160, 182 (1949) dissenting opinion).
21. *Wilson* v. *Schnettler*, 365 U.S. 381, 394 (1961) (dissenting opinion).
22. *Ibid.*, p. 396.

ing in 1950, Justice Frankfurter admonished his brethren: "Freedom of speech, of the press, of religion, easily summon powerful support against encroachment. The prohibition against unreasonable search and seizure is normally invoked by those accused of crime, and criminals have few friends."[23] Justices Murphy and Douglas spoke in a similar vein. "It is easy," said Murphy, "to make light of insistence on scrupulous regard for the safeguards of civil liberties when invoked on behalf of the unworthy."[24] "A rule protective of law-abiding citizens," added Douglas, "is not likely to flourish where its advocates are usually criminals."[25]

In search cases, then, exclusion of the illegally seized evidence is not intended to serve any immediate individual interest, that is, the interest of the particular individual who claims that his Fourth Amendment rights were violated and whom the evidence clearly incriminates, but rather the long-range interests of individual privacy.[26] One person who is unquestionably a criminal is set free in order that others, law-abiding men, may be safe in their homes. The justices are required to bear in mind that the Fourth Amendment "often may afford a shelter for criminals. But the forefathers thought this was not too great a price to pay for that decent privacy of home, papers and effects which is indispensable to individual dignity and self respect."[27]

What are the tests by which the justices must be guided in determining the constitutional reasonableness of a search? At best, these are quite unsatisfactory. The Constitution does not define a reasonable search, and, indeed, it is arguable that the only solid historical guidance provided the justices in interpreting the Fourth Amendment is the knowledge that it was intended to outlaw the general warrant. Beyond that, the Supreme Court must determine reasonableness as a matter of sound judicial policy consonant with the purposes of the amendment. But since the amendment not only forbids unreasonable searches but also sets forth, in its second clause, stringent warrant requirements, should not the question of reasonableness usually be determined by the presence or absence of a warrant? It is this matter which has divided the justices in a number of cases since the late nineteen forties, particularly those involving questions of search in-

23. *Harris* v. *United States,* 331 U.S. 145, 156 (1947) (dissenting opinion).
24. *Davis* v. *United States,* 328 U.S. 582, 597 (1946) (dissenting opinion).
25. *Draper* v. *United States,* 358 U.S. 307, 314 (1959) (dissenting opinion).
26. This is the view the Court today takes of the exclusionary rule. It is, of course, possible to take a different view, as the Court itself once did. For discussion see pp. 78–79, *supra.*
27. Justice Jackson dissenting in *Harris* v. *United States,* 331 U.S. 145, 198 (1947).

cidental to arrest.[28] In the one view, reasonableness may be determined without reference to the prior procurement of a warrant. In the other view, the warrant requirements must be strictly adhered to and are almost always determinative of the reasonableness of a search, except for narrowly circumscribed emergency situations. To determine reasonableness quite independently of the existence of a warrant is to grant a discretion to officers which the amendment did not intend, and to remove the judiciary as a restraining force in the search process.

According to the first view, reasonableness "depends upon the facts and circumstances—the total atmosphere of the case."[29] This is the sort of test (though, realistically speaking, it is no test at all) which would leave the justices almost entirely at large in defining the Fourth Amendment and would permit them to construe the amendment without reference to the historical events which gave it birth. Because of such reasoning, the scope of search incidental to arrest was expanded to a point where it was no longer justifiable in terms of its old rationale, the protection of the arresting officer and the securing of the person arrested, and the rationale was replaced by judicial policy-making subject to the differing views of different judges, the changing viewpoints of the same judges, and the felt necessities of the day.

But even if, according to the other view, which predominated until 1947 in Fourth Amendment interpretation, searches not conducted under the intervening hand of the magistrate are condemned by history, what conclusive guidance does history have to offer on the constitutionality of wire tapping or of administrative inspections without warrant, or even on the need for the exclusionary rule itself? On such questions the justices will be required to muster wisdom and insight to interpret the Fourth Amendment in the light of its purposes as they conceive them, all the while weighing the relative importance of the various considerations competing for their favor, whether these be law enforcement and individual privacy, as in wire tapping, or the public health and individual privacy, as in administrative inspection. Answers to such questions do not come mechanically in an emotionally charged subject matter. Here it is not the history of the Fourth Amendment alone that will count, but the whole tangled web of human history and experience, as they are understood by the justices. No simple formulas can be devised and

28. E.g., *Harris* v. *United States*, 331 U.S. 145 (1947); *United States* v. *Rabinowitz*, 339 U.S. 56 (1950).
29. *United States* v. *Rabinowitz*, 339 U.S. 56, 66 (1950).

applied to the resolution of these issues. The inadequacy of formulas is suggested by the canon of Fourth Amendment interpretation set forth by Chief Justice Taft in 1925. The amendment, he said, "is to be construed in the light of what was deemed an unreasonable search and seizure when it was adopted, and in a manner which will conserve public interests as well as the interests and rights of individual citizens."[30] The difficulty with this formula is that in some situations today the conservation of public and private interests might not be achieved by construing the amendment "in the light of what was deemed an unreasonable search" in the eighteenth century.

Fourth Amendment adjudication is further complicated by the variety of the issues subsumed under the heading of search and seizure. It is possible for a justice to construe liberally the protection of the Fourth Amendment where federal searches are concerned, and yet feel constrained, out of considerations of federalism, to oppose extension of the exclusionary rule to the states. He may be convinced of the unconstitutionality of wire tapping and yet regard administrative inspections and involuntary blood tests as meeting constitutional standards.[31] Illustrative of the point are the three search cases, each raising a different question, decided on June 27, 1949. On that day, *Wolf* v. *Colorado*[32] forbade the states to engage in unreasonable searches but did not require them to exclude evidence so obtained; *Lustig* v. *United States*[33] found that a state search had involved federal participation in violation of the silver platter doctrine; and *Brinegar* v. *United States*[34] sanctioned the warrantless search of an automobile in the presence of probable cause. Yet no one member of the Court joined the majority opinion in all three cases, and no one member dissented in all three cases. Justice Black, alone among the justices, agreed with all three decisions, but in the Lustig case he concurred on separate grounds.

Nor does individual judicial performance in Fourth Amendment cases (and in Fourteenth Amendment cases relating to the Fourth) necessarily correspond with performance in other civil liberties cases. By way of illustration, a notable feature of the Roosevelt Court was the liberal activist bloc of "the four," Justices Black, Douglas,

30. *Carroll* v. *United States*, 267 U.S. 132, 149 (1925).

31. The preceding sentences sum up Justice Frankfurter's position. Justice Black, on the other hand, believes that blood tests and administrative inspections are constitutionally prohibited but that electronic eavesdropping is not. Justice Clark voted to extend the exclusionary rule to the states, yet on the whole he has construed the protection of the Fourth Amendment much more narrowly than did Justice Frankfurter.

32. 338 U.S. 25 (1949).

33. 338 U.S. 74 (1949).

34. 338 U.S. 160 (1949).

Murphy, and Rutledge, who usually took a far more sympathetic view of the rights of the individual, and accordingly tended to minimize the community's interest in preventing the unlimited exercise of those rights, than did their fellow justices. In procedural matters, too, the probable guilt or innocence of a defendant was of little consequence to "the four" in their evaluation of the constitutional sufficiency of the procedure employed at the trial. With the death of Justices Murphy and Rutledge in 1949 and their replacement by justices antagonistic to the liberal activist tenets, "the four" became "the two," and the phrase "Black and Douglas dissenting" for a few years acquired almost the same currency as had, at one time, the phrase "Holmes and Brandeis dissenting," which is now a part of constitutional lore. Yet similar as these justices were in their approach to many civil liberties issues, they were markedly divergent in their approach to search and seizure questions. Justice Murphy construed the protective function of the Fourth Amendment in a broader fashion than did Justice Rutledge,[35] and the same statement might be made even more emphatically of Justice Douglas in contrast with Justice Black.[36]

Ultimately, as with other vaguely phrased constitutional guarantees, the construction that the justices place on the Fourth Amendment in any given situation will depend on the importance they attach to the value it safeguards. "It is . . . true of journeys of the law," Justice Frankfurter has said, "that the place you reach depends on the direction you are taking. And so, where one comes out of a case depends on where one goes in":

> It makes all the difference in the world whether one recognizes the central fact about the Fourth Amendment, namely, that it was a safeguard against recurrence of abuses so deeply felt by the Colonies as to be one of the potent causes of the Revolution, or one thinks of it as merely a requirement for a piece of paper.[37] A decision may turn on whether one gives that Amendment a place second to none in the Bill of Rights, or considers it on the whole a nuisance, a serious impediment in the war against crime.[38]

If the amendment is indeed accorded a place "second to none" in the Bill of Rights, some of the Court's decisions are legitimately subject to serious criticism. Nevertheless, in seeking to curb illegal searches and seizures through the instrumentality of the exclusionary

35. See, e.g., their contrasting views in *Oklahoma Press Pub. Co.* v. *Walling*, 327 U.S. 186 (1946), and in *Brinegar* v. *United States*, 338 U.S. 160 (1949).
36. See, e.g., their contrasting views in *Trupiano* v. *United States*, 334 U.S. 699 (1948), and in *Wolf* v. *Colorado*, 338 U.S. 25 (1949).
37. *United States* v. *Rabinowitz,* 339 U.S. 56, 69 (1950) (dissenting opinion).
38. *Harris* v. *United States*, 331 U.S. 145, 157 (1947) (dissenting opinion).

rule—its most creative act in this area of constitutional law—the Court has come to grips with a moral problem of the first order confronting society. The ordinary criminal represents no one but himself; his sins are personal. The law officer, however, embodies in his person the community's dedication to law and order. When he sins, the law loses its moral grandeur. A major moral test of law is that it afford equal protection to all and special privileges to none. When the community itself, through the agency of its law officers, disregards the law, the moral superstructure is undermined. "The contrast between morality professed by society and immorality practiced on its behalf," in the words of Justice Frankfurter, "makes for contempt of law."[39]

Now that the troublesome and divisive issue of state searches has been settled, by bringing the due process guarantee against unreasonable searches into alignment with the Fourth Amendment, the Court will need to devote much energy to the task of fashioning constitutional rules for the states to follow. It also seems safe to say that another of the Court's main tasks in the future will be to define the Fourth Amendment, in terms that will give it meaning, to protect against those threats to privacy which arise not from searches in the traditional sense but from "figurative" searches, such as wire tapping and electronic eavesdropping, and from whatever new contrivances science may yet devise. This is the problem to which Justice Brandeis addressed himself so forthrightly and with almost prophetic vision in the Olmstead case[40] almost forty years ago. The needs of the day have swept away much that was sacred in the American heritage; the barriers of privacy have crumbled on many fronts. It will be the task of the Supreme Court to attempt to preserve those which are left.

39. *On Lee* v. *United States,* 343 U.S. 747, 758–59 (1952) (dissenting opinion).
40. *Olmstead* v. *United States,* 277 U.S. 438, 471 (1928) (dissenting opinion).

# SELECTED BIBLIOGRAPHY

A complete bibliography of scholarly literature relating to search and seizure would require a separate volume. This bibliography, therefore, makes no pretense to completeness; it does not list all the items which were consulted, nor even all those cited in the footnotes. It is limited to those official documents, books, and articles which the author found most useful in the preparation of this volume.

The principal source materials for this study are, of course, to be found in those volumes of the United States Reports, beginning with 3 Cranch (1805–6), which contain the decisions of the United States Supreme Court on the subject of search and seizure.

## OFFICIAL DOCUMENTS


DISTRICT OF COLUMBIA. *Report and Recommendations of the Commissioners' Committee on Police Arrests for Investigation.* District of Columbia, 1962.

FEDERAL BUREAU OF INVESTIGATION. *Crime in the United States: Uniform Crime Reports—1964.* Washington, D.C., 1965.

NATIONAL COMMISSION OF LAW OBSERVANCE AND ENFORCEMENT. *Report on Lawlessness in Law Enforcement.* Washington, D. C., 1931.

U. S. COMMISSION ON CIVIL RIGHTS. *Hearings before the United States Commission on Civil Rights, Hearings Held in Detroit, Michigan*, December 14 and 15, 1960.

U. S. HOUSE OF REPRESENTATIVES. *Hearings before Subcommittee No. 3, Committee on the Judiciary, on H.R. 408, H.R. 477, H.R. 3552, and H.R. 5149.* 83d Cong., 1st Sess., 1953.

———. *Hearings before Subcommittee No. 5, Committee on the Judiciary, on H.R. 762, H.R. 867, H.R. 4513, H.R. 4728, and H.R. 5096* (Ser. 2), 84th Cong., 1st Sess., 1955.

U. S. SENATE. *Hearings before a Subcommittee of the Committee on the Judiciary, on S. 838, S. 2753, S. 3229, and H.R. 8649.* 83d Cong., 2d Sess., 1954.

———. *Hearings before Subcommittee on Constitutional Rights, Committee on the Judiciary, Wiretapping, Eavesdropping and the Bill of Rights*, Parts 1 and 2. 85th Cong., 2d Sess., 1958; Parts 3, 4, and 5, 86th Cong., 1st Sess., 1959.

———. *Hearings before Subcommittee on Constitutional Rights, Committee on the Judiciary, on S. 1086, S. 1221, S. 1495, and S. 1822.* 87th Cong., 1st Sess., 1961.

———. *Hearings before the Committee on the Judiciary, on S. 2813 and S. 1495.* 87th Cong., 2d Sess., 1962.


## BOOKS


ADAMS, CHARLES FRANCIS. *The Life and Works of John Adams.* Boston, 1856. Vols. II, X.

ALLEN, FRANCIS A. *The Borderland of Criminal Justice: Essays in Law and Criminology.* Chicago, 1964.

AMERICAN CIVIL LIBERTIES UNION, Illinois Division. *Secret Detention by the Chicago Police.* Glencoe, Ill., 1959.

*Annals of Congress*, 1st Cong., 1st Sess. Compiled by Joseph Gales. Washington, D.C., 1834.

BARTH, ALAN. *The Price of Liberty.* New York, 1961.

BEISEL, ALBERT R., JR. *Control over Illegal Enforcement of the Criminal Law: Role of the Supreme Court.* Boston, 1955.

BERGH, ALBERT ELLERY (ed.). *The Writings of Thomas Jefferson.* Library ed. Washington, D.C., 1903. Vol. VII.

BLACKSTONE, SIR WILLIAM. *Commentaries on the Laws of England.* Edited by William Draper Lewis. Philadelphia, 1900. Vol. IV.

BOWEN, CATHERINE DRINKER. *John Adams and the American Revolution.* Boston, 1950.

———. *The Lion and the Throne: The Life and Times of Sir Edward Coke, 1552–1634.* Boston, 1957.

BUTTERFIELD, L. H. (ed.). *Diary and Autobiography of John Adams.* Cambridge, Mass., 1961. Vol. III.

———. *Adams Family Correspondence.* Cambridge, Mass., 1963. Vol. II.

COKE, SIR EDWARD. *Institutes of the Laws of England.* London, 1804. Part 4.

COOLEY, THOMAS M. *A Treatise on the Constitutional Limitations.* 7th ed. Boston, 1927. Vol. I.

DAHL, RAYMOND A., and BOYLE, HOWARD H., JR. *Procedure and the Law of Arrest, Search and Seizure.* Milwaukee, Wis., 1961.

DASH, SAMUEL, KNOWLTON, ROBERT E., and SCHWARTZ, RICHARD F. *The Eavesdroppers.* New Brunswick, N. J., 1959.

DEVLIN, PATRICK. *The Criminal Prosecution in England.* New Haven, Conn., 1958.

DOUGLAS, WILLIAM O. *The Right of the People.* New York, 1958.

ELLIOT, JONATHAN (ed.). *The Debates in the Several State Conventions on the Adoption of the Federal Constitution.* 5 vols. Philadelphia, 1861.

FARRAND, MAX (ed.). *The Records of the Federal Convention of 1787.* 4 vols. Revised ed. New Haven, Conn., 1937.

FELLMAN, DAVID. *The Defendant's Rights.* New York, 1958.

HALE, SIR MATTHEW. *The History of the Pleas of the Crown.* 1st Amer. ed. Philadelphia, 1847. Vols. I, II.

HURST, JAMES WILLARD. *Law and Social Progress in United States History.* Ann Arbor, Mich., 1960.

JACKSON, ROBERT H. *The Supreme Court in the American System of Government.* Cambridge, Mass., 1955.

KAUPER, PAUL G. *Frontiers of Constitutional Liberty.* Ann Arbor, Mich., 1956.

LAFAVE, WAYNE R. *Arrest: The Decision To Take a Suspect into Custody.* Boston, 1965.

LASSON, NELSON B. *The History and Development of the Fourth Amendment to the United States Constitution.* Baltimore, 1937.

MCKECHNIE, WILLIAM SHARP. *Magna Carta: A Commentary on the Great Charter of King John.* 2d revised ed. New York, 1958.

SIEBERT, FREDERICK SEATON. *Freedom of the Press in England: 1476–1776.* Urbana, Ill., 1952.

SMITH, PAGE. *John Adams.* New York, 1962. Vol. I.

THORPE, FRANCIS NEWTON (ed.). *The Federal and State Constitutions.* Washington, D.C., 1909. Vols. III, IV, V, VI, VII.

TREBACH, ARNOLD S. *The Rationing of Justice: Constitutional Rights and the Criminal Process.* New Brunswick, N.J., 1964.

VARON, JOSEPH A. *Searches, Seizures and Immunities.* 2 vols. Indianapolis, Ind., 1961.

WIGMORE, JOHN HENRY. *A Treatise on the Anglo-American System of Evidence in Trials at Common Law.* 3d ed. Boston, 1940. Vol. VIII.

WILSON, WOODROW. *Constitutional Government in the United States.* New York, 1921.

## ARTICLES AND PERIODICALS

ALLEN, FRANCIS A. "The Wolf Case: Search and Seizure, Federalism, and the Civil Liberties," *Illinois Law Review*, XLV (March–April, 1950), 1.

———. "The Exclusionary Rule in the American Law of Search and Seizure," *Journal of Criminal Law*, LII (September–October, 1961), 246.

———. "Federalism and the Fourth Amendment: A Requiem for Wolf," *The Supreme Court Review* (1961), p. 1.

AMSTERDAM, ANTHONY G. "Search, Seizure, and Section 2255: A Comment," *University of Pennsylvania Law Review*, CXII (January, 1964), 378.

ATKINSON, THOMAS E. "Admissibility of Evidence Obtained through Unreasonable Searches and Seizures," *Columbia Law Review*, XXV (January, 1925), 11.

———. "Prohibition and the Doctrine of the Weeks Case," *Michigan Law Review*, XXIII (May, 1925), 748.

BARRETT, EDWARD L., JR. "Exclusion of Evidence Obtained by Illegal Searches: A Comment on People v. Cahan," *California Law Review*, XLIII (October, 1955), 565.

———. "Personal Rights, Property Rights and the Fourth Amendment," *The Supreme Court Review* (1960), p. 46.

BEANEY, WILLIAM M. "The Constitutional Right to Privacy in the Supreme Court," *The Supreme Court Review* (1962), p. 212.

BENDER, PAUL. "The Retroactive Effect of an Overruling Constitutional Decision: Mapp v. Ohio," *University of Pennsylvania Law Review*, CX (March, 1962), 650.

BENNETT, JAMES V. "A Cool Look at 'the Crime Crisis,'" *Harper's* (April, 1964), p. 123.

BLACK, FORREST R. "A Critique of the Carroll Case," *Columbia Law Review*, XXIX (November, 1929), 1068.

———. "Burdeau v. McDowall—A Judicial Milepost on the Road to Absolutism," *Boston University Law Review*, XII (January, 1932), 32.

BLAKEY, G. ROBERT. "The Rule of Announcement and Unlawful Entry: Miller v. United States and Ker v. California," *University of Pennsylvania Law Review*, CXII (February, 1964), 499.

BRADLEY, EDWIN J., and HOGAN, JAMES E. "Wiretapping from Nardone to Benanti and Rathbun," *Georgetown Law Journal*, XLVI (Spring, 1958), 418.

BREITEL, CHARLES D. "Controls in Criminal Law Enforcement," *University of Chicago Law Review*, XXVII (Spring, 1960), 427.

BROEDER, DALE W. "The Decline and Fall of *Wolf v. Colorado*," *Nebraska Law Review*, XLI (December, 1961), 185.

———. "Wong Sun v. United States: A Study in Faith and Hope," *Nebraska Law Review*, XLII (April, 1963), 483.

BROWN, PETER MEGAREE, and PEER, RICHARD S. "The Wire-tapping Entanglement: How To Strengthen Law Enforcement and Preserve Privacy," *Cornell Law Quarterly*, XLIV (Winter, 1959), 175.

BROWNELL, HERBERT J. "The Public Security and Wiretapping," *Cornell Law Quarterly*, XXXIX (Winter, 1954), 195.

BRUCE, ANDREW ALEXANDER. "Arbitrary Searches and Seizures as Applied to Modern Industry," *The Green Bag*, XVIII (May, 1906), 273.

CHAFEE, ZECHARIAH, JR. "The Progress of the Law, 1919–1922," *Harvard Law Review*, XXXV (April, 1922), 673.

COLLINGS, REX A., JR. "Toward Workable Rules of Search and Seizure—An Amicus Curiae Brief," *California Law Review*, L (August, 1962), 421.

CORWIN, EDWARD S. "The Supreme Court's Construction of the Self Incrimination Clause," *Michigan Law Review*, XXIX (November, 1930), 1; (December, 1930), 191.

DALBEY, DWIGHT J. "Taking Inventory," *FBI Law Enforcement Bulletin*, XXXIV, No. 7 (July, 1965), 12.

DASH, SAMUEL. "Cracks in the Foundation of Criminal Justice," *University of Illinois Law Review*, XLVI (July–August, 1951), 385.

DEREUIL, LOUIS J. "Applicability of the Fourth Amendment in Civil Cases," *Duke Law Journal*, Vol. 1963 (Summer, 1963), p. 472.

DICKERSON, D. M. "Writs of Assistance as a Cause of the American Revolution," in Richard B. Morris (ed.), *The Era of the American Revolution: Studies Inscribed to Evarts Boutell Greene* (New York, 1939), p. 40.

DONNELLY, RICHARD C. "Comments and Caveats on the Wire Tapping Controversy," *Yale Law Journal*, LXIII (April, 1954), 799.

———. "Proposals for Meeting the Challenge of Interstate Organized Crime: Electronic Eavesdropping," *Notre Dame Lawyer*, XXXVIII, No. 6 (1963), 667.

DOUGLAS, WILLIAM O. "Vagrancy and Arrest on Suspicion," *Yale Law Journal*, LXX (November, 1960), 1.

EDWARDS, RICHARD A. "Criminal Liability for Unreasonable Searches and Seizures," *Virginia Law Review*, XLI (June, 1955), 621.

EINHORN, EDWARD MARTIN. "The Exclusionary Rule in Operation—A Comparison of Illinois, California and Federal Law," *Journal of Criminal Law*, L (July–August, 1959), 144.

EVANS, GREGORY U. "Search and Seizure Incidental to a Lawful Arrest," *William and Mary Law Review*, IV, No. 2 (1963), 121.

FAIRFIELD, WILLIAM S., and CLIFT, CHARLES. "The Wiretappers," in Max Ascoli (ed.), *Our Times: The Best From The Reporter* (New York, 1960), p. 50.

FAIRMAN, CHARLES "Does the Fourteenth Amendment Incorporate the Bill of Rights? The Original Understanding," *Stanford Law Review*, II (December, 1949), 5.

FOOTE, CALEB. "Tort Remedies for Police Violations of Individual Rights," *Minnesota Lew Review*, XXXIX (April, 1955), 493.

———. "Law and Police Practice: Safeguards in the Law of Arrest," *Northwestern University Law Review*, LII (March–April, 1957), 16.

GALLER, GERALD H. "The Exclusion of Illegal State Evidence in Federal Courts," *Journal of Criminal Law*, XLIX (January–February, 1955), 455.

GEORGE, B. J., JR. "'The Potent, the Omnipresent Teacher': The Supreme Court and Wiretapping," *Virginia Law Review*, XLVII (June, 1961), 751.

GOLDSTEIN, HERMAN. "Police Discretion: The Ideal versus the Real," *Public Administration Review*, XXIII (September, 1963), 140.

GOLDSTEIN, JOSEPH. "Police Discretion Not To Invoke the Criminal Process: Low Visibility Decisions in the Administration of Justice," *Yale Law Journal*, LXIX (March, 1960), 543.

GORSKI, JEROME C. "The Exclusionary Rule and the Question of Standing," *Georgetown Law Journal*, L (Spring, 1962), 585.

GRANT, J. A. C. "The Tarnished Silver Platter: Federalism and Admissibility of Illegally Seized Evidence," *UCLA Law Review*, VIII (January, 1961), 1.

GRAY, HORACE, JR. Appendix, in Quincy's *Massachusetts Reports, 1761–1772.*

HAISLIP, GENE. "Judicial Reaction to Evidence Obtained by Harsh and Unusual Means," *William and Mary Law Review*, IV, No. 1 (1963), 1.

HALL, JEROME. "The Law of Arrest in Relation to Contemporary Social Problems," *University of Chicago Law Review*, III (April, 1936), 345.

HANDLER, EMMERICH. "The Fourth Amendment, Federalism, and Mr. Justice Frankfurter," *Syracuse Law Review*, VIII (Spring, 1957), 166.

HENNINGS, THOMAS C., JR. "The Wiretapping-Eavesdropping Problem: A Legislator's View," *Minnesota Law Review*, XLIV (April, 1960), 813.

HOOVER, J. EDGAR. "A Comment on the Article 'Loyalty among Government Employees,'" *Yale Law Journal*, LVIII (February, 1949), 401.

———. "Rejoinder by Mr. Hoover," *Yale Law Journal*, LVIII (February, 1949), 422.

———. "Cooperation: The Key to Effective Law Enforcement in America," *Syracuse Law Review*, XII (Fall, 1960), 1.

INBAU, FRED E. " 'Fair Play' in Criminal Investigations and Prosecutions," *Northwestern University Tri-Quarterly*, III, No. 2 (1961), 3.

JOHNSON, EARL, JR. "Organized Crime: Challenge to the American Legal System," *Journal of Criminal Law*, LIII (December, 1962), 399; LIV (March, 1963), 1; LIV (June, 1963), 127.

KAMISAR, YALE. "*Wolf* and *Lustig* Ten Years Later: Illegal State Evidence in State and Federal Courts," *Minnesota Law Review*, XLIII (May, 1959), 1083.

———. "The Wiretapping-Eavesdropping Problem: A Professor's View," *Minnesota Law Review*, XLIV (April, 1960), 891.

———. "On the Tactics of Police-Prosecution Oriented Critics of the Courts," *Cornell Law Quarterly*, XLIX (Spring, 1964), 436.

KAPLAN, JOHN. "Search and Seizure: A No-Man's Land in the Criminal Law," *California Law Review*, XLIX (August, 1961), 474.

KNOWLTON, ROBERT E. "The Supreme Court, Mapp v. Ohio and Due Process of Law," *Iowa Law Review*, XLIX (Fall, 1963), 14.

KNOX, JOHN C. "Self Incrimination," *University of Pennsylvania Law Review*, LXXIV (December, 1925), 139.

KOHN, ALAN C. "Admissibility in Federal Court of Evidence Illegally Seized by State Officers," *Washington University Law Quarterly*, Vol. 1959 (June, 1959), p. 229.

LEAGRE, RICHARD M. "The Fourth Amendment and the Law of Arrest," *Journal of Criminal Law*, LIV (December, 1963), 393.

MAGUIRE, ROBERT F. "How to Unpoison the Fruit—the Fourth Amendment and the Exclusionary Rule," *Journal of Criminal Law*, LV (September, 1964), 307.

MANWARING, DAVID R. "California and the Fourth Amendment," *Stanford Law Review*, XVI (March, 1964), 318.

———. "The Impact of *Mapp v. Ohio*." Unpublished paper delivered at the 1964 Annual Meeting of the American Political Science Association, Chicago, Illinois. September 9–12, 1964.

MCGARR, FRANK J. "The Exclusionary Rule: An Ill Conceived and Ineffective Remedy," *Journal of Criminal Law*, LII (September–October, 1961), 266.

MILLER, FRANK W., and TIFFANY, LAWRENCE P. "Prosecutor Dominance of the Warrant Decision: A Study of Current Practices," *Washington University Law Quarterly*, Vol. 1964 (February, 1964), p. 1.

MORRIS, ARVAL. "The End of an Experiment in Federalism—A Note on Mapp v. Ohio," *Washington Law Review*, XXXVI (Winter, 1961), 407.

NAGEL, STUART S. "Testing the Effects of Excluding Illegally Seized Evidence," *Wisconsin Law Review*, Vol. 1965 (Spring, 1965), p. 283.

NELSON, KNUTE. "Search and Seizure: Boyd v. United States," *American Bar Association Journal*, IX (December, 1923), 773.

PACKER, HERBERT L. "Policing the Police: Nine Men Are Not Enough," *The New Republic*, CLIII, No. 10 (September 4, 1965), 17.

PARSONS, JUDSON A. "State-Federal Crossfire in Search and Seizure and Self-Incrimination," *Cornell Law Quarterly*, XLII (Spring, 1957), 346.

PAULSEN, MONRAD G. "Law and Police Practice: Safeguards in the Law of Search and Seizure," *Northwestern Law Review*, LII (March–April, 1957), 65.

———. "The Exclusionary Rule and Misconduct by the Police," *Journal of Criminal Law*, LII (September–October, 1961), 255.

REICH, CHARLES A. "Midnight Welfare Searches and the Social Security Act," *Yale Law Journal*, LXXII (June, 1963), 1347.

REMINGTON, FRANK J. "The Law Relating to . . . Detention, Questioning and Frisking of Suspected Persons . . . ," in Claude R. Sowle (ed.), *Police Power and Individual Freedom: The Quest for Balance* (Chicago, 1962), p. 11.

REYNARD, CHARLES A. "Freedom from Unreasonable Searches—A Second Class Constitutional Right?", *Indiana Law Journal*, XXV (Spring, 1950), 259.

RICHARDSON, JAMES R. "Rochin and Breithaupt in Context," *Vanderbilt Law Review*, XIV (June, 1961), 879.

ROGERS, WILLIAM P. "The Case for Wire Tapping," *Yale Law Journal*, LXIII (April, 1954), 792.

ROTHBLATT, HENRY B. "The Arrest: Probable Cause and Search without a Search Warrant," *Mississippi Law Journal*, XXXV (March, 1964), 1

ROZENZWEIG, MARGARET LYBOLT. "The Law of Wire Tapping," *Cornell Law Quarterly*, XXXIII (September, 1947), 73.

SCURLOCK, JOHN. "The Law of Arrest in Missouri," *University of Kansas City Law Review*, XXIX (Summer, 1961), 117.

———. "Searches and Seizures in Missouri," *University of Kansas City Law Review*, XXIX (Summer, 1961), 242.

SILVER, EDWARD S. "The Wiretapping-Eavesdropping Problem: A Prosecutor's View," *Minnesota Law Review*, XLIV (April, 1960), 835.

SOBEL, NATHAN R. "A Comment on the Law of Search and Seizure," *The Pleader* (1962), issued by Kings County, New York, Criminal Bar Association.

Symposium, "A Forum on the Interrogation of the Accused," *Cornell Law Quarterly*, XLIX (Spring, 1964), 382.

TRAYNOR, ROGER J. "Mapp v. Ohio at Large in the Fifty States," *Duke Law Journal*, Vol. 1962 (Summer, 1962), p. 319.

WAY, A. FRANK, JR. "Increasing Scope of Search Incidental to Arrest," *Washington University Law Quarterly*, Vol. 1959 (June, 1959), p. 261.

WEINSTEIN, JACK B. "Local Responsibility for Improvement of Search and Seizure Practices," *Rocky Mountain Law Review*, XXXIV (Winter, 1962), 150.

WESTIN, ALAN F. "The Wire-Tapping Problem: An Analysis and a Legislative Proposal," *Columbia Law Review*, LII (February, 1952), 165.

———. "Wiretapping: The Quiet Revolution," *Commentary*, XXIX (April, 1960), 333.

WHITTAKER, LLOYD T. "Is This Trip (to the Supreme Court) Necessary?" *Journal of Public Law*, IX (Spring, 1960), 260.

WIGMORE, JOHN H. Comment, *Illinois Law Review*, XXIII (December, 1928), 377.

WILLIAMS, EDWARD BENNETT. "The Wiretapping-Eavesdropping Problem: A Defense Counsel's View," *Minnesota Law Review*, XLIV (April, 1960), 855.

WILLIAMS, GLANVILLE L. "The Exclusionary Rule under Foreign Law: England," *Journal of Criminal Law*, LII (September–October, 1961), 272.

WILSON, O. W. "Police Arrest Privileges in a Free Society: A Plea for Modernization," *Journal of Criminal Law*, LI (December, 1960), 395.

———. "Police Authority in a Free Society," *Journal of Criminal Law*, LIV (June, 1963), 175.

———. "How the Police Chief Sees It," *Harper's* (April, 1964), p. 140.

WILSON, PAUL E. "Perspectives of Mapp v. Ohio," *Kansas Law Review*, XI (May, 1963), 423.

WOLF, PETER H. "A Survey of the Expanded Exclusionary Rule," *George Washington Law Review*, XXXII (December, 1963), 193.

## LAW REVIEW NOTES AND COMMENTS

"Judicial Control of Illegal Search and Seizure," *Yale Law Journal*, LVIII (December, 1948), 144.

"Limitations on Seizure of 'Evidentiary' Objects: A Rule in Search of a Reason," *University of Chicago Law Review*, XX (Winter, 1953), 319.

"Philadelphia Police Practice and the Law of Arrest," *University of Pennsylvania Law Review*, C (June, 1962), 1182.

"Search and Seizure in Illinois: Enforcement of the Constitutional Right of Privacy," *Northwestern Law Review*, XLVII (September–October, 1952), 493.

"Search and Seizure in the Supreme Court: Shadows on the Fourth Amendment," *University of Chicago Law Review*, XXVIII (Summer, 1961), 664.

"Search, Seizure and the Fourth and Fifth Amendments," *Yale Law Journal*, XXXI (March, 1922), 518.

"The Administration of Complaints by Civilians against the Police," *Harvard Law Review*, LXXVII (January, 1964), 499.

"Two Years with the Cahan Rule," *Stanford Law Review*, IX (May, 1957), 515.

"Wire Tapping," *Law Notes*, XXXII (January, 1929), 183.

"Wiretapping and the Congress," *Michigan Law Review*, LII (January, 1954), 430.

# INDEX

## Subject Index


A

Adams, John, 33, 34, 37
Administrative inspection: of dwellings, 15, 245 ff; of business records, 81–82
Admissibility of illegally seized evidence: in common law, 60, 62, 184; in foreign jurisdictions, 127, 132–33. *See also* Exclusionary rule
Allen, Francis A., 140, 163, 264
Announcement of authority by officers, 166–67
Arrest: in common law, 27; included in Fourth Amendment, 44–45; warrant requirements for, 45, 169; warrants seldom used in, 45; search incidental to, 87, 98–117, 168; "stopping" as, 97–98, 170; prompt arraignment following, 169–70; for "investigation," 178–79; for vagrancy, 179–80; administrative, 256
Atkinson, Thomas E., 85
Automobiles, search of, 87–98, 168

B

Barrett, Edward L., Jr., 187
Beisel, Albert R., Jr., 117, 180
Benson, Egbert, 41–42
Bill of Rights; in Constitutional Convention, 39; agitation for, 39–41; adopted, 41–42; and the states, 44, 118, 121–22
Black, Forrest Revere, 70, 90
Black, Hugo L.: on relationship of Fourth Amendment's clauses, 43; on meaning of due process, 121–22
—in *District of Columbia* v. *Little* (1950), 248; in *Linkletter* v. *Walker*, 172; in *Mapp* v. *Ohio*, 162; in *On Lee* v. *United States*, 236; in *Rochin* v. *California*, 135; in *United States* v. *Rabinowitz*, 110; in *Wolf* v. *Colorado*, 129
Blackstone, Sir William, 198
Blood tests, involuntary, 141–43
Bradley, Edwin J., 206
Bradley, Joseph P.: in *Boyd* v. *United States*, 52 ff
Brandeis, Louis D.: on meaning of Fourth Amendment, 47–48; on importance of Boyd case, 61
—in *Burdeau* v. *McDowell*, 69, 70; in *Gambino* v. *United States*, 71–72; in *United States* v. *Lee*, 201n
Breitel, Charles D., 224–25
Brennan, William J., Jr.: on importance of Boyd case, 61; on wire tapping warrant, 233n
—in *Abel* v. *United States*, 258; in *Ker* v. *California*, 166–67; in *Lopez* v. *United States*, 240–43; in *Ohio* ex rel. *Eaton* v. *Price* (1959), 254; in *Ohio* ex rel. *Eaton* v. *Price* (1960), 255; in *Pugach* v. *Dollinger*, 217–18
Brown, G. Edmund, 189
Brownell, Herbert J., 225
Burton, Harold H.: in *Brinegar* v. *United States*, 98n; in *District of Columbia* v. *Little* (1950), 248; in *Kremen* v. *United States*, 111n; in *McDonald* v. *United States*, 107; in *On Lee* v. *United States*, 237
Business records, inspection of. *See* Administrative inspection
Butler, Pierce: in *Olmstead* v. *United States*, 205

C

Camden, Lord. *See* Pratt, Chief Justice
Cardozo, Benjamin N.: opposed to exclusionary rule, 84; on meaning of due process, 121
Celler, Emanuel, 232
Chafee, Zechariah, Jr., 88
Clark, Tom C.: in *Chapman* v. *United States*, 113; in *Irvine* v. *California*, 139; in *Ker* v. *California*, 113, 165–66, 171; in *Kremen* v. *United States*, 111n; in *Linkletter* v. *Walker*, 172; in *Mapp* v. *Ohio*, 158 ff
Clarke, John H.: in *Gouled* v. *United States*, 67–68

Coke, Sir Edward, 23, 26, 54, 119
Commission on Government Security, 221
Common law: rules of arrest and search, 26–27; admissibility of illegally seized evidence under, 60, 62, 184; forbids eavesdropping, 198
"Consent" to search, 168–69
Crime: rate, 174–75; firearms as cause of, 183; public indulgence of, 184. *See also* Illegal arrest and search; Police
Curtis, Benjamin R.: on meaning of due process, 119

D

Dash, Samuel, 222, 231
Day, William R.: in *Adams* v. *New York*, 62–63; in *Burdeau* v. *McDowell*, 69; in *Stroud* v. *United States*, 201n; in *Weeks* v. *United States*, 63–65
Devlin, Lord Justice, 133
Dewey, Thomas E., 155
Dollinger, Isidore, 112
Douglas, William O.: on wire tapping warrant, 233n; Fourth Amendment needs judicial vigilance, 265, 266
—in *Abel* v. *United States*, 257–58; in *Davis* v. *United States*, 81; in *Frank* v. *Maryland*, 251–53; in *Jones* v. *United States* (1960), 47n; in *McDonald* v. *United States*, 107; in *Mapp* v. *Ohio*, 159, 162; in *On Lee* v. *United States*, 237; in *Pugach* v. *Dollinger*, 218; in *Rea* v. *United States*, 146–47; in *Rochin* v. *California*, 135; in *Schwartz* v. *Texas*, 213; in *Silverman* v. *United States*, 238; in *Stefanelli* v. *Minard*, 146; in *Wilson* v. *Schnettler*, 158; in *Wolf* v. *Colorado*, 129n; in *Zap* v. *United States*, 81
Due process clause. *See* Fourteenth Amendment, due process clause of

E

Eagleton, Thomas F., 228
Eavesdropping. *See* Common law; Electronic eavesdropping; Wire tapping
Edwards, George, 184n, 196n
Electronic eavesdropping: unresolved constitutional problems, 232–33; prevalence of, 233–34; decisions on, 235–43; Justice Department position on, 244. *See also* Federal Communications Act, Section 605; Wire tapping
Exclusionary rule: for federal searches, 60, 62–86; basis of, 77–80, 128–29; for non-constitutional violations, 79–80; attacked, 84, 190; defended, 85, 191; significance of, 86, 269–70; adopted by some states, 125, 151; alternatives to, 128–30, 186–88; applied to states, 158–72; effect on law enforcement, 188–90, 195–97; selective, 191n; in Scotland, 192n; in wire tapping cases, 206 ff. *See also* Illegal arrest and search

F

Federal Bureau of Investigation, 188–89, 221, 255–57
Federal Communications Act, Section 605: enactment, 206; decisions on, 206–20; attempts to liberalize, 224–25; opposition to liberalization of, 225–26; position of Justice Department on, 227–30; effect on Olmstead doctrine, 243. *See also* Electronic eavesdropping; Federal Communications Commission; Wire tapping
Federal Communications Commission, 226n, 228
*Federalist, The*, No. LXXXIV, 40
Fellman, David, 178
Field, Stephen J.: *In re Jackson*, 201n
Fifth Amendment: in relation to Fourth, 53 ff; 77–79; 162, 241–43, 248; history of self-incrimination clause, 58–59
First Amendment: in relation to Fourth, 241–42
Foote, Caleb, 187
Fourteenth Amendment, due process clause of: historical antecedents, 119; early decisions on, 119–20; development of, 120–21; conflicts over interpretations of, 121–22; as limitation on state searches, 126–72. *See also* Exclusionary rule; Fourth Amendment
Fourth Amendment: text of, 13, 48n; importance of history in understanding, 19–20; purpose of, 20, 47–48; antecedent English history, 20–30; antecedent American history, 30–37; drafted and adopted, 41–42; requires warrant whenever feasible, 43–44; relationship of its clauses, 43–44; and private searches, 44, 68–69; and state searches, 44, 126–72; and arrest, 44–45; state provisions analogous to, 38–39, 124; standards required by, 45–47;

protects against forfeiture, 52; unresolved problems, 167 ff; summary of Court's interpretation of, 263 ff. *See also* Exclusionary rule; First Amendment; Fifth Amendment; Fourteenth Amendment, due process clause of
Frankfurter, Felix: on relationship of Fourth Amendment's clauses, 43; on basis of exclusionary rule, 77; on meaning of due process, 121-22; on importance of Fourth Amendment, 127, 266, 269
—in *Abel* v. *United States,* 111–12, 256–57; in *Chapman* v. *United States*, 113; in *Davis* v. *United States*, 81–82; in *Elkins* v. *United States*, 153 ff; in *Frank* v. *Maryland*, 249–51, 258 ff; in *Harris* v. *United States*, 104; in *Irvine* v. *California*, 139–40; in *Lustig* v. *United States*, 72–73; in *Nardone* v. *United States* (1939), 209; in *On Lee* v. *United States*, 236; in *Rathbun* v. *United States*, 216–17; in *Rochin* v. *California*, 135–36; in *Stefanelli* v. *Minard*, 145–46; in *Walder* v. *United States*, 75n; in *Wolf* v. *Colorado*, 126 ff; in *Zap* v. *United States*, 82
Freund, Ernst, 246

G

General search warrant: in England, 21 ff; judicial restrictions on, 26–29; denounced by Commons, 30. *See also* Writ of assistance
Gerry, Elbridge, 39, 41
Gray, Horace, Jr., 36
Gridley, Jeremiah, 33–34

H

Hale, Sir Matthew, 26–27
Hall, Jerome, 124
Hand, Learned: on search incidental to arrest, 100
—in *United States* v. *Polakoff*, 215, 217n
Harlan, John M. (1833–1911): on meaning of due process, 121
Harlan, John M. (1899–): in *Ker* v. *California*, 113–14, 166; in *Lopez* v. *United States,* 238–39; in *Rea* v. *United States*, 147; in *Mapp* v. *Ohio*, 162–63
Hastie, William H.: in *Hanna* v. *United States*, 149
Hennings, Thomas C., Jr., 225
Henry, Patrick, 40
High Commission, Court of, 22
*History of the Pleas of the Crown*, 26
Hogan, Frank, 181, 230n
Hogan, James E., 206
Holmes, Oliver W., Jr.: on importance of Fourth Amendment, 263
—in *Olmstead* v. *United States,* 202–3; in *Silverthorne* v. *United States*, 66
Hoover, John Edgar, 181, 196, 221
Hutchinson, Thomas, 34, 35, 36

I

Illegal arrest and search: extent of, 123–24; 176–80, 185–86; federal-state cooperation in, 150, 154–56, 161; most serious at state level, 176–77; reasons for, 177; vagrancy laws as instrument of, 179–80. *See also* Exclusionary rule
Inbau, Fred E., 175n, 180
*Institutes of the Laws of England*, 119

J

Jackson, Robert H.: on importance of Fourth Amendment, 95; on illegal searches, 96, 265; on public opinion and police misconduct, 186; on why victims don't file suit, 187; forbids, then permits, Justice Department wire tapping, 227
—in *Brinegar* v. *United States,* 95–96; in *Harris* v. *United States*, 105; in *Irvine* v. *California*, 137 ff; in *On Lee* v. *United States*, 235–36; in *United States* v. *Di Re*, 92–93
Jefferson, Thomas, 39
Johnson, Earl, Jr., 182
Johnson, Lyndon B., 195
Justice Department: creates Office of Criminal Justice, 195; and wire tapping, 200, 227–30

K

Kamisar, Yale, 155
Kennedy, Robert F., 230
Knox, Jno. C., 69–70

L

Law enforcement. *See* Police
Licensing laws, English, 21 ff
Lillburn, John, 58–59
Livingston, Robert R., 37

M

McNabb-Mallory Rule, 169–70
McReynolds, James C.: in *Carroll* v. *United States*, 89–90
Madison, James, 41
Magna Carta, Chapter XXXIX, 25–26, 119
Mansfield, Chief Justice: in *Leach* v. *Money*, 29
Manwaring, David R., 193
Martin, Luther, 39
Mason, George, 39
"Mere evidence": rule forbidding seizure of: 53 ff, 82–83, 233
Miller, Samuel F.: on meaning of due process, 120
—in *Boyd* v. *United States*, 55
Minton, Sherman: in *Schwartz* v. *Texas*, 212–13; in *United States* v. *Rabinowitz*, 108–9
Mitchell, William D., 227
Murphy, Frank: on wire tapping warrant, 223n; on importance of Fourth Amendment, 266
—in *Goldstein* v. *United States*, 211; in *Harris* v. *United States*, 104–5; in *Lustig* v. *United States*, 73; in *Trupiano* v. *United States*, 106–7; in *Wolf* v. *Colorado*, 129–30

N

Nagel, Stuart S., 196

O

Otis, James, Jr., 34–35, 37
Otis, James, Sr., 33, 36

P

Palmer, A. Mitchell, 199
Papers, seizure of, 53 ff, 80–83
Particularity of description in warrant: in common law, 27; Fourth Amendment standards of, 46
Paulsen, Monrad G., 164
Paxton, Charles, 32, 33, 35, 36
"Personal privilege" doctrine. *See* Suppression of evidence, "standing" to ask for
Pitt, William, 25, 30
Police: difficulties faced by, 173–74; seek to avoid warrant restrictions, 175 ff; attract poor personnel, 180n; inadequate salaries of, 180–81; costs of, 181; inadequate training of, 181; kept weak by politics, 181–82; scandals, 181–82; discretion, 182; must enforce multitude of laws, 182, 183n; nonessential tasks of, 182; co-operation, 183–84; no state supervision of, 183–84; public antagonism to, 184; public apathy to problems of, 184; reforms in Chicago, 190n; in Detroit, 196n. *See also* Crime; Exclusionary rule; Illegal arrest and search
Pound, Roscoe, 131
Pratt, Chief Justice (Lord Camden): honored, 29
—in *Entick* v. *Carrington*, 29, 53–55, 59–60; in *Huckle* v. *Money*, 28; in *Wilkes* v. *Wood*, 28
Prettyman, Barrett E.: in *District of Columbia* v. *Little* (1949), 247–48, 262
Privy Council, 21–23
Probable cause: in common law, 27; Fourth Amendment standards of, 46–47, 88–89, 94–96, 168; in automobile searches, 88–90, 94–96, 168
"Property interest" doctrine. *See* Suppression of evidence, "standing" to ask for

R

Reed, Stanley F.: in *Lustig* v. *United States*, 73n
Reisman, Leonard, 178
Roberts, Owen J.: in *Goldman* v. *United States*, 211–12; in *Goldstein* v. *United States*, 210–11; in *Nardone* v. *United States* (1937), 206–7
Rogers, William P., 231
Roosevelt, Franklin D., 227
Rothblatt, Henry B., 194
Rutledge, Wiley B.: in *Brinegar* v. *United States*, 94–95; in *Wolf* v. *Colorado*, 129n

S

Scotti, Alfred T., 224
Scroggs, Chief Justice, 24, 25
Search incidental to arrest, 87, 98–117
Section 605. *See* Federal Communications Act, Section 605

Sewall, Chief Justice, 33
Silver, Edward S., 174n
Silver platter doctrine, 70–73: discarded, 149 ff, 161n; reverse, 145 ff, 157–58, 161n; in wire tapping, 214. *See also* Twin sovereignties doctrine
Star Chamber, Court of, 21–23, 54, 58
States, the, and the Fourth Amendment. *See* Exclusionary rule; Fourteenth Amendment; Fourth Amendment; Illegal search and seizure; Writs of assistance
Stewart, Potter: on Court and law enforcement, 173
—in *Elkins* v. *United States,* 150 ff; in *Silverman* v. *United States*, 237–38
Stone, Harlan F.: forbids Justice Department wire tapping, 200, 227
—in *Olmstead* v. *United States,* 205
Suppression of evidence: motion for must be "timely," 64, 67–68; derivatively obtained, 66–67, 208–9; "standing" to ask for, 73–75, 210–11; 219–20; appeal from order granting or denying motion for, 68n. *See also* Exclusionary rule
Sutherland, George: in *Byars* v. *United States*, 71

T

Taft, William H.: on basis of exclusionary rule, 77; on Fourth Amendment interpretation, 268
—in *Carroll* v. *United States,* 88 ff; in *Olmstead* v. *United States*, 201–2
Thatcher, Oxenbridge, 33
Traynor, Roger J.: on exclusionary rule, 173
—in *People* v. *Cahan,* 185–86
Treasury Department, 200, 228
Twin sovereignties doctrine: in double jeopardy and self-incrimination, 144n. *See also* Silver platter doctrine

U

"Unreasonable" searches and seizures: meaning of, 42–44, 53 ff, 87, 108–12, 266–68

V

Vinson, Fred M.: in *Harris* v. *United States*, 103–4; in *Trupiano* v. *United States*, 106

W

Warrants: differences in requirement for in arrest and search, 45; seldom used in arrests, 45; standards for issuance, 45–47; exceptions to requirement for, 87–117; seldom used in searches, 116; issuing process defective, 194
Warren, Earl: in *Benanti* v. *United States,* 214–15; in *Lopez* v. *United States*, 239–40; in *Rathbun* v. *United States*, 216
Washington, George, 41
Weinstein, Jack B., 176, 195
Westin, Alan F., 220, 231
Whittaker, Charles E.: in *Chapman* v. *United States*, 112–13; in *Wilson* v. *Schnettler*, 157
Whittaker, Lloyd T., 261
Wickersham Commission, 123, 195
Wigmore, John, 58–59, 84, 150, 205
Williams, Glanville L., 133
Wilson, James, 39n, 40
Wilson, Woodrow, 184
Wire tapping: federal laws to forbid, 199, 205, 206 ff.; early use of, 199–200; position of Justice Department on, 200, 237–30; decisions on, 200–20; prevalence of, 220–22, 231; congressional hearings on, 222 ff; in New York, 230–31; efforts by states to forbid, 231–32; unresolved constitutional problems, 232–33. *See also* Electronic eavesdropping; Federal Communications Act, Section 605; Federal Communications Commission
Writ of assistance: makes first appearance, 22; authorized by Parliament, 24, 32, 36; in Massachusetts, 31–37; in other colonies, 36–37; Continental Congress protests use of, 37–38; alluded to in Declaration of Independence, 38; outlawed in six states, 38–39. *See also* Fourth Amendment; General search warrant
Writs of Assistance case. *See* Paxton's case in Index of Cases

## Index of Cases

Where a case is discussed at some length, page numbers are indicated in boldface.


### A

*Abbate* v. *United States*, 359 U.S. 187 (1959), 144n
*Abel* v. *United States*, 362 U.S. 217 (1960), **111–12, 255–58**
*Adams* v. *New York*, 192 U.S. 585 (1904), **62–63**
*Agnello* v. *United States*, 269 U.S. 20 (1925), 99
*Aguilar* v. *Texas*, 378 U.S. 108 (1964), 47, 171
*Amos* v. *United States*, 255 U.S. 313 (1921), 68n, 169

### B

*Barron* v. *Baltimore*, 7 Peters 243 (1833), 44, 118
*Bartkus* v. *Illinois*, 359 U.S. 121 (1959), 144n, 155n
*Beck* v. *Ohio*, 379 U.S. 89 (1964), 99n, 171
*Benanti* v. *United States*, 355 U.S. 96 (1957), 156, **214–15**, 228n
Bonham's case, 8 Coke's Rep. 107 (1609), 35
*Boyd* v. *United States*, 116 U.S. 616 (1886), 43, **49–61**, 62–63, 80, 83, 87, 91, 109, 203, 243, 248, 250, 263
*Breithaupt* v. *Abram*, 352 U.S. 432 (1957), **141–43**
*Brinegar* v. *United States*, 338 U.S. 160 (1949), 46, 92, **93–96**, 168n, 264, 268, 269n
*Brown* v. *United States*, 276 U.S. 134 (1928), 81
*Burdeau* v. *McDowell*, 256 U.S. 465 (1921), 44, **68–70**
*Burford, Ex parte*, 3 Cranch 448 (1806), 44, 49n
*Byars* v. *United States*, 273 U.S. 28 (1927), **70–71**, 144, 213

### C

*Carroll* v. *United States*, 267 U.S. 132 (1925), 44n, 87, **88–91**, 263
*Chapman* v. *United States*, 365 U.S. 610 (1961), **112–13**, 169
*Cleary* v. *Bolger*, 371 U.S. 392 (1963), 171n
*Clinton* v. *Virginia*, 377 U.S. 158 (1964), 171n
*Commonwealth* v. *Dana*, 2 Met. (Mass.) 329 (1841), 62

### D

*Davidson* v. *New Orleans*, 96 U.S. 97 (1878), 119–20
*Davis* v. *United States*, 328 U.S. 582 (1946), **81–82**, 103n
*Di Bella* v. *United States*, 369 U.S. 121 (1962), 68n
*Dinan* v. *New York*, 371 U.S. 877 (1962), 219n
*District of Columbia* v. *Little*, 178 F.2d 13 (D.C. cir. 1949), **247–48**
*District of Columbia* v. *Little*, 339 U.S. 1 (1950), 246, **248**
*Draper* v. *United States*, 358 U.S. 307 (1959), 45, 47

### E

*Elkins* v. *United States*, 364 U.S. 206 (1960), 74, **149–56**, 157, 264
*Entick* v. *Carrington*, 19 Howell's State Trials 1029 (1765), **29, 53–55, 59–60**, 250
*Escobedo* v. *Illinois*, 378 U.S. 478 (1964), 243n

### F

*Fahy* v. *Connecticut*, 375 U.S. 85 (1963), 171n
*Feldman* v. *United States*, 322 U.S. 487 (1944), 144n
*Fox* v. *Ohio*, 8 Howard 410 (1847), 144n
*Frank* v. *Maryland*, 359 U.S. 360 (1959), 15, **248–53**, 258, 259
*Frisbie* v. *Collins*, 342 U.S. 519 (1952), 170n

G

*Gambino* v. *United States*, 275 U.S. 310 (1927), 70, **71–72**, 144
*Giordenello* v. *United States*, 357 U.S. 480 (1958), 47
*Go-Bart Importing Co.* v. *United States*, 282 U.S. 344 (1931), 101–2
*Goldman* v. *United States*, 316 U.S. 129 (1942), **211–12**, 235
*Goldstein* v. *United States*, 316 U.S. 114 (1942), 74n, **210–11**, 214, 219, 228n
*Gouled* v. *United States*, 255 U.S. 298 (1921), **67–68**, 82–83, 201, 237n
*Grau* v. *United States*, 287 U.S. 124 (1932), 46
*Griswold* v. *Connecticut*, 381 U.S. 479 (1965), 243n
*Groban, In re*, 352 U.S. 330 (1957), 260n

H

*Hale* v. *Henkel*, 201 U.S. 43 (1906), **80–81**
*Hanna* v. *United States*, 260 F.2d 723 (D.C. cir. 1958), 149
*Harris* v. *United States*, 331 U.S. 145 (1947), 99, **103–15**, 264
*Haywood* v. *United States*, 268 F. 795 (7th cir. 1920), 74n
*Henry* v. *United States*, 361 U.S. 98 (1959), 96n, 97
*Hester* v. *United States*, 265 U.S. 57 (1924), 91
*Huckle* v. *Money*, 2 Wilson, 205 (1763), 28
*Husty* v. *United States*, 282 U.S. 694 (1931), **91**

I

*Irvine* v. *California*, 347 U.S. 128 (1954), **137–41**
*Isbrantsen-Moller Co.* v. *United States*, 300 U.S. 139 (1937), 81

J

*Jackson, In re*, 96 U.S. 727 (1878), **49n**, 201
*Johnson* v. *United States*, 333 U.S. 10 (1948), 107n, 112, 168n
*Jones* v. *United States*, 357 U.S. 493 (1958), 112
*Jones* v. *United States*, 362 U.S. 257 (1960), 47, **75**, 219

K

*Ker* v. *California*, 374 U.S. 23 (1963), 15, 99n, **113–14**, **165–67**, 171, 264
*Ker* v. *Illinois*, 119 U.S. 436 (1886), 170n
*Knapp* v. *Schweitzer*, 357 U.S. 371 (1958), 144n
*Kremen* v. *United States*, 353 U.S. 346 (1957), **111**

L

*Lanza* v. *New York*, 370 U.S. 139 (1962), 165
*Leach* v. *Money*, 19 Howell's State Trials 1002 (1765), 29
*Leyra* v. *Denno*, 347 U.S. 556 (1954), 239n
*Linkletter* v. *Walker*, 381 U.S. 618 (1965), **172**
*Lopez* v. *United States*, 373 U.S. 427 (1963), 236n, 238–43
*Lustig* v. *United States*, 72–73, 268

M

*McCulloch* v. *Maryland*, 4 Wheaton 316 (1819), 203
*McDonald* v. *United States*, 335 U.S. 451 (1948), **74**, **107**
*McNabb* v. *United States*, 318 U.S. 332 (1943), 79–80, 146–47, 169–70, 236
*Mahon* v. *Justice*, 127 U.S. 700 (1888), 170n
*Mallory* v. *United States*, 354 U.S. 449 (1957), 169–70
*Malloy* v. *Hogan*, 378 U.S. 1 (1964), 144n
*Mapp* v. *Ohio*, 367 U.S. 643 (1961), 15, 44, 78n, 79n, 157, **158–64**, 219, 264
*Marcus* v. *Search Warrant*, 367 U.S. 717 (1961), 46n
*Marron* v. *United States*, 275 U.S. 192 (1927), 83n, **100–1**, 263
*Massiah* v. *United States*, 377 U.S. 201 (1964), 243n
*Miller* v. *United States*, 357 U.S. 301 (1958), 80, 166

*Monroe* v. *Pape,* 365 U.S. 167 (1961), 177, 187
*Murphy* v. *Waterfront Commission,* 378 U.S. 52 (1964), 144n
*Murray* v. *Hoboken Land Co.,* 18 Howard 272 (1855), 52, 119

N

*Nardone* v. *United States,* 302 U.S. 379 (1937), **206–7**, 218, 228n
*Nardone* v. *United States,* 308 U.S. 338 (1939), **208–9**, 213
*Nathanson* v. *United States,* 290 U.S. 41 (1932), 47
*National Safety Deposit Co.* v. *Stead,* 232 U.S. 58 (1914), 62, 126

O

*Ohio* ex rel. *Eaton* v. *Price,* 360 U.S. 246 (1959), **253–54**
*Ohio* ex rel. *Eaton* v. *Price,* 364 U.S. 263 (1960), **254–55**
*Oklahoma Press Pub. Co.* v. *Walling,* 327 U.S. 186 (1946), 81n, 269n
*Olmstead* v. *United States,* 277 U.S. 438 (1928), 15, 79, **200–5**, 232, 243, 263
*One 1958 Plymouth Sedan* v. *Pennsylvania,* 380 U.S. 693 (1965), 171
*On Lee* v. *United States,* 343 U.S. 747 (1952), **235–37**

P

Paxton's case, Quincy's *Massachusetts Reports,* 51, 1761–1772, **33–35**, 250, 496
*People* v. *Cahan,* 282 P.2d 905 (Cal. 1955), **185–86**
*People* v. *Chiagles,* 142 N.E. 583 (N.Y. 1923), 83n
*People* v. *Defore,* 150 N.E. 585 (N.Y. 1926), 84
*People* v. *Gonzales,* 124 P.2d 44 (Cal. 1942), 185
*Preston* v. *United States,* 376 U.S. 364 (1964), 92n, 99n, 103
*Pugach* v. *Dollinger,* 365 U.S. 458 (1961), **217–18**

Q

*Quantity of Books* v. *Kansas, A,* 378 U.S. 205 (1964), 46n

R

*Rathbun* v. *United States,* 355 U.S. 107 (1957), **216–17**
*Rea* v. *United States,* 210 F.2d 237 (10th cir. 1954), **145–46**
*Rea* v. *United States,* 350 U.S. 214 (1956), **145–48**
*Rios* v. *United States,* 364 U.S. 253 (1960), **97–98**
*Rochin* v. *California,* 342 U.S. 165 (1952), **134–36**

S

*Scher* v. *United States,* 305 U.S. 251 (1938), 91
*Schwartz* v. *Texas,* 344 U.S. 199 (1952), 156, **212–13**, 217, 218–19
*Segurola* v. *United States,* 275 U.S. 106 (1927), 68n
*Sgro* v. *United States,* 287 U.S. 206 (1932), 168n
*Shapiro* v. *United States,* 335 U.S. 1 (1948), 81n
*Silverman* v. *United States,* 365 U.S. 505 (1961), **237–38**, 264
*Silverthorne* v. *United States,* 251 U.S. 385 (1920), **66**
*Smith* v. *Maryland,* 18 Howard 71 (1855), 49n, 188n
*Spano* v. *New York,* 360 U.S. 315 (1959), 239n
*Stacey* v. *Emery,* 97 U.S. 642 (1878), 46
*Stanford* v. *Texas,* 379 U.S. 476 (1965), 46, 171
*State* v. *Krinski,* 62 A. 37 (Vt. 1905), 125
*State* v. *Sheridan,* 96 N.W. 730 (Iowa 1903), 125
*State* v. *Slammon,* 50 A. 1097 (Vt. 1901), 125
*Steele* v. *United States* No. 1, 267 U.S. 498 (1925), 46
*Stefanelli* v. *Minard,* 342 U.S. 117 (1951), **145–46**, 217–18
*Stoner* v. *California,* 376 U.S. 483 (1964), 169, 171
*Stroud* v. *United States,* 251 U.S. 15 (1919), 201n

T

*Taylor* v. *United States,* 286 U.S. 1 (1932), 112
*Trupiano* v. *United States,* 334 U.S. 699 (1948), **105–7**, 264

U

*United States* v. *Di Re*, 332 U.S. 581 (1948), **92–93**, 264
*United States* v. *Jeffers*, 342 U.S. 48 (1951), 75, 219
*United States* v. *Kirschenblatt*, 16 F.2d 202 (2d cir. 1926), 83
*United States* v. *Lee*, 274 U.S. 559 (1927), 201n
*United States* v. *Lefkowitz*, 285 U.S. 452 (1932), 83n, 101, **102**
*United States* v. *Murdock*, 284 U.S. 141 (1931), 144n
*United States* v. *Pearce*, 275 F.2d 318 (7th cir. 1960), 47n
*United States* v. *Polakoff*, 112 F.2d 888 (2d cir. 1940), 215, 217n
*United States* v. *Rabinowitz*, 339 U.S. 56 (1950), **107–11**, 264
*United States* v. *Ventresca*, 380 U.S. 102, 108 (1965)

W

*Walder* v. *United States*, 347 U.S. 62 (1954), 75n
*Weeks* v. *United States*, 232 U.S. 383 (1914), 14, **63–66**, 70, 83–84, 87, 99, 125, 144, 213, 218
*Weiss* v. *United States*, 308 U.S. 321 (1939), **208**
*Wilkes* v. *Wood*, 19 Howell's State Trials 1153 (1763), **28**
*Wilson* v. *Schnettler*, 365 U.S. 381 (1961), **157–58**
*Wolf* v. *Colorado*, 338 U.S. 25 (1949), 14, 44, 73, 77, **126–34**, 144, 159, 212, 218, 219n, 264, 268
*Wong Sun* v. *United States*, 371 U.S. 471 (1963), 67, 168n

Z

*Zap* v. *United States*, 328 U.S. 624 (1946), **81–82**, 103n

# THE JOHNS HOPKINS UNIVERSITY STUDIES IN HISTORICAL AND POLITICAL SCIENCE

EIGHTY–FOURTH SERIES (1966)

1. Search and Seizure and the Supreme Court: A Study in Constitutional Interpretation
   By JACOB W. LANDYNSKI

THE JOHNS HOPKINS PRESS

BALTIMORE

# THE JOHNS HOPKINS UNIVERSITY STUDIES IN HISTORICAL AND POLITICAL SCIENCE

A subscription for the regular annual series is $8.00. Single numbers may be purchased at special prices. A complete list of the series follows. All paperbound unless otherwise indicated.

FIRST SERIES (1883)—Bound Volume.. O. P.

1. Introduction to American Institutional History, An. By E. A. Freeman..... O. P.
2. Germanic Origin of New England Towns. By H. B. Adams.......... O. P.
3. Local Government in Illinois. By Albert Shaw. Local Government in Pennsylvania. By E. R. L. Gould...... O. P.
4. Saxon Tithingmen in America. By H. B. Adams....................... O. P.
5. Local Government in Michigan and the Northwest. By E. W. Bemis.... O. P.
6. Parish Institutions of Maryland. By Edward Ingle.................... O. P.
7. Old Maryland Manors. By John Hemsley Johnson ..................... O. P.
8. Norman Constables in America. By H. B. Adams .................. O. P.
9-10. Village Communities of Cape Ann and Salem. By H. B. Adams....... O. P.
11. Genesis of a New England State. By A. Johnston .................... O. P.
12. Local Government and Schools in South Carolina. By B. J. Ramage... O. P.

SECOND SERIES (1884)—Bound Volume O. P.

1-2. Method of Historical Study. By H. B. Adams......................... O. P.
3. Past and Present of Political Economy. By R. T. Ely........................ O. P.
4. Samuel Adams, the Man of the Town Meeting. By James K. Hosmer..... O. P.
5-6. Taxation in the United States. By Henry Carter Adams.............. O. P.
7. Institutional Beginnings in a Western State. By Jesse Macy............. O. P.
8-9. Indian Money in New England, etc. By William B. Weedon............ O. P.
10. Town and Country Government in the Colonies. By E. Channing......... O. P.
11. Rudimentary Society Among Boys. By J. Hemsley Johnson.............. O. P.
12. Land Laws of Mining Districts. By C. H. Shinn..................... O. P.

THIRD SERIES (1885)—Bound Volume. O. P

1. Maryland's Influence Upon Land Cessions to the U. S. By H. B. Adams.. O. P
2-3. Virginia Local Institutions. By E. Ingle ............................. O. P.
4. Recent American Socialism. By Richard T. Ely........................... O. P
5-6-7. Maryland Local Institutions. By Lewis W. Wilhelm.................. O. P
8. Influence of the Proprietors in Founding New Jersey. By A. Scott...... O. P.
9-10. American Constitutions. By Horace Davis ......................... O. P.
11-12. City of Washington. By J. A. Porter ........................ O. P.

FOURTH SERIES (1886)—Bound Volume O. P.

1. Dutch Village Communities on the Hudson River. By I. Elting...... O. P.
2-3. Town Government in Rhode Island. By W. E. Foster. The Narragansett Planters. By Edward Channing...... O. P.
4. Pennsylvania Boroughs. By William P. Holcomb ....................... O. P
5. Introduction to Constitutional History of the States. By J. F. Jameson.... O. P.
6. Puritan Colony at Annapolis, Maryland. By D. R. Randall........... O. P.
7-8-9. Land Question in the United States. By S. Sato ..................... O. P.
10. Town and City Government of New Haven. By C. H. Levermore...... O. P.
11-12. Land System of the New England Colonies. By M. Egleston......... O. P.

FIFTH SERIES (1887)—$8.00

1-2. City Government of Philadelphia. By E. P. Allinson and B. Penrose...... O. P.
3. City Government of Boston. By James M. Bugbee.......................... O. P.
4. City Government of St. Louis. By Marshall S. Snow................. O. P.
5-6. Local Government in Canada. By John George Bourinot............ O. P.

7. Effect of the War of 1812 Upon the American Union. By N. M. Butler. . O. P.
8. Notes on the Literature of Charities. By Herbert B. Adams. . . . . . . . . . . . . . O. P.
9. Predictions of Hamilton and De Tocqueville. By James Bryce. . . . . . . . . . O. P.
10. Study of History in England and Scotland. By P. Fredericq. . . . . . . . . . . . . O. P.
11. Seminary Libraries and University Extension. By H. B. Adams. . . . . . . . . . . O. P.
12. European Schools of History and Politics. By A. D. White. . . . . . . . . . . . . O. P.

SIXTH SERIES (1888)

History of Co-operation in the United States O. P.

SEVENTH SERIES (1889)—Bound Vol. O. P.

1. Arnold Toynbee. By F. C. Montague O. P.
2-3. Municipal Government in San Francisco. By Bernard Moses. . . . . . . . . . . O. P.
4. Municipal History of New Orleans. By William W. Howe. . . . . . . . . . . . O. P.
5-6. English Culture in Virginia. By William P. Trent. . . . . . . . . . . . . . . . O. P.
7-8-9. River Towns of Connecticut. By Charles M. Andrews. . . . . . . . . . . . . . . O. P.
10-11-12. Federal Government in Canada. By John G. Bourinot. . . . . . . . . . . . . O. P.

EIGHTH SERIES (1890)—Bound Vol. . . O. P.

1-2. Beginnings of American Nationality. By A. W. Small. . . . . . . . . . . . . . . . . O. P.
3. Local Governments in Wisconsin. By D. E. Spencer. . . . . . . . . . . . . . . . . . . 1.00
4. Spanish Colonization in the Southwest. By F. W. Blackmar. . . . . . . . . . . . . . O. P.
5-6. Study of History in Germany and France. By P. Fredericq. . . . . . . . . . . 3.00
7-9. Progress of the Colored People of Maryland. By J. R. Brackett. . . . . . . . O. P.
10. Study of History in Belgium and Holland. By P. Fredericq. . . . . . . . . . . O. P.
11-12. Seminary Notes on Historical Literature. By H. B. Adams and Others. . . O. P.

NINTH SERIES (1891)—Bound Volume O. P.

1-2. Government of the United States. By W. W. and W. F. Willoughby. . . O. P.
3-4. University Education in Maryland. By B. C. Steiner. The Johns Hopkins University (1876-1891). By D. C. Gilman . . . . . . . . . . . . . . . . . . . . . . . O. P.
5-6. Municipal Unity in the Lombard Communes. By W. K. Williams. . . . O. P.
7-8. Public Lands of the Roman Republic. By A. Stephenson. . . . . . . . . . . . . . . . 2.50
9. Constitutional Development of Japan. By T. Iyenaga. . . . . . . . . . . . . . . . . . O. P.
10. History of Liberia, A. By J. H. T. McPherson . . . . . . . . . . . . . . . . . . . . O. P.
11-12. Indian Trade in Wisconsin. By F. J. Turner . . . . . . . . . . . . . . . . . . . . . . O. P.

TENTH SERIES (1892)—Bound Volume O. P.

1. Bishop Hill Colony. By Michael A. Mikkelsen . . . . . . . . . . . . . . . . . . . . . . O. P.
2-3. Church and State in New England. By Paul E. Lauer. . . . . . . . . . . . . . . . . O. P.
4. Church and State in Maryland. By George Petrie. . . . . .Paper 1.00; Cloth O. P.
5-6. Religious Development of North Carolina. By S. B. Weeks. . . . . . . . . 1.50
7. Maryland's Attitude in the Struggle for Canada. By J. W. Black. . . . . . . O. P.
8-9. Quakers in Pennsylvania. By A. C. Applegarth. . . . . . . . . . . . . . . . . . . . . O. P.
10-11. Columbus and His Discovery of America. By H. B. Adams and H. Wood . . . . . . . . . . . . . . . . . . . . . . . . 1.50
12. Causes of the American Revolution. By J. A. Woodburn. . . . . . . . . . . . . . O. P.

ELEVENTH SERIES (1893)

1. Social Condition of Labor. By E. R. L. Gould . . . . . . . . . . . . . . . . . . . . . . O. P.
2. World's Representative Assemblies of Today. By E. K. Alden. . . . . . . . . . . 1.00
3-4. Negro in the District of Columbia. By Edward Ingle . . . . . . . . . . . . . . . O. P.
5-6. Church and State in North Carolina. By Stephen B. Weeks. . . . . . . . . . . . . O. P.
7-8. Condition of the Western Farmers, etc. By A. F. Bentley. . . . . . . . . . . . . 3.00
9-10. History of Slavery in Connecticut. By Bernard C. Steiner. . . . . . . . . . . . . O. P.
11-12. Local Government in the South. By E. W. Bemis and Others. . . . . . . . O. P.

TWELFTH SERIES (1894)—Bound Vol. O. P.

1-2. Cincinnati Southern Railway. By J. H. Hollander . . . . . . . . . . . . . . . . . . . O. P.
3. Constitutional Beginnings of North Carolina. By J. S. Bassett. . . . . . . . . .O. P.
4. Struggle of Dissenters for Toleration in Virginia. By H. R. McIlwaine. . . O. P.
5-6-7. Carolina Pirates and Colonial Commerce. By S. C. Hughson. . . . . . . . . O. P.
8-9. Representation and Suffrage in Massachusetts. By G. H. Haynes. . . . . . . . . O. P.
10. English Institutions and the American Indian. By J. A. James . . . . . . . . . . O. P.
11-12. International Beginnings of the Congo Free State. By J. S. Reeves. . O. P.

THIRTEENTH SERIES (1895)

1-2. Government of the Colony of South Carolina. By E. L. Whitney. . . . . . . . O. P.
3-4. Early Relations of Maryland and Virginia. By J. H. Latané. . . . . . . . . . . . O. P.
5. Rise of the Bicameral System in America. By T. F. Moran. . . . . . . . . O. P.

6-7. White Servitude in the Colony of Virginia. By J. C. Ballagh.......... O. P.
8. Genesis of California's First Constitution. By R. D. Hunt............... O. P.
9. Benjamin Franklin as an Economist. By W. A. Wetzel............... O. P.
10. Provisional Government of Maryland. By J. A. Silver.................. O. P.
11-12. Government and Religion of the Virginia Indians. By S. R. Hendren. O. P.

FOURTEENTH SERIES (1896) — Bound Volume ....................... O. P.

1. Constitutional History of Hawaii. By Henry E. Chambers................ O. P.
2. City Government of Baltimore. By Thaddeus P. Thomas .............. O. P.
3. Colonial Origins of New England Senates. By F. L. Riley............ O. P.
4-5. Servitude in the Colony of North Carolina. By J. S. Bassett.......... O. P.
6-7. Representation in Virginia. By J. A. C. Chandler ........................ O. P.
8. History of Taxation in Connecticut (1636-1776). By F. R. Jones....... 1.25
9-10. Study of Slavery in New Jersey, A. By Henry S. Cooley................ O. P.
11-12. Causes of the Maryland Revolution of 1689. By F. E. Sparks.......... O. P.

FIFTEENTH SERIES (1897)

1-2. Tobacco Industry in Virginia Since 1860. By B. W. Arnold............ O. P.
3-5. Street Railway System of Philadelphia. By F. W. Speirs............ O. P.
6. Daniel Raymond. By C. P. Neill.... 1.25
7-8. Economic History of B. & O. R. R. By M. Reizenstein ............... O. P.
9. South American Trade of Baltimore. By F. R. Rutter.................. 1.50
10-11. State Tax Commissions in the United States. By J. W. Chapman.......... 3.00
12. Tendencies in American Economic Thought. By S. Sherwood......... O. P.

SIXTEENTH SERIES (1898)

1-4. Neutrality of the American Lakes, etc. By J. M. Callahan............ O. P.
5. West Florida. By H. E. Chambers.. O. P.
6. Anti-Slavery Leaders of North Carolina. By J. S. Bassett............. O. P.
7-9. Life and Administration of Sir Robert Eden. By B. C. Steiner............ 3.00
10-11. Transition of North Carolina from a Colony. By E. W. Sikes......... O. P.
12. Jared Sparks and Alexis de Tocqueville. By H. B. Adams............ O. P.

SEVENTEENTH SERIES (1899)

1-2-3. History of State Banking in Maryland. By H. B. Bryan.............. O. P.
4-5. Know-Nothing Party in Maryland. By L. F. Schmeckebier............ O. P.
6. Labadist Colony in Maryland. By B. B. James ............................ O. P.
7-8. History of Slavery in North Carolina. By J. S. Bassett.............. O. P.
9-10-11. Development of the Chesapeake and Ohio Canal. By G. W. Ward... O. P.
12. Public Educational Work in Baltimore. By Herbert B. Adams............. 1.50

EIGHTEENTH SERIES (1900)

1-4. Studies in State Taxation. By J. H. Hollander........Paper 4.00; Cloth 5.00
5-6. Colonial Executive Prior to the Restoration. By P. L. Kaye............ O. P.
7. Constitution and Admission of Iowa into the Union. By J. A. James.... O. P.
8-9. Church and Popular Education. By H. B. Adams......................... O. P.
10-12. Religious Freedom in Virginia: The Baptists. By W. T. Thom.... O. P

NINETEENTH SERIES (1901)

1-3. America in the Pacific and the Far East. By J. M. Callahan........... O. P.
4-5. State Activities in Relation to Labor. By W. F. Willoughby............ O. P.
6-7. History of Suffrage in Virginia. By J. A. C. Chandler................ O. P.
8-9. Maryland Constitution of 1864. By W. S. Myers.........................O.P.
10. Life of Commissary James Blair. By D. E. Motley ..........................O.P.
11-12. Governor Hicks of Maryland and the Civil War. By G. L. Radcliffe.. O. P.

TWENTIETH SERIES (1902) — Bound Volume ........................... O. P.

1. Western Maryland in the Revolution. By B. C. Steiner.................. O. P.
2-3. State Banks Since the National Bank Act. By G. E. Barnett............ O. P.
4. Early History of Internal Improvements in Alabama. By W. E. Martin. O. P.
5-6. Trust Companies in the United States. By George Cator................ O. P.
7-8. Maryland Constitution of 1851. By J. W. Harry......................... O. P.
9-10. Political Activities of Philip Freneau. By S. E. Forman.............. O. P.
11-12. Continental Opinion on a Proposed Middle European Tariff Union. By G. M. Fisk.............................. 1.50

TWENTY-FIRST SERIES (1903)—Bound Volume ............................. O. P.

1-2. Wabash Trade Route. By E. J. Benton ................................ O. P.
3-4. Internal Improvements in North Carolina. By C. C. Weaver........ O. P.

5. History of Japanese Paper Currency. By M. Takai .................... O. P.
6-7. Economics and Politics in Maryland, 1720-1750, and the Public Services of Daniel Dulany the Elder. By St. G. L. Sioussat .......................... O. P.
8-9-10. Beginnings of Maryland, 1631-1639. By B. C. Steiner........... O. P.
1-12. English Statutes in Maryland. By St. G. L. Sioussat................. O. P.

TWENTY-SECOND SERIES (1904)

1-2. Trial Bibliography of American Trade-Union Publications, A. By G. E. Barnett............ ........ O. P.
3-4. White Servitude in Maryland, 1634-1820. By E. I. McCormac......... O. P.
5. Switzerland at the Beginning of the Sixteenth Century. By J. M. Vincent. 1.00
6-7-8. History of Reconstruction in Virginia. By H. J. Eckenrode........ O. P.
9-10. Foreign Commerce of Japan Since the Restoration. By Y. Hattori..... O. P.
11-12. Descriptions of Maryland. By B. C. Steiner......................... O. P.

TWENTY-THIRD SERIES (1905)

1-2. Reconstruction in South Carolina. By J. P. Hollis................... O. P.
3-4. State Government in Maryland, 1777-1781. By B. W. Bond, Jr. ......... O. P.
5-6. Colonial Administration Under Lord Clarendon, 1660-1667. By P. L. Kaye O. P.
7-8. Justice in Colonial Virginia. By O. P. Chitwood..................... O. P.
9-10. Napoleonic Exiles in America, 1815-1819. By J. S. Reeves............ O. P.
11-12. Municipal Problems in Medieval Switzerland. By J. M. Vincent....... 1.00

TWENTY-FOURTH SERIES (1906)—Bound Volume ................... O. P.

1-2. Spanish-American Diplomatic Relations Before 1898. By H. E. Flack.. O. P.
3-4. Finances of American Trade Unions. By A. M. Sakolski................ O. P.
5-6. Diplomatic Negotiations of the United States with Russia. By J. C. Hildt ......................... O. P.
7-8. State Rights and Parties in North Carolina, 1776-1831. By H. M. Wagstaff .......................... O. P.
9-10. National Labor Federations in the United States. By William Kirk.... O. P.
11-12. Maryland During the English Civil Wars. Part I. By B. C. Steiner ... O. P.

TWENTY-FIFTH SERIES (1907)—Bound Volume ....................... O. P.

1. Internal Taxation in the Philippines. By J. S. Hord.................... 1.00
2-3. Monroe Mission to France, 1794-1796. By B. W. Bond, Jr........... O. P.
4-5 Maryland During the English Civil Wars. Part II. By Bernard C. Steiner O. P.
6-7. State in Constitutional and International Law. By R. T. Crane....... O. P.
8-9-10. Financial History of Maryland, 1789-1848. By Hugh S. Hanna.... O. P.
11-12. Apprenticeship in American Trade Unions. By J. M. Motley.......... 2.50

TWENTY-SIXTH SERIES (1908)

1-3. British Committees, Commissions, and Councils of Trade and Plantations, 1622-1675. By C. M. Andrews. O. P.
4-6. Neutral Rights and Obligations in the Anglo-Boer War. By R. G. Campbell ........................... O. P.
7-8. Elizabethan Parish in Its Ecclesiastical and Financial Aspects. By S. L. Ware .......................... 2.00
9-10. Study of the Topography and Municipal History of Praeneste, A. By R. V. D. Magoffin................. 2.00
11-12. Beneficiary Features of American Trade Unions. By J. B. Kennedy.. O. P.

TWENTY-SEVENTH SERIES (1909)

1-2. Self-Reconstruction of Maryland, 1864-1867. By W. S. Myers....... O. P.
3-4-5. Development of the English Law of Conspiracy. By J. W. Bryan...... 3.50
6-7. Legislative and Judicial History of the Fifteenth Amendment. By J. M. Mathews ........................ 2.50
8-12. England and the French Revolution, 1789-1797. By W. T. Laprade...... O. P.

TWENTY-EIGHTH SERIES (1910) — Bound Volume ................. O. P.

1. History of Reconstruction in Louisiana. (Through 1868). By J. R. Ficklen.. O. P.
2. Trade Union Label. By E. R. Spedden 2.00
3. Doctrine of Non-Suability of the State in the United States. By K. Singewald 2.50
4. David Ricardo: A Centenary Estimate. By J. H. Hollander............... O. P.

TWENTY-NINTH SERIES (1911)

1. Maryland Under the Commonwealth: A Chronicle of the Years 1649-1658. By B. C. Steiner...Paper 2.50; Cloth O. P.
2. Dutch Republic and the American Revolution. By Friedrich Edler..... O. P.
3. Closed Shop in American Trade Unions. ume ........................ O. P.

THIRTIETH SERIES (1912)—Bound Vol-
By F. T. Stockton................ O. P.

1. Recent Administration in Virginia. By F. A. Magruder................. 3.50

2. Standard Rate in American Trade Unions. By D. A. McCabe.......... 5.00
3. Admission to American Trade Unions. By F. E. Wolfe.................. 3.50

THIRTY-FIRST SERIES (1913)

1. Land System in Maryland, 1720-1765. By Clarence P. Gould.............. O. P.
2. Government of American Trade Unions. By T. W. Glocker................ 4.00
3. Free Negro in Virginia, 1619-1865. By J. H. Russell.................. O. P.
4. Quinquennales: An Historical Study. By R. V. D. Magoffin. Paper 1.00; Cloth 1.50

THIRTY-SECOND SERIES (1914) — Bound Volume .................. O. P.

1. Jurisdiction in American Building-Trades Unions. By N. R. Whitney.. 4.00
2. Slavery in Missouri, 1804-1865. By H. A. Trexler.................... O. P.
3. Colonial Trade of Maryland. By M. S. Morriss....................... O. P.

THIRTY-THIRD SERIES (1915)

1. Money and Transportation in Maryland, 1720-1765. By Clarence P. Gould... 3.50
2. Financial Administration of the Colony of Virginia. By Percy Scott Flippin. Paper 1.25; Cloth 2.00
3. Helper and American Trade Unions. By John H. Ashworth............. 2.00
4. Constitutional Doctrines of Justice Harlan. By Floyd Barzilia Clark.....4.00

THIRTY-FOURTH SERIES (1916)

1. Boycott in American Trade Unions. By L. Wolman.................. O. P.
2. Postal Power of Congress. By Lindsay Rogers ........................ 4.00
3. Control of Strikes in American Trade Unions. By G. M. Janes. ......... O. P.
4. State Administration in Maryland. By John L. Donaldson............... 4.00

THIRTY-FIFTH SERIES (1917)

1. Virginia Committee System and the American Revolution. By J. M. Leake 3.00
2. Organizability of Labor. By W. O. Weyforth ....................... 4.50
3. Party Organization and Machinery in Michigan Since 1890. By A. C. Millspaugh ....................... 4.50

THIRTY-SIXTH SERIES (1918)

1. Standard of Living in Japan. By K. Morimoto ....................... O. P.
2. Sumptuary Law in Nurnberg. By K. R. Greenfield......Paper 2.00; Cloth 4.00
3. Privileges and Immunities of State Citizenship. By R. Howell.......... 2.00
4. French Protestantism, 1559-1562. By C. G. Kelly...................... 3.50

THIRTY-SEVENTH SERIES (1919) — Bound Volume .................. O. P.

1. Unemployment and American Trade Unions. By D. P. Smelser, Jr........ O. P.
2. Labor Law of Maryland. By M. H. Lauchheimer.......Paper 3.00; Cloth 4.00
3. American Colonization Society, 1817-1840. By E. L. Fox............... O. P.
4. Obligation of Contracts Clause of the United States Constitution. By W. B. Hunting ....................... 2.00

THIRTY-EIGHTH SERIES (1920) — Bound Volume .................. O. P.

1. United States Department of Agriculture. By W. L. Wanlass. Paper 3.00; Cloth 5.00
2. Amalgamated Association of Iron, Steel and Tin Workers. By J. S. Robinson 3.00
3. Employment of Plebiscite in Determination of Sovereignty. By J. Mattern. 4.00

THIRTY-NINTH SERIES (1921)

1. Capitalization of Goodwill. By Kemper Simpson..................... O. P.
2. Rise of the Cotton Mills in the South. By Broadus Mitchell.............. O. P.
3. International Molders' Union of North America. By Frank T. Stockton..... 4.00

FORTIETH SERIES (1922)—Bound Volume ....................... O. P.

1. Presidential Campaign of 1832. By Samuel R. Gammon, Jr............ 3.50
2. Canadian Reciprocity Treaty of 1854. By C. C. Tansill................ 2.00
3. Recent Problems in Admiralty Jurisdiction. By Edgar T. Fell.......... 3.50
4. Creation of the Presidency, 1775-1789: A Study in Constitutional History. By Charles C. Thach, Jr.............. 3.50

FORTY-FIRST SERIES (1923) — Bound Volume ...................... O. P.

1. Paper Money in Maryland, 1727-1789. By Kathryn L. Behrens........... O. P.
2. Shop Committee in the United States. By Carroll E. French........... 2.50

3. Bavaria and the Reich: The Conflict Over the Law for the Protection of the Republic. By J. Mattern............ 2.50
4. James Henry Hammond, 1807-1864. By Elizabeth Merritt............... 3.00

FORTY-SECOND SERIES (1924)

1. Contemporary French Opinion on the American Civil War. By W. Reed West ........................ 2.00
2. Frederick Law Olmsted: A Critic of the Old South. By Broadus Mitchell O.P.
3. Constitutional Doctrines of Justice Oliver Wendell Holmes. By Dorsey Richardson .................... 2.00
4. Reformation in Poland: Some Social and Economic Aspects. By Paul Fox. 3.00

FORTY-THIRD SERIES (1925)

1. Agrarian Movement in North Dakota. By Paul R. Fossum............... 3.50
2. Virginia Frontier, 1754-1763. By Louis K. Koontz........................ O. P.
3. Ordinance Making Powers of the President of the United States. By James Hart. .................... O. P.

FORTY-FOURTH SERIES (1926)

1. Sumptuary Legislation and Personal Regulation in England. By F. Elizabeth Baldwin......Paper 4.00; Cloth 5.00
2. Doctrine of Continuous Voyage. By H. W. Briggs.................. 4.00
3. Wage Policies of Labor Organizations in a Period of Industrial Depression. By V. J. Wyckoff................ 2.50

FORTY-FIFTH SERIES (1927)

1. State as a Party Litigant. By R. D. Watkins ........................ 4.00
2. Relation of Thomas Jefferson to American Foreign Policy. By W. K. Woolery 2.50
3. Ecclesiastical Censure at the End of the Fifteenth Century. By W. K. Gotwald ........................ 1.50
4. Constitutional Status and Government of Alaska. By G. W. Spicer........ 2.50

FORTY-SIXTH SERIES (1928)

1. Mission of William Carmichael to Spain. By S. G. Coe.............. 2.00
2. Workers (Communist) Party and American Trade Unions. By D. M. Schneider ........................ 2.50
3. Virginia Constitutional Convention of 1901-1902. By R. C. McDaniel..... 3.50
4. Protection of Citizens Abroad by Armed Forces of the United States. By M. Offutt ........................ 3.00

FORTY-SEVENTH SERIES (1929)

1. Congressional Investigating Committees. By M. E. Dimock.... ...... O.P.
2. Study of Judicial Administration in the State of Maryland, A. By G. K. Reiblich ........................ 3.00
3. Financial History of Baltimore, 1900-26. By L. O. Rea................ 2.50
4. Franco-German Relations, 1878-1885. By R. H. Wienefeld.............. 4.00

FORTY-EIGHTH SERIES (1930)

1. Economic and Social Aspects of Federal Reclamation. By Dorothy Lampen 2.50
2. Russo-American Relations, 1815-1867. By Benjamin Platt Thomas... ...... O. P.
3. Maryland Legislature. By Harry Joseph Green ........................ 2.00
4. Southern Commercial Conventions, 1837-1860. By Herbert Wender..... 4.50

FORTY-NINTH SERIES (1931)

1. Departments of the American Federation of Labor. By Albert Helbing... 2.50
2. State Legislative Committees: A Study in Procedure. By C. I. Winslow..... 3.00
3. French Opposition to the Mexican Policy of the Second Empire. By F. E. Lally ........................ 3.50
4. Henry Charles Carey: A Study in American Economic Thought. By A. D. H. Kaplan .................. 1.50

FIFTIETH SERIES (1932)

1, Hours of Labor. By Lazare Teper... 2.00
2. Some Presidential Interpretations of the Presidency. By Norman J. Small. 4.00
3. Governor of Maryland, The. By Charles J. Rohr.........Paper 3.00; Cloth 5.00
4. Yellow Dog Contract. By Joel I. Seidman ........................ 2.00

FIFTY-FIRST SERIES (1933)

1. Studies on Scipio Africanus. By Richard M. Haywood.................. 2.00
2. Right of Search and the Slave Trade in Anglo-American Relations, 1814-1862. By Hugh G. Soulsby......... 3.50
3. American Policy of Recognition Towards Mexico. By S. A. MacCorkle.. 2.00
4. Mathew Carey: A Study in American Economic Development. By K. W. Rowe ........................ 3.00
5. Hezekiah Niles as an Economist. By R. G. Stone..................... 2.50

FIFTY-SECOND SERIES (1934)

1. Italy's Relations with England, 1896-1905. By J. L. Glanville.......... 3.50
2. Capital Issues Committee and War

Finance Corporation. By Woodbury Willoughby .................... 2.50
3. Maryland Business Corporations, 1783-1852. By J. G. Blandi............ 2.50
4. American Doctrine of State Succession. By H. A. Wilkinson............... 2.50

FIFTY-THIRD SERIES (1935)

1. Juristic Status of Egypt and the Sudan. By Vernon A. O'Rourke............ 3.50
2. Workmen's Compensation in Maryland. By Evelyn Ellen Singleton.......... 2.50
3. Mutual Savings Banks in Baltimore. By Robert W. Thon, Jr............. 2.00
4. Contribution of the Ideologues to French Revolutionary Thought. By Charles H. Van Duzer............ 2.50

FIFTY-FOURTH SERIES (1936)

1. Movement for the Acquisition of All Mexico, 1846-1848. By John D. P. Fuller ......................... 3.50
2. Gas Light Company of Baltimore. By George T. Brown.................. 2.50
3. Journeymen Barbers' International Union of America. By W. Scott Hall 3.50
4. Supreme Court and Political Questions. By C. G. Post............... O. P.

FIFTY-FIFTH SERIES (1937)

1. Germany and Morocco Before 1905. By Francis T. Williamson.......... 4.00
2. History and Development of the Fourth Amendment of the United States Constitution. By Nelson B. Lasson...... O. P.
3. Influence of Border Disorders on Relations Between the United States and Mexico, 1876-1910. By Robert Gregg 4.00
4. Floating Debt of the Federal Government, 1919-1936. By Edward Raguet Van Sant ...................... 3.50

FIFTY-SIXTH SERIES (1938)

1. Commercial Banking and the Stock Market Before 1863. By Joseph Edward Hedges.................. 3.00
2. Industry and Commerce of the City of Rome (50 B. C.–200 A. D.). By Helen Jefferson Loane............ O. P.
3. Investment Value of Goodwill. By Lawrence N. Bloomberg........... 1.50
4. Historical Scholarship in the United States, 1876-1901: As Revealed in the Correspondence of Herbert B. Adams. By W. Stull Holt................ 4.50

FIFTY-SEVENTH SERIES (1939)

1. History of Criminal Syndicalism Legislation in the United States, A. By Eldridge Foster Dowell........... 3.50
2. Wholesale Marketing of Fruits and Vegetables in Baltimore. By Robert G. Deupree...................... 4.00
3. History of the Woman's Peace Party. By M. L. Degen................ 4.00

FIFTY-EIGHTH SERIES (1940)

1. Malaria and Colonization in the Carolina Low Country, 1526-1696. By St. Julien Ravenel Childs.............. 4.50
2. Municipal Indebtedness: A Study of the Debt-to-Property Ratio. By Leroy Shattuck, Jr...................... 3.00
3. Security Affiliates of National Banks. By W. W. Peach................ 3.50

FIFTY-NINTH SERIES (1941)

1. Investment Management. By John A. Loftus.......................... 2.50
2. Baltimore 1870-1900: Studies in Social History. By C. Hirschfeld........ 2.50
3. National Bituminous Coal Commission. By R. H. Baker............ 5.50

SIXTIETH SERIES (1942)

1. From Barter to Slavery: The Economic Relations of Portuguese and Indians in the Settlement of Brazil 1500-1580. By Alexander Marchant...... O. P.
2. Geopolitik: National Self-Sufficiency and Empire. By J. Mattern....... O.P.
3. Question of Expatriation in America Prior to 1907. By I-Mien Tsiang... 2.50
4. Public Trusteeship. By Norman Heaney 2.50

SIXTY-FIRST SERIES (1943)

1. Maryland During and After the Revolution. By Philip A. Crowl........ O. P.
2. Charles J. Bonaparte, Patrician Reformer. By Eric F. Goldman....... 3.00
3. Studies in the History of the English Feudal Barony. By S. Painter...... 4.00
4. Economic Thought of Woodrow Wilson. By W. Diamond.......... O. P.

SIXTY-SECOND SERIES (1944)

1. Andrea Barbarigo, Merchant of Venice, 1418-1449. By Frederic C. Lane.... O.P.
2. Growth of German Historicism. By Friedrich Engel-Janosi............ O.P.
3. Wheats of Classical Antiquity. By N. Jasny ............................ 3.50

SIXTY-THIRD SERIES (1945)

1. Henry Barnard's American Journal of Education. By Richard E. Thursfield. 5.00
2. Roman Rhetorical Schools as a Preparation for the Courts Under the Early Empire. By E. Patrick Parks....... 1.50

3. Slave States in the Presidential Election of 1860. By Ollinger Crenshaw O. P.

SIXTY-FOURTH SERIES (1946)

1. Great National Project: A History of the Chesapeake and Ohio Canal. By W. S. Sanderlin.................. O. P.
2. Richard Hildreth. By Donald E. Emerson .............................. 3.50
3. William Rufus Day: Supreme Court Justice from Ohio. By Joseph E. McLean ........................ 3.00

SIXTY-FIFTH SERIES (1947)

1. British Block Grants and Central-Local Finance. By Reynold E. Carlson.... 4.50
2. Landowners and Agriculture in Austria, 1815-1848. By Jerome Blum........ 5.00

SIXTY-SIXTH SERIES (1948)

1. French Freemasonry Under the Third Republic. By Mildred J. Headings.. 5.00
2. Science and Rationalism in the Government of Louis XIV, 1661-1683. By James E. King.................. O. P.

SIXTY-SEVENTH SERIES (1949)

1. Capitalism in Amsterdam in the 17th Century. By Violet Barbour....... O. P.
2. The Patent Grant. By Burke Inlow.. O. P.
3. Saint Mary Magdalene in Mediaeval Literature. By Helen Garth......... 3.00

SIXTY-EIGHTH SERIES (1950)

1. The Organization of State Administration in Delaware. By Paul Dolan... 3.50
2. The Theory of Inter-Sectoral Money Flows and Income Formation. By John Chipman ........................ O. P.
3. Congressional Differences over Foreign Affairs, 1921-41. By George Grassmuck ...................... O. P.

---

*Bound Volumes Discontinued Beginning with the Sixty-Ninth Series.*

---

SIXTY-NINTH SERIES (1951)

1. Party and Constituency: Pressures on Congress. By Julius Turner........ O. P.
2. The Legates of Galatia From Augustus to Diocletian. By Robert K. Sherk.. 2.50

SEVENTIETH SERIES (1952)

1. Federal Examiners and the Conflict of Law and Administration. By Lloyd D. Musolf ...................... 4.00
2. The Growth of Major Steel Companies, 1900-1950. By Gertrude G. Schroeder ...................... O. P.

SEVENTY-FIRST SERIES (1953)

1. The Revolt of 1916 in Russian Central Asia. By Edward D. Sokol......... 4.00
2. Four Studies in French Romantic Historical Writing. By Friedrich Engel-Janosi ......................... O. P.

SEVENTY-SECOND SERIES (1954)

1. Price Discrimination in Selling Gas and Electricity. By Ralph Kirby Davidson ......................... O. P.
2. The Savings Bank of Baltimore, 1816-1866. By Peter L. Payne and Lance E. Davis ........................... 3.50

SEVENTY-THIRD SERIES (1955)

The Paris Commune in French Politics, 1871-1880. By Jean T. Joughin. Two vols. ....................... O. P.

1. Volume I: The Partial Amnesty
2. Volume II: The Final Amnesty

SEVENTY-FOURTH SERIES (1956)

1. Robert Oliver, Merchant of Baltimore, 1783-1819. By Stuart Weems Bruchey 6.00
2. Political Theory and Institutions of the Khawārij. By Elie Adib Salem....... 3.00

SEVENTY-FIFTH SERIES (1957)

1. Britons in American Labor: A History of the Influence of the United Kingdom Immigrants on American Labor, 1820-1914. By Clifton K. Yearley, Jr. 5.00
2. The Location of Yamatai: A Case Study in Japanese Historiography. By John Young .................... O. P.

SEVENTY-SIXTH SERIES (1958)

1. Trends in Birth Rates in the United States since 1870. By Bernard Okun. O. P.
2. The Dynamics of Supply: Estimation of Farmers' Response to Price. By Marc Nerlove ...................Cloth 5.00

SEVENTY-SEVENTH SERIES (1959)

1. Republicans Face the Southern Question—The New Departure Years, 1877-1897. By Vincent P. De Santis..Cloth 6.00
2. Money, Class, and Party: An Economic Study of Civil War and Reconstruction. By Robert P. Sharkey..Cloth 5.50

SEVENTY-EIGHTH SERIES (1960)

1. The Nobility of Toulouse: A Social and Economic Study. By Robert Forster. .................... Cloth 5.00
2. The Union Pacific Railroad—A Case in Premature Enterprise. By Robert William Fogel. .... Paper 3.00; Cloth 3.50

SEVENTY-NINTH SERIES (1961)

1. Enterprise and Anthracite: Economics and Democracy in Schuylkill County, 1820-1875. By Clifton K. Yearley, Jr. Cloth 5.00
2. Birth Rates of the White Population in the United States, 1800-1860: An Economic Study. By Yasukichi Yasuba. Paper 5.00

EIGHTIETH SERIES (1962)

1. The Road to Normalcy: The Presidential Campaign and Election of 1920. By Wesley M. Bagby Paper 4.00; Cloth 4.50
2. The Decline of the Venetian Nobility as a Ruling Class. By James C. Davis. Paper 3.50; Cloth 4.00

EIGHTY-FIRST SERIES (1963)

1. The First Ottoman Constitutional Period: A Study of the Midhat Constitution and Parliament. By Robert Devereux. ................... Cloth 6.00
2. Elbeuf During the Revolutionary Period: History and Social Structure. By Jeffry Kaplow. ............ Cloth 6.50

EIGHTY-SECOND SERIES (1964)

1. A Rural Society in Medieval France: The Gâtine of Poitou in the Eleventh and Twelfth Centuries. By George T. Beech ..................... Cloth 5.00
2. United States Policy and the Partition of Turkey, 1914-1924. By Laurence Evans ..................... Cloth 7.95

EIGHTY-THIRD SERIES (1965)

1. The Right to Vote: Politics and the Passage of the Fifteenth Amendment. By William Gillette .......... Cloth 4.50
2. A Baronial Family in Medieval England: The Clares, 1217–1314. By Michael Altschul ............. Cloth 7.50

EIGHTY-FOURTH SERIES (1966)

1. Search and Seizure and the Supreme Court: A Study in Constitutional Interpretation. By Jacob W. Landynski. Cloth 8.50